TRAVELS THROUGH AQUA, GREEN, AND BLUE

A memoir by

MARY E. GREGORY

Travels Through Aqua, Green, and Blue
Copyright © 2020 by Mary E. Gregory.

Cover Design by Michael Roberts
Interior Design by FormattedBooks.com

ISBN: 978-1-7354116-0-6 (Paperback)
ISBN: 978-0-578-72167-5 (eBook)

Library of Congress Registration Number / Date: TXu002207565 / 2020-07-14

Urban Honesty Press
www.urbanhonestypress.com
Contact: info@urbanhonestypress.com

Find me at:
www.maryegregory.com

To my sweet husband, Pierre, without your dedication to providing me a good life, free of most household duties, this book would not have been possible.

To my brother, Paul, for giving me the title of this book and for being one of the most sincere people I know.

To my sister, Sam: may love always conquer all.

Thank you all, from the bottom of my heart.

AUTHOR'S NOTE

This is my story of childhood trauma and triumph. It is genuinely aligned with what I believed at the ages I was when these experiences unfolded for me. I share a lot of my past, but I realize one cannot remember every detail from every situation. I admit that now. I also honor and respect the possibility that others may reflect upon these events differently. To protect the privacy of family and friends, I have changed many of their names.

For those who are at the precipice or deep in the valley of your transformation, I sincerely hope that you find inspiration in my story as I take you deep in the valley of my changes.

—Mary

CONTENTS

Chameleons are able to adapt to their environment and hide in plain sight. They do this in order to survive. Despite times where they are clearly outnumbered or being toyed with, they remain adaptable, still, and resilient, and end up living another day.

INTRODUCTION

I came into this world half-baked. That's what I like to call being born with a birth defect. I was born with a bilateral cleft lip and palate. When I was younger, and until I was in third grade, I would call it a "cliff lip and pilot." My mother never corrected me either; it seemed she was fine with, or tickled by, my interpretation. Sometimes I'd explain to people, "You know, like a pilot going over a cliff." I thought it was a nice enough visualization to help explain my deformity, as it related to an impending plane crash, an image others were familiar with. But most times, I would say, "I was just born this way." It was simple enough and seemed to convey the fact that even I didn't really know why I looked the way I looked. But I knew I stood out.

"Experts suggest that parents discuss with their children ways to handle negative social situations related to their cleft lip or cleft palate. A child who is entering school should learn the proper (and age-appropriate) terms related to the cleft. The ability to confidently explain the condition to others may limit feelings of awkwardness and embarrassment and reduce negative social experiences."[1]

I'd had a few surgeries to repair my cleft palate when I was a baby, but my nose was still wide and flat. And except for a small stubby tooth that came out sideways and resembled a shark tooth, I didn't have my four front teeth. I had two large vertical scars on my upper lip—the result of my surgeon trying to give me a Cupid's bow. It was like staring at a real-life Picasso painting, with my odd symmetry and form suggesting just enough normal features to distinguish I was human, but enough out of place to pique one's curiosity.

I had two holes on the inside of my lip that connected straight into my nasal cavity. I had a hole in the roof of my mouth that also led right into my nasal cavity. Eating was a logistical nightmare and took a bit of art and patience.

Because of all the holes in my mouth, when I ate, things often got stuck. I would have to constantly suck food out of all these cavities, or else they'd find a way up and out of my nose. I turned these holes into a type of parlor trick at elementary school lunchtime. I would bet kids at my table that I could make milk come out of my nose. I'd usually wager one of their snacks to do it. It only took one push and—voila! "Come see the lady who we call the Niagara Milk Falls, ladies and gentlemen!"

But one of the things I hated most was eating in front of people, especially other kids. I was always told that I looked like a rabbit when I ate. That's likely why a cleft lip used to be called a *harelip*: "A congenital cleft or fissure in the midline of the upper lip, resembling the cleft upper lip of a hare, often occurring with a cleft palate."[2] Using this term is considered derogatory and offensive now, but it was pretty common until about the late '80s to use it.

Having a facial deformity was getting harder and harder for me to ignore as I got older and entered first grade. I quickly realized I would have to learn to live with this face and the negative reactions of others. Yet, I held on to the dream that one day I would look normal.

"Research has shown that during the early preschool years (ages three to five), children with cleft lip and cleft palate tend to have a self-concept that is similar to their peers without a cleft."[3] "Self-concept may be adversely affected by the presence of a cleft lip or cleft palate, particularly among girls."[4]

Since my mid-twenties—after over ten reconstructive maxillofacial and oral surgeries since the age of fourteen—I have carried my deformity pretty well, and most people only subliminally know something is wrong with my symmetry.

To get through a large part of my life, though, I had to be a chameleon. If I drew too much attention to myself, I would be prey to all the bullies, even the non-practicing bullies. If I didn't put myself out there enough and act like I didn't care, I'd also look like prey. Some taunts really didn't affect me, but others were downright scarring.

"Changing skin color is an important part of communication among chameleons. A chameleon's skin changes colors in response to its emotions, such as anger or fear, changes in light, temperature, or humidity."[5]

I was once told I looked uglier than a dog by a boy I worked with during my first summer job training as a junior lifeguard when I was fourteen years old. This was in response to a survey the other boys were conducting on who was the prettiest in our group. I was, of course, the ugliest. My face just seemed to elicit derogatory comments from complete strangers, too, even from old ladies who were minding their own business on the city bus. Generally, you'd expect them to have seen it all, and therefore, could see me and let it go, resist the urge to comment on my face. But no, I often got questions from old people about my face or just state-the-obvious remarks like, "Looks like you got a harelip, young lady." No shit, Sherlock.

At the time of my early adolescence, Run-DMC's "Mary, Mary" was popular, and I would hear this little jingle, "Mary, Mary, why you buggin'?" about five times a day. It got to the point where someone would only have to say the beginning, and I would finish the end with "…why ya buggin'?" Another good one was for the Cherry Merry Muffin dolls; their jingle was, "Cherry Merry Muffin, she cooks sweet, smells sweet, looks sweet, too." Again, they'd only have to start out with the "Cherry Merry Muffin" part, and I would finish the rest. Somehow the fact that I participated in those two jingles built me up some cred with the guys in my middle school, since they were the only ones who would shout those jingles at me from great distances whenever they saw me. I learned early on that being able to take a teasin' wasn't all bad, much better than when it was insults alone. I figured, if you can laugh at yourself when It's safe, then you can build a reserve of dignity for when it isn't. Be adaptable.

There were many times, though, where I was the strategic point of attack. The vulnerable amongst the powerful. The ones who didn't know me, or just despised looking at me, often got their chance to publicly ridicule me. This was generally when I was in class or stuck on the school or city bus with nowhere to go. Oh, the city bus, where free-for-all insult slinging was a boy's favorite pastime. I'd be stopped in my tracks just to be told, "Damn bitch, you fuckin' ugly." That was a common insult, "ugly bitch," or "ugly witch," or a general, "What the fuck happened to your face, bitch?" The least profane, but still insulting, was being called a "snaggle-tooth," or "flat nose." Though these might be excellent times to correct my bullies and tell them about the "medical" term for my condition, I generally sided with taking the insult and getting away with as much dignity as I could muster. Be resilient.

But we were also poor and dirty kids. Our shoes were often old and raggedy; they talked while we walked because they were so worn down the glue had come off the seams that held the heel or the front of the shoe closed. So, they flapped open and slapped shut when we walked and made a loud clapping sound. They were run down from all the walking everywhere around town we did. Since we usually didn't have a running car, our feet got us most places.

To the keen eye of a young kid, it was obvious we were poor. Those were times where I could be, and often was, stripped of my dignity and left to lick my own wounds. Not just one insult could be slung about my face, but a series could be air-bombed about my dirty clothes, my raggedy shoes, my poor ass, my skinny ass, my fat mom, my actual station in life. I was poor and on welfare. I was prey. My bullies would intimidate me physically by pushing on my shoulders, grabbing my arms, pushing the back of my head, or getting close enough to my face to tell me they would fuck me up once we got off the bus if I had anything to say back to them. When off the bus, my older sister by almost two years, Samantha, would usually be my cover and stand between them and me as my protector, keeping our pace brisk, but making sure we avoided *running* because all that would do was elicit a chase. Be still.

I would often go home and count the ways that I was worthless: I'm left-handed, I'm too tall, I'm too skinny, I have no boobs, I'm poor, I've got terrible clothes, I only wear Pro Wings (the affordable way someone poor could wear knock-off L.A. Gears), I've got this pimple on my nose, I'm ugly. The list would go on and on. I would cry it out, journal my sorrows in my little diary with a little lock, and hope to get a hug and reassurance from my mom. I'd have to push the feelings of inadequacy deep into my heart pocket and go out there and live another day.

Part 1

TRAVELS THROUGH AQUA

I feel I began on this earth with a lot of potential. I wasn't anyone special, Just the child of a southern preacher and the youngest of three. I was as adventurous, curious, and excited about my little life as the next kid. During my early childhood, I experienced a world that now seems like it came from a fictional novel. On paper, I shouldn't have the life I do now. I shouldn't have my Pollyanna optimism, my warmness toward complete strangers, or my very rational mind. But great strength comes from great moments—often scary, lonely, yet powerful moments.

I should start off by saying that I have a very good life. I have a best friend that I've known since the first day of sixth grade. I'm going to be celebrating my twentieth wedding anniversary this August. I'm going to New Orleans for the first time ever and will be enjoying the Jazz Festival. I have all of these events lined up, all of these extraordinary, fun life experiences. I would say that I am very lucky.

As a way to tame the chaos in my life recently, I've been doing a lot of meditation, a lot of soul searching and journaling. All of that brought me to finally writing my memoir. I'm sitting here on my couch at 5:30 in the morning, watching my cats try to catch a moth that's circling around the room trying to avoid the rapture of my halogen floor lamp. I'm speaking into my phone to record the first inspirational moments of my memoir.

I'm thirty-six years old. Yet today, sitting here, I feel unfulfilled. My work is exciting, yet stressful. My commute is long, but I listen to audiobooks and music every day so I feel like I'm personally developing. During the past year, while driving two hours through the concrete jungle to get to my Hollywood office, I've listened to over fifteen audiobooks. The titles range from *Fifty Shades of Grey* (which I regretted purchasing after about an hour of listening to it) to books like *Think and Grow Rich* and *Outwitting the Devil* by Napoleon Hill, *The Miracle Morning* by Hal Elrod (the reason why I'm up at 5:30 in the morning), *The Five Love Languages* by Gary Chapman, *Chicken Soup for the Soul* and *The Success Principles* by Jack Canfield, *Awakening Your Inner Genius* by Sean Patrick, *The Power of Now* by Eckhart Tolle, and *American Gods* by Neil Gaiman.

There's still something missing in my life. There's a part of me that still feels like it's waiting to be born. Maybe it's the writer in me, the one who's been waiting to come out of the closet? Or maybe it's the never-been-a-mother in me? Like this will somehow awaken something inside and give me a reset-my-childhood-for-free card. Whatever it is, I've got to set out to find it. Through writing this book, I believe I will.

THE BEGINNING

When I was five years old, several traumatic events—that I believe broke her—hit my mother Linda like a succession of freight trains. While she was married to my father, she was forced to own a stigma that she wasn't emotionally prepared to own. One bigger than her and one bigger than our society at the time. What came next was much like a study on the fragility of the human mind and our instinct to run far away from societal judgement.

My father was the preacher of our church in Nashville, Tennessee. Brother Jack, as they called him, was also the music director and played piano and the church organ for many of the Wednesday night church meetings and Sunday services. He was almost six feet, four inches tall, had a slim build, with dark brown hair and blue eyes and a big brown mustache that parasailed off of his wide and easy smile. His voice was calm and soft, quick to sympathize and assure you. We were a faithful family, devoted to the church and what it meant to serve God. Everyone had a role, and we seemed to be playing our part.

My brother Paul was the oldest and, at the time, was nine years old. He was tall and lanky with light hazel eyes. He was born to be a country boy, though we lived in the suburbs. His hair was brown like maple syrup and sat on his head like he'd just taken off an army helmet. It was long enough in the front to reach his eyebrows, the tips of his ears, and the nape of his neck. No matter what you asked him, his whole face always seemed to be thinking hard about your question. He sported corduroys and blue jeans, the knees tattered with holes, some patched, and some patches with holes in them still. He was endlessly dusting off dirt and leaves from his grass-stained jeans. Paul was born with a rare skin condition, which fully expressed itself when he was around seven years old. His entire body was covered in brown birthmarks, some small, some large, but they were everywhere, and it looked like someone decided to splatter warm chocolate syrup on his body. In the family, we called it, "profesha, profesha, multiple birthmarks." Said just like that, all scientific-sounding, though when I went searching for it when I was older, I couldn't find a skin disease called that. I did find an image of a woman who had skin like my brother's. It turns out it was actually called LEOPARD syndrome.

My sister Samantha, who I called Sam, was small and petite with light blonde hair bordering on platinum. Our mom always told us that her hair hadn't grown in until she was two years old, and that everyone said she looked like a real-life toddler baby doll with her striking, deep-set green eyes and little teeth that looked like chiclets. She had light-brown freckles that fell across her nose and rosy cheeks like tiny peanut butter-colored snowflakes. They were more natural, delicate, and stereotypical freckles than my brother's. She got the pale skin and high cheekbones from the German side of our mother's family, along with the short stature and thicker form like my mother's sisters, who only grew to five feet, two inches to five feet, six inches tall, compared to our mom's larger stature of five feet, ten inches.

My sister was an independent thinker and doer from an early age, but still sensitive and respectful of her elders. She took on chores without ever being asked, and she kept herself and her belongings organized. She seemed to be born with the knowledge of self-reliance, an 'I can fix anything' attitude, but with a dash of shyness that made her overall behavior tame. Obeying the rules got her noticed, praised, and fulfilled her need for attention, the right kind of attention for someone with her level of shyness. She was a natural-born older sister, though, at least when we were younger. I looked up to her and wanted to be around her as much as possible. She, on the other hand, wanted independence from her annoyingly ever-present little sister.

I had the tall and lanky genes from my father's side, with round blue eyes and blonde-ish hair, what my mom called dishwater blonde, which always made me feel like I somehow got left in the sink too long when they were giving out real hair colors. I didn't have any real identifying beauty marks, except the one. I had an adventurous tomboy disposition, but the good-girl follow-the-rules obedience from the faith I'd grown up to respect and fear. My hair was long and stringy, approaching wavy but finally settling on tangled. I was my older siblings' gullible and obedient little sister.

One vivid memory when my sister got the best of me stands out. It was a hot summer day, Sam told me that whoever could drink their soda first would win…something…so I ran to the kitchen and poured out my 7UP bottle that we just got from the porch soda machine at the neighborhood convenience store up the street. It went right down the sink, every single last fizzy ounce of it. Thinking I had won whatever prize she was offering, if she even did offer one, I pranced to the living room where she was standing. Tipping my glass bottle, only a single drop crawling out to the floor to freedom.

"Tada, I won!" I exclaimed and showed her my emptied bottle with a victorious stance. My sister stood there laughing, a full bottle of 7UP in her hand, the round, green bottle filling her entire small hand, her lips curled around the opening as she swallowed. As she laughed at my gullibility, her chuckle amplified through the inside of the bottle and I realized she was smarter than me.

For as long as I could remember, everyone was always extra nice to me whenever I was with my father, handing me candy and a quick wink whenever he'd stop to talk to one of the deacons, church staff, or members as we walked the long hallways of the church. He was always performing sermons, volunteering, and doing other preacher duties for the church, such as the monthly baptisms for adults wanting to be born again and for the little children when it was their time to be saved.

I was only four and a quarter years old for my baptism. I had learned from my sister to use quarters in your age if you wanted to seem older, though at the time, I didn't know exactly how many quarters I was, so I only used the one. The large clear tub of water that sat at the front of the church, glistening under the lights, made it easy to see the small waves that both rippled and jiggled softly against the edges of the plastic tub. The bright white light shining on the water made it majestic-looking, clear yet mysterious, like one of my large blue marbles. This big body of blue peacefulness somehow made me feel special. You could see right through the water even while standing in the back of the church. The blue was so blue up there against all the wood paneling, the organ pipes, and long floor-to-ceiling dark red drapes, the contrast was stunning. It was like a blue watery moon in the sky of our church.

I was one of several kids getting baptized that night, but I wasn't the first. I had a lot of pride knowing my dad was going to be baptizing some of the other kids and a few adults that night. I watched each person as they walked up and willingly devoted themselves to Christ, got dunked, and walked out soaking wet, transformed. It was interesting observing the ritual while standing in line for my turn. Once it was mine, I walked toward my dad and got closer to the water. I could see it splashing around and dripping off the sides like rain on a car windshield. I felt a great sense of hesitation, and my legs suddenly got heavy and wobbly. My dad encouraged me to walk toward him, as he could see my growing reluctance with each step. I didn't realize there was so much water when I gazed at it earlier, but being right near it overwhelmed my young self. He guided me closer to him, close enough to grab my hand and then to guide me up the stairs and into the water. It was deeper than I had expected. Even though I was nearly five years old, I was as tall as a seven-year-old and hadn't expected to be neck deep when fully committed. I stuck my neck up and gasped a little; my toes struggled as they barely felt the bottom. This wasn't at all what I expected. My father bent down and grabbed my chest with his forearm, cradling my chin with his hand, firmly squeezing my nose closed with his thumb and index finger. I was breathing in huge breaths from my mouth now. With one hand holding the back of my head, he lifted me up enough so that my legs went out beneath me. The swiftness and strength he used to move me was frightening, and just before he plunged me into the water, I yelled out at the top of my lungs, "No!!!!!!"

When I was brought back up, all I could hear was an erupting laughter from the entire church. My father was smiling as he helped pull me out of the bath. I coughed and gasped for air and dripped on my way out, suddenly weak and embarrassed. My mother's arms were not far away, and, despite my wetness, she let me cling to her like an octopus. I felt overwhelmingly helpless and small, though I knew I had done a big thing.

When I was six, in the year 1985, my dad decided to bring himself to the cross, as he later told me, and finally accepted his sexuality. He wanted to be reborn as his true self, as a gay man. Looking back, I am not exactly sure how he revealed this news, but I remember when an emotional tidal wave came through our home. And if we knew anything, we knew that everything had changed.

My dad had spent most of his life denying his true self, believing that God was testing him. He felt that he had to be married and have a family to show God that despite what feelings he had for men, he would and could be a faithful follower, resisting the temptations of his sexuality. But it was becoming too hard. He was now forty-two and had found a different and welcoming community where he could be himself. He was going to be open for the first time in his life.

He knew he was gay when he was about seven or eight years old. Back then, he grew close with a neighborhood boy. They slowly began to express their fondness for each other in how they dressed similarly, in their interests, even the music they liked. Eventually, it became clear to both of them that their feelings were more than just mutual. What they felt was emotional, tender, and affectionate. Their connection became deeper when they were ten years old and kissed for the first time. But it was the 1950s, and society wasn't aware enough to accept an openly gay person. Those who weren't openly gay, but had mannerisms of someone who was "soft" or "sensitive," tried to blend into society by sticking to their religion and dating the opposite sex.

My dad's musical abilities were inherited from his father, Jack Sr., a locally famous musician who played the clarinet, saxophone, and was the band leader for the Nashville WSM radio show, "Waking Crew," which he had led since before World War II. He also played each weekday on WSM TV's "Noon" show.[6] My grandfather was born during the great depression, and from the age of four until he was an adult, he lived in a Tennessee boy's home. His mother, Elizabeth Gregory, for whom I was given my middle name, was unwed. The family rumor had it that a local boy, who was well off and of a higher social class, was the father. He refused to claim my grandfather as his son, though. Elizabeth was of little means, and the financial burden of rearing a child on her own during the great depression, was too much. She visited my grandfather often, however, and was a part of his life as much as she could. She later married in her early forties and was referred to as Granny Gordon by the family. A man came by the boys home with instruments and taught my grandfather how to play the clarinet and by the time he was fifteen years old, he was proficient at playing the instrument. Jack Sr. was entrepreneurial and as a kid he would sell apples on the side of the road to make a little pocket change. As an adult, he would ensure that there were always fresh fruits in his home, never letting any fruit rot and frequenting orchards and farmers markets to procure them. My grandfather later married a woman named Beverly and had three children, my father being the middle child and the first boy. The family called my dad Jackie.

When my father was in his twenties, while serving in the Army, he opted to become a conscientious objector and served as a civilian service clerk in Alaska for four years, at an Army Community Hospital. When he met my mother, he was twenty-six and she was just sixteen. They fell deeply in love, as he later recalled to me. And, seeing their wedding photos, there was no doubt in my mind why. She was beautiful. My mother was a soft-spoken woman as well. Her height complemented his; she had long blonde hair and her full shape favored someone with her height and bone structure. She had a wide smile and blue eyes like him; they invited you to trust and elicited an ease that made her very likable. Her cheekbones were round and full of possibilities and optimism. They were married just over a year after meeting and started a family just a few years after that.

My father did a good job hiding himself behind a wife and children, and he lived as a devout religious man. My father coming out was not only a major blow to my mom's self-esteem, it gave those around her the power to be better than her. No matter their own problems, none would match up to my mom's.

Because I was only six when this announcement was made, I looked to my mom's behavior to show me how to handle this new awareness, and this new life. Her pain was the prism of all her failures. She laid in bed sobbing for hours and then screaming angrily at God for cursing her life. On many occasions, I crawled into her bed and tried to console her. I saw myself as a ladybug, just hoping she would see me and think she was lucky.

My mother spent a lot of time sleeping, removing herself from her family. It was hard for her to talk about what was happening because there were no support groups for the wives of gay preachers. So she retreated into her head. This new life label was humiliating for her because it was not about a cheating husband; that you could get sympathy for. It was about a man she couldn't keep straight. It was a time when the average person didn't understand what HIV or AIDS meant, or where it came from or how you could get it. Our society at large invented the labels and their meaning and the fear around them. To the average person, the disease was for gay people who were being punished for being sinners. And if you were somehow associated with gay people, well, you were put in that circle, too.

Our family now had to own being associated with people with HIV and AIDS. We had a father, and husband, that was gay—and the cherry on top, he was also a preacher. Now, people my mother knew would turn away from her in the street. Those she'd known from church for years looked at her sideways or cut their conversations short. They didn't know how to interact with her now that Jack was out of the closet. She was alone. And so was he. Yet we still went to church for a few months after the news broke. It was likely a hard pill to swallow for the average person, but our mother wasn't the average person.

Mom was a preacher's wife, a mother of three, and already struggling with the first signs of schizophrenia. So much was unknown about mental illness in the mid-'80s, and it was often socially stigmatized. Mental health was associated with being locked up in a padded room with a straitjacket. Women were often depicted as crazy when they were overly emotional and could be locked away in mental facilities for their entire lives for mental illnesses we treat commonly today. While my mother grieved, she began to show signs of schizophrenia. But her disease would not be addressed for almost twenty years.

I think temporary insanity would be the best way to describe what happened next. Until then, I'd never seen our mother shout or get angry, unless she was running around the house to get us kids to take a nap or snapping at us to quiet down when we'd get excited at a restaurant. Now she was yelling at us for anything, it seemed; like how long it took us to get out of the house and go to school or church, the mess we made with our clothes. She even told us what a burden we were to cook and clean for and how we could never do anything right. Paul seemed to get the worst of it. He was ten years old and had the longest relationship of any of us kids with our mother, but he was a male, and so she started to point her anger at him on a more frequent basis.

Just a few months after Dad had moved out, the news about a gay preacher became an especially good article to print. Until then, Mom had only ever seen a newspaper print of her hosted tea parties which boasted of finger foods and names of fellow church women in attendance. Now she had her shame delivered in the weekend paper.

Paul, Sam, and I were already outside playing after we'd finished up breakfast. We knew better than to make noise in the house. I'd come in to get some water, and Mom was still sitting at the kitchen table. She'd spent the better part of the morning in the kitchen reading an article published about our father. She sat there, staring at the picture of her husband in the newspaper. She shook her head as she read the article, almost like she was sad for the family whom the story was about.

I was curious about what she was reading. Her face showed no signs of conclusion; she maintained a crinkle between her eyes and just kept shaking her head from side to side. I sat in silence staring at her face and wondering if her head would ever stop shaking. She let out a few big sighs and placed the paper down on the table, keeping her hand on the top as if she was swearing an oath on the Bible. She slowly got up from the table, never noticing me sitting there, and walked toward the bedroom to go lie down. I sat in my seat until I could hear the bedroom door close. I pushed my chair back, walked over to her chair, and stood on it as I peered at the newspaper article. The picture was clearly my dad. He was walking down the street, a microphone in his face, and a flash of light lit up the side of his face like a media-evading movie star. I stared at the picture like I would a new toy box, letting my imagination run wild with every detail, every word. I thought, *What was my dad feeling? Where was he going? How was the reporter right there as he was walking down the street? Had he followed him?*

Dad's brow was furrowed and deep, like he had a headache. The reporter next to him had a small grin on his face, like he had "caught" something. I said the word I recognized out loud to try it on for size; until that point I had only heard people say it. "Gaaaaay." I realized I couldn't say it without smiling. I decided the reporter was calling my father gay, and my father's worried face was because he was being openly outed to our entire community.

I attempted to read the article, but most of it didn't make much sense. A few words I knew, "Baptist Church, preacher, married, Linda Gregory, mother of three..."

I had lost myself in the picture when the phone rang, and I quickly raised my head. I darted to the chair along the kitchen wall that sat under the yellow phone, with its dirt-encrusted, tangled cord. I picked the phone up and placed the receiver over my ear. It cupped my small ear completely. The round bottom part of the phone that you spoke into rested on my chest. I held the phone handle with both hands.

"Hello, the Gregory residence," I said politely.

"Hello, is this Mary?"

"Yeeass," I said with my young, southern voice and drawl.

"This is your grandma, Edith. Can you get your momma on the phone?" she asked.

"Hello Grandma. I'll go get her, but she went down to take a nap a little while ago. You still want me to wake her up?" I wasn't sure whether Momma would get mad at me for interrupting her rest.

"Yes, Mary. Go get your momma up," she insisted.

Two large french doors led to the bedroom. I put both my hands around one of the vintage glass doorknobs and leaned back with both my feet firmly planted; this gave me force to pull both doors open at the same time. A loud creaking sound made its way into the silent air of the bedroom. Mom was lying on the bed. She had drawn the curtains, and there was a faint humidity in the air.

"Momma, Grandma is on the phone," I whispered softly at the edge of the bed up toward her face.

"Tell her I'm sleeping. I can't talk right now," she said slowly.

"Well, she said I needed to wake you up," I said matter-of-factly.

She let out a long and heavy sigh.

"I'll take the phone here in the bedroom," she told me. I scurried to the kitchen and picked up the phone that had been dangling from its mangled cord.

"Hello Momma," Mom said in a low and tired voice. I gripped the telephone with both my hands and tried to be silent while listening on the line.

"Linda, did you see that article about Jack in the paper? Oh my lord, what are you going to do? You can't keep going to that church. They're going to be cruel to you, Linda."

"I don't know, Momma. I'm not sure what I'm going to do. We need to finish the divorce and we'll see," Mom said sadly.

"Well, Linda, I don't know what to say. How are you and the kids going to make it? How are they going to grow up with a gay father?" Grandma said with a concerned tone.

"I don't know. They've got me, and we have the house, and as long as Jack can pay child support, we'll find a way, I suppose." Her tone was continuing down, long and slow like it was getting stuck in a jar of vaseline. I knew she didn't want to have this conversation right now. Not with the morning she had. I decided to take the phone off my ear and softly put it back into its yellow cradle on the wall. I sat down on the chair, and my legs hung heavily over the edge. I was six years old when my entire world changed.

I looked all around the kitchen. Everything looked different now. Objects around the house that I had taken for granted now became real objects that were part of something bigger. I noticed the bulbous brown doorknobs screwed into the yellow-flower-wallpapered kitchen cabinets. A cabinet left open above the counter revealed cans of food; peas, sweet corn, sweetened condensed milk, and fruit mixed cocktail—my favorite way to eat fruit. I thought about the mix of pineapple chunks, soft pink cherries, and slithery peach slices combined with the medley of other inferior fruits, like small hard chunks of pears and green grapes. I'd eat each bite as it was cradled in a large spoon dripping with sugary syrup, precisely measured with the perfect ratio of cherry to other fruit. Then when the cherries were gone—there were never enough cherries—I'd pick peaches to other fruit, then pineapple to other fruit, until there was just the sweet syrupy motherload to drink right from the can.

I saw a large drawer full of potatoes that had been left open, the top of the plastic bag poking out like fresh mushrooms sprouted from the forest. The buffalo-checkered linoleum tiles on the floor seemed to stare back at me angrily for all the wear and tear I'd put on them while playing. The wood carvings on the feet of the small, round kitchen table looked like panther's paws standing at attention, though no longer shining from fresh lacquer and the joy of new beginnings.

I felt a small pull in my stomach. I hung my head down and hugged my legs tight. I stayed in that position for a little while, marinating in a feeling of comfort and security. I stayed in this position until the pull went away.

Time passed, but time did not heal. It ultimately took a full year or so for the divorce to finalize, and our mom's behavior became more and more erratic. We would come home from school and find her sitting at the kitchen table, staring at a light bulb, completely lost in her head. It was rare to have someone come over to check on us, and the house was officially out of control.

Dishes piled in the sink, the trash hadn't been taken out for weeks, and little trash piles sprouted up all over the kitchen floor, leaving a putrid smell developing from where maggots hatched out of fly eggs. The laundry baskets were overflowing, and there was a sea of clothes along the floor that you would have to shuffle your feet through to just walk through the house. Empty glasses and bowls encrusted with the remains of cereal and oatmeal were scattered around the TV and on the floor.

The three of us kids made every effort to get ourselves to and from school. We were no longer going to Bible school at the church. We would find a way to dress ourselves and walk to and from the bus stop every day. Some days we wore socks, and some days we didn't. Some snowy days we had hats or gloves to protect us from the cold; some days we didn't because we simply couldn't find them in the house anymore. It was becoming noticeable to others that we were being neglected. One day when we came home, Mom was waiting there for us at the door. She looked upset, as though we'd lost the family fortune on a bad bet.

"Did you tell your teachers that you were hungry?" she asked.

We all looked at each other, unsure of what to say.

"I didn't, Momma," I said, being the first to claim my innocence.

"Well, the school just called and said they're worried about you kids. They said you're looking hungry. They said you're not properly dressed for the weather," she explained. We all looked at each other, then looked down at what we were wearing. We realized it was the truth—we were not dressed properly for the weather that day. But none of us spoke up to point out the obvious. There were certainly grumbles in our bellies on most nights, and if not for school breakfast and lunch, we would have been starving.

After a long silence, my brother Paul declared,

"They called you because I can't do this anymore, Momma. We need help. I can't keep taking care of the girls. You need to start getting out of bed and getting us to school. You need to start cleaning the house. We don't have any more clean clothes, and we haven't for a while, Momma."

Paul was just ten years old at the time, but he was the oldest in the family and, though he would have rather been doing his own thing, took on the big protective brother role. He looked exasperated and flushed as we all stood there in the entranceway. His eyes began to leak tears down his cheeks and create small wet stains on his shirt. There was a long pause as our mom stared at the three of us. You could see that she was beginning to come back to reality and to really see us for the first time in a long time. It had been two seasons since Dad had moved out, and the cold made the change even more bitter.

We must have looked like a real sad state of affairs. The krinkle between her eyes started to relax for just a moment, and her face, it crumpled in places I had never seen, and she dropped to her knees fast, like she'd been hung, and started crying harder than I'd ever heard anyone cry before. It felt like the walls were shaking. She pulled the three of us into her arms and grabbed our shirts and made fists. That feeling was in my stomach again; my colors were changing. We all stood there in the hallway, stacked up on each other like wood in a fire, and cried. As I cried, I felt the pull start to slowly fade away.

Over the next few weeks, things started to improve. The house was slowly getting cleaned up, and Mom got up each morning to take us to school, some days she was even waiting for us at the bus stop near our house. She would prepare small snacks for us when we got home and was sure to make me "yucky milk" whenever I asked for it. Sam called it "yucky milk" because she thought it was disgusting. It was two parts sweetened condensed milk and one part water. It tasted like a creamy dessert, like the mother's milk I never suckeled because of my deformity made it impossible to latch on. Mom's attentiveness helped us begin to feel like the earth had stopped its shaking.

It was soon thereafter, just about a month later, when our father was granted visitation rights and a whole new level of discomfort permeated the house.

He only got to see us once a month. He would just take my brother, sister, and me all out to dinner, maybe take us to a store to buy us some shoes or clothes, or we'd go to his apartment for a short visit. Most times he would drop Sam and me off at home and let Paul spend the night with him. Our mom seemed okay with this arrangement at first.

It was only after about three visits with Dad that it was becoming clear that they couldn't share custody and that the sight of our father was leaving her angry for days. It was like sharing us with Dad was becoming harder to face than she thought—just his presence would trigger her. They would fight when he picked us up and when he dropped us off. One visit I even met one of his *friends* who was leaving his apartment as we arrived—an unfortunate encounter, I'm sure—and like any six-year-old, I went home and told Mom about the brown man I met in Dad's apartment. This didn't go over well. She rang his apartment all night, and when he did pick up, she exploded on him with expletives that left me buzzing. I knew Dad had a boyfriend, but that really didn't mean anything to me. The only thing I knew of my father was that he would put antiseptic on my wounds from this tiny green bottle, and I was always scared because it stung so bad. I only knew that I wanted him to come by the house and fix my Alligator bike because the chain wasn't working, so every time I rode my bike down the hill next to our house I had to slow myself down by putting my feet on the ground right before turning the corner. Sadly, it seemed only a matter of time before Mom would lose patience with this new and imposed arrangement, which was merely established in exchange for the child support it brought in.

One afternoon, Mom piled us kids into the loaner car Dad gave her since ours had broken down recently. We were each sitting patiently, arms folded across our laps, each taking a moment to look out our own windows and daydream. Sam and I sat in the back seat, and Paul sat in the passenger seat, as a privilege of being the oldest. Mom backed slowly out of the driveway. It wasn't like her to take us on random trips through the neighborhood, but we were all so starved for Mom's attention that we went despite any guarantees of ice cream or a trip to Centennial Park. As the car pulled slowly in front of our church, we looked at each other, confusion ricocheting across our faces. In my mind, I heard the faint sounds of a bomb falling in the distance, slowly getting louder, as if it was locked on our location and coming to land on us. She parked a hundred feet in front of the bus stop just outside the church.

"What are we doing here?" Paul asked. We were no longer attending the church; it had been too difficult to face the questions and the disgrace.

"This fucking church wants to treat me like an outcast, even though I'm not the faggot. Well, fuck 'em!" The blood rushed to her face, and I realized that rage had set in and revenge was all that would satisfy our mom. The sound of the bomb grew closer.

She opened her car door and walked over to the trunk. She pulled out a few signs on long wooden sticks and walked over to the back passenger seat where Sam and I were sitting and opened the car door.

"Get out!" she screamed. The mind bomb hit, rattling me to my core. Sam and I slid ourselves across the back seat and got out of the car. With confusion still on our faces, we looked at our mother and awaited further orders.

"Here, Paul, you grab this sign." He grabbed it and held it to the ground so he could read it. His expression changed from its usual thinking configuration to listless disappointment. It read, "My father is a faggot." The first detonation.

"Samantha and Mary, you're going to sit at the bus stop and hold these signs up," Mom said as she handed each of us signs on the long wooden sticks. Sam and I walked over to the bus stop and sat down. I realized what we were there to do—we were there to picket our father and our church. The second detonation. I had seen things like this on TV, but I didn't think I would ever do it. This is what adults did, not kids. I sat there at the bus stop and looked back at my brother. His head was down, and the sign he held draped over his shoulder so it was not readable.

"Put your sign up, Paul!" Mom screamed. He grudgingly lifted it up as he slowly walked to the bus stop to sit next to Sam and me.

We each sat there holding up signs. My sister's said, "This Baptist Church has homosexuals working here." Mine said, "Jack Gregory is gay."

The three of us sat there, transforming during every excruciating moment, each of us taking on this experience in our own way. This was an act of war—on our father and our church. We were her little army. After a few moments, a few cars honked. This reminded me of when truckers would come up and down our street, and my dad had showed me that if I put my arm in the air and pulled it down, pretending to pull on a cord truck drivers used to honk, they'd honk back. He was right, they did. But

I didn't want these cars to honk at me, especially because of these signs. Eventually our signs sank to our chests, our legs wrapped around the long wooden sticks, and our chins sat on top of the cardboard signs.

Any fond memory of my life before this moment was now becoming harder and harder to access. I had good memories that I tried to recall in that moment, like Grandma's bee farm, my grandfather's little red change wallet made of rubber, when life was simple and I was just a preacher's daughter. Each memory I was holding on to for dear life. But each moment I sat there I was slowly starting to feel less and less close to those memories, as if those memories were not mine. I was beginning to feel angry at my mom for making me feel this way, for changing me, and for making me say things I didn't mean. *Why is she doing this,* I thought.

"I want to go home," I told our mom.

"These people are the reason your father's gay. It's because of this church. We're not going anywhere, Mary."

I looked at her and put my sign down on the ground. I stomped toward the car with long strides, arms swinging. I scooched my way across the back seat and folded my hands across my chest. I sat there stewing as my hot tears streamed down my cheeks, my love for my parents now tarnished. Now, it was incarnated in the hot, stingy liquid falling from my eyes uncontrollably, like a fresh tap directly from my heart.

A few moments later, Paul and Sam opened the passenger car door and looked at me.

"Hey Mary, you okay?" Paul asked as his arm hung over the car door. I didn't say a word as I glanced at him. Paul and Sam got into the car, and we all sat next to each other in the back seat. No one said a word. After a few moments, our mom pulled the driver's side door open and peered in at us. She had all our picket signs under her arm and threw them over the front passenger seat. Her eyes were covered in a glaze of tears, and I could tell she was holding them back by the crumpling in her face and the heat that made her cheeks bright red. She sat in the driver's seat with her hands gripping the wheel, taking deep breaths. After a few moments of this silence, she let out a heavy and almost remorseful sigh and started the car.

No one spoke the entire ride home. My mind swirled with thoughts of the church and how now it was taking on this whole other meaning. The church was where I went to preschool, where I was told I shouldn't write with my left hand—but did anyway—where I had a crush on Christopher, the platinum blond boy in my class, who I liked so much that I wanted to be a boy just so he would play with me. It was where I would get spicy cinnamon Dentyne gum from the old fat guy who ushered folks into the main worship hall. It was where I survived my baptism. Now, it was becoming a confusing place in my heart and mind, filled with accused liars and deceivers. I was being forced to shift my life entirely from everything I had ever known. Everything I had ever known to be true was becoming a lie. My parents and my life were changing right before my eyes.

BEE STINGS

Any kind of visit to Grandma Edith's was usually unpleasant. It was nice to see our family, but she never really seemed to like us. She was a beautician and owned a beauty salon. Edith had white hair as high as a beehive, and a face that looked like she had just sucked on a sour lemon, with an attitude to match. She was of good stock, always wearing a dress, support stockings, and comfortable white shoes. Edith always seemed tired, as if her busy life was catching up to her. My grandfather, Walter, had Parkinson's disease and had been deteriorating for years and grandma was his principal caregiver. He was always pale and sweaty, with a lop of black hair stuck to his glistening forehead. He was a tall and slender man, with sucked-in cheeks and hollowed brown eyes. I always wished I had known him longer before this disease got its tight hold on him. The thought of catching it often raced through my mind and would scare the bejesus out of me. I was told he got the disease from being stung by a swarm of bees. Over a thousand stings, they said! I tried to recreate that situation in my head, but knowing that they were bee farmers, it never seemed to add up. It was probably just something they told us kids to help us make sense of it all.

It was great to get his attention, though. A spark would shine out of his eyes, and he would give me a smile. In those moments, I felt loved. As much as he had the sweats, and as much as Grandma had to change his sweaty sheets almost ten times a day, there was an immense amount of love between the two of them. They had five kids together. My mom was the youngest of five, and almost fifteen years younger than her oldest sibling, Uncle Hank. Mom had told me she had been a daddy's girl. When we would see Grandma Edith it was usually because Mom needed some time alone. Paul, Sam, and I drove Grandma nuts. She'd start yelling that she was going to whip our behinds if we didn't keep it down in the house. Countless times she would run into the bedroom where my sister and I were jumping on the bed, being loud and obnoxious, and corner one of us so she could pull out the switch. That thing would make so much noise as it swung through the air before smacking you on the bottom. She always made sure she got you on your bare bottom, too. A good whelp would come out and you'd be told to shut up! The red heat of tears running down our faces, and the burning sensation from our freshly whacked bottoms, got us in order pretty quickly.

Mom once told us that Grandma was afraid of drowning; that's why she never took a bath. She would only wash herself in the sink with a washcloth. It was interesting to me that a woman with such a strong personality and such resilience had such a silly vulnerability. I often wondered where this fear came from. She certainly didn't seem to be afraid of anything else.

Grandpa was the complete opposite from Grandma. He was a nice and gentle man. He cared for us deeply, and before he was too disabled, he would take us kids with him to the barbershop and to the store. He was actually able to drive for a little while, albeit it was a wobbly car ride. He carried a bright red change purse made of rubber. It was thick rubber and had a slit down the middle. When he squeezed it, it would open and show me all kinds of coins he had stacked on each other. They filled the inside of it completely. He would pull it out of his pocket, drop his hand down to our faces, and we'd marvel as he opened it up and told us to take a quarter.

"Really, Grandpa?" we'd ask.

"Sure, go on, get a candy from the machine," he would tell us.

We'd drop a coin in a gum machine, turn the shiny metal knob and crank away, each turn getting us closer and closer to a sweet treat. I was in love with gumball machines. I loved the clinking sound they made as my quarter fell into the compartment where all the other coins lived. It was a sound unlike anything else and gave me a small thrill inside.

Going to Grandma Ediths's house when they were harvesting honey was quite the experience. I only recall enjoying this experience once, however.

On that day, many of my mom's sisters were at my grandparents' house. There were pots all over the kitchen; honeycombs and golden honey sunbathed in mason jars on the counter. I watched lustfully, like children do when they see sweet treats before them, while honey settled slowly around the combs as my aunt Ruth tilted the pot of honey into the jars. Grandma was walking from the bee farm back to the house, holding huge trays of honey and combs. Bees were flying everywhere. I was scared and fascinated all at the same time.

Grandma refused to wear any kind of bee suit because, in her opinion, there was nothing to be afraid of. I followed her into the kitchen through the back door. Most of the bees had flown back into their boxes, and all that was left was a caramel-colored tray of wax and honey. She pulled off a piece of the honeycomb and handed it to me. The honey dripped down my hand, and I looked up at her. She had little pieces of bee on her hands and fingers and around her nails. A wing stuck to her knuckle and little speckles of the stuff that bees are made of peppered her nail bed. She seemed so strong and powerful in that moment. She told me to bite into it, to chew the comb but not to swallow it. I took a big savory bite out of that hunk of honeycomb. I'll never forget the surge of flavor that enveloped my mouth. My teeth slid through the comb, and a small half-moon chunk stared back at me. As I chewed, more and more gushes of honey filled my mouth. I had to swallow honey quickly enough to make room for the ever-changing wax formation that was happening in my mouth. Ultimately, the comb clumped together into a soft lump, the consistency getting harder than gum by every chew. I stared at the small piece left in my hand, mesmerized by the shape of interlocking catacombs that stored little pieces of gold. As the last bite of honeycomb was pinched between my fingers, a small amount of honey oozed down my hand. There couldn't have been a lovelier fate for this child's heart.

I finally pulled the wax out of my mouth, and observed the tooth-marked wad of white wax. I was impressed that the form had been created from the hovering swarms of bees and by the caramel-colored sweet liquid gold that still dripped down my fingers.

My sister's experience wasn't as divine. She was minding her own business when a rogue bee, no doubt upset at our pillaging, targeted Sam. It was her first bee sting. She screamed out that she had been stung, holding out her little index finger. All the aunts came over to her, and one pulled out the stinger, while my mom whisked her inside for some more care. Edith peeked out of the back door and said to me, "I told you girls not to be scared of them darn bees. They won't sting you if you just ignore them. They can sense when you're scared." I decided at that moment never to be afraid of bees again. Perhaps I'd be like Grandma. Not scared of anything. Except maybe drowning. She must have been Baptized too.

BIG BROTHER AND FOOD STAMPS

The small neighborhood store just up the street from our house had a soda machine on the porch that sold cold glass-bottled Coke and 7UP for just a quarter. Many times in the summer, we'd all walk up to the store just to buy a cold pop from the machine. Something about opening the door, sliding out a pop, the sound of the cap popping off, and watching the misty release of carbonation made my little heart sing a little.

We experienced our first winter without our dad and the car he loaned us no longer ran. The winters in Nashville brought rain and snow and did a real number on our house. Without having a family car, or the means to buy one, we were stuck relying on kind people Mom knew from the church to do our grocery runs. On one day in particular, there was a blizzard outside, and over the course of a few hours, it had dumped several inches of snow onto the roads and sidewalks. We were low on everything in the house, and Mom was unable to call in a favor. She turned to Paul to talk him into the task.

"Here is eight dollars. Be sure to keep the money in the booklet. They'll pull the money out when it's time to pay, okay?" she explained to him. I don't think Paul had ever paid for a family shopping trip by himself before, and definitely not with food stamps. He nodded that he understood. He took the paper booklet, put it into the side pocket of his jacket, and zipped it up. He threw on his hat with the furry earflaps, and his thick maroon-colored gloves. He then headed out into the blizzard on his important mission.

I kept thinking about how cold he must have been. Just the thought made me shiver. I was worried for Paul. No one was on the road, and all you could hear once the door opened was the sound of wind and ice crystals smacking against the house and trees. The skies were an eerie gray, and the air was cloudy white. Perfect for the imagination of a child's scary monster to show itself.

I thought my brother was so brave. He seemed to understand what having the "man of the house" title meant. I waited patiently by the door for his return, envisioning his journey down the sidewalk to the country store, how he was battling the blizzard, and how he'd triumphantly walk through the front door. I wanted him to be safe, so I tried my best to walk with him in my mind. I tried to keep the thought of him turning into a real snowman out of my mind, even though the visual slipped in from time to time. He was nearly all white by the time he walked through the door. His arms puffed out from the jacket he was wearing, one hand holding a jug of milk, the other hand holding a bag full of food; eggs, bread, cereal, bananas, and oatmeal.

The harsh winter made me fantasize about warmer times. When our family would play in the backyard together. Sam and I would get on the swings, our father lying in the sun with cucumbers on his eyes, sporting his little Speedo while catching some rays in the lawn chair.

Going back into time and remembering when we were all enjoying the house as a family was what I did when I needed to remember "the good times."

During the divorce, Dad hadn't come around much, and Mom never seemed to be fully present. We certainly didn't eat at the table for dinner anymore. One day, my dad was at the house, picking some things up. I was explaining to him my Evel Knievel trick with my bike, and how I put my feet on the ground to slow down as I swung around the corner in a dramatic stunt. He said he would fix the chain when he could and that maybe next time he came over, he would do it. He never came back to fix the chain, and as the weeks passed, I began to lose my expectation that he ever would.

Each year around Thanksgiving my school would ask us for canned goods to donate to a family in need for the holidays. That year I did my best to grab a few canned goods from our mostly barren cupboards. My mom helped me pick out a few things that we could give besides canned food, like a bag of rice and some saltine crackers. I brought them to school, proudly pulling out each item from my paper grocery bag. The next day the teacher asked the class who wanted to go with her to deliver the food. I raised my hand so high and eagerly my butt came out of the seat. I wanted to be part of giving someone in need some of the food from my house. I could imagine a little old lady's joy at receiving my crackers and a can of my fruit medley. Going on the car ride with my teacher was especially exciting. Any kind of car ride I got excited about because I never really got to ride in a car, and I loved the feeling of it. How quickly everything passed by you, and how much there was to see. We started off by taking three bags of food to an elderly woman who lived by herself. We had another three bags full of food. "One more stop," my teacher said. We drove for a short while and pulled up to my house. In bewilderment, I looked at her.

"Why are we at my house, Mrs. Beaucanon?"

"We're here to donate food to your house, Mary, because you're one of the families that need help this year."

Part of our life without Dad meant we were pretty poor. If he paid child support, it never went very far. Food stamps helped, but when you had three young children who drank a gallon of milk a day and a mother who didn't work, well, $300 in child support only went so far.

The deferred maintenance on the house was really bad. When it rained, it poured in the house. The dining room had large brown circles where droplets had leaked through the ceiling many times before, and these were in several locations around the house. When it rained, we hurried to grab big buckets, bowls, and pots to catch all the rain. In a way, it was fun. My mom would turn it into a game. She would say, "Where in the house can you find water?" I would leap up and run through each room to find a leaky ceiling.

"I found some, Mom, here in the living room," I would say proudly as I pointed to the newly discovered leak. We all ended up taking shifts of dumping water duty while the rain came down. Huddling in the living room for heat, we each occupied ourselves in different ways. Mom was getting the TV working with bunny rabbit ears and aluminum foil. I was playing a board game with my sister. Checkers was my favorite. I could play for hours with Paul and Sam. Though Paul would mostly draw and watch TV with Mom. After a few days of rain, it would let up, and the carpets would have a chance to dry. We would be back at school once it was possible to get on the streets again without a car. The weather always seemed so harsh when I was a child. I never seemed to have the right clothes, the right shoes, the right accessories, or the transportation to get through it. Depending on the conditions, I would invariably be stuck with wet clothes when it rained or be freezing when it was snowing. Even still, I loved the rain and the snow. When I did have the right clothes on, it was grand! Stomping in puddles was a sheer delight and so was making angels in the snow. These were purely joyous moments for me as a child.

The old ladies next door to our house were quite friendly. They had mothballs in their lawn, which always gave their yard and their house a weird smell. I wondered why they needed so many mothballs everywhere. Whenever my sister and I were feeling especially adorable, we would walk next door, ring the doorbell, and ask in unison, "Can we have some butterscotch, please?" We'd stand there with our wide smiles, hands behind our backs, looking up at the old lady neighbors as they joyfully welcomed our request.

The older sister, Esther, would yell to her sister inside, "Ethel, the neighbor girls want some butterscotch. Can you bring a few pieces?" Sometimes we would be invited in. Their museum-style home had a soft yellow glow that emanated throughout the house and onto the front porch. Sometimes I scared myself with the thought that maybe if I took their invitation to come inside, I could get trapped, that maybe their kindness was some kind of setup, like in *Hansel and Gretel*. But then inevitably, as I

27

pondered the risks, one of the sisters would bring out some butterscotch to the front porch where we were standing. We'd tell them we had to go and scurry out like happy little mice. The yellow wrappers around the yellow candy always seemed funny to me because it was correctly advertising the color of the candy inside. Red cinnamon candy did the same thing, which I liked more than butterscotch. Sam, however, was butterscotch's biggest fan.

'67 DODGE DART

The day my mom showed up in a '67 Dodge Dart, the path to our new life was really just beginning. It was aqua-colored and seemed kind of cool with its white-walled tires and chromed grill.

My dad had left an old black Lincoln Continental in the driveway that didn't run anymore. I loved to go inside of it and explore. It was like a relic of times passed, when he still lived with us. I would go inside of it to get away from the outside world, peacefully allowing myself to explore it. I would look through the glove compartment and sift through his papers. I'd find cool things under the seats. I'd grab the steering wheel and pretend I was driving. I'd reach down and pull out the cigarette lighter and look at the spirals and wonder how it worked. There was something familiar about being in my dad's old car. The smell felt like a mix of old newspapers, dust, and leather. All the little gadgets and knobs and chrome and wood finishes sparked my imagination like nothing else. When I was in his car, I felt I was close to him. I would read the carefully folded papers in the glove box. Line by line the registration information, running my fingers over the letters in his name–*JACK*–and then the words that told me our street address–*NEBRASKA AVENUE.*

When my mom pulled up in the Dart, I was playing explorer in the Lincoln. I leaned up through the window to see the car shift from side to side while it settled into the rock driveway next to the Lincoln. It was interesting and exciting seeing my mom driving a car, since this was not a sight I was used to anymore, not since Mom and Dad divorced. I rolled down the window, putting all my weight into it to turn the knob round and round with both hands. Perhaps this meant things were going to get better? But, shortly after Mom arrived, she declared news I hadn't expected.

"We're leaving Nashville, and we're going to go visit some family before we go," she said.

"Where are we going after that?" I asked.

"I don't know yet, but it's going to be better than here," she said. Her decision to leave seemed swift, and quickly brought me down from my original excitement. As I exited my dad's Lincoln and pushed the door closed with both my hands and body, I realized that I would soon be leaving it and my father behind, along with the life I knew.

That was the first time I experienced regret–such a short word for how bad I'd felt. Granted, I was only six years old, but my mind was already keenly focused on my life. My mom told me to go inside the house and grab some things I would want to bring.

There were a few things I really loved, like the Mickey Mouse phone we had in the dining room. It was something nice we had. I would pick up the phone and turn the dial around and around, making a game of which number I was calling, mostly having them start in the 8's, 9's, and 0's so I got to roll my finger fully around the rotary and watch it roll back and hear the recoil sound. I actually felt silly wanting to take the phone. Why would I take our phone in the car? Sure, I loved that phone, but my mom was talking about leaving, and I knew what she meant. That we were leaving for good. The only other thing I thought of to take was the grandfather clock that hung in the living room but my dad had broken into the house a few days before and stolen it. He had taken a few things while we were out of the house, but I remember that being one of them. There was now only an outline on the wall where it used to hang.

Dad was really upsetting our mom in those days. Just his presence enraged her. I think he broke in to save all of us kids another physical encounter between the two of them. It was my first experience of having my home broken into. You see your house a totally different way after that. You see it how someone else sees it. You notice the things that are untidy, the vulnerable spots that were once just a normal area, now disturbed by an intruder. I thought there was no need for me to take anything that would remind me of what I was leaving behind. And so, I never went into the house to grab anything.

Everyone piled into the car. I remember watching my brother and sister get into the car with their heads hung low, carrying small bags of things they wanted to bring. It was a pretty short period of time from when my mom said we were leaving until we actually got on the road. I remember, as we pulled out of the driveway, feeling like I should have gone inside. I should have taken a look around the house one last time. Felt the house one last time.

The farther we went down the road and the smaller the house appeared in the distance, the more I realized we were leaving our home, our town, and our life as we knew it. I was going to be traveling through unknown lands in this aqua-colored car.

It would be another thirteen years before I would see my father again.

AUNT CAROLINA'S

G oing out of town would mean we would stop at a few relatives' houses. The first stop was Aunt Carolina's, my father's sister.

Aunt Carolina had a husky dog that grabbed you by the hand and walked you to their front door from the driveway. He was a blind dog, so this was his way to make sure you knew he still had dibs on the house. I was always scared of this dog, but my sister and brother had no fear. I couldn't figure out how they weren't afraid to place their little kid hands in its mouth. No way would I do this. Getting bitten by a dog was a serious fear of mine. After endless amounts of assurance that the dog wouldn't bite me, I still held my ground and waited in the car until the dog was in the house, and then I would wait for someone to escort me inside.

Aunt Carolina was married to a motorcycle cop named Cleo. He was the skeptical tough type, but he loved my aunt dearly. And he loved her two children, Lenora and Winston. Aunt Carolina's nickname was "Dearie." A name she approved after Lenora made her a grandmother. She didn't want to be called, "Grandma." She was too young and pretty for that. Lenora and Winston were the oldest of all the cousins from both sides of the family, by at least ten or so years, so it always felt like they were happy to see their baby cousins, and we were always well received. There were two more cousins from Dad's younger brother Alan, but we weren't close to him or our cousins. Aunt Carolina would always have candy ready once we stepped through the door, and she always wanted to know everything that was going on in our lives.

Every time we would come over, the first thing we wanted to do was go to cousin Winston's bedroom. His room had everything; a TV, an Atari, a stereo, a record player, and the mother of all things cool, a waterbed. He always lets us play in his room and take over his space. I would plop down on his bed and let my body move as the waves made splashing sounds. My brother and sister would do the same, and the three of us would giggle and laugh in excitement as we tried to traverse the sea that was his bed. I stared at the posters he had lining his wood-paneled walls; Prince's "Purple Rain" and Michael Jackon's "Thriller." This was a boy's room. It maintained a masculine color palette, which consisted of flannel sheets and dark drapes, and a few items around to decorate; just the necessities—like combs, a wallet, keys, and watches—were on his dresser.

This time, though, Aunt Carolina stopped us all from running into Winston's room. She told us that she had something to tell us first. We all sat on her long couch, the three of us kids sitting there, waiting to hear what she had to say, like obedient little church kids.

"Listen, your cousin Winston is sick, and you ain't gonna be able to go see him today."

"Why's he sick, Aunt Carolina?" Paul asked with a puzzled look on his face.

"He's got a bad disease that's making him really tired."

"But we just want to say bye before we leave," Paul said.

Mom looked at Aunt Carolina to indicate it was up to her to approve the request. She nodded, "Well, all right, but don't be too long." We all leapt from the couch and ran around the corner to Winston's room. Paul opened the door slowly. We all peeped in the room to see Winston lying on his bed, his back toward the door.

"Winston, it's us. We're leaving, and we want to say goodbye. Hey, Winston, wake up," Paul continued to whisper. Winston stirred a little and turned toward us. "Hey guys, come on in," he said softly.

"Where you guys going?" he asked while rubbing his eyes open. He patted his hand down on his waterbed to signal for Paul to come sit down. I could hear the water splashing. Paul hopped on the bed next to Winston and put both hands behind his head while sitting up against a pillow. His body and Winston's were bouncing up and down slowly in the waves.

"I don't know where we're going. Mom bought a car and wants to leave town. We're saying bye to everyone," he said so matter-of-factly. I stood at the side of the bed, not wanting to get on, not wanting to make it a final goodbye.

"Let's go, kids," Mom shouted from the living room. As we left Winston's room and walked through the hallway, Mom and Aunt Carolina were softly talking in the living room. Aunt Carolina was telling Mom she wanted to tell us kids about what Winston had. When they saw us, Mom turned to Aunt Carolina and gave her permission.

"Now, I want you kids to know that Winston is sick. He's got a virus that is really bad, and there's no cure for it. He went to the doctor, and they said he has HIV. Do you know what HIV is?" she asked us cautiously. I knew this word because I had heard it a few times since Dad had come out of the closet. The language used around me to describe gay people hadn't been subtle, and no one had held back on the derogatory terms that first came to their mind when the subject was brought up. I had seen a few ads and commercials talking about the disease and whether it could be caught on toilet seats. It dawned on me in that moment that cousin Winston must have been gay, too.

We left her house on that note, and my mind swirled with all that this meant. I really wanted to run back into his room and fling my arms around him for a big, huge hug. But I didn't. I didn't go back into his room. I just followed everyone out to the car and looked out the window as we drove away. The blind dog stood there obediently next to Aunt Carolina and Uncle Cleo. The dog seemed to hold some kind of wisdom that I could finally see, and that I was no longer afraid of. I would never see Winston again. I later learned when I was much older that Winston was one of the earliest reported cases of HIV in the Nashville area. He had a great relationship with a man who stayed by his side for years until he passed away in 1991 from AIDS-related illnesses.

UNCLE HANK

The next stop was Uncle Hank's, Mom's older brother. He lived about thirty miles from Nashville, with his wife Gladys and two girls, Natalie and Jessica. He looked like a greaser; black boots, blue jeans, and a white T-shirt with a pack of smokes rolled into the sleeve.

We stayed for a few days in his baby blue double-wide trailer that sat on cinder blocks. They had a picture of Elvis in the dining room that was bigger than the one they had of Jesus on the opposite wall. His wife Gladys had a sweet voice but was nervously shy, or maybe just unconfident, but in those days, she was just considered obedient. She waited for cues from uncle Hank before she made any decisions around the house, except when it came to the kids. Her aim was to keep us kids occupied by making sure we had enough food to eat and toys to play with that we stayed out of the rooms that she and Hank liked to occupy. It was nice to be catered to like this. I could ask Gladys for anything and she would find a way to accomodate me. Since Uncle Hank didn't want to handle anything with the kids, he was usually occupying himself with woodworking projects in his garage.

Natalie and Paul were the same age, and Jessica was a little younger than me. We all loved to play together. Jessica had a bouncing toy horse in her room. She also had a chest full of dress-up clothes and a toy box full of Barbie dolls and Mr. Potato Heads and LEGOs. Sam, Jessica, and I could play hide and go seek for hours.

Uncle Hank was artistic. He made treasure boxes out of cedar wood and carved beautiful designs on their lids. The most wonderful smell wafted through the air as the cedar box began to burn under his soldering knife. I loved that smell. I sat there watching Uncle Hank engrave a heart on a box that he ended up giving to our mom as a present when she returned to pick us up. For my brother, he engraved an eagle on his cedar box. Uncle Hank's hand moved effortlessly as the designs seemed to come to life under his knife. The burning cedar stayed with me for years after, and I could almost smell it each time I looked at those designs.

AUNT RUTH

Aunt Ruth was the closest in age to Mom and five years older. She was the shortest of all of Mom's sisters, too. Their house was at the corner of a winding road that swung left and only gave you just a moment to turn into their long, steep driveway that led to the back of their house, where they had a small set of chairs on the back porch. When you walked in, you were right in their dining room, and to the right was their kitchen. There were knickknacks everywhere, and a sign that read, "Bless This Mess," hung on the wall. A mason jar of bacon grease sat off to the side of their stovetop. They had an empty five-gallon refillable water bottle in the corner of the kitchen; this is where everyone threw their spare change and occasional bill. The front of the house sat on top of a ledge, and it had long stilts to hold it up. It faced a pond off to the left, and the rest was green rolling hills and several other decks that all faced toward the same shared pond.

Their den was downstairs, and so was my aunt's office. You had to walk down over thirty heavily carpeted steps to get downstairs or so it seemed. Their den felt like a warm and cozy cave, with green shag carpet and wood-paneled walls. There was a TV set with an Atari hooked up, and books lined the many shelves around the room. Magazines were in baskets next to each of their large armchairs. They had two kids, John and Chloe, who were both older than my brother—John by five years and Chloe by three. John was really into science and planes, and Chloe had posters of horses all over her bedroom wall. Her room was the epitome of a girly-girl's room. It looked like something from a kids' commercial with the matching bed covers and curtains, dolls everywhere, and stuffed animals stacked neatly on her bed.

We weren't close to our aunt Ruth and her family—and we rarely ever saw any of them, though I'm not sure how much they talked on the phone—but she was welcoming and wanted to make us feel at home. They were a smart family, way smarter than we were. Aunt Ruth's husband was a geologist. Aunt Ruth was a math teacher. Their kids were smart. Brainiac smart.

We had arrived at their house late; dinner had already been served and the kitchen cleaned up. But Aunt Ruth started fixing us up some plates once we all walked into the dining room. We would be staying the night and sleeping in their den, so we were told. I'd felt like we had invaded their home. We hadn't really grown up around our cousins, so the next day when they woke up to us hanging out in their den, watching their TV, they didn't know what to make of the situation. But soon, though, my brother and cousin John started playing Atari. My sister and I hung out in Chloe's room, looking at all her posters of horses, playing with her dolls. I wasn't sure why she liked horses so much, but I imagined that it was because she could actually go ride one, being that she was more in the countryside than we were in Nashville.

The agreement was that us kids would stay there a few days while our mom settled some loose ends. We were going on a week now that our mom was dropping us off at family members' houses and then taking off. Maybe because she finally had wheels, she could get away for a while and enjoy some freedom from us kids? Maybe she was going back to our house to grab the Mickey Mouse phone? But while she was gone, I was unsupervised, and I decided that I'd go fishing for change in the kitchen.

Late at night I would sneak into their kitchen and slowly roll the five-gallon jug of coins on its side. I would put my small fingers inside and reach for quarters, taking ten or fifteen at a time, slowly taking their quarters each time I could, hoping no one would notice. I had been wrapping them up in a napkin, hiding them in my winter jacket pockets. Over the course of just two or three days, I had probably stolen about thirty dollars in quarters.

Once Mom arrived back at Aunt Ruth's, she announced we were leaving and getting back on the road. We quickly gathered our things and said goodbye to our cousins. I was especially clever about getting my jacket into the car first, as I didn't want the sound of clinking quarters to tip them off. I decided that once we were far from Aunt Ruth's, I would confess to Mom what I had done. As we rode out in the '67 Dart, I started counting down the minutes until I could confess my dirty deed. I wanted the distance from Aunt Ruth's house to be far enough that it wouldn't make sense for us to go back and give her the money. After an agonizing fifteen minutes, I pulled out the two carefully wrapped napkin bundles of quarters from my pockets and laid the coins on my lap. Since I was sitting in the front seat, the sound caught my mom's attention, and she glanced at my lap. Her eyes widened as she gazed at the mound of quarters I had.

"Where did you get all that money, Mary?" she demanded.

"I took it from Aunt Ruth's change jug. They had all this money in there, and we're poor, and I thought we could use it," I confessed.

"Now, you know stealin' ain't right, Mary," she said as she gave me a disappointed glance.

"I know, but we need the money, Mom." I gave her my most endearing wide-eyed pouty face. She thought for a while, staring at the road ahead.

"Well, we can't turn around now. They didn't need the money like we do. I'm sure they ain't missin' it." A huge sigh of relief rushed from me.

"So what do you think we should do with the money, Mom?" I asked. My brother raised his hand and exclaimed, "Let's go to Burger King!" A chorus of agreement echoed throughout the car, and we all waited to hear the verdict.

"Well, all right, that sounds nice," Mom said as she glanced over at me, a small smile across her face. I turned around to look at my brother and sister and flashed them my biggest grin. Somehow I had pulled off the biggest heist of my life! As the cheeseburgers settled into my stomach, I felt an overwhelming sense of guilt. I wasn't proud of myself. I knew it was wrong to steal, but I knew why I did it. I was tired of us being poor and not having control over when we would eat. Having some money felt good. I never wanted to steal again, but the problem was I didn't know how long I was going to be poor either.

AUNT SOPHIE

Our last stop was to Aunt Sophie's. She was my grandmother's little sister, on my mother's side. Unlike Grandma Edith, she was a sweet, soft woman, but still strong and unafraid. She lived just twenty miles from Chattanooga. Her town wasn't very big, and as you got into her neighborhood, there were long roads lined with trees, big gaps between the houses, and lots of land for animals. Aunt Sophie had a farm with all kinds of animals; horses, chickens, and even a fair amount of kittens running around. It was exactly like everything I had ever heard about a farm. I hadn't remembered Aunt Sophie, so this was my first impression of this woman, and I was pleased.

She lived in a single-wide trailer, not too big. Just enough. Aunt Sophie's house had burned down a few years before, but they had left it sitting on the farm, burned and all, though they had hoped to rebuild it. After we arrived, she walked us up to the burned house to have a peek inside. It was weird to see everything black and charred, just like the day it had burned down over five years ago.

Aunt Sophie described what had happened like a tour guide would describe the history of an old castle or village ruins.

"There was an electrical fire that started while we were asleep. Our fire department is volunteer only you know, and when they arrived it took them about fifteen minutes to get the fire out. But it was too late."

I imagined her being unable to put the fire out and standing there while she watched her house burn. This seemed far worse than a break-in, but it was still a violation.

"You can see where all our family pictures were over there on the side table and the wall. Our armchairs are still there, too. That's where my husband and I would sit at night and watch TV." I listened intently as she described all that she lost in the fire.

Later that day, we were all sitting outside in front of this huge tree in an open part of their yard. There was a little swing hanging from it. I sat on it and swung a while as my mom and Aunt Sophie talked. My brother started climbing the tree. "You better stop climbing that tree, Paul. You're gonna fall off and break your arm," Aunt Sophie told him in a wise manner.

"I'm not going to fall off, Aunt Sophie. I've been climbing trees for a while now," he said confidently. A few minutes later, I hopped off the swing and followed Aunt Sophie inside. Mom and Sam were already back in the house getting ready for supper. As soon as we were inside, we heard a loud scream from Paul.

We all rushed outside to find him lying at the base of the tree holding his arm. Mom rushed over to him and picked him up. His arm was broken and hanging in such a way it looked way longer than it should have been. I looked at Aunt Sophie like she was some kind of magic woman, a fortune teller. How did she know he would fall and break his arm? Aunt Sophie's daughter took Paul and Mom to the emergency room, and Sam and I waited for them patiently with Aunt Sophie at the house. When he returned, he looked battered and tired. His cast was white and bulky. He had a look of shame on his face—probably because he knew Aunt Sophie's prediction had come true and he was just too knuckleheaded to listen to her. We stayed with her for an extra day so Paul could rest some more, then we headed back on the road.

BYE BYE, TENNESSEE.
HELLO, NEW YORK.

Leaving Tennessee and getting on the road meant a mayhem of maps, gas stations, and lots of coffee. Paul would always end up being the pumper at the gas stations. Each time, the money Mom handed him got smaller and smaller. I wasn't sure where we were going; we just drove. After a few days of being on the road and sleeping at rest stops every night, I really started wanting a bed. Eventually, I woke up from a night nap to our mom yelling. "Look, we're in the Big Apple!" she said, fully charged with excitement, her finger pointing toward the city. We had just gotten on the Brooklyn Bridge. Boy, was it impressive! We all pressed our faces to the window to see as much of the city as we could. Despite the late hour, it was so bright and busy. It felt as though we were floating in a ship above the sky. Mom drove slower now. The feeling of being on a bridge that size was starting to make her feel uneasy, and she told us to settle down so she could concentrate.

Once we were off the bridge, the first stop was to ask someone where we could find the Travelers Aid office. Luckily for us, it was open 24/7. They assessed our situation after a brief discussion with Mom, then a tall Black woman came from behind the counter and said she would take us to the store around the corner to pick up some food. We followed her in our car. It wasn't until we were in the liquor store that I realized how hungry I was. I didn't know if I should grab Oreos or a banana. I was used to gas station selections, so I went with them both and an apple juice. The woman explained that we could stay in a shelter at the church up the street for the night. In the morning, we could come back and she would have a hotel voucher for us.

Once we arrived at the church, we were shown where we could sleep. She pointed us to the pews. We all looked over at the sea of homeless people wrapped up in blankets and lying along the seats. The smell of sour clothes and musk assaulted my senses. Were we going to have to sleep here?

"Because you're so late, we can't have you all sleeping in the same area," the woman said to Mom.

"We have to stay together," Mom told her.

"I'm sorry, we just don't have the room. You can see how full we are."

"We can't sleep here then. We can't all fit on one of these," Mom said as she pointed at the long, skinny wooden pews. "Thank you for your help, but we're leaving." Mom grabbed the top of my jacket and pulled me with her as she walked away. She turned around to Paul and Sam to make sure they were following us. As soon as we reached the outside, the cool air hit us hard, but it was a welcome relief from the stuffiness and hopelessness in the church. The church seemed more eerie, unknown, and lonely to me now. I hadn't ever imagined that this was what they were used for at night, to shelter those who had no place to go. Sleeping in our car until the morning seemed like our only option now, and I was perfectly fine with that. The piles of empty coffee cups and food wrappers that littered the car floor, the piles of clothes and pillows that were thrown across the seats, was a welcoming and familiar sight now. At least we still had a place to go.

When the morning came, we went back to Travelers Aid and marched in to get our hotel voucher. The woman who helped us last night was not there, but my mom intended on giving someone a piece of her mind for suggesting that the church was an option for a woman with small kids. She had been up all night ruminating. She'd sigh heartily every few minutes; her exhaled warm breath hovered in the air against the cold of the car. The blankets we had and the insulation from the car didn't hold up against the New York cold. Mom explained her grievances to the man working the counter, and he apologized. He said he would make a note of it in their logs and the next time they would recommend a different place for women with children. That seemed to satisfy her.

The vouchers were only good for three nights. He also gave us the address of a shelter for women with children in Yonkers. "That's going to be your best bet until you can get on public assistance," he advised. All I wanted to do was sleep in a bed. The three days seemed to go by slowly. Each day we went to the welfare office to wait in line to get seen and to move through the process. Those were long days. You needed an address to get aid, so the shelter was going to be our only way to qualify. Mom's plan was that after the first check arrived, we would leave the shelter and find an apartment.

The shelter felt like a hospital. Each room held up to three families. Bunk beds lined the rooms and could fit eight people. The rooms had metal lockers along one wall where people kept their belongings. We were paired with a Black family with two boys and a girl. Our moms chatted briefly about why they were there, and once they parted, we started getting settled in. I'd never really seen my mom talk to Black people before now. Where we lived and went to school and church, there weren't many people of color. I'd keenly observed Mom's interactions then. Now that we were in New York, I realized that everyone who had helped us so far was Black. At first, it seemed that us kids would get along without any issues. The kids were around the same age as the three of us, so naturally we were interested in seeing if we could pair up and play. Over the course of a few days, it was apparent that they didn't want to be our friends. If we would say "Good mornin'," they would completely ignore us. I'm sure we seemed as different to them as they did to us. We'd gotten word the day after living in the shelter that within a few days we would have our first government check and could find an apartment and get out of there.

I had grown accustomed to being stared at because I looked different. One afternoon, while I was reading a book on my bunk, the three kids stared at me from the hallway. At first I didn't think much of it, since they often observed people. Likely, they were far from home, too. They came up to me, and one asked, "Do you want to play hide and seek?"

"Sure," I said as I looked up from my book. The girl started to count, and the other two boys started looking for places to hide. The oldest boy indicated I should go in the locker to hide. I was too claustrophobic to do that, but he opened the door, and the other boy pushed me inside and slammed it shut. I started banging on the door. "Open this door! Help! Open the door!" I screamed and banged as they all laughed outside. It was completely dark in there except for the small light coming from the top of the locker vents and the cracks along the sides. I kept screaming, but no one was coming. After a few moments, the kids left the room and it was just me. I was growing more and more scared and decided I was going to get myself out of there. I pressed my back against the back of the locker while I pushed my feet against the door with all my might. I got the jam of the door to bend in just enough to put my hand around it. I grabbed the bent section with both my hands and started to pull it back like a sardine can. I was able to pull back the metal just enough to get my head through. I gasped at the fresh air and light. I screamed for help directly into the four corners of the big room. When still no one came, I decided I was going to get out by myself. I tried to push my body through the hole I had created. The metal scratched my arms and ribs, but I kept pushing myself through, contorting my body like I was shedding a second skin. My thighs and kneecaps and then my feet finally came out, and I laid on the cool linoleum floor. Soon, a few people came running into the room. My brother and sister had been outside playing and hadn't heard my screams until a few moments before.

"What happened, Mary?" my brother asked.

"Those...kids...pushed me in the locker...and...wouldn't let me out," I told him in between deep breaths and crying. My forehead was dripping with sweat. I was taken to the administration office to tell them my story. They patched up my scrapes with antiseptic and Band-Aids. I really wished that my dad was there to clean my scratches and scrapes with his little green bottle of antiseptic—I preferred his stings to theirs. My mom had been out looking for apartments and didn't come back for a few more hours. The office administrator decided that they would move the other family out of the room we were sharing for now and would talk to the mother of the kids. No one seemed alarmed about the incident. It made me feel guilty about asking for help.

Once Mom got back to the shelter, she decided we were going to live in a motel until she found a place. The check came in the mail that next day. So we drove through Queens trying to find an apartment in an area that was close to a school. We parked in a small parking lot and we were all standing next to the car when a tall, handsome blond man walked over to us.

"Hi there. I'm James, and you are?" he asked with a friendly tone and extended a hand out to shake my mom's.

"I'm Linda," she said, blushing.

"I see you got a classic '60s Dodge Dart. I work on cars, so if you ever need anything, just let me know," he offered.

"Well, I do have some issues right now. It's been overheating," she shared.

"Open the hood for me and I'll take a look," he said as he pointed to it and walked right in front of the car. He wore blue jeans and a white T-shirt and had a bandana hanging from his back pocket. His cigarettes were rolled in his sleeve. I could see my mom really liked this attention. She was smiling more than I had seen her smile in a really long time. My mom was a large woman, over 250 pounds at the time. She was just thirty-two years old, had that long blonde hair, those big blue eyes, that wide smile and perfect teeth, all accented with high cheekbones and an innocent, sweet girl kind of voice when she was in a good mood—which made her pretty charming when she wanted to be. They talked for a while in front of the car, noticeably flirting.

I remember feeling electricity between them. He invited us over to his place for dinner that night. After dinner, he offered to let us stay there. I wasn't sure Mom was going to accept, since there didn't seem to be many places to sleep in his one-bedroom apartment. But from the looks of it, it was also better than a shelter or a church. She decided to accept his offer. Sam and Paul got comfortable at the foot of the bed on the floor, where

James had laid down pillows and blankets for them. Mom and I got the bed. I was the baby of the family after all. Some time later, James came into the room, probably expecting everyone to be fast asleep.

I had almost drifted off when I felt his weight on the bed, and I moved a little with a small sigh as he got close to my mother. I wanted him to know that I was in the bed, too. I could feel his hands moving, and their bodies squirming, which shook the bed enough that I knew what they were doing. As quietly as I could, I slid off the side of the bed and onto the floor, taking my blanket with me. The bed began to rattle, and noises started coming from my mom. Neither my siblings nor I made any movements or noises. I think we all had the same thought: maybe life would be better if we had a man in our lives.

WHERE'S THE BEEF?

The next day, we moved into a motel, just for a short time until we found an apartment. Mom would leave the room during the day to look for work, and we'd stay inside trying to stay warm and wait for food. It was a bitterly cold winter, one that came to be known as the "Winter Cold Wave of 1985." Florida called it the "Freeze of the Century" after 90 percent of the citrus crops were destroyed—a two-billion-dollar loss. Even Ronald Reagan's inaugural speech was held indoors at the Capitol Rotunda due to the cold. We really didn't have the clothes to handle that kind of weather and often found ourselves taking warm showers every few hours. The room didn't have a heater, so we huddled in the bed under the blankets together to keep warm.

Mom ended up finding a job at Burger King. She flipped burgers during the late shift from 4 p.m. to 10 p.m. When she came back to the room after work, she'd have a bag full of cooked hamburger meat leftover from her shift. Luckily, all we needed was ketchup and we would devour the semi-warm beef patties. At the time, the "Where's the Beef?" commercials were playing all over television. I was proud that my mom worked at Burger King, even though the ads were for Wendy's. From time to time, she would bring home a Chicago-style pizza. I fell in love. I loved the way they cut the slices into easy-to-grab squares and how each bite had a good ratio of crust to pizza fixins. Once the lid opened, I would quickly grab two pieces and put them on my plate, then grab a third to eat. Once that piece was done, and if there were any pieces left, I would take a new slice from the box and start eating it before touching the original two pieces I had on my plate. I was so hungry I wanted to make sure I had enough for later.

The motel room had its problems. One day, there was a leak, and scalding hot water covered our floor. Slowly, the water started creeping from under the carpet and across the floor like lava. We had to jump on the bed and wait there until our mom came home because the floor was too hot to even walk on. That night, we got a better room. And after that, we moved in with "The Greek."

THE GREEK

I'm not quite sure where my mom met George Kosinski. He had white hair and a big white handlebar mustache. His belly was large, and he had a smile on his face at all times, which seemed suspicious to me. Why was he so happy? He could have been mistaken for Santa Claus, especially when he laughed. His accent was strong, but the way he pushed out his words with effort and conviction made me pay attention to everything he said. He was much different than the young greaser. Maybe Mom wanted more than just a mechanic or one-nighter? We stayed with Hank on and off while we transitioned from living in motel rooms to our own place. He had a small house that sat on the corner of his street at the bottom of a hill. It had a big black stove in the living room, and he would stuff wood inside of it to keep the house warm and to cook food. He also had a medium-sized black dog. It was young, but not a puppy, and it had a good disposition. I had never had an animal before, besides Sugar Foot, a little white poodle my brother had found wandering the neighborhood when we lived in Nashville. We had it for about three days, then it eventually went "missing." I woke up from a nap, looking for Sugar Foot, and my mom said it must have run away. I was scared of big dogs, but George's dog was just the right size. I took to him immediately.

I really wanted to teach this dog how to give a handshake. Every time we were over at George's, I would go outside with the dog, have him stand in front of me, and I would teach him how to give me his paw and shake my hand. For about a week I did this. I would put food out for the dog, but before I gave it to him, I would put out my hand, and I would say, "Shake." He would lift his paw into mine, and I'd proceed to grab it and shake it. We'd look at each other with satisfaction because of this new understanding between us. I was able to make something, anything, do what I wanted, and I'd felt proud of myself. Perhaps he felt proud to make me happy, too? Each day, I looked forward to going to George's house, to see the dog, to teach it tricks, and to be proud of myself.

One day, on a very cold and snowy evening, George had the big black stove full of wood. It was heating up the house, as well as some food in a big pot on top of it. I accidentally bumped into George's stove, hitting it with my wrist. You could hear a searing sound as my flesh met with the stove. I pulled it away quickly, but I had already burned it. I had a red circle on my right wrist the size of a watch. George, in all his infinite Greek wisdom, quickly told my mom the Greeks' remedy for burns.

"Linda, Greeks don't put ice or water; we use salt to disinfect the wound. Let me put salt on it and you will see. It will heal right up. We have been doing this for thousands of years," he exclaimed. My mom, in all her infinite southern wisdom, listened to him and had me lay out my wrist while George put salt on my burn.

The pain was excruciating, and the burning sensation only amplified the longer the salt stayed on my skin. I could only take it for a minute or two before I ran to the kitchen sink and let cold water run over it. My mother kept up this "remedy" for a few days until the circle on my wrist turned green and oozed. I had a large red halo around the burn. The day we were moving out of our motel room to stay with The Greek, I looked at my mom and said, "I need to go to the doctor. This still hurts, and look at it—it's infected." She really looked at it and agreed. We went to the emergency room, and I received an ointment that made the pain go away almost immediately. When asked about what happened, the story about my burn incident made sense to the doctor. When they pressed on why it was so infected, Mom simply told them, "You know how kids are; they can't keep Band-Aids on." Strangely, no mention of salt. I put the ointment on for a few days, and the almost glow-in-the-dark, green, slimy layer of infection eventually slid off. Underneath was more disturbing. My skin was red, wet, and spiderweb-like with its coloration pattern of white speckles, seared blue veins, and blurred redness. I didn't know what to make of this foreign wound; it was unlike any I had before. After a few days, the infection was gone, but I was left with the spider's web that criss-crossed my skin in an intricate pattern that I'd never seen before.

Mom ended her relationship with George shortly thereafter. They had a huge argument one night, and he told her she had to leave. It was one of the first times I heard Mom called "crazy." They had a much longer relationship than she had with The Greaser—that was just a one-night stand—but with The Greek, she had called him her boyfriend. Mom had recently found an apartment, so after months of motels, we were finally moving into our own place.

P.S. 17

Mom enrolled us in a school called, P.S. 17—P.S. stood for "Public School." It was in Queens just a few blocks from George's place. I was late to second grade by a few months, and because of my age and aptitude tests, which I didn't think went too well, they still let me into second grade. Paul, Sam, and I all had to take the aptitude test. I was nervous. The only thing I thought I would excel at was if they asked me to spell supercalifragilisticexpialidocious. My brother had taught me that.

They took me to the auditorium to take the grade exam. One of the proficiency tests was to write the numbers one to twenty-five on a piece of paper. It seemed too simple of a test for someone my age, yet I proceeded to do it. In my nervousness, though, I wrote the number twenty twice. This error was circled in red ink by the examiner, who seemed disappointed in this mistake. The other test was to look at twenty or so images of objects for thirty seconds and then tell the examiner how many I remembered. I was able to remember just ten of them, and this, too, seemed to disappoint the examiner. I started to feel like an idiot and thought I wouldn't be able to pass any of these tests. But as the tests went on, I was able to finish them, and after about an hour or so, I was finally given a classroom to report to.

The moment I arrived outside the classroom door, I was terrified. Being the new kid struck fear into me—the fear that I'd never be accepted. I looked, dressed, and talked differently than everyone else. My second-grade teacher was a pretty brunette, who wore pretty clothes and had a pretty smile and a pretty teacher's pet. I was a dirty kid.

The teacher introduced me to the class. "This is Mary Gregory, and she's from Tennessee. Does anyone know where that is?" A few kids raised their hands. "James, where do you think that is?" she asked.

"That's in the South, Mrs. Tanner," he shared.

"Yes, that's right, James. Mary is from the South. Everyone please say hello to Mary," she said in her most teacher-ish voice.

"Hi Mary," the class said in unison.

"Hi," I said with as much enthusiasm as I could muster.

My first few days were terrible. Each day, we would pick up trays of food from the hallway and bring them back to a row of tables in our classroom that were designated for eating. Each day, I kept dropping my tray before I got to the table. The first time I dropped it I must have missed a step. Everything went all over the floor. The teacher was nearby and said, "You got milk on my shoes, Mary."

"I'm sorry, I don't know what happened. I just tripped and the tray fell. I'll clean it up," I said as I looked up at her.

"You better, Mary. You only get one lunch, and I'm sure you want to eat," she added. I was already kneeling down when she put her boot in front of me to wipe off the splash of milk that landed on it.

The next day, the same thing happened. This time, I tried to clean it up before she saw me by using my sleeve to gather up all the food on the floor. I was so nervous about being spotted by my teacher that it escaped me that all the kids were looking at me and beginning to laugh. I gathered the tray of food as best I could and brought it back out to the hallway. I went into the restroom and began to cry. I was never going to fit in at this school. Why was I dropping my food on the floor? This was two days in a row now that I was going without lunch, and I was getting really hungry. I cried out what I could, rinsed off my clothes, and let out a big sigh. I stared at myself in the mirror. I was going to have to make this life work, I realized, because we were never going back to Nashville.

"Children who are judged as attractive tend to be perceived as more intelligent, exhibit more positive social behaviors, and are treated more positively than children with cleft lip or cleft palate.[7] "Children with clefts tend to report feelings of anger, sadness, fear, and alienation from their peers, but these children were similar to their peers in regard to 'how well they liked themselves.'"[8]

Later that night, I tried to find out why we would never go back home. Mom's argument to me was simply that we couldn't.

"My family doesn't want us, and the church has turned their back on us. I have to make sure they never find us or else they'll take you all away from me. Is that what you want, Mary?" she said. I was so afraid of losing my mother. I was a young and vulnerable child, and had no other choice than to be solely dependent on my mother. She was everything. I knew in my heart, though, that our family must have loved us, at least a little.

Our mom often spoke badly about our father and made sure my brother felt the wrath of her disdain for Dad, and all men. She would tell my brother constantly that he was a faggot just like his father. She pushed him away, and when he couldn't run away from the house or the car, that's when it was the worst. My brother would lash out; he would curse her and behave badly, acting just the way she expected. I always knew why, and I wanted to support him, but I knew my mom held all the cards. I wanted to believe that things were better than they could have been back home, but we were living in such a dark place. We were hungry, we were poor, and we were far, far away from home.

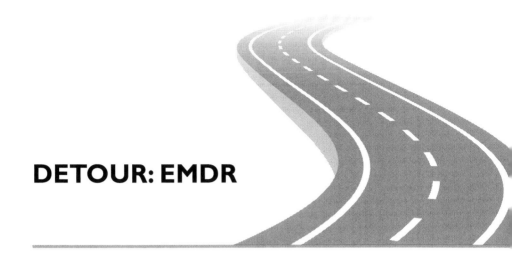

DETOUR: EMDR

Later in life, while writing this book, I stirred up a lot of emotions about my childhood. I was thirty-seven years old and into my second year of writing it. I was going through a tough time in my marriage, too, partly because my introspection had revealed that several areas of my life were not being fulfilled. I realized I had changed a lot as a person—especially in the past ten years or so—and I wanted my life to reflect those changes. I yearned to be more aligned with who I had become and to find the voice to say what I wanted, and the courage to stand by it.

I had started a new job at my company in a new role—which had a huge learning curve—so I was generally feeling inept. I also realized I was still carrying around many insecurities about myself that stemmed from my childhood. I sought therapy after my mother died a month after I turned twenty-nine, but the therapist was not a good fit. So after a few sessions, I stopped going. But now I was at a new crossroads in life and needed help.

I was holding myself together, secretly agonizing every day over my conflicting feelings, and no one seemed to know I was depressed. Even I didn't really know the depth of my despair. After experiencing a terrible panic attack that lasted almost eight hours, I reached out to my old business partner, to share my troubles and to see if he had a recommendation for someone who could help. He knew many of my troubles quite intimately. We owned a startup together for several years, and he was there for me when four of my family members passed within a four-year time period.

He recommended a therapist who he thought would push past all the barriers I had put up, and help me. I needed that. I needed someone who wasn't just going to be intrigued by my life story; I needed someone who had heard of problems like mine before and had some real solutions for me. I needed that desperately. So, I left the therapist a message on the heels of my panic attack. She called me back right away and penciled me into her next available appointment.

The office building was a basic five-story '70s design with sleek marble lobby walls and marble floors that made every clack of my heels echo loudly throughout the main lobby. It felt like I was in a mausoleum. No one manned the lobby; it was self-serve. The elevator was simple—no elaborate, upgraded design inside the cage—just brown walls on both sides and a large mirror facing the doors so I got a look at myself when I walked in. It was an old mirror, too, that had a cloudy film over it. I was alone in this elevator, but still turned my head after I stepped in. Even through the cloudiness, I didn't want to vainly stare at myself. When I got to my therapist's floor, it was nothing special either. It had long hallways on either side with satin beige paint on the walls and brown trim around the office doors. There was bland office-y artwork on the walls—flowers, roses, but with that '80s rose-color pastel palette that made me scoff out loud at what I thought was the laziness of the building managers. Reinvestment is an investment, after all. Oh well. The hallway reminded me of the apartments we used to live in as kids in New York, with its obnoxious and unwelcoming fluorescent tube lighting that let out a faint buzzing sound and didn't quite light everything up. It gave off a creepy vibe that made you want to hurry to your door.

Opening the therapist's door was like stepping into a different world, like Alice falling through a rabbit hole into Wonderland. I immediately felt the peacefulness of the room, like it was assuring me that I was in the right place. The light was dimmed by floor halogens, letting out a warm glow. The stark difference between this room and the hallway made me swiftly close the door behind me. There was a noise-canceling machine on the floor to my right, next to a tallish fake plant in the small front foyer, giving the appearance of privacy. She had a small sign outside her office door, which was the first door you saw when you walked in. It said, "Flip the switch when you arrive." So I did. My attention was drawn to a small black table in the hallway with a tea set on it. There were several varieties of tea conveniently displayed in a black wooden box. I grabbed a Good Earth Sweet & Spicy herbal tea and a small paper cup, then walked a little farther down the hall to a small waiting area with four chairs, two sets facing each other. There was a water cooler in the corner and several magazines laid out on a small glass coffee table in the middle. I was intrigued when I saw a Forbes magazine sitting on top of the pile. *Huh,* I thought, *we got some real brains in here.* My tea bag label dangled off the side, and I filled my small paper cup with scalding water, then topped it off with a splash of cold water from the cooler, so my fingers wouldn't burn while holding the cup.

Dr. Dawson walked out after five long minutes or so, floating past me like a hummingbird to grab some water from the cooler between her appointments.

"Mary Gregory?" she asked.

"Yep, that's me."

"Please, go into my office. I'll be right there."

She was a lovely sight. Her room was lovely, too. A soft light with a reddish glow enveloped me the moment I walked into her comfy one-hundred-square-foot room. I was compelled to look around, and my gaze stopped on the medium-sized oak wood desk she had against the wall, no doubt where she sat peacefully to write her summary notes after sessions. There were paintings on the wall that I could tell were made by real artists, not just prints of some scenic cliché location meant to make you calm. Those didn't work for me. Dr. Dawson had long fiery red hair that was punkish in color, and she wore a goth-ish style flower-patterned dress with sparkly Mary Jane shoes. She gave off an air of authenticity and had a feng shui type of demeanour that quickly dispelled my nervousness. She shared that she had spent many years providing art therapy to paranoid schizophrenics during her clinicals and that she found they were very creative people. As she spoke, she pointed to a piece on her wall, which had been done by one of her patients during that time. I trusted that we were bonded by a history of experience with the minds and behaviors of schizophrenics, though mine was only with the experience of my mother. I immediately felt that Dr. Dawson's positive experiences would help me to see a different side of my mother.

We discussed my panic attack, the book I was writing, my mother, my sex life, my marriage, and the weight of my crossroads. We talked at length and almost without stopping in the fifty minutes allotted for my session, allowing the final five for wrap-up and payment. She didn't take insurance, and the price was one hundred and seventy-five dollars per session with a minimum of two sessions a month. Her office was in Encino, which took an hour to get to from my Hollywood office. I thought about the long days ahead of me twice a month, but I only had to wonder for a moment about whether the sticker shock and commitment was really all that shocking; it wasn't.

After a few sessions, Dr. Dawson told me that I had PTSD from the trauma I experienced in my childhood. I was genuinely shocked. The only people I had ever heard of with this type of disorder were soldiers. She educated me on this topic, and I read all I could about it on Wikipedia and other online sources. She even shared her own experience with trauma and told me that there were many situations beyond war that imprinted themselves on one's mind and caused grief for years after the event occurred. She determined that many of my insecurities were stemming from trauma in my early life. In particular, the time of my life when I went to P.S. 17 and kept dropping my tray at lunch.

She recommended an EMDR session, a method of treatment for people with PTSD. EMDR stands for Eye Movement Desensitization and Reprocessing. It sounded a little like a Scientology term, like a "reprogramming" or something, but I was still intrigued, especially when I read how this method helped so many people before me overcome their trauma. I had listened to many books about the mind right before and during my therapy sessions. Titles like, Napoleon Hill's *Outwitting the Devil*, *Make it Stick* by Peter C. Brown, *Consciousness Explained* by Daniel C. Dennett, *Awakening Your Inner Genius* by Sean Patrick, and *Moonwalking with Einstein* by Joshua Foer. I was fascinated with the mind and how it worked, and how powerful it was on a subconscious level. I was open to this type of therapy, but I had homework to do before we could have the session.

She explained to me that for my memory to become "disconnected" with the physical responses I was experiencing, I needed to change my memory of the traumatic event. To do this, I needed to place people from my current life into my memory, into that scene, that traumatic event. Those people would then be called upon by me to step into the memory and play their part as I walked through the traumatic event and remembered how it made me feel. Simultaneously, the dual attention stimuli technique would be employed by way of sounds beeping in one ear and then the other—beep, beep, beep, beep. This allowed the memory to be sent to both parts of the brain, and for a new memory to replace the old one. By placing those people who possessed a particular comforting quality into my memory, along with one safe place, I could change my negative responses to that memory on both the subconscious and conscious levels. If that memory were to come up in the future, my mind would play the new version of the memory. I would recall every component of it, but the new memory would place those safe people into my traumatic event, providing me the positive support I needed at that time. Dr. Dawson explained after the session that, until now, I couldn't see how profoundly this traumatic event had affected my life, but that over the weeks and months or even years, I would see small differences—possibly big differences—in the way I felt, and how people treated me. I was intrigued by this theory. It had been nearly thirty years since the incident I was there to address, so my mind would need time to show how the absence of negativity would positively affect my life.

There were three people and one place I needed to identify. Here are my paraphrased notes for this assignment.

1. Safe Place:

   Your safe place could be as simple as your bed, with comfy pillows and blankets, your pet, or dumb TV on. Or, it could be as fantastical as another planet with a *Lord of the Rings* feel, including gnomes, fairies, etc. At the end of the day, all that matters is that you can connect to a sense of safety when you imagine it.

   My Notes: I feel safest at home; with Booboo (my hubby) around and my cat Tabby on my lap.

2. Wise One:

   The wise one could be a Mother Theresa or Dalai Lama type, or it might simply be a friend that you feel has figured out how to live a good life.

   My Notes: Wise one: Richard. He is to me the rock of the earth.

3. Protecting Figure:

   The same rules apply. It could be the Incredible Hulk or an uncle who was good at standing up for you or physically protecting you. You just need to be able to connect to a sense of protection.

   My Notes: Edwin. He is an Incredible Hulk type; very strong. We've done a Tough Mudder together, and during one of the obstacles, he picked me up over his shoulder and ran across the field. He works on the facilities team and is always lugging around furniture or hanging up TVs for executives and cleaning up after company-sponsored parties. He would protect me.

4. Nurturing Figure:

   This can be someone you know, like your mom or a caring and supportive friend. It could be someone from TV or film, like Glinda the Good Witch. It could be an animal, like a cuddly and benevolent bear that holds you or an animal you could ride. It doesn't matter. What *does* matter is that you can connect to a real sense of nurturance when you imagine this figure.

My Notes: Aunt Carolina (my father's sister). She loves everything I post on Facebook and is always assuring me of how sweet I am. She was there for me and wanted me in her life, especially when I came back to Tennessee for the funerals of my mother and father.

We scheduled one more regular session before the EMDR therapy session. EMDR takes ninety minutes. There are a lot of ground rules so the therapist can be sure you're ready. After the session, I was advised to lay low. Take care not to work. She explained I would be really tired, and the most important part was to not be hard on myself.

My husband and I were taking a break of sorts during the time I had my first EMDR session. Our break was a small one, just a few days while I watched my friend Matt's place in the Hollywood Hills. Matt and his husband Stewart were on vacation in Greece and needed someone they trusted to watch the house and dog sit their two German Shepherds. Matt was a former colleague of mine whom I'd met during his new hire lunch at California Pizza Kitchen. We sat next to each other with a table of six other folks on our team and immediately hit it off when I told him that I didn't mind double-dippin' with the chips and guacamole. He laughed and said, "That's what a southern person would say." I told him that I was originally from Nashville. He then shared he was born and raised in Louisiana.

Later that afternoon, we went out for a coffee. I shared a little of my history as a child, a little about my family, my father. That's when Matt confided in me that he was gay. He asked that I keep that a secret at work, which I agreed to do. We started sharing our spouses' leftovers at lunch, playing ping pong together in the break room, going out for drinks and to the gym across the street from work to play racquetball. We even hiked Havasupai Falls together—one of the most physically taxing experiences of my life.

I had watched Matt and Stewart's place once before, for just a night, but this time it would be four days and a good opportunity to test whether the heart would grow fonder being away from my husband Pierre. I worked in Hollywood just eight minutes away. Staying there was a great opportunity to save my usual two-hour commute, which also lent me to being the perfect house and pet sitter.

The night of the EMDR session, I knew I would get home late—our sessions usually didn't start until 7:30 p.m.—and most people wouldn't be up or available for a "talk" if I needed a lifeline that night. But my husband was a night owl; I knew he would be up.

I settled myself into Dr. Dawson's couch like I normally would. She explained all the components of the session. She showed me the headphones I would wear that would emit the ear-to-ear low drone beeping sound and vibrations during the session. I explained to her who I chose as my safe people and place and why I chose them. Then we began. I put on the headphones, and she started to test out the vibrations, turning up the sound and vibrations to a level I felt comfortable with. She started slow, having me describe the scene at school. Having me explain what was going on during that time so I could start evoking my emotions. "I was feeling scared in my new school. My teacher looks at me as if I'm a piece of dirt. I don't want anyone to know we're living in a hotel," I tell her. That same old feeling of being sorry for myself surfaces.

"Mary, you had been through a tough few months. Of course you're scared. Who could we bring in right now to help you feel better? Someone who would understand what you're going through right now?"

"Richard. I can bring in Richard." The vibrations and noise acted as reminders that I was in an EMDR session, but I continued to focus on the scene.

"What does Richard do or say to you?"

"He tells me that he's sorry I'm going through this tough time. He says that one day this would all be over, that I would be happy in a new life. He says that he understands what I'm going through and that he's there for me to talk to at any time."

"Feel this moment, what it feels like to be understood and to have someone care for your well-being, Mary. Someone who understands how hard it is for you right now in this moment of your life." A tugboat was getting pulled from my stomach; an ache in my chest was hardening. I felt like I was squeezing out sadness like you would the last bit of toothpaste from the tube. I sat there visualizing and living in this moment, feeling the pain and feeling that someone understood me and cared for me. I had someone realizing what I needed so badly during that time of my life. He was giving me a sense of safety and hope. My trauma and pain was starting to pull apart from my mind and body, to expel itself from me like a curse. Slowly, the infected layers were being treated, the wounds wrapped in clean dressing. Once the tug went away, we moved on to the rest of the trauma from the memory.

"Mary, now that you know Richard is there, understanding you and assuring you that your life will be better, what happens next? What are you feeling?"

"When I drop my tray, other kids laugh at me. My teacher just stares at me and expects me to clean it up myself. I only have a few clothes, but I'm so ashamed that this is the second time I'm dropping my tray and that I just use my sweater to clean up the mess. I should have gotten a towel. My teacher should have come over to help me, but I'm by myself to figure it out, and I was hungry, really hungry. I wanted to get back to the table so I could finish the carton of milk I still had."

"Mary, who would you need right now?"

"I need someone strong. Someone who would tell the other kids to stop laughing, who would help me pick up the mess. Someone to help me grab another tray of food, even if I wasn't allowed to get another one. Someone to tell my teacher to stop being so mean to me."

"Okay, let's bring in Edwin. What would he do? What would he say?"

"Edwin would come from the hallway once he heard the crash of the tray on the floor. He'd say in a loud voice, 'Mary, how you doing today? Need some help?' I'd tell him that I did need help. He'd bend down next to me and tell me that he would take care of it. 'Just sit there, Mary. I'll have this cleaned up in a second.' A few of the kids start to snicker and laugh. He tells them right away, 'Hey! Don't laugh at Mary. She's a really nice person, and this was an accident. Any one of you could have dropped your tray. I don't tolerate bullying, guys, you know that! Now, one of you guys go and grab Mary another tray of food.' A few kids get up to grab me food."

"Do you start to feel better, Mary?"

"Yes, I really do. I feel like he really stood up for me. He helped build respect for me with the other kids. He made them have compassion for me. He made it feel like a mistake to drop the tray and not something I did because I was stupid."

"That's good, Mary. Enjoy this feeling for a while. Look at his face, look at his smile, and know and feel he will protect you. What about your teacher? What is she doing?"

"She's still in the corner, snickering at me. But when Edwin gets up to throw away the food from the floor, he walks over to her. I can just barely hear what he says, 'Mrs. Tanner, respectfully, can I ask you why you're looking at Mary this way?' The teacher says it's because I keep dropping my tray and she's wondering why I am being so stupid. She says that I don't look like the rest of her students, and she thinks I shouldn't be in her class."

"What does Edwin say back to her?"

"He says, 'Mrs. Tanner. Mary doesn't look like the rest of your students because she was born with a birth defect. This has nothing to do with her intelligence. I know Mary. She's really smart. You're an adult, and her teacher; you should be behaving in a way that models how a grown woman should behave. The way you are acting now is like a mean child. To me, that seems like you're the ignorant one. You need to be kind to her, and if I hear that you've looked at her the wrong way, made fun of her, or encouraged the other kids to be mean to her, I'll be back here with the principal.' I'm shocked by what Edwin says, but she agrees that she will change her behavior."

"How do you feel about this, Mary?"

"I am feeling better. I can actually smile in this moment. I'm sitting on the bench where we eat lunch, and I'm feeling comfortable with myself. I feel protected. I feel that I have someone sticking up for me. I know that

Edwin has now made the other students care about me, and now he's made my teacher care about me. If she cares, I know the other kids will, too."

"Sit in this moment, Mary. Feel what this feels like. Enjoy the emotions of being protected and cared for in this way." I bask in this feeling for a while, the vibrations and beeping sounds only faintly recognizable at this point, and I let everything sink in. My brain feels like watercolors on a canvas, each color mixing and swirling across paper like smooth dolphins swimming next to a speeding boat.

"I am a little girl, with a clean sweater on. My nerves are calm. The other kids are being nice to me, even helpful and compassionate. My teacher had a change of heart; she realized her negative ways and wants to change for the better. She learned something, too. She came over to me and put one hand on my shoulder and another on the top of my head and caressed my hair. The physical touch melts my body, and I feel like home, like Tennessee home. I hadn't been touched like that in a long time. It's very caring and calming."

We went through several other scenes, placing in the memory my safe place, my safe people, and the acknowledgment of my yearning for my family back in Tennessee. My aunt Carolina assured me I would meet her again soon and that she still loved me. Everyone came into play when I needed them.

"Now, let's go back through the scene again, Mary. I want you to go through it all again. If anything negative comes up, we'll talk through it and we'll continue to use your safe people and places." I walked through the memory a few more times until the trauma in the scene no longer felt negative. There was no crying, no pulling, no tightening. I then opened my eyes, feeling almost reborn. I let out a big sigh and looked at Dr. Dawson. She looked back at me with a sincere compassionate expression. We let silence fill the room. I would have likened this experience to an intense workout, that feeling when you've gone hard and your body is shaking a little, buzzing even. You need to pull all your senses together to even walk a straight line.

"This was good. I feel a lot better," I told her. She reminded me that I needed to take it easy. No stress. Just relax. I let out another big sigh to show confirmation and thanked her. I felt that I had grown up a little, that I had changed and I was stronger now. *This must be what truly confident people feel like,* I thought.

I drove the forty-five minutes back to the Hollywood Hills and pulled into Matt and Stewart's long and steep driveway. It was now almost 10:30 p.m. The dogs started barking as they heard me pull up. I entered through their security gate, which lets you into their large red-brick courtyard. The dogs immediately jumped and sniffed me with enthusiasm as I wiggled my way through them. I walked a few feet to their beautiful and expensive large red door on the side of their house. I'd luckily remembered to keep the porch light on. I let myself in, and their dogs trailed in eagerly past me. Matt and Stewart own a beautifully open three-bedroom home from the '50s. High thirty-foot ceilings, simple '50s furnishings, and artwork peppered the house. Literature lined the walls with built-in bookshelves stacked floor to ceiling with film and recipe books. Stewart is a famous movie producer for some rather major movies, some that had personally resonated with me growing up as a young adult. They had a black grand piano that sat behind their floor-to-ceiling light gray brick fireplace. Matt loved to play when I would visit, and I loved sitting there and watching him. Stewart didn't have the patience for Matt's spontaneous Chopin renditions, so having me over gave him license to revel in his inspiration and talent. Just off to the left of the entranceway, the soft light from a heated pool was visible. I had spent a few afternoons swimming in there, being handed freshly blended margaritas or white wines while swirling around with some friends who were visiting Matt from Italy, or hanging out with Matt and his twin brother when he was in town during a layover from the airline he worked for as a pilot.

I let my bags fall to the floor. I was neater than that, but that night I didn't really care. I tapped and flipped the multitude of light switches that lit up various recessed lights throughout the house while I sauntered into their elaborately remodeled kitchen off to the left of the long entranceway. The south side of their house was all windows, floor to ceiling, so I took a moment to peer at the vast stretch of dark trees barely lit by the soft under-lights that lined that side of the house. *Tomorrow morning will look beautiful,* I thought. I opened their wine fridge and pulled out one of the "fifty dollars or under" bottles Matt said I could have my way with. There were two rows of them; one white, one red. "Just don't touch Stewart's eighty-dollar-plus bottles on the top three shelves," Matt's voice faintly reminded me. I smiled. *I won't,* I thought. Two-Buck Chuck is what I usually popped nightly at home; fifty dollars was just fine. I poured a large glass of wine in one of Stewart's rather large wine glasses. The kind that I was reminded not to break because they were Stewart's expensive glasses. My whole left hand cupped the bottom of the glass, making me feel quite elegant and capable. I took a sip and savored the complex flavors that melted on my tongue and palate as I pressed the final bit of grape juice down my throat. I stood there in the kitchen and looked down at the dogs, who were admiring my being there, in wonderment it seemed. They weren't sure what I was doing, but it seemed fascinating to them.

I grabbed the bottle and walked over to their living room couch that faced the tall fireplace. I set down both the wine bottle and the glass carefully, and the dogs started settling into their spots near me on the floor. I laid back into the couch and spread out my knees and arms so that I knew I had this space all to myself. I looked around this beautiful house and realized the trust bestowed unto me and the gift to have this moment to relax and just be. I finished about half of the bottle as I laid on the couch, phoning my husband to share my experience and to feel a piece of home through his voice. I'd felt complete after the call and quickly sank deep into sleep. I woke feeling slightly hungover, what usually happened when I drank good wine, but I also felt another type of different. A relief type of different.

SELLIN' BULL HORNS

Making money was our main objective as kids living in New York. It ended up being easier than expected. Queens had its share of drunks, so money was all over the place. Paul, Sam, and I started picking up bottles and cans around the neighborhood, before and after school. We'd go to 7-Eleven, where they exchanged cans for five cents and bottles for ten cents. It was simple, too; you brought in the bottles and cans to the counter, and they exchanged them right then and there for cash. Once we exchanged our goods, we'd turn around and buy convenience food and candy. We'd usually make around three to four dollars among the three of us, and that was enough for each of us to get a hotdog or hot sandwich, and even pick up a candy bar.

It was a simple philosophy in my neighborhood that those who partied didn't recycle. The bottles of beer we found were lying around, near, or in trash cans. There were usually large brown forty-ounce bottles of beer everywhere. As we were on our daily hunt, the old beer smell had a way of lingering in the air that made the bottles easy to spot. No matter how much we emptied the cans and bottles before putting them in our bags, the drippings of beer puddled at the bottom of the bags and made for a messy experience as we sat them on the 7-Eleven counter. The sour beer smell wafted through the air as I anxiously waited for them to count each of our deposits. Once the final bottle or can had been counted, and our transaction was finished, the workers would pull the sticky bag from the counter and toss it into the trash.

In all of our hunting for bottles and cans, we found other things. On one particular hunt, next to a few bottles of beer, I found a roach clip with a small joint still clutched in its grip. I put it in my pocket to show to Mom. Paul found a small working radio alarm clock, and Sam found a painting of a clown on black velvet. As I kept looking around, inside the trash cans and dark corners, I found a pair of real bull horns. They were dark and long with determined and powerful points on each end. I slung it over my shoulder, and it gave me some strength, by association. It had leather wrapped around the center of it with a divot in the back so you could hang it on the wall. After dropping off the bottles and cans, we went back to our little apartment to take a better look at our findings. We hadn't expected to find anything other than bottles and cans.

"We can sell these down the street, near all the shopping centers," said Paul.

"But what if we can't?" I asked.

"Then we'll bring them back home and decorate the apartment."

It was cold outside, and I didn't want to be out there any longer than we needed to, We didn't have the right clothes for this winter, but a hot meal sounded really nice, if we could sell our treasures.

We soon hit the streets to sell our goods. The streets were a constant hustle and bustle, with people who walked really fast and with purpose. Old men seemed to all have one hand in their pockets, jangling their coins. They'd dig deep into their pockets, and grab their coins like you would sand on the beach, then close their hand up while spreading open their fingers so the change would fall like winnings from a slot machine. I was fascinated by this display of wealth. Oh, what I would give to lay out all those coins on my bed, organize them by value—stack all the quarters in one pile, then dimes in another—each coin in its own pile, each pile representing a dollar amount. Once I was satisfied with the number and the organization of it all, I'd smash it all together again and find a new way to count it. When each man walked by jingling his money, I'd estimate how much he had in his pocket. "Oh, that sounds like four dollars and twenty-seven cents; it sounded like there were a lot of quarters in there. I bet he's got mostly pennies; that wasn't that thick of a jingle. Maybe that's more like two dollars and thirty-four cents," I'd say, to Paul's and Sam's amusement. That counting game amused me, too, and kept me busy while we stood out there in the cold looking for customers. I looked around at everyone, trying to pick out the right one to buy my bull horns.

"We want to sell each thing fast. It's cold out here," said Paul. "Your target price is five dollars." I walked up to one of the pocket jigglers.

"Hey, mister, I have a good deal; bull horns for your living room?" I said as I held the horns out in front of me like a freshly caught fish.

"Oh, those are nice, young lady. How much?" The pocket jiggler said with no hesitation.

"Just five dollars," I answered.

"I'll take 'em then," he said with his straight-forward New York attitude.

I was amazed at how quickly that worked. Paul also quickly sold his radio to a young college-looking guy, and Sam sold the black velvet clown painting to a woman who was with her young daughter. Within minutes, we had fifteen dollars in our collective pockets. We ran home like the devil was after us and waited for Mom to get home from work.

The moment she opened the door, we all ran up to her to tell her how successful we had been selling our junk; we were all beaming with accomplishment. Mom looked down at all of us as she went to put down all her things on the bed.

"Okay, kids, you did a great job tonight. But I wasn't able to bring home any hamburgers, so I'm going to need you to help get some dinner," she said.

"Oh, we can help with that!" Paul said victoriously. We all bundled up as much as we could and walked ourselves a few blocks to 7-Eleven. It was nice and warm, bright and clean—a stark difference from our apartment. Wafts of heated hotdogs and burgers lingered in the air and influenced our purchases. With fifteen dollars in our pockets, it felt like we could buy anything. We each got to choose what we wanted. Besides large New

York pizza slices you could get at the corner pizza shop, my other favorite was a New York plain bagel smothered with cream cheese. I reached into the bin where they had piles of different kinds of bagels; onion, sesame, blueberry, and plain. I pulled out a large plain bagel. The fresh bagel had a distinctive bread smell, softly rising out of the round top, which was tight like flexed skin. I inhaled its dominating scent, and a grumble went through my stomach in anticipation of what was to come. I cut it in half and placed it in the toaster. I spread a small serving of cream cheese on each half. It was thick, and the cheese melted just a bit where it hit the toasted warm inside. I took a huge bite and let the cold cheese and slightly warm toasted bagel hit the roof of my mouth. For a moment, I was in heaven. I ran my tongue along the entire bagel where cream cheese had poured out after my bite. Then I wrapped the rest of the bagel in a paper towel and we headed back to the apartment to eat our dinner.

I was good at finding money, too. One day, we all hung out by the local grocery store to help people to their cars and unload their groceries. Usually people would give us a quarter tip. While I was waiting at the exit of the store, I saw a woman throw away a soda can in the trash. I walked over, put my hand in the trash, and pulled out the soda can, along with a ten-dollar bill stuck to a receipt. This felt like winning the lottery. I immediately imagined all the food and candy I could buy. I ran over to Samantha to show her the ten-dollar bill. It was so green. I held each side with my fingers, holding the bill in front of her face. "Look, I found this in the trash! Can you believe it?" I exclaimed, my face beaming with joy. We ran home with lightning speed as thoughts of pizza and junk food ran through our minds. Sure enough, once I shared my story with Mom, she agreed that it should be pizza and ice cream night.

SOUP KITCHENS AND CHICK-O-STICKS

We spent a lot of time in the lines at food banks. The cold made it difficult in those long lines, which you needed to stand in hours before the soup kitchen opened just so you had a seat at the table. Even during the day, there were trash cans filled with fire all around the area where we stood in line for lunch. It was a large lot that led to a warehouse where they had lines of tables set up. Each trash can was manned by some homeless man or woman. They helped keep us warm. My siblings and I all took turns running over to the lit-up cans and putting our hands around the flames to warm ourselves.

One of the old guys saw us three sorry-looking kids and decided to brighten up our day a little. He walked up to my mom and said between his missing teeth, "Hey, momma, your kids like candy?" My mom was already pulling us in tight, not knowing if this guy was a creep or not. He opened up his jacket to show us that instead of watches, he had Chick-O-Sticks. We all looked up to Mom to give her our most pleading looks. She agreed that we could have one.

"Can your son come over and play a game of chess?" he asked her after we each grabbed a candy from his black mitten hands.

"Yes, that's okay, but he can't go too far, and once we start moving in this line, I want him to come back over," she instructed.

"Yes, momma, I'll bring him back in one piece and smarter than when he left," the old man exclaimed. Paul went over to the chess tables where a bunch of old men were playing. Twenty minutes later, we still hadn't moved. Paul walked back over to us by himself.

"Well, I learned how to play chess," he shared in a matter-of-fact kind of way.

"Was it hard?" I asked. I knew there was no way I would be allowed to leave Mom's side to go learn how to play chess with those dirty old bums. I did, however, want to go try.

"Naw, it wasn't hard at all. You just have to learn what each piece is, and which way it can move. The hard part is winning," Paul said. I looked over at the men sitting in front of each other, playing this game that I found quite mysterious. *Wasn't this something rich people played*, I thought. *Maybe Paul's smart enough to be rich one day?* I looked over at the Chick-O-Sticks man, all the old men, and I realized that though they didn't have money, they had their minds, and they just shared something with Paul that he hadn't had in a long time: attention.

We all started moving inside the kitchen to eat. Rows and rows of people walked through the cafeteria to grab the food being offered. We each grabbed a bowl of minestrone soup, potatoes, a slice of bread, a piece of fruit, and a milk. Then we walked to one of the tables and sat down. The heat from the bowl warmed my nose and face, and my body began to thaw out.

One thing about soup kitchen food is that it's not very seasoned. And soup kitchen bread always tastes slightly moldy. It's usually donated bread, so it's already a little past the recommended shelf life. Despite dipping it into a hot soup, the mold flavor still remained.

When you're hungry, though, food becomes very tasty in different ways. It takes on a new life. It fixes the pangs, it fixes the imbalances in your mind, and it adds a layer of normalcy to your life that you didn't have before eating it. You can think. Until that need is met, all you can think about is food. I would be at this point several times in my life, but this was the beginning.

THE BRONX

We ended up moving to the Bronx that Spring. Mom found us a place in a huge apartment building set among other tall gray apartment buildings. There were no trees around, just lots of people hanging out outside. We were in between welfare checks, so we temporarily lived with the apartment manager until we could get an apartment of our own. The entire building was mostly Puerto Ricans and Blacks. The manager was a short Puerto Rican man who was single with two kids and a dog. There was a buzz of activities everywhere. Outside the building, there was a man spray-painting constellations using various mediums. He added glitter to make the paintings come alive and sparkle. I was fascinated by how he moved while he was painting. Every dot and every spray had a purpose, and it was a treat watching the artwork come alive.

After a few days of living in a building, we would have learned the elevator etiquette, but, since the elevator never worked, we became familiar with the stairwell etiquette right away. We would meet our neighbors in the stairwell. We also discovered we could make a lot of money doing errands for elderly neighbors because of the amount of steps in the building. Small liquor store errands put a little jingle in my pocket.

I turned seven years old while living in that building. It was August. We had a small party in the manager's apartment. I remember how aware I felt then, the moment I turned seven. The candles were blown out, and later, I laid on the floor with the manager's dog. I looked at him and gave him a peck on the nose. He bit me. A small bite, but enough for me to realize the pain from the chomp of a dog's bite. I was shocked, yet became very aware of a dog's fickleness. I stared at the dog while I held my chin where he bit me, just long enough for me to know I had learned a lesson. I learned you can't stare at a dog in the face for too long before they get suspicious of you. He wasn't like The Greek's dog either. This dog was bigger, older, and seemed to have had enough of kids. It was almost the end of summer by the time we got our own apartment.

Living in the Bronx was no joke. You know those scenes where the kids are playing in the street while the fire hydrant sprays water to cool them off because of the sweltering heat? Yeah, that was a fair depiction of how it was. We did that many days during the summer just to stay cool. Having survived the winter, I was now surviving a New York summer.

There was a family that my mom had befriended. The woman was a Jehovah's Witness. She had a few kids that my brother, sister, and I would play with. She was a single mom like our mom. Sometimes we would have dinner together. Us kids would play hide and seek and jump rope outside the apartment building. One day, the woman decided to get us out of the neighborhood and take us to Coney Island. It was a hard sell to our mom, who didn't trust anyone with us. She generally trusted us with ourselves, but not with other people. She felt everyone was either a molester or a faggot or a kidnapper and couldn't be trusted. But somehow, she trusted her friend.

Paul, Sam, and I were all so excited. We were going to get to go on the subway! It wasn't a long trip either; at least it felt shorter in comparison to the car odyssey out of Tennessee. Once the doors opened, we all piled outside and aimed for the pier. The smell of the ocean air was so energizing. This was my first time seeing an ocean, and I was dumbstruck. I looked around at all the people walking the pier and enjoying themselves at the beach. The woman watching us encouraged us to walk near the waves and enjoy the ocean and the sand. She set up our spot on the sand while we all dashed to the ocean. There were five of us kids in total, and we ran to the ocean like we wanted to hug it. With our arms flailing, and sand kicking up everywhere, we ran like monsters toward the ocean. I had never been on a beach before, so I reveled in all the wonderful textures, smells, and sounds. There was hot sand under my feet, waves crashing onto the shore, and I watched little bubbles coming up from the wet sand as little bits of air found their way out. All day, the three of us Gregorys were having such a great time. By the end of the day, we each had a sufficient burn on our faces, shoulders, and backs. Sunscreen was definitely an afterthought, or not even a thought, on this trip.

Exhausted and ready to go home, we walked ourselves back to the subway to go back to the Bronx. While standing in the subway train, I observed all the people coming in and out of the subway cart. Because it was so crowded everywhere, I was standing near the doors, holding on to a handle. I saw a man sit down in a newly opened seat and begin reading his paper. Another guy was standing, holding the handle near the subway door, across from me with his back near the door. At the next stop, the doors opened and he stuck his head out, looking to the left. Interested and wanting to know what he was looking at, I did the same thing. I leaned forward and stuck my head out of the sliding glass doors, then looked to the left. Unfortunately, I wasn't paying attention and the doors closed on my neck.

My head was stuck between the sliding doors, and the train started moving forward. All I could hear were people screaming and yelling for someone to open up the door. We were heading toward the tunnel at a fast pace, and there wasn't much time before we would enter the black abyss. I was screaming for someone to help, the rushing air cool on my face as we quickly glided through the underground. It seemed extra dark because I didn't want to open my eyes. I felt tugs on my body, different tactics to pull me back into the subway cart. Voices were loud and angry, intensified from trying to stop what was likely a horrific outcome if I somehow collided with a physical structure outside those doors. After what felt like an eternity, the doors were pulled open, and my head was pulled inside the subway. I realized it was the guy reading the paper. I was so embarrassed that I couldn't even look at him as he looked at me to see that I was okay. I had my head so far down that my chin was nearly touching my chest. I could see his black slacks and black shoes and could hear him asking me if I was okay. I could see my tears fall onto the floor. I buried my head into the side of the woman who had brought us there in the first place, and with my sheepish voice said, "Yes, I'm okay."

The tears burned my cheeks as they rolled out of my eyes, hot with embarrassment. I only briefly peeped out from her side to see the rest of the train passengers long enough to try to get a glimpse of the man who saved me. I could still see his slacks and shoes, and as I curiously tried to keep looking up to see his face, I was stopped by my own self-imposed limitations. I kept my head on her shoulder and chest, resting there until I could no longer feel the outside world. I wanted to be lifted out of that subway and be back at home. My siblings were trying to talk to me, but I did not utter a word. I was quiet the entire way home. As we walked from the subway station back to the apartment building, all I wanted to do was sleep. When I walked into the apartment, my brother and sister quickly explained what had happened to our mother.

Mom was so upset at me for risking my neck, as it were, for my own curiosity, and she was right. I had been stupid. I learned a lesson from that experience. Don't just do what others are doing; think first to make sure there's no danger. The other big lesson; the next time someone saves you, be sure to look them in the eye and thank them. I often think about that gentleman that literally saved my neck and wonder what type of impact I may have had on his life. Was that the highlight of his life? Does he tell his friends and family about the story often? I'll never know, but I do know the impact he had on me.

SELLIN' SNAKES

"**U**nlike other animals, chameleons continue to grow throughout their lives. As their old skin gets too small, they will shed it in bits and pieces, dissimilar to snakes that shed their skin all at once."[9]

Paul had figured out that you could go to the huge open space behind our apartment building and catch snakes. He found out that the grass snakes were not poisonous. He had caught a few and sold them to people for five bucks each. At first, my sister and I were skeptical, but he convinced us to go into the big open area, full of debris people left there instead of taking it to the dump, and start looking for snakes.

"Listen, it's easy, and they won't bite. I've been selling them to people almost every day for the past week," Paul explained. He showed us where to look. We spotted ones with red and green stripes, and some with red and white spots. He showed us how to pull them out of the grass right behind their necks and throw them in a paper bag. Once you picked them up, the tails would wrap around your hand, and if you let go of their necks, they would just slither along your arm, and surprisingly not try to bite you. Sam and I each caught two snakes that day and sold them for five dollars each, almost as quickly as we had caught them. It was easy to be ambitious in New York.

After our snake hunt, and feeling confident, Paul showed Sam and me a little path behind some bushes where he said there was a guy selling cigarettes. I didn't think we should be adventuring beyond the openness of the park-like area, but Paul led the way, and our curiosity got the best of us. We followed him deep into the unwalked parts of the park. Sure enough, after a few turns, there was an older man leaning up against a bush, rolling up cigarettes and tossing them onto a tin top with a small handwritten sign that said, "fifty cents each." I watched the old man put his hand into a tin can, spread the loose tobacco on the paper and roll it up, then lick the paper to seal it. I wasn't sure the saliva was necessary; I felt like it was a gross step. Paul tossed him fifty cents, picked up a smoke, and put it in his ear. That's when Paul started smoking; he had recently turned eleven years old.

THE BOY WITH THE BLOOD DISEASE

Steven's skin was caramel colored, he was probably Italian. He was skinny like me, and he was my age. We all called him "String Bean." His brother was around Paul's age, and they were often out playing without Steven. I had met them one day while taking the steps. Almost every day, Steven would knock at our door and ask if I wanted to play. We quickly realized that the best thing we had going was each other. We would go all the way up to the roof and hang out and look at the city. We sat and talked about our lives, where we came from, what our parents were like. His mom was a single mother, like most women I knew. He told me he had a rare blood disease and that's why he was so skinny. That he had to have transfusions all the time because his blood didn't bring enough oxygen into his body to support his organs. I remember this made me like him even more because he seemed kind of like me. He had a life unlike any other person I had ever met. He was vulnerable. I felt really close to him, and the thought that he may die from his disease made me incredibly sad, and appreciative of our time together.

Some days, we would play hide and seek and run under the bottom stairs and hide. One day, he leaned over and asked me, "Do you want to kiss?" Stunned but curious, I said, "Yes." Our lips gently met. We mimicked what it looked like in the movies, pressing our lips together and moving our heads from side to side. We got closer together, he wrapped his arms around me, and we started caressing each other. He put his hands under my shirt so that he could run them along my back, and I did the same to him. We started kissing some more. His hands went down my pants, and he squeezed my butt cheeks.

I got scared, pushed away from him, and started to run downstairs. We both ran all the way down twelve flights of stairs and hid underneath the staircase while we gained our breath. I sat there, huddled up, not sure whether what we did was enough to get me pregnant, and because I felt so many feelings for Steven, maybe this meant we were going to get married? I sat there, huffing and puffing, insecure but electrified by what had just happened.

"Did I do something wrong?" he asked.

"No, not at all," I said. "I just don't know what that meant, you touching me like that."

"I don't know either. I just wanted to."

We sat there, crouched underneath the staircase, and I looked at him. He had a life unlike any other person I had met; was mine that bad after all? He seemed to appreciate these moments, because his were timed.

SPINAL TAP

I had just turned seven and I was feeling some normalcy in my life. I knew that I could make money selling snakes, and even sell things on the street. I was excited about my new age, the things I could do, and the things that *seven* allowed me to be. One day after school, after a day of selling snakes, and after watching Paul smoke a few cigarettes he bought from the bum in the bushes, we waited in front of the building for our mom to get home. Once we spotted her, we hopped into her fading aqua-colored Dodge Dart. I began to explain to her the extravagance of our snake sales. I explained how we had sold a black snake with red stripes to a man in a black suit. How a few kids asked Paul to give them his green snake. Paul's pants pockets had a few crumpled-up dollars in them, each with a story he could tell us. I was riding in the back seat; Paul was up in the front seat, as the older brother should be. I turned my head to the right to look at Sam when I suddenly felt a pain running from the top of my forehead all the way down to my shoulder blades. At once, I could feel a sharp sting moving up my neck. I tried to move it straight, but doing so hurt so bad that I kept my neck in the twisted position.

"Mom, my neck is stuck," I said as my eyes widened and panic flew across my face.

"What? You can't move your head?" she asked me in such a direct tone that I had to give her an answer immediately.

"I can, but it hurts really bad to move it… I feel the pain all down my spine."

"We're going to the emergency room, Mary." The government assistance we had received was enough to cover medical emergencies, and she was sure this was one of them.

The burning sensation I felt as I cranked my head back to center was so painful that I only moved it in small incremental moves. By the time we reached the emergency room, I had finally moved my head forward and straight. However, moving it any other direction caused a sharp pain sensation. Like every ligament in my neck was on fire.

Mom signed me in as my brother and sister waited patiently in the emergency room, not really knowing what was happening.

When I was finally called, about two hours later, and after a brief discussion with the doctor about my symptoms, I was immediately rushed to a different team to get a spinal tap. They were looking at a possible case of spinal meningitis. I was wheeled into the room to undergo the procedure. It basically consisted of me sitting at the edge of the table, with my head leaning toward my knees, making my back and spine as wide and open as possible. A nurse placed a paper over my back, which would be used as a barrier between pokes. The point was to get to my spinal fluid. When the needle first entered my spine, I felt a tight pinch. I knew I had to just endure this pain because there was a greater good. I was going to find out what was happening to my neck, and once I found out, I would be better and get back to my snake searches. I had to endure the poking a few times, because the needle didn't find the spinal fluid right away.

After the procedure, my head began to hurt, and I was soon experiencing my first migraine. I laid there, hoping for the booming to subside, the light sensitivity to wash over me, and with all that hope, I eventually fell asleep. I awoke to my mom standing over me, rubbing the hair around my temples, and asking me about how I was doing. It turned out that I had a strain of viral meningitis. Luckily, it was curable, and less intense than a bacterial or fungal infection. The hospital stay had been nice. I could ask for Jell-O anytime I wanted, and I did. I stayed at the hospital for just one day and was released with a neck that was mostly back to normal and a newfound understanding of dirt. That washing your hands was important. That touching dirty bottles and cans meant you needed to be safer and more aware before putting those dirty hands near your mouth and skin and eyes. I realized that there were probably many kinds of diseases slithering around those snakes. I also realized that I had more strength and pain tolerance than I had previously thought. I had gone through a spinal tap, without crying. I reveled in my newfound maturity.

YONKERS

We were only in the building another few weeks before we left for Yonkers. I never had a chance to say goodbye to Steven.

In Yonkers, we lived in a really huge hotel room, like an extended-stay apartment. It was the end of the summer, and school had just started back up. During the day, our mom was out of the motel room looking for an apartment, and we spent the day finding something we could eat and figuring out how to cook it. We had a hot plate. That always made cooking possible because no matter where you stayed, you could always find an outlet. One day, we decided to cook ramen. We had finished boiling the water and added the ramen to the pot, then let it cook for a little while as the compacted dry noodles unraveled. We then added the packet of seasoning. After a minute, we poured the ramen into our bowls and began to eat. We never thought to turn off the hot plate. After eating, we all started playing near the beds. The glowing red hot plate was sitting on the nightstand between the two queen-sized beds. Our big thing as kids was to play wrestling and make spaceship forts. I tried my best Hulk Hogan maneuver on Paul, which didn't hold him down for long. Sam and I ganged up on him and accidentally pushed him onto the hot plate. And I stress *accidentally*. His butt was on it long enough that we could hear a searing sound. The heat managed to burn through his underwear and create little black rings in the shape of the hot plate spirals. He screamed out in pain and quickly ran to the bathroom. After sitting in a tub full of cold water, while Sam and I threw in as much ice as we could from the hotel ice machine, he stood up and bravely showed us his butt cheeks. There was a large red ring that outlined his right butt cheek, just the same shape as our good ole hot plate.

When Mom got home, she could sense something was wrong. We had picked up the entire hotel room and were quietly sitting on the edge of the bed and watching TV. Paul didn't want to tell Mom because he was the oldest and was supposed to be watching us. Any kind of trouble and it was his, well, *ass*. But I broke. I told her what had happened, and Paul showed her his burned ass cheek. She reminded us that this is the kind of trouble you can get into when you're horsing around all the time. There was definitely no salt put on his burn.

One morning, a week or so later, Paul frantically woke us all up.

"Mom, the school bus is outside. I need clothes for camp." I don't think anyone realized he was going to camp. Adventures like that seemed like they were for other people. Like in the movies; wooden cabins, hiking near a spring, learning to tie knots, and hiding candy under your bunk. I really wanted to go do something like that, too.

"How long are you going for?" my mom asked.

"It's just for the weekend," he yelled as he hurried through the hotel room to collect anything that looked clean. This wasn't some kind of paid-for camp. This was through the school, and though we were all in school at the time, nothing seemed permanent, let alone extracurricular activities like camp. There were no clean clothes in our drawers; there were only clothes piled high everywhere, and everything was dirty. He grabbed his belongings, some dirty underwear, some old socks, a few T-shirts, a blanket, and stuffed it all in a large black trash bag. He flew out of the hotel room and got on the bus for his trip. The waft of his dirty belongings hit me. I was embarrassed for him, though I knew he could handle himself. Just like that, he was off on an adventure, and we were all still in our crummy hotel room.

Mom lived in her head mostly, ruminating over conversations or events in her recent or distant past. When she came out of her deep thoughts, everything around her was a shock; sometimes she'd even startle herself with a verbal, "Ahhhh." Her attention deficit disorder was very severe. It was so hard to have a conversation with her because she couldn't keep her attention on you long enough before going back into her head. A typical habit of hers, after watching TV on the couch for a short while, was to get up and pace around the house. There was never any point in watching a movie or having a long conversation with her because she was never really all there. She would often find some food and start eating. This seemed to calm her nerves. Only in very extreme cases was she present, and when you got her in those moments, it felt like a victory.

She had a hard time spelling, and her handwriting was very curvy and sloppy. I got really good at reading it, and could even forge her signature and handwriting. I would always try to help her learn, though. I was a great speller, and to encourage interactions with her, I would put together lists of words that we would sound out phonetically. Then she would try to spell them. We would go over each word until she could spell them correctly. I even graded them and gave her encouragement when she spelled a word right.

She would get very excited over any modicum of stress. Battling my mom's overreactions, outbursts, and general depressed disposition was draining. One day in particular, it seemed I had my mom's attention. I had convinced her to read me a story. We got on the bed and laid there with me snuggled into her shoulder. The kids' book I chose didn't matter any to me; it was that we were close, and she was being tender, and focused. As she was reading to me, I was starting to feel whole. My love tank started to fill up. As I was enjoying the closeness with my mom, then the hotel room door opened. It was a man we had never seen before. He asked for someone by name, though the name did not sound familiar. My mom jumped out of the bed and told him he was in the wrong room and to leave. He did, and he closed the door behind him, and just like that, my moment with my mom was over. Her paranoia had been activated.

"Who left the door open? I bet this guy is a detective for your father. We have to get out of here," she said.

"Mom, this was a mistake. We left the door unlocked. He could have been going to a room just next door," I explained.

"No, they're getting close to finding us. We need to leave," she said. By this time, we had been gone from Tennessee for almost a year. There was no word from our family, not that I had heard. I wasn't sure if she was calling back home from time to time, but we never spoke with anyone that was kin. It was a short while later when she found us an apartment to live in.

MUSINGS: PERSONAL LEADERSHIP

When I think about the people that I gravitate toward—the ones that other people can't seem to get along with—it's always the ones who are leaders and are very sure of themselves. To me, this is a quality that I absolutely know is successful. It's a quality that I can see a mile away, and it's an indication that a person has many other great qualities. I am receptive to these leadership qualities, and because I am developing my own sense of leadership, I need those people around me. More times than not, those people need someone like me around, too. To build them up, to inspire them, to open their minds to other people and experiences. To show them that this leadership quality does not have to alienate everyone.

DUMPSTER DIVING

The apartment Mom found was an upstairs apartment, and the building was just off an alley. From the first day we moved in, there were signs this place might not work out. I smashed my nose into the furnace after running and tripping in the hallway and bled all over the hallway carpet. Our typical MO was to find the nearest community center and welfare office and get our bearings with the local soup kitchens and food banks. We knew we would need them eventually.

Mom was getting clever at finding food, however. She had gotten wind of the fact that grocery stores threw out food after just a few days from their best-by date. We were used to standing in line to get day-old bread, canned vegetables, and stale crackers or cookies. Her strategy would be going right to the source, and avoiding all that standing in line hungry business. She came home the first time she dumpster-dived with bags of old bananas. The first thing she made for us was banana pudding. It was really good. "I mean, you need aged bananas anyways," she explained. The second time, we all joined in.

We all stood there, staring at the huge dumpster where someone from the store had just dumped things like bananas, lettuce, bell peppers, cucumbers, boxes of crackers, bread, cookies, you name it. My mom, despite being nearly 300 pounds by then, was fairly spry. She jumped in and started rummaging through the dumpster, handing us "good" food when she found it. I was scared that someone from school would see me, but I was also really hungry and really excited about this new way of getting food that might avoid another long line at the food bank or soup kitchen. Then I jumped in. Digging through the dumpster was quite an adventure. At least these were the same things I would eat from the soup kitchens. While I searched for food, all I thought was that this was for all the times I had been hungry, and that this was an answer, a remedy, even if it was a desperate measure. There is a smell of old, stale, and smelly vegetables that overpowers a dumpster. I remember all those smells because everything I pulled out smelled like that. I knew that it would fill my belly, and for that, I was a willing participant. But I wasn't eager to do it again. Though I knew being hungry is like lacking oxygen. It's thin air to your soul. You are weak; you're stunted. I was now more okay with the long food bank lines and would reserve the dumpster diving as a backup plan only.

ALMOST LOST
THE DODGE

When we went to the local recreation center, Mom met a guy. He was Native American, tall and strong-looking, with long hair he tied up. I found him attractive and had a little crush on him. The guys who hung out at those centers were often recovering addicts, and there were often lots of men, so the energy was filled to the brim with "bad guy" mojo. Mom started to smoke cigarettes and drink, which I'd never actually seen her do before. She had people over all the time. It got so bad one day that the Native American guy took the car for the night and hadn't returned with it. That car was our only vessel to move about the country—and a bed and a roof when we needed it. Mom wasn't going to call the cops. She was already too paranoid about us being taken away from her and having to go back to Tennessee. Paul, Sam, and I each took turns looking down the alley to see if he would come back. I was kicking around dust on the ground during my turn, I saw something. Pushed flat by dirt and rocks was the slightest glimmer of a few coins. My eagle eyes peered down further and saw there were bills on the ground, too. I knelt down, picked up the coins, and dusted off the bills. Indeed, this was money—like, real money. I grabbed what was there and uncovered twenty-seven dollars. There was a twenty, a five, and two one-dollar bills. I felt I had struck it rich! How long had that money been sitting there, just blending in with the dirty alley? A few moments later, I looked up to see the Dodge Dart turning into the alley and coming toward our apartment. I yelled out to my siblings to come to the alley. I stepped to the side so he could park it. A pile of people came out; two women and two guys. My mom was watching from the apartment window. "Here are your keys, Linda," he said as he threw them up to her. She caught them as he walked into the building. I knew he had been with those other women by the way he walked out of the car, like he had just won a car race. We all rushed upstairs to see what Mom was doing. The Indian man hadn't come up to the apartment, though. I assumed he just kept on walking and went home with his new friends. Mom was frantically gathering our things and told us that we were leaving. I barely had time to tell her I had found money before we were all piling into the car. We would always leave right when the government checks arrived, and luckily it was that time of the month. Instead of paying rent, we filled up the gas tank and hit the road. This time, I thanked the Gods we were leaving. I couldn't have been happier. The Dodge Dart pulled away from the dusty alley, and I didn't look back. Pulling away made me feel relieved. We were leaving New York for good.

Chameleons change the actual structure of their cells, which changes how light reflects off their skin. When responding to an attack, they can change to green, black or blue.

Part 2

TRAVELS THROUGH GREEN

N one of us knew where we were going. As we got on the freeway, "On the Road Again" by Willie Nelson came on. Even at the age of seven I knew how ironic that was. We had been on the road to who knows where for a good while when Paul finally asked Mom the big question.

"Where are we going?"

"We're going to California," she said.

"But why?" Paul asked.

"There's a beach there," she said excitedly. Her wide, fixed smile hung there for a few moments, not changing until we all brought a smile to our faces in support of her effort. A part of me was hoping she would say we were going back to Tennessee.

The trip to California was long and it felt like the days turned into nights on a blended stream of moon, stars, headlights, and then sun. Mom let us drink coffee. It was quite the eyebrow-raiser in some parts of the country, especially when we would walk up to the counter, each holding a large coffee in a styrofoam cup at eight o'clock at night. We didn't mind though. We earned that coffee—besides, with tons of sugar and creamer it was a lot like a warm, sweet treat.

We had the occasional fight in the car because we were cranky from traveling. We didn't know lots of typical travel songs, just Sunday school songs mostly. We belted out, "This Little Light of Mine," and "He's got the Whole World in his Hands," and "Jesus Loves Me." It was like we were on a road trip to the promised land.

We would always find a place to sleep at a truck stop, a rest area or even a parking lot. When road conditions were good, it seemed like these were everywhere, but when conditions were bad, it felt like an eternity until you could get off the road. One night, as we were traveling through Arizona, the conditions were worse than our mom had ever experienced. It was raining so hard you could barely see out the window, and not very far at that. There were high mountains all around and the two-lane road seemed rocky with all the wind that raced through it. There was little brush or tree cover to filter the wind. Mom was panicking. She wasn't skilled enough to handle more complex road conditions than what our suburban neighborhood had challenged her with. She was the kind of driver who braked a little in case the green light turned yellow and was afraid to drive the speed limit, even in normal conditions. She began to cry.

"I can't see anything. I don't know where I can pull over," she said as her worrying voice built up volume. Paul was holding up a map and frantically looking for places we could pull off. I was getting scared. It was raining very hard and those old headlights didn't do much for night vision. Our wipers could barely keep up; they only got enough water off the windshield to show a momentary blur before it was drenched again. Sam looked worried, too.

Mom was not prepared for this level of danger. Semi-trucks passed us on the left and swooped out in front of us, honking their horns in exasperation. How they were able to drive at such high speeds, I could not imagine.

As if the situation couldn't get any worse, all of a sudden Mom belted out, "The brakes are out!"

That's it, I thought. I had had enough. From the rain, to the terrain, the car, the shitty wipers, to the woman behind the wheel—I decided, in that moment, that I was prepared to die. I was going to leave it all up to fate. I leaned against the door and curled into my side. The rain made the metal door vibrate. I closed my eyes and went to sleep.

A moment later, as if I had been reborn, I woke to the sound of my mom and brother talking outside the car. I opened my eyes to a beautiful sight.

I didn't die.

The sun was out, and everything around was beautiful. Cliffs and red rock were everywhere, the world was brown and beige, and the sky was bright blue—a stark difference from the night before when it was black and nothing seemed like it would ever be warm again.

We were parked in a gravel turnout, hugged by tall cliffs on one side. Out the windshield I could see the road on the horizon; it seemed to go on for days. I felt overwhelmed to have survived a prescribed car crash, evading it by my surrender. I sat in the car for a while and soaked in the reassurances of my brother and mother's voices. Where was Sam? I scanned the area and could see her kneeling next to the side of the cliff, examining rocks. I stared at her for a while then opened the car door. I felt lighter as I stood and took in the clean air. I felt more emboldened from having survived near death (or so I thought).

"Mom, didn't the brakes go out?" I asked.

"Yes," she said.

"So what happened? I thought we were going to die." I looked at her with one eye closed to the sun's glare.

"I started pumping the brakes. All of a sudden they started working," she said plainly.

Paul seemed fairly calm about it, as if they'd already gotten over the incident hours before—which they must have. There was no trace of the evening's weather anywhere, like it had never happened. I kicked some small rocks.

"Let's all go get some breakfast," Mom said loud enough for Sam to hear.

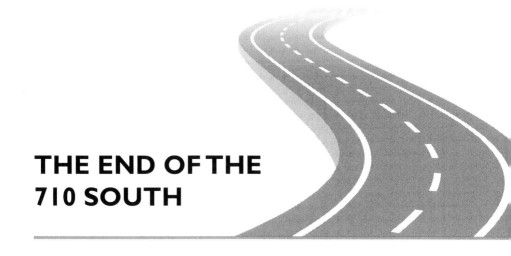

THE END OF THE 710 SOUTH

The two-week journey across the country had taken a toll. I just wanted to sit in a bath with a couple of Barbie dolls and fall asleep in a warm, clean bed. It was very late when we first saw the 710 freeway sign above an overpass. *Long Beach Freeway.*

"Long Beach, that's where we're going! I've always wanted to see the beach!" our mom excitedly declared.

So that was that. We traveled on the 710 South until it ended. We got off the Shoreline Village Drive exit and pulled into a parking lot. In the distance were big white boats—The Queen Mary ship was among them, and I marveled at how beautiful it was. I had a sense that we were safe, now—maybe even done traveling. Mom turned off the headlights and we all went to sleep.

Tap tap tap.

It was three o'clock in the morning when the Shoreline Village security guard tapped on the driver's side window. Mom rolled her window down.

"This is not a public parking area, lady. This is private property."

"I'm sorry. We just got off the freeway a few hours ago and didn't see the sign. We're new in town. We're coming from New York," she told him softly. She was using her sweet, soft southern accent, which got her out of a lot of sticky situations.

"Well ma'am, since you're traveling from out of town, I can understand the confusion...but you can't park here tonight."

"Do you know where we can find a Travelers Aid office?" she asked.

"Sure. There's an office open 24/7, just down the street off Pacific Avenue. You'll be able to get some help there," he explained.

Mom started the car and we drove through the empty roads of downtown Long Beach.

The Travelers Aid office was in a quaint, '50s-style bungalow. The porch light beamed warmly along the porch and stairs, and more soft light glowed beyond fluffy white curtains. It felt like home. We walked inside—strangely, the door was unlocked. It felt like we were at a bed and breakfast. Mom went up to the desk and was given fifty dollars in food vouchers, then directed toward a mission house for women and children just up the street.

It was very late when we got there. Two small nuns opened the door to the mission once we arrived and took us to a private room meant for families. I liked that we didn't have to share a room with anyone else. I crawled into a warm bunk bed piled thick with blankets and quickly fell asleep.

When morning came, we woke up to the call for breakfast, which sounded like a great idea. The kitchen smelled of food and bustled with the sounds of spoons hitting ceramic bowls and food peeling from pans and falling onto plates. There was a large pot of coffee sitting in the coffee maker, alongside several kinds of juices and a gallon of milk. There were several boxes of cereal to choose from, and I was excited at the thought of eating Froot Loops *and* Honey Combs for breakfast. My heart filled with joy as I poured a tall glass of apple juice and filled my cereal bowl with milk. I filled my belly until it popped out.

During the day we had to leave the mission. They said this gave everyone time to look for a job or a place to live, but when you're new in town and have little money, six hours in an unknown town can feel like an eternity, especially when lunchtime comes around. We walked around the neighborhood and found the Main Library; from there, we were able to find local food banks. This was a predominantly Hispanic and Black neighborhood, much like New York—except these people were Mexicans, not Puerto Ricans. There was more space, too: the streets were wider, and the apartment buildings were only two or three floors high, not more. I wondered how Mom always seemed to find neighborhoods that were so different from Nashville. I took in the concrete, the smells, the looks from others as we walked down the street. *This may work,* I thought, *if we can find the welfare office.*

MY CAR ADDRESS

We found a Baptist Church near the mission. We were asked to go to the registration office. This church was huge and had a large, open lobby with several doors that led into the nave. This was where the congregation ended up after Bible study.

"Once you register your family, Linda, your kids need to go upstairs and attend Bible study with the kids their age. They'll be asked to register with their age groups," she instructed. Paul, Sam, and I went upstairs to one of the desks at the end of the hallway.

"We're new," Paul said, matter-of-factly.

"Okay. You need to fill out this form, so we know what group to put you in," the girl at the desk said as she handed Paul a pink index card with a bunch of questions on it. He handed it to me.

"You fill it out."

I grabbed it and began to write.

> Name: Paul, Samantha, and Mary Gregory.
> Age: 11, 9, and 7.
> Address:

I thought hard about this. I didn't want to lie, but besides the mission, we had spent the past month traveling across the country in our car. The car seemed like my address. So I wrote: *car*.

I finished filling out the rest of the card and handed it back to the young girl manning the kids' registration desk. Her eyes rolled down the card, then hit the address. She made a disgusted face, riddled with confusion. I was embarrassed before she even said a word.

"Your address is your car," she asked, in a long and drawn out statement.

"Yeah. Right now we're living in the mission down the street, so we don't have an address," Paul said sternly.

"Okay...well, Paul, you're going to be in the room with ten-and-overs. Samantha and Mary, you're going in the under-tens' room with Kristi," she said, pointing toward our rooms. I reluctantly parted ways with Paul.

The under-tens' room was buzzing with noise and full of kids I didn't know.

"The next time I can, I'm going downstairs to the grown-up room to sit with Mom," I whispered to my sister.

"You can go if you want to. I'm staying up here," she said. Once the coast was clear, I dashed downstairs, snuck in the back door, and spotted my mom sitting in the back corner. I slowly slithered up next to her.

"What are you doing here, Mary?" she asked in a low whisper, startled that I wasn't where she thought I would be.

"I don't want to be up there. I don't know anyone," I said. She paused, giving me a hesitant, yet understanding stare.

"If you're going to sit with me, you have to be quiet," she insisted. I looked at her silently, to show my obedience. After a few minutes, she leaned over and whispered in my ear, "There's doughnuts and coffee on the back table, go help yourself."

I smiled up at her in excitement, then made my way to the back table. I collected a doughnut with pink icing and a coffee (with three sugar cubes and a big pouring of powdered creamer). I vowed to myself that I would be the quietest sugar-loaded seven-year-old Mom had ever seen.

OUR LANDLORD ON MAGNOLIA

After about a week of living in the mission, Mom found a place on Magnolia and 6th Street. The neighborhood was a mix of apartment buildings and single-family homes in varying muted blues, browns, and white stucco. Many of the apartment buildings were square fortresses with apartment doors around all sides—these targeted elderly tenants. Downtown was going through the early stages of gentrification, and high-rise condos were being built in neighborhoods closest to the beach. Some were selling for over $200,000, according to the advertisement draped across the one being built just under a mile away from our apartment.

Our apartment building was one in a long row of six, one-story apartments that reached from 6th street to the alley. Ours was the one right next to the alley. The building looked like it could have been one side of a small motel. It sat right behind our landlord's huge Craftsman house. We rented a studio apartment with a Murphy bed we all shared. The apartment was shotgun-style, so you could see the entire apartment from the porch. Though there wasn't much, we *were* only six blocks from the ocean.

We were all still periodically wetting the bed. The rule was: once you wet the Murphy bed, you were banned and had to sleep on the couch or on the floor. After all, we only had the one bed (and Mom hadn't discovered plastic sheets yet).

None of us talked about our feelings much; we just focused on getting through life in one piece, while avoiding hunger as much as possible. I would talk to Sam about how unhappy I was with my clothes and shoes, or how I wanted the things I saw on television, but as we grew more aware of the likelihood that those possessions would never be ours—and that our lives would never be like what we saw on television—we both grew frustrated. The deeper disappointments, we kept to ourselves.

Our circumstances had created fissures within the family. Anything could become a weapon: bedwetting, our looks, our clothes. Possessions took on a whole new level; if you had something of value, something clean, something newish, or anything that was better than what another sibling had, you had to guard it with your life. The consequences of breaking, using, or even *touching* said items became an all-out war.

Sam and I stayed closer to each other than we did to our brother, who had a completely different standard of what he guarded as "prized possessions." Paul hung tight to his cedar box from Uncle Hank, and his bike. It was hard relating to him, since he was the oldest and already fully fed up with our situation. He was only eleven or so, but old enough to voice that he wasn't happy with Mom's decisions. That often led to them fighting and yelling. She would scream at him that if he wanted to go back to his "faggot father," he could. Paul would often leave the house in a huff and spend the night out on the streets. Many times, he found a hot meal and a place to stay at his friends' houses. It was starting to become normal that he wasn't around.

Paul ended up at a different elementary school than Sam and me. The first few months at a new school flew by, and before long it was Christmas break. All the kids were talking about what they wanted from Santa, but Sam and I knew better. We never expected presents. We wanted them, but we were well aware of our financial situation by this point, so no one ever pushed. We didn't have a tree, or lights, but the night before Christmas, we heard a tap at our apartment door. We were all in the living room watching television. We never had visitors, so we all huddled behind the door as

Mom opened it a crack. She was paranoid of anyone who knocked at the door, and it was always an ordeal when it happened. Whether she was afraid of the police, the child protection agency, welfare, or you name it, she responded the same every time: by asking us who was at the door and why someone would be knocking at it. We, of course, never had an answer.

"Hello Linda. I wanted to drop off a few presents for the kids. Can I come in?" our landlord said from the porch, just loud enough for us to hear him inside. We had been peering through the sliver in the curtain and suddenly became relaxed when we heard who it was.

"Oh, hi, Tim. Yes, please come in," our mom said as she slowly opened the door wider.

Our landlord held gift bags in each arm. We had only been living in the apartment for five months, but that was long enough for our landlord to know we didn't have much. He handed my sister and me a bag each, and we pulled out huge teddy bears. Each one had on a fancy button up vest and trousers. Mine was white with red pants and a green vest and Samantha's was brown with a beige vest and dark brown pants. He handed Paul a present, too, but it wasn't a bear—it was a bag full of clothes. He gave him a shirt, pants, shoes, and socks. He handed Mom an envelope. She grabbed it, thanked him, and placed it inside her purse.

After he left, she opened the envelope and her eyes widened, a huge smile appearing across her face.

"Look, look guys, look what he gave me," she said as she opened the envelope wide enough for us all to peer inside. It was a fifty-dollar bill. "We're going out to dinner!"

All three of us kids belted out a huge, "Hooray!" We quickly threw on our shoes and bolted out of the apartment. We walked to The Grinder, which had the best clam chowder and gave you as many oyster crackers as you wanted. It was a glorious dinner.

When times were tough, we ate things like beans, peanut butter, sliced potatoes, pasta with Prego sauce, and—of course—government cheese, but we didn't have a lot of meat, fruit, or vegetables. We relied on school breakfasts and lunches to get us through the day. This didn't stop our mom from finding ways to overeat. She was gaining weight, noticeably. I never understood how she kept getting fatter while we were all thin as rails.

Paul had made friends with the older kids in the neighborhood right away and rode his bike around town with them. I'm not exactly sure how he got a bike, but he was resourceful, so I never put anything past him. I really wanted to join them, and desperately wanted a BMX bike (but a knock-off would also do). I would have been happy with any sporty boy bike. It was another eight months before it was my eighth birthday, and I got a BMX-type bike I rode everywhere. I had gotten pretty good at riding it, so my brother and his friends finally let me tag along.

They didn't ride their bikes like I rode mine. They were rougher—jumping off curbs, riding in the streets, riding with no hands, taking turns weaving in between each other. They rode through dangerous areas, like the condo high-rise construction site in front of our house.

The first and only night they let me ride with them, I fell off my bike and onto some debris in the construction site. I hit my arm and ribs so hard, it took the wind out of me. I wanted to act tough, though, because it was a treat hanging with my brother and his guy friends. I sucked it up and got back on my bike. The pain on my face was probably pretty clear. I was sure I wasn't going to be invited again—not because of my wipeout, but because I just couldn't keep up. The strength of a boy at twelve verses a girl at eight—no matter how tough she wants to be—is just not the same.

There was a platinum blond family, or as my brother called them, towheaded, with three kids down the street. The younger brother and sister were who Paul, Sam, and I played with. The oldest sister was sixteen, pretty, and shapely. My brother, now at the pivotal age of twelve, had a crush on her.

Their older sister would often flirt with the workers at the construction site, walking by in her tight Jordache jeans, white halter tops, and long, platinum-blonde hair. One day, we all watched as she gave the hottest construction worker a special time in his truck. For some reason, she didn't realize or care that we were all on our porch watching the show. The door was open to his truck, and he was leaned back. All we could see were her feet on the ground. After about ten minutes, his head surfaced and so did hers.

With all the construction debris around our apartment, Paul realized that the small, round, metal pieces that popped out of drills—which he called, "slugs"—were just as good as quarters when you popped them into vending machines. This was a revelation! We used them to buy the newspaper for our mom on Sundays, mainly so Sam and I could clip endless coupons. The coupons felt like little pieces of money, and allowed me to exercise my organizational skills. I categorized them by product type and value offered, then by the nearest expiration date, which I kept on top.

The slugs worked in the soda machines at Shoreline Village, too—even the cigarette machines at The Grinder, according to my brother. We tested these slugs everywhere we could. Paul always had a handful he would dole out to us. We tried them in public telephones, which would sometimes return real quarters after we put the slugs in and hit the phone hard on the receiver. When you put the slugs in a newspaper machine, if you forcefully pulled open the door like you were mad at it, it would spit our real quarters, as if to say, "Oh, I'm sorry, here's your change." These hacks my brother found were like winning the little lottery.

IVS AND HOOKERS

There were many characters in our neighborhood. A few stood out in particular—for instance, the middle-aged Black man who was always being pushed around town on a gurney by some pretty woman. He would always lie on his stomach, his IV dangling in the open. I always wondered what disease he had. He would always wave at people, smiling. I decided he was some kind of pimp in his younger years—the King of All Pimps. He made sure he was still respected by keeping up appearances and walking around town with a lovely lady, I imagined.

Another character in the neighborhood was a fat white guy who wore lots of gold chains around his neck, though they seemed fake because they were so yellow and didn't look like the *real* gold chains in New York. His shirt was always open enough for you to see all his chains—as well as a patch of glistening, sweaty skin and lots of hair. He was always walking around the neighborhood with Black girls who were really pretty and taller than him. I was sure he had also been a pimp, or still was. Every time I went to the corner store, I always seemed to run into either the guy on the gurney or the fat white guy. But all the kids in our neighborhood went to the liquor store by themselves. At any one time, some kid was buying his mom cigarettes, or even a beer. All you had to do was bring a note, and if it looked legit enough, they'd sell you anything you wanted. Though my mom didn't smoke or drink, she did have us run to the store to grab things for her. If there was some extra change lying around, I'd run to the liquor store in a heartbeat, even if it was to grab one five-cent Atomic Fireball; a small red cinnamon-flavored miniature jaw breaker that felt like it burned a hole through your cheek after you had it there for about thirty seconds.

Our neighborhood had crazies, too. One in particular always stayed with me: a tall, blonde woman who walked in circles around trees. What was so strange about her was that, besides being dirty, she seemed normal. She hadn't been disfigured because of an accident or years of drug abuse. Her skin was darkened from years in the sun and intermittent showering I decided, but she still had a softness to her. Unlike other bums in the neighborhood, she wasn't known for bouts of crazy talk or aggressive behavior; she was quiet, and kept the crazy in her mind while circling around a tree for hours. I would sometimes see her on a bus bench sleeping, downtown on the Promenade or near the bus station. I wondered if she had kids and family that missed her. Maybe she was a school teacher, or a housewife pushed to the brink of insanity. I always wanted to know her story. I never found it out.

IT'S FLYING PIPES!

It was 1986 and Chinese slippers were all the rage. This was great for us, because they were only two dollars. They were cool, too. *Karate Kid* had come out and everyone was wearing them.

One afternoon we were playing with the towheaded kids. We found a pipe from the construction site, and we decided to throw it up in the air and into a tall tree to see what leaves and branches we could break. Paul went first, and he got pretty high into the tree, knocking against branches and small leaves came down showering us like snow. Next Sam threw it up, and it came down without doing much damage, like it found a hole in the tree and went through it and then came back out. I was next. I threw it high into the tree for the first time, but didn't knock anything loose from it, just like Sam. I quickly grabbed the pipe from one of the girls who was next, eagerly wanting a redo.

"Let me try to throw it up higher, just one more time," I said.

I wanted to be the strongest, and thought if I threw it hard enough, I could get it to reach the top of the tree. I put my hand to the ground, the pipe gripped hard in it, the starting position exemplifying my intent of a powerful throw. I swung my arm up and released the pipe way up into the air and watched it as it traveled fast and deep into the tree. It flipped and glistened as the sun struck its metal surfaces. I lost sight of the pipe, though, and when it came down moments later, it struck the corner of my forehead. I touched my head and felt the warmth of blood oozing out. When I looked at my hand and saw my blood I fell to the ground. The world had become a lot hazier.

"Are you okay, Mary?" Paul asked frantically while I helped myself up with his hand. I started to think about how much trouble I was going to be in if Mom knew I had hurt myself.

"I'm okay, but it hurts a lot. I'm really dizzy," I told him.

I started to feel my throat swell up. I was ready to cry, despite everyone standing there watching me. I started to walk toward the apartment, but I was too dizzy and fell on the ground again. Sam grabbed me under my arm and wrapped my arm around her shoulder. I put my hand over my head and stood up. Hot blood was running down my forehead and dripping off my cheek.

"You're going to have to go to the hospital," Samantha told me.

Dammit.

The moment we walked into the apartment, my mom could see I was injured.

"I fell and hit my head," I quickly said before my sister could say anything.

"Let me see," Mom said. She held her hands out to grab my head. It felt like I had a huge hole in my head.

"You sure did hit your head pretty hard. This is a good one, Mary. We just need to wash it off and hope you don't have a concussion," she said as she investigated the area further.

At this point there wasn't any pain, just a throbbing sensation. Samantha handed Mom a washcloth, then grabbed some ice. Mom wiped the blood off my head, threw the ice inside the washcloth, and pressed it against my head.

"Just keep this towel on there. That'll stop the bleeding and keep down the swelling."

My head throbbed from the pain of both the ice and the wound. I wanted to fall asleep, but Mom insisted I stay up. She kept the TV on to be sure I was up all night with her until she felt it was safe for me to fall asleep. The wound healed up over the next week and a half, and for a few years I had a nice little knot on my head to remind me of my stupidity.

MUSINGS: MOTHERLY MENTOR

Cleaning the house was a family affair. Tired of waiting for our mother to get the inspiration, my sister and I would often get fed up and start cleaning the place ourselves. Once we got started, however, we'd inspire our mom to join in.

Sometimes she'd get out of her head for a while and show us how to clean. One day it was pots.

"You take S.O.S. pads, dip them in water, and scrub scrub scrub," she said.

We took the pots to the front porch and started scrubbing. It was so much fun to scrub our dirty pots, caked with last week's cooking. I would clean a thousand pots just to have that moment again—a good moment where Mom was present and wasn't yelling, upset, or depressed. I only remember a couple dozen moments like that with her.

When you can't rely on your mother to be your rock, it builds a fiercely independent person. I believe I still seek an older female mentor, but not a motherly figure. There's no vacancy for a mother in my heart.

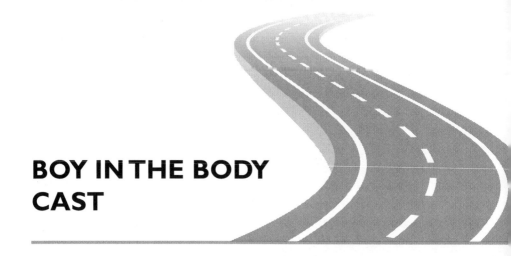

BOY IN THE BODY CAST

It was the late '80s, and whites and hispanics—and most races, really—
didn't mix their cultures much. In general, it seemed to me like most
adults were racist and for the most part, no one seemed to be doing anything
about it. Insults were made about every culture by every culture, and this
was normal. I always thought this was because everyone was ignorant about
each other and our cultures, but now I realize that people were just scared of
what they didn't know and what they'd be called if they mixed too heavily
into another group's culture. There were harsh critics to this mixing from
all sides, and if those mixes produced children, well then everyone could
come together for criticism's sake. But just as there was all of this racism,
there was equally an eagerness for all us kids in the neighborhood, from
different cultures and of different races and backgrounds to play together;
even if we knew what our parents' bigotry was, we all didn't really care
enough to stop playing with each other. We found commonality in our
city's culture, which was a melting pot of Cambodians, Mexicans, Samoans,
Vietnamese, Blacks, Chinese, Caucasians, and more.

A Mexican family lived next door to us. They had two sons; one was
around my age, the other around my brother's. One morning, while I was

out front playing, the father walked by, toward their apartment. He was holding the youngest son, who was in a full body cast.

"Hey, what happened?" I asked the older brother, who trailed behind.

"He was hit by a car," he said with a solemn look. I never really talked to the youngest brother, but I had sympathy for him. Their family was quiet and more traditional, and we must have seemed like rabid animals to them, out playing till the sun came down, yelling in the house and always dirty. Their father was probably quite right to have the boys not playing with us.

How did he get hit by a car? I've been running around the streets for ages; am I just lucky that I haven't been hit by a car?

The youngest son stared at me as he passed by and gave me an embarrassed look, like, "I know, I got hit by a car. Don't look at me."

I gave him the best reassuring look my eight-year-old self could muster: one of bewilderment. I'd never seen anyone in a full body cast before.

As I stared at him being carried toward his apartment, the blanket that had been covering him slipped off his side and revealed his bare butt, outlined by the cast. I had a sense of empathy and looked away from him long enough to ensure that if he looked back, he could confirm I hadn't seen him.

TIME TO MOVE, AGAIN

E ventually it became time for our apartment building to be demolished so another big condo could be built. We would have to move out, and though we had gotten ourselves established, Mom had an itch to try a new city out. Our landlord already had plans to move his entire house—quite literally—to another part of town, and told us that we only had thirty days to find a new place to live. Once the welfare check arrived, we packed up and left. It was raining as we got on the 710 North. Mom pointed the Dart to Vegas. Maybe it was the bright lights or something she read, but our apartment being demolished meant that it was time to up and leave town. Again.

ALL YOU CAN EAT

The rain made the trip to Vegas feel like a thousand miles long. I thought of all the things we were leaving behind—all the things that had started to become familiar to me.

It felt like we arrived in Vegas the day after we left Long Beach. It was possible that Mom was the slowest driver that ever existed. We walked Las Vegas Boulevard, looking at all the sidewalk entertainment. I was amazed at all the lights and action. We found a buffet at Circus Circus and all sat down for dinner. It was nice to see troves of food on people's trays, knowing we had license to pile up our own plates. Endless rows of meat and fixins', soups, salads, and desserts made my eyes pop out of my head and my stomach churn in anticipation. I loaded my plate with a T-bone steak, potatoes, yams, gravy, and green beans. I went back for a salad and topped it with croutons, shredded cheddar cheese, black olives, and blue cheese. I ended my meal with a banana split, my favorite. I had never eaten all I could eat before, and it was glorious.

We watched the free trapeze performances in the casino after dinner. I loved how their bodies moved in harmony, how they fell into each other with such grace and trust, and how no one seemed afraid of the heights. I was afraid for them; falling down seemed like such a scary proposition to me.

Long swings hung from the ceiling, and a cool breeze wisped by my cheeks as the trapeze artists swung by. There was a big net across the bottom of the stage, in case one of the performers were to slip and fall. I quickly covered my eyes each time they fell—which they sometimes did on purpose. They wore beautiful costumes. Even the men looked beautiful in their sparkling leotards of brilliant, festive colors, like emerald green and ruby red, all covered with shiny diamonds. I stared at my sister as her eyes filled with wonder; I could see her dreaming of being a performer like them, being a beautiful woman who swung on swings with beautiful, leotard-clad men.

Mom found a place in Vegas after several weeks of Travelers Aid vouchers, hotels and welfare office visits. The apartment was sad and dingy and had brown carpet, just like all the other places. It had a basic kitchen with dark brown cabinets and nothing memorable, except that it had one bedroom, a step up from most places we had stayed at. The entire neighborhood felt soulless. By then, the entire Vegas experience—the strip, the lights, the temporary nature of the visitors and the services designed to serve the temporary—so far was leaving me queasy. This feeling of impermanence found its permanent anchor in me, in this town.

Paul was getting along well with kids his own age in the neighborhood. He showed Sam and me all the cool things to do at Circle K. You could get a large drink and fill it with every single kind of soda from the fountain. That was called a "suicide." I couldn't understand why it was called a suicide, but every time we had a $1.07, we would run over to Circle K and make a *suicide*.

There were a lot of guys his age in the neighborhood, and *G.I. Joe*, *Thundercats*, and *He-Man* were on television every weekday. He had made a few friends and would go to one of their houses after school to watch at least one of these shows. Paul was often at a friend's place for dinner, so it was usually just my sister and me in charge of making dinner at the apartment. Sam was a resourceful cook. If there was something available in the kitchen to cook, she would use it to make a meal. We often ate sliced potatoes fried in oil and would dip them in ketchup or mustard. I was in awe of her culinary expertise, and served as an eager mouth to taste her creations.

Mom enrolled us in a year-round school and started working at the Golden Nugget on Fremont Street. The concept of a year-round school didn't sit well with me. Why would you make a kid go to school in the summer? I also wasn't exactly excited about having to meet new kids again. It was always an opportunity to be bullied. The kids were already well into their school year, though it was August. I was going to join a third-grade class, and would already be behind by a few months. I had luckily scored high enough in the entrance exam to be placed in a class with smarter kids, and the initial teasing was significantly less than I was prepared for. The introduction by the teacher was simple and the class got started quite quickly. I was able to immerse myself in the book she was reading to the class.

At recess, I was hoping to see my brother and sister, but somehow I couldn't find them on the playground—which was the largest playground I'd ever seen. There were several basketball courts, jungle gyms, monkey bars, and tether balls. I zeroed in on a boy from my class. I stood there in the field and watched as four or five girls chased him around. They all wanted to kiss him. His name was Jay, and he had a striking resemblance to Michael Jackson. I smiled as he dodged them, then surrendered and fell to the ground as the girls jumped on top of him and planted kisses on his cheek. I watched with some amusement because I had never seen girls behave this way. At that moment, I realized it was probably a big pain in the ass being really attractive.

As it turns out, Jay was very kind. He invited me to his ninth birthday party that was happening that weekend. He did so by sitting an invitation on my desk and asking if I could make it as soon as I sat down for class. It felt like everyone was waiting for my answer and I quickly flushed with excitement and said I would come. Things seemed so very different now. Maybe I was going to make new friends after all.

The day of the party, all the cool kids were there. I wasn't sure how I fit into this bunch. I could have easily felt like an outsider, but didn't. I walked through his house, room by room, past people that were talking or standing around. I stumbled upon his bedroom after someone pointed to it and said he was probably there. There were a few guys from school hanging out in there. They were all playing a video game on his Atari. As I opened the door, they all looked at me.

"Hey Jay. Happy Birthday. Thanks for inviting me," I said quickly.

"Come in and close the door," he told me. I sat next to him on his bed and got comfortable while I watched them play their game. I felt at ease with him and his friends. It had been a long time since I had felt so accepted, especially among kids who were far better off than me.

"Do you play basketball?" he asked me. I actually hadn't, but I had a curiosity for it.

"Yeah, I like to play."

"Cool. Come to the court on Monday and play with us."

"Okay. I will, thanks."

A surge of happiness ran through my body. As kids came by his room and opened the door looking for him, they glanced at me sitting next to him. He never made an awkward move away from me. I started to feel normal.

After a while, Jay turned to me and said, "Thanks for coming to my party. I was hoping you would come."

I didn't know what to say, and probably flushed red. The door swung open and one of the kids said, "Cake and ice cream in the kitchen, come on!"

Everyone fled the room except for him and me.

"So, this is a cool party," I told him.

He looked at me and said, "Yeah, it is."

Then he leaned toward me, laid his lips on mine, and started to kiss me. *Michael Jackson is kissing me!* I couldn't believe it. I had some practice kissing in New York with Steven, maybe he could tell? Is that why he wanted to kiss me? Maybe I seemed like an experienced girl, like someone who knew what she was doing. Maybe I was just having a good hair day.

What if someone comes into the bedroom?

A surge of panic came over me. If they saw us kissing, it would be talked about at school, and then my sister and brother would know. I jumped up quickly.

"I've got to go," I told him.

I left his room and the party quickly. I ran home like the devil, it was only a few blocks away from our apartment. What had I done? What did this say about him and me? I sank into the couch when I got home. Mom was at work, and Sam and Paul were probably at the park. I felt really good, but a little embarrassed. How could someone that looked like him like a girl that looked like me? I thought about his face, his kind words, and his smooth advancement toward me. I thought about what it all meant until everyone came home.

The next day, when I went to school, Jay acted like the kiss never happened. He was back on the field, being chased by girls. He never ended up playing basketball with me. Though to some degree, I understood this rejection. What did I expect he would do, tell the school he loved me? Hold my hand during recess? But I still felt a sting. But there were no aunts or grandmas or moms who were going to comfort me as I held up my heart and cried out in pain, this stinger just kept on stinging.

PLEDGE OF ALLEGIANCE

Reciting the Pledge of Allegiance was mandatory in school, meaning everyone just did it. "I pledge allegiance to the flag of the United States of America and to the Republic for which it stands, one nation under God, indivisible, with liberty and justice for all." One morning, I decided *not* to pledge allegiance. I was feeling let down by my world. I wondered what was good about reciting a pledge that said we were one under God, because God is what said my father was a sinner and that sin broke my family apart. Were we indivisible, unable to be separated or divided? I saw divisions everyday; in our home, in society, in our schoolyard. And could I claim we were justice for all? Seeing what I'd seen in soup kitchens and ghettos? Knowing what I knew I thought I was being a rebel, and standing up for myself and my integrity. One other kid decided to join me in silence when we passed glances while the others recited. My teacher didn't find this amusing. Our punishment was to say the Pledge of Allegiance out loud, alone, while the entire class watched us. I felt humiliated by this punishment. There seemed to be no power I could evoke by exhibiting my own protest. My own First Amendment right, the one protecting free speech, though I didn't know anything about these official rights at the time, seemed like some fuzzy rule that only adults could evoke. Adults wanted you to say the words that were their truths, like when my mom handed me that picket sign a few years earlier, but those weren't my words. And these weren't my words either, at least not on this day. But I said those words and sat back in my chair pissed off that I'd been once again forced by an adult to represent their message. I fell in line and recited my Pledge of Allegiance the next day.

BACKWARD F

Maybe it was because I was left-handed, maybe it was because I was a little dyslexic, maybe it was because I had a really fucking hard life, but whatever the reason—I had problems writing a cursive capital *F*. For some reason, my F's came out backward, like they were written in a mirror. When my teacher saw my backward *F*, she decided to teach me a lesson.

She asked me to come to the front of the class. She gave me a piece of chalk and said, "I want us to teach Mary how to write in cursive. She's having problems with it."

The entire class laughed. I let out a big sigh.

"Write a capital *F*, Mary."

I turned to the chalkboard and proceeded to write an *F*. I stepped back and turned toward the teacher, determined not to look at my classmates. She then wrote a cursive capital *F* on the board. Sure enough, it was the mirror image of mine.

She looked at me and said, "Just look at my letter *F*, and copy it."

I held the piece of chalk in my hand, close to the board, and started at the top. I struggled with the first parts of the letter, the curves wanting to go one way and my brain wanting them to go another.

"No, Mary, turn the other way. Start on the right, then turn down to the left,"

I finally wrote out the letter *F* the way she wanted. It didn't feel right, but I did it. The class stopped snickering by now, and was dead silent.

"Again, Mary."

The second one I wrote was a little easier. I concentrated on how the movement of the letter flowed, and less on how it looked.

"Good job, Mary. This is looking more like a cursive *F*," she exclaimed. "One more, Mary. You can do it."

I closed my eyes and visualized the cursive *F* on the board—all the movements that it took to arrive at the letter she had written for me to copy. I opened my eyes and proceeded to write my final *F* on the chalkboard. I did so with ease. I handed her the piece of chalk, and turned to the class. Everyone was staring at me, a bit of sympathy on each of their faces.

"That's good, Mary. You can go back to your seat now," the teacher told me.

I walked quickly back to my desk feeling a tide of shame washing over me. It's true that I did, at that moment, permanently change how I wrote a capital *F*—however, I'm not sure that her tactic was the best. I'd never felt that many eyes on me before, at least not when it came to my thinkin' hat. I felt like I was back in second grade and dropping my tray.

I felt like I needed a guide on how to survive teachers. So far, I hadn't had any that really understood me. Many of my teachers acted like my deformity meant I must have been slow or limited in my intellectual or emotional development. A cleft lip and palate always made you look stranger than most, I would agree with that, but certainly not any more mentally deficient than anyone else. But I had a big ego for such a young person. I didn't let them get away with treating me differently. Sure, it hurt me inside, but I stood up for myself. I did my schoolwork and I did it well, to show them I was better than those who looked normal—but they would always find a weakness in me. That was because, well, I was weak. I had dirty clothes, beat up shoes, a grumbling stomach, and a broken heart. *If only there were teachers that didn't suck,* I thought.

After a few months in that class, the teacher who made me write *F* on the board went out of her way to praise me for some artwork I had drawn of lava and volcanoes. She insisted my artwork was beautiful and even held it up to the class to signal her interest. In some ways I was embarrassed, not knowing what to do with all this positive attention. I stared at my drawing in her hands, and captured her smile as she walked up and down the rows of desks to show the other students my artwork. I tried to see and understand what she saw and was so impressed by. I could see the emotions brought out by the colors I'd used; deep blues, reds, and yellows. An erupting volcano in the distance, the lava dripping off the sides and slithering in a river that led right toward the viewer. One of my fears was being consumed by lava. Lava seemed like a cruel natural phenomenon, to move so slow but be so deadly and unstoppable. I'd seen a National Geographic about volcanoes not long before, and was horrified to see the black creeping wave of lava slowly unfolding toward a home in Hawaii; ultimately burning it to the ground. It reminded me of the 1958 movie, *The Blob*. The Blob was drawn toward people, and then consumed them in a wobbly, bouncing, giggly slime.

My teacher's interest in my art made me feel special, and I liked being seen through her prism of talent. I decided in that moment that my creative side would shine, and I allowed it to wander and express itself; in other colorings I did or even in writing assignments. The teacher became more and more impressed with my reading and writing skills and went out of her way to call on me to read passages from books or to read a story I'd written as one of our writing assignments. I realized it was possible to make someone see you completely differently, maybe not even not see your handicap, if you were able to impress them with a talent.

LONELY DAYS

After school one day, Paul, Sam, and I decided to hang out at the park before going back home. Mom was always working, so she was never home when we got out of school. Sam and I swung on the swings, singing aloud the latest pop song. Paul was playing with his friend, throwing and kicking a ball several yards down from us. I saw a guy sitting near a tree, his head laid back against the trunk while soaking in the sun. He had one of his legs laid out, relaxed. I noticed he had on the smallest of running shorts, and it was easy to see that he was going commando—his genitals were exposed. I looked at my sister, and with my eyes I steered her toward the guy near the tree. The man bent his head down and peered at us, but looked away quickly. We hopped off the swings and ran over to where Paul was playing to tell him what we saw. Paul looked over at the tree and could see the man—and his exposed privates.

"Hey! Cover yourself up!" he yelled at the man. He turned to my sister and me, and said, "Let's go home. It's already late, and I'm sure Mom is worried about us."

It was already getting dark. We all ran back to the apartment. The reality of life, the raw vulnerability of the world was following us. Paul opened the door. The lights were all out except for the last bit of light coming into the living room from the opened blinds.

Mom was in the living room, lying on a mattress she put on the floor. She'd been writing, and was crying, a desperate look on her face. Several pieces of paper in front of her were filled, every line, with her worries. The pages were full of her unusual handwriting that consisted of both large and small cursive, even from word to word, the messy sentences continuing in the margins with vague continuity, words crossed out or written over by new words with darker lines and underlines.

"I thought they took you away from me," she said to us. It had been at least three hours since we could have come home after school, but we weren't used to her being there anymore. We all rushed into her arms, tackling her like kittens would their mother. We all began to cry. "I thought Child Services took you all. I'm such a bad mother. I thought I'd lost you."

She looked at us and cried vulnerably, in a way that reminded me of the look she had in the hallway of our house in Nashville when the school had called about us being neglected.

"What are we doing here, Mom?" Paul asked. "Can we just leave this place?"

Mom stared at him, hesitating. She let out a big sigh.

"I think we need to leave this place, too," she conceded.

My mom was only thirty-three, with three kids and no real income except what she made at the Golden Nugget. Her only life outside of us was the time she might have had after work—maybe grabbing a beer, maybe having a love affair. During that time, we mostly only saw her at night—and only sometimes, since she never had a predictable schedule. We kids looked after each other, most of the time. It would get lonely and I would often cry myself to sleep, desperately seeking a feeling of completeness only a mother's comfort can give. Sleeping in the apartment most nights with just the moon's light coming into the living room through our simple curtains could make me feel all alone.

Mom told us that her welfare check was coming the next day, and that after she cashed it we would leave. My brother, sister and I all looked at each other and, without saying a word, we all said, "Thank God."

We then rambled on about the guy who just showed us all his man bits, and I shared my Pledge of Allegiance and the "cursive F" story and how nothing was good about this place except for the cheap buffet food and the circus act.

Las Vegas was filled with lost hope. It saturated the air like smog and I was sick of it.

We didn't have to go to school the next day. We all just waited for the mail lady. By the time the check plopped into our mailbox at 3 p.m., we were already packed up and ready to go. After Mom cashed the check, I asked her, "Where we goin', Mom?"

"Long Beach. Let's go back to Long Beach."

A part of me was still hoping she would say *Nashville,* so that maybe we could go see Dad again. We were going into our third year on the run and running away was the way it was. My more aware years were now away from Nashville and I had doubts about the life we could have if we went back. That, combined with my mother's paranoia, made it so that a larger part of me thought we'd be taken away from her, and the idea of that was more frightening than my longing to see my father again.

LONG BEACH, AGAIN

Long Beach was becoming home.

It was already a couple months into the school year, and I was in a new third-grade class. We did the Travelers Aid and welfare office dance once again.

No one was happy at the welfare office. After hours of waiting, when they finally saw us, Mom told them about how we traveled from Vegas and didn't have any kind of furniture. She was able to secure a one-time check of $750 to furnish an apartment, but they wouldn't send it until she could show proof she was renting. This was an incredible amount of money and meant we could buy some real beds and couches, a coffee table, a dining room table. Somehow, though, we didn't qualify for food stamps.

As a family of four, we were approved for $7,500 per year of cash benefits. That was $650 per month split into two checks of $325; received on the first and the fifteenth of the month. Our rent was $380 a month for a one bedroom apartment. Because of bus fares and incidentals like shoes, clothes, electricity, and water bills, that $650 just wasn't enough. So we did the soup kitchens and food banks dance again, too.

There were, luckily, many food banks in Long Beach. Some gave you bread, cheese, powdered milk, and peanut butter. You would have to wait in line from early in the morning in order to get a bag full of food. Others served lunch only, which still required standing in line for two hours to get one lunch sack. Then others gave you a food box. Those were the grand prize. Those would have beans, rice, cereal, fruit, bread that didn't smell moldy, cheese, desserts, snacks, and more. Those required standing in line from before lunch until at least six o'clock in the evening for the chance of getting one of the limited food boxes they had available that day. If you didn't make the cut that day, your six hours standing in line were for naught.

Our neighborhood was home to a YMCA, a middle school, a few diners, and a couple of missions. We lived in a two-story apartment building. It was nothing special. There were five apartments on each floor, and our apartment was on the second floor, right in the middle: apartment #8. We shared a large courtyard with another building, and the kids played there. There was a high, black, metal gate in the front that usually had a broken lock. It was a predominantly Mexican neighborhood. We were one of only two white families living in the apartments.

There were small houses sprinkled around the block that looked out of place. Those houses were remnants of a time when the neighborhood was much different, and seemed to give the street a softer feel. Each of the houses had big front yards and wooden fences, almost like they could have come from Nashville.

The apartment building next to ours was home to a family that owned a food truck—the kind that sold candy, popcorn, fruits, and other sundries. It mostly sat outside our apartment building and was de facto one of our neighborhood stores.

The owners of the truck had three kids. The oldest was a very handsome guy with thick black hair, a Superman build, and bedroom eyes. The other two were twins, a boy and a girl. The twins each had what I had: a cleft-lip and palate. Theirs didn't look like mine, though; their eyes were large and far apart, their foreheads bigger, their noses extra large and their scars for Cupid's bow were much thicker scars than mine. They spoke funny, too, like their muffled voices were being spoken through some kind of device.

They were all in their teens when we moved into the neighborhood, and while they treated everyone nicely, I felt like the twins treated me extra nicely. Looking the way we looked, the least we could do for each other was to be kind. They didn't go to school, though. They worked on the family sundry truck. Public school wasn't kind enough for them, and they were probably better off kept away from the harsh, unkind world of children in large groups.

Because their family was so well respected in the neighborhood, other kids didn't make fun of them. They were part of the neighborhood, and we were all part of one big family. The girl always held herself with confidence. She had a beautiful body: her hair was long and dark brown, and she wore tight-fitting clothing that showed all her curves. Despite the fact that she couldn't do anything about her face, she was still confident. That resonated with me. I didn't have the body yet, nor the clothes, but at least I could carry myself with confidence. If she could, I could, too.

Shortly after we moved in, a woman from two apartments down knocked on our door. She introduced herself to our mom and offered to babysit us. She said she was living with her boyfriend's family and that she had an infant son, but saw that Mom had three young kids and might need a night off once in a while. I was skeptical of her. Sure, we were three young kids in the house with a single mother, and the neighbor lady was a likely babysitter candidate, but Paul was twelve years old and we didn't need a babysitter if he was around, which he was some of the time. Besides, Sam and I could handle ourselves, as long as no one intentionally messed with us. Our mom told her that if there was a time when she needed her services, she would reach out.

About a month after we moved into the building, the time came for the neighbor to babysit us. The experience was worse than I expected. Not only did she make us stand in a corner most of the evening because she said we were being too loud, she also made us put mayonnaise in the wall corner and put our noses in it. I'm pretty sure my brother's dislike for mayonnaise started that night. When our mother returned that evening, I quickly tattled on the babysitter, who stood there as if she thought I was the biggest liar she'd ever seen and denying the claims of mistreatment. My mother didn't take her side, but she didn't scold the woman either. She gave her the twenty dollars she promised her and then asked her to leave very calmly. I stood there shocked. We had been told our whole lives to stay away from people because they will probably hurt us, and now someone has, and she pays them?

"I know she did what you said she did. I'm not going to have her babysit you all anymore, okay?" Mom assured us. All three of us kids agreed that if we didn't have to endure someone like that again, we could forgive this misjudgement on our Mom's part.

Why are people so mean to other people? I realized that night that once someone has power over another soul—and especially a more vulnerable soul—the true nature of that person would reveal itself.

Those who dislike themselves and their life are hurt souls. But people who have hurt souls and power, then use their power inappropriately and hurt others, to temporarily feel better about their own life, that's a whole other kind of pain.

From the outside, bullies appear to be a pillar of strength. It's the exact opposite, however. The moment you stand up to them, bullies usually back down rather quickly and become the very essence of their own pain. Ultimately, you will end up pitying them.

Sam and I were friends with all the kids in our building, as well as almost every kid in the other buildings that lined our side of the street. We'd play Chinese jump rope in the courtyard and always found creative ways to pass the time. We'd do face painting and water coloring, or create a maze through our apartment; we'd do just about anything that would engage our imaginations and keep our thoughts away from our current situation.

This neighborhood was a place I truly felt accepted. Everyone was really proud of their own home and their own traditions. Most of the apartment building was filled with first-generation families from Mexico—moms, dads, kids, and grandparents all lived together. Moms stayed at home to raise the kids, and the dads went off to work every day. Some were mechanics. Some were cowboy-lookin' guys who were called Rancheros. Most of the adults didn't speak much (or any) English, and it was the kids who were their translators. The family unit was important, and so was mealtime.

Luckily for us, that meant that there was always food being cooked by an abuela or mom. They'd usually feel bad for Sam and me and give us a plate. This is when I first had Spanish rice fresh from the skillet, and fresh homemade salsa with chilis ground using a mortar and pestle. The salsa was so hot it made my eyes water and mouth burn. I'd swear I wouldn't eat it again, but then a few days would pass and fresh salsa was being made again, and I'd go right back to eating it.

MUSINGS: THE THIRD CHILD EFFECT

I'm pretty sure that my birth put the nail in the coffin of my mom's body. Mom was only 200 pounds when she had me, which, for a five-foot-ten woman, isn't actually that bad. Today, I'm six feet, one inch tall and almost 170 pounds. Yet Mom, at five-foot-ten, was over 350 pounds (sometimes tipping 400) for most of my childhood. How did she nearly double in size after having me? A failed marriage, mental illness, despair, and poverty. That's how, I suppose.

GOT ANY HAND-ME-DOWNS?

I went back to my previous elementary school to finish the third grade. Everyone already knew each other, and it seemed like the class was so much harder than in Vegas. The teacher was nice, though (finally).

My first day back, my mom had given me a letter to give to the teacher. I hadn't actually read it before handing it to her that morning. My teacher read it to herself, then looked down at me with a sigh. She closed the note up and told me to sit down while she made an announcement.

"Class, this is Mary Gregory. She has just moved back here from Las Vegas. You may remember her from last year. Her mother has sent me a note asking for some help," she announced. I felt like I was folding into my seat like kneaded bread. *What could Mom have asked for help with?*

"Since she is newly back in town, her mother asks if any of you could help out by donating any old shoes or clothes you may have."

It felt like time had slowed down.

"Yes, Michelle." The teacher pointed to a student with her hand up.

"I've got some old clothes I can bring to class tomorrow."

"Who in this room—raise your hands—wants to help Mary?" the teacher asked, scanning the room optimistically.

The overwhelming majority of hands darted into the air. I was amazed. I felt incredibly accepted. My fears of being the poor one, the ridiculed one, all began to fade. In that moment, I learned a lot about humanity. I learned that if you share your situation with others and acknowledge your vulnerability, people don't always just take advantage of this weakness. If you aren't too afraid or too proud to ask for help, you can receive exactly what you need. I started to see a different side to people, and I felt that a part of my life was being reborn.

SCHOOL BUS BLUES

By fourth grade, Sam and I were old enough to take the city bus. If we were running behind and couldn't walk the twenty blocks up the street to catch the school bus, we took the "1 Easy" city bus from the corner of Magnolia and Pacific Coast Highway (PCH), which was just a few blocks up from our apartment. The city bus was mostly great; it got us to school in just twelve minutes. Whenever it was time to go home, however, we were relegated to the dreaded school bus. The school bus blues consisted of a few things beyond your control. It was the '80s and many kids had Jheri curls, so depending on who had been sitting in your seat that morning, you could be relegated to a greasy spot right where your head lay. The really high backs didn't allow you to slump or slouch at all, so if you sat in that seat, you were getting the grease. I liked Michael Jackson, though, and he had a Jheri curl, which I found really attractive. Though I would momentarily hesitate if I had to sit in a spot with a Jheri curl stain, I'd think of Michael Jackson, and it wouldn't be that bad.

The school bus was where I learned a lot about people. Because of the characters I had to deal with, I would have rather taken the city bus over the school bus any day. Folks on the city bus mostly kept to themselves, and there was usually a dilution of kids to adults—but on the school bus, everyone was fair game. Our driver was an old woman who looked bitterly unhappy with her job. When she opened the door to greet us in the morning, it was always, "Get in kids, and hurry up." When the doors closed and we pulled away from the curb, we would get the speech: "Now I don't want you kids fighting or kicking the seats. Sit your asses down until we get to school."

For a moment we would be model citizens. That didn't stop the chaos, however. In the secret underground world of the school bus, the art of nuance was practiced continuously. I would watch the driver's eyes, and in the split second she wasn't looking, I would pop some candy in my mouth. I was clever at chewing delicious Now and Laters so slowly she never saw. Others, however, had designs on the not-so-subtle art of bullying. It didn't matter if you were a girl or a boy; if a bully didn't like you, they would find a clever way to throw something at you, kick your seat, pull your hair, or even pick a fight with you.

One day in particular had been a more annoying ride than usual. This was the week Sam decided she wanted a spiral perm so she could look like Jennifer Grey in *Dirty Dancing*. She'd gone to a local beauty school downtown, hoping to get it done on the cheap. The perm turned out so tight she looked like a blonde version of Little Orphan Annie. She even had the same freckles sprinkled on her cheeks. The movie had played on local television that week, and no one wasted an opportunity to call her Annie.

One boy in particular was relentless. "Hey, Annie. Annie. Hey Annie," he whispered to Sam on the bus.

"Shut up!" she yelled back at him.

"Oooooohhhhh," said the entire bus. The boy gave Sam a nasty look and when he sat back in his seat behind us, I looked back, and I could see his face; it was full of anger, and he shook his head from side to side, as if he was plotting his revenge.

"When the bus stops, walk in front of me," Sam told me.

"Why?"

"I think he's going to try and fight us when we get off. I don't want you to get hit."

When the bus stopped and all the kids stood up, I got in front of Sam in line. A few seconds later, the boy pushed through the people in the aisle and went to hit Sam in the back of the head. She turned around in time to push him into an empty seat and began to throw her fists down on him. She was hitting everywhere: his face, his head, his arms, his stomach. There were still enough people in front of us getting off that the school bus lady couldn't see the fight. It was all over in about a minute. Sam pulled herself off of him and stood there, staring at the bully.

"I told you to shut up," she said.

He stared up at her and didn't say a word. He looked sweaty and ashamed and still had his arms up from defending his face. The kids who were in the back of the bus and who had seen the fight all stared at Sam in awe. No one had to say a word. As each person from the back filed out of the bus, they gave him a disappointed look, some shaking their heads.

The bully problem had been solved, and it left me feeling like I had the coolest sister in the world.

Sam and I ran high on moxie over the next few weeks, and the boy Sam beat up never got back on the school bus again. It felt like we had won our place in the "don't fuck with us" category.

Fights on the school bus were common occurrences, because the only adult was driving that bus, and she was not paying attention to the kids. When the guys got too aggressive—like pushing and pulling hair, endlessly teasing, or making fun of my face—Sam would eventually snap and challenge the bullies.

"Shut up, or I'll punch your face into your asshole," she would tell them out of exasperation.

The only thing our school bus driver cared about was that we all stayed in our seats. If you wanted your life to be easy going, you sat in the front of the bus in earshot of the driver, so she could tell bullies to knock it off directly. If you were late, or were picked up on the route later than most kids, you had to sit in the back of the bus, and *good luck*. That's where all the assholes sat. If you were slick enough, you could move to another seat when the bus driver wasn't looking. That was like getting away with murder, and was a maneuver only the bravest would try. Sam and I always sat together when we could, it ensured the least amount of trouble possible.

VUI

I had made friends with a small Vietnamese girl in my third-grade class named Vui. She rode the school bus with us, and lived in a house that was on our walk home. She was a latchkey kid like us, but she didn't have any siblings, so there was no one there to keep her company. Sam and I would walk her home, and she'd sometimes invite us inside to eat a snack. The smells hit us the moment we walked in the door. Her house was the first Asian home we'd ever been in. It smelled like rice and fish, and the odor lingered in the air.

Vui's house was simple: a small rug here and there, a black kitchen table, four chairs, Vietnamese art on the walls with wall drapes, a small television on a small stand, and a big, round bamboo rice holder on the kitchen floor. She did her best to host us. She would offer us a bowl of vegetables or chicken prepared the night before and put it on top of rice. She introduced us to white rice with soy sauce drizzled on top. There was still a fishy smell to the rice, even if there was none in the bowl. I deeply enjoyed the salty and smoky flavor it added to the rice, even though the fish aroma was peripheral. Until then, the only thing I knew to put on white rice was sugar; which was how my mother and brother ate it when they spent time together in the late evenings watching TV, though I didn't like the way that tasted.

Vui showed me a different way that a home dedicated to certain foods smelled like those foods even when you weren't cooking. This seemed to be a more dedicated, assuring way to eat and to live. I've been in many homes since, and the ones that make me smile and feel at home are the ones that smell like the food they must eat everyday. When they smell of fresh homemade bread, or strong spices like chili powder, cumin, garlic, onions, paprika, or even grease, I know there's a tradition there.

English was her second language, and she loved when we talked because I would explain to her the words and expressions of the English language. She would listen to me intently as I explained the reasons; often she didn't understand the details, but I loved her eagerness to learn, her politeness. Her accent was very strong, but I had a lot of patience and I really wanted to understand her. We both struggled with being laughed at for our accents or mannerisms. I would get laughed at each time I walked through the halls or the playground and said, "Good mornin'" to any of my classmates. Apparently this sounded too country for the other kids, so after a few teasings, I had to change it to "Hi."

We learned a lot about each other by sharing what our lives were like. She could relate to my life in New York, and my sadness for missing my father. She shared how her family escaped from Vietnam, and how many of her family members had died. She missed them and wished she could see her family again, but that she knew it would be a very long time until that would ever be a possibility. Her parents told her not to think about it.

Vui showed me another side to my own life's struggles, which helped give me strength to keep going. We fled my mom's war, one that had nothing to do with me—but Vui had fled a real war. Were the results the same? Is your family dead if you think you'll never see them again? I decided war is relative.

CREATIVELY YOURS

I really hit my creative streak in third grade. I decided to try my hand at writing comic books. Pac-Man was something simple I could draw, so I created stories around Mr. and Mrs. Pac-Man and their family. I would draw the little boys in tuxedos and the girls in cute dresses with little pink bows on their heads. After a few weeks, I had a full comic book with a complete storyline. I would carry it around with me, stapling in new pages of construction paper when an idea came to me and I wanted to add it to the story.

One day on the playground, I had the opportunity to show my comic book to the school's principal. I walked up to him and introduced myself. I quickly dug into my backpack and pulled out the comic book I'd created.

"I wrote a story about Mr. and Mrs. Pac-Man. See here, they met one day while walking around their neighborhood."

I held up the booklet so he could see my drawing of a scene on a suburban street, lined with trees like our old neighborhood in Nashville. Mrs. Pac-Man was on her bike, and Mr. Pac-Man was holding a basketball. I flipped the page.

"See, here, this is when he rescued her from the ghosts."

Mr. Pac-Man was holding many cherries by their stems, throwing them toward the ghosts. Some had already turned blue, because he had activated their frightened mode. Mrs. Pac-Man stood behind him, smiling.

"And see here, here's when they got married. They had children, too: two boys and three girls," I explained enthusiastically, showing him their wedding and flipping the page to show their boys and girls playing in a Pac-Man game, with no ghosts chasing them.

"Keep pursuing art, Mary. You've got a great imagination," he said as he patted me on the shoulder and turned away to talk to the recess lady. I was filled with joy. My principal liked my work.

Later that week, I was given an assignment to write a story about anything I wanted. We were going to present the story in front of class the following week. That weekend, as I sat at the kitchen table thinking about what I wanted to write about, I looked around at the piles of Mom's papers, some old clothes I could use as fabric, some pieces of yarn, and a bottle of glue that I had been using to put on my fingers, just so I could peel it off. I decided to write about a character called *Sue Glue*. The story went like this: Sue Glue was made from a bottle of Elmer's Glue. Super Glue had become so popular that Elmer's Glue was no longer needed. Even the glue stick was considered better than her, because it had a lid, unlike her top that always had a little bit of wet glue on its head. Moms complained that she was too messy. This meant that she and her family could no longer make a living with arts and crafts, forcing them into poverty. I drew Sue Glue and added long orange yarn to her head. I even made her a dress out of the scrapes of fabric lying around.

I pulled out my mom's typewriter and started to write Sue Glue's story. She had picked it up from a thrift store, and though not every letter worked, and the ribbon was old, it was still a beautiful machine. The typewriter was black, clunky, and each key seemed too far apart for my small fingers. I loved the sound it made, though: the clinky, clanky, extra effort it made to swing each letter to the paper, like a pitcher throwing their fastest pitch. I had written two pages before I knew it. I decided that I would add extra flavor to my presentation by memorizing it. I spent all weekend reading the story aloud, making changes along the way, and committing the story to memory.

The morning of the story presentation, I had an overwhelming sense of stage fright. I hadn't performed like this before. Sure, I acted like a clown at home, but now I had to remember my lines. The teacher called my name, and I walked up to the front of the class. I saw Vui sitting at her desk in the far right corner of the room and decided that she would be the person I would focus on while giving my presentation, because of her demure quality.

As I stood in front of class, I placed Sue Glue on the table in front of me and began my presentation. Vui started to giggle. I was translating a story of a girl who was far from home, and no longer fit in, but she was a bottle of glue with long yarn hair and had a funny accent. I think my story was too much for Vui to handle. She started laughing so hard that I began to laugh. I knew what I had written was funny, but I didn't think it was *that* funny. Her laugh was infectious—maybe because Vui was always so quiet in class that the other students couldn't believe she was drawing attention to herself. This ignited a chain reaction, but I kept on with my story, barely able to complete most sentences without her slapping the table or giggling into her shirt. Soon the entire class was laughing, even the teacher. I soon finished my story and sat back down in my seat. My face was red from laughter and the lack of oxygen. I was sweating, and the classroom felt incredibly hot. I looked over at Vui, who was smiling like I had never seen her smile before. I caught eyes with her and smiled. I had accepted my life in that moment, and so did she. I knew I wasn't the only person going through a hard time, missing their family, far away from everyone they once knew. And yet, somehow, we could find a way to laugh about it and even make others laugh about it, too. There is something cathartic and joyful about sharing the layer underneath with everyone you meet.

My teacher pulled me aside later that day and told me she loved my story and especially loved that I went the extra mile to memorize it. That really boosted my self-esteem. I felt special. I felt encouraged to keep up my resourceful ways to be creative. I realized that even with the limited resources I had, I was able to be creative. What was within me could be shared.

LONG AND LANKY

By the time I was nine years old and in the fourth grade, I was already five feet, five inches tall. At the end of the school year, we had a fitness competition for the fourth, fifth, and sixth graders. I really wanted to compete. I had never been in a competition before, and I was excited about the possibility of winning. I signed up for two competitions. One was for the standing long jump and the other was for the half mile. I had never practiced a standing long jump before, but I figured it wasn't too difficult, considering all you had to do was jump from one point to the other. If I was any good with the long legs I had, I'd get pretty far.

The real competition was between myself and Tia, a tall Samoan girl in my class. Tia went first. Surprisingly, she had quite the leap! When I stepped up to jump, I didn't even get close to her mark. Her leap was almost twice as long as mine. When we went again, I got further, but nowhere near hers. I ended up getting second place. I wasn't the best leaper, but I knew I could run.

I put my mind to winning the half mile. As the race started, Leon, who was in my class, gave me the thumbs up from the sideline. Since we were in the same class together, he knew how athletic I was, and how fast I could run. When the competition started, I went full force. *Half a mile is two times around the playground. I've got this.* After the first lap, I didn't even feel winded. I looked back and I was clearly way ahead of everyone. I soared through the second lap without breaking a sweat, and I was handed the blue ribbon as I crossed the finish line.

I had won a competition! I was the *best* at something. I couldn't wait to get home and show Mom. I marveled at what was written on the back of the ribbon: Name: Mary Gregory; Class: Mrs. Robbins; Event: Half Mile. It was royal blue and had gold lettering that said, "First Place." I played it out in my mind, the joy my mom would express the moment she saw me walk into the house with my blue ribbon.

It wasn't until almost the end of the day, when the lessons were over, that I realized I had lost my first place blue ribbon. I looked everywhere for it: my pockets, my desk, my backpack, the floor. Leon sensed I was panicking and got my attention.

He whispered, "Did you lose your ribbon?"

"Yes, I can't find it."

"I'll help you look for it when we can leave."

I nodded to him, sinking into my seat and now feeling terrible. He had also won a blue ribbon that day for running the mile. When the class ended, he helped me look for it through the entire classroom. We then looked all through the playground. Time was getting tight and I had to catch the school bus home. My glory walk into the house was slowly beginning to fade. The shiny blue ribbon was gone. I realized how anticlimactic it would be to tell my mom I had won and not have the ribbon to prove it. When I got home, I showed her my second place red ribbon, and told her the story of my first place victory. She was still just as proud of me.

"Mary, you can win anything you want," she said.

THE MISADVENTURES OF WALKING HOME

Vui was quickly replaced as my best friend when two new girls got on the school bus one morning. They were tall, Black, and skinny, and wore almost matching outfits. At first I thought they were twins. Their names were Myesha and Keya. They were a year and a half apart, just like my sister and me. Myesha was Sam's age, and Keya was mine.

Myesha and Keya lived just a few blocks out of our way home. Our walks became adventures. Countless times we would egg each other on to jump a wall and grab some fruit from someone's backyard, or we would scrounge together money to buy sodas and candy at the liquor store. Mostly, we just talked about life. They also didn't have a father around, and when we asked them where he was, they said they didn't know. Their mom was a nurse and worked all the time, so just like us, they were left to take care of themselves most days. One thing Sam and I appreciated was that their house was always so clean. They had nice clothes, nice shoes, a nice room that the two of them shared, a kitchen full of food, and even a Betamax VCR! To a true poor kid, they seemed to have it all, *and* they were cool and pretty. We were two sets of sisters who had each other's backs. When we were all together, we were a brute force.

We soon set up a sleepover so we could expand on our newfound friendship. We somehow convinced our mother to allow us to spend the night at their house. It only worked because their mom didn't have a boyfriend, and we were able to guarantee that a man didn't live in the house. That night, their mom rented scary movies, and Sam and I got to experience a VCR for the first time in our lives. It was so awesome!

There was hesitation on our part when they wanted to spend the night at our house though, since getting it cleaned and ready for a sleepover was going to be a lot more work for us. We'd have to find a way to hide the mess; our entire house would need to get cleaned (including the fridge), the mounds and mounds of laundry would have to get done (or cleverly stored away—without a smell), Mom's papers stacked on the kitchen table would have to get cleared, and then there was the situation of Mom herself. We'd need to make sure her hair was brushed and she wasn't stinky.

We managed to pull off one sleep-over, but the night was not a success. An unfortunate part of having my facial deformity was that I was a mouth breather, so I snored. Loud. I kicked when I slept, too, partly from not getting enough oxygen. Keya slept on my bed with me, and by the time the morning arrived, she was ready to cry. She told me that I had kept her up all night, kicking her and snoring. I never thought that I could ruin this sleepover. I had worried so much about all the other things, the "poor people" things that I thought would matter, but not that. Damn my deformity.

Walking home from school and dealing with street bullies was a part of life. My sister and I always knew it was a tricky prospect, depending on the block we walked down. If we were walking home with Myesha and Keya, the four of us represented enough of a force that we were generally left alone, but near the end of the school year, however, Myesha and Keya moved away to a new school. For about a month, after they left, four bullies decided we were their prey. I must have had a beacon on me, because from the first day we walked past the ringleader's apartment, he saw my face, and I knew then we would be tortured.

He was a tall boy, around my brother's age, and his followers were all kids a few years younger than him. He lived just one block before we would cross PCH and be in our own neighborhood. He would wait in front of his apartment building with the three smaller kids behind him, waiting. If we were more clever that day, we would walk a few streets off and take another route home, but often times when we were lazy or confident or just plain forgetful, we'd walk down the regular street, and we were caught by the bullies. At first it was just them throwing simple insults as we walked by, like calling us stupid girls or ugly bitches. But quickly thereafter they leveraged the movie, *The Mask*, which had been playing on television that week. Soon I became the brunt of their brutal verbal attacks. As we walked by they called me "Rocky," the main character's name in the movie. His face was scarred and disfigured. His mouth and teeth were deformed and he had a large lump on his head. They followed us, throwing insults the whole time.

"Mask, mask, mask," they kept yelling at me. "What's the matter scarface, you gonna cry?"

"Keep walking," my sister told me.

Then they started to shove us. We decided that if we didn't hit back, they'd leave us alone, but when one of them socked me in the arm my sister quickly turned around and punched the kid in the arm, too. We had to run like lightning to get away from them. We knew they would leave us alone once we crossed PCH, if we could beat them to the end of the block.

By the end of the week, though, things had escalated. Our tricks to avoid them were failing; they had scouts on each corner, and when they spotted us a block away, they all quickly ran in our direction. But one day they caught up to us, and one of them pulled at my backpack to stop me. We weren't close enough to the light to cross.

"Leave us the fuck alone," my sister shouted at them, holding her ground.

"Fuck you, you ugly bitch," the ringleader shouted back at her.

"Let's go, Mary. These guys are assholes."

I pulled myself from their grip.

"Fuck you, freckles," said the ringleader to Sam.

He shoved her hard, and she fell down to the ground. I looked around, but no one was going to help us. No one. Sam quickly got up and shoved the guy. His shoulder swung back, but his body didn't move. Sam and I looked at each other, then ran as quickly as we could away from them. We got enough of a lead that as we approached Pacific Coast Highway, they slowed down and stopped chasing us.

When we got home we decided that the only way to get out of this bullying cycle was to change our route home permanently. We started walking another five blocks out of the way, making the walk home longer but ensuring that for the time being, those boys wouldn't be bothering us anymore. After a month of doing that, we were brave enough to walk the straight path home. To our surprise, the boys weren't anywhere to be found. We luckily never saw them again. Assholes.

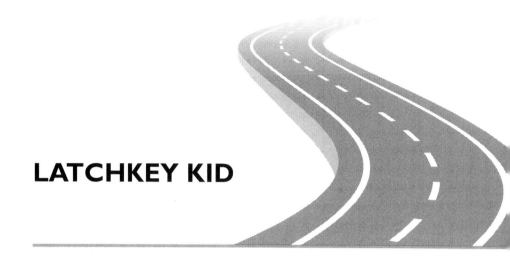

LATCHKEY KID

You can gain a level of empowerment and insight from being a latchkey kid; knowing you're being trusted to watch over yourself is a great responsibility. You can even be your own security, even if you thought you had to get it solely from someone else. This develops your street smarts, which is a crucial part of preparing for life.

Being a latchkey kid, you earned a level of independence and confidence. You had to navigate people and your environment, know how to get yourself home, and understand how your neighborhood and the neighborhoods beyond worked. You discovered that there are people who don't fit into a personality type that you are comfortable with, yet you needed to navigate them to get yourself home.

You are confronted with people in worse situations than your own. You may find that at the very moment when you need help, the most unlikely person comes to your aid—like they had been watching your journey from afar. You may find that you have the opportunity to help someone who needs it more than you, as you've been watching *their* journey from afar as well.

I once walked a small boy across a busy intersection after the light went out. Cars had been stopping in the intersection and I could see that he hadn't crossed the light when he could have, and he was hesitating, rightfully so. I navigated the cars and crossed the street toward him. I knelt down and asked where he needed to go, and he pointed to where I had just crossed from. I let him know I would help him cross the street, and then grabbed his hand. When we got across, he looked worried and like he was going to cry, no doubt he was told not to talk to strangers, and here I was ushering him across a busy street. I assured him he was safe and that he would get home okay. He nodded and I turned to continue my walk home and he went his way.

I FEEL THE EARTH MOVE UNDER MY FEET

On October 1st, 1987, Sam and I had gotten to school early enough to have school breakfast and play double-dutch with the girls out front. At 7:42 a.m., everything around us started to violently shake. It was as if I was looking at life through a bouncing camera. Kids were running out of the buses still lined up against the curb and were screaming as they shook forcefully from side to side. A younger girl was crying, scared to death. I ran over to her and grabbed her hand. Together, we ran over to a grassy area. I put my arm around her and held her, keeping her protected. The Earth shook for several minutes before it finally stopped. Chaos was all around; you could smell it. Kids were crying and trying to understand what had just happened. We were all filled with adrenaline. I searched around for my sister, using just my eyes. I found her and waved one hand at her while holding the little girl I was protecting. She ran toward me. Our bus lady ran out of the bus screaming over and over.

"Oh my God. What happened?" She looked terribly frightened and confused. Nothing about this day was going to be normal.

Just an hour later, our mom showed up at the school. She insisted we go somewhere else.

"It was like I was in a shoe box, being tossed around. Everything around me was blurry and everything was falling down from the walls," she said.

We had never experienced an earthquake before, and this was quite the introduction. Mom was rattled, and so were we. The safest place she felt we could be was our birthplace in Long Beach; Shoreline Village. I suppose you would think being near water after an earthquake didn't make sense, but she felt that's where we began in Long Beach, and it only seemed natural to her to go back there to feel safe and regroup.

"Where's Paul?" I asked Mom as she drove toward Shoreline Village in our Dodge Dart.

"He's already back at the apartment; we're gonna go by there and pick him up. He has some quarters," she said, matter-of-factly. Paul was thirteen and no longer in school anymore, he'd dropped out of middle school and Mom didn't seem to fight him on it either.

We all arrived at a nearly empty Shoreline Village and rested our worried heads at one of the coffee shops. Paul's cedar box from Uncle Hank sat on the table. He opened it up to show us his quarters. He was paid in quarters for delivering newspapers, and had quickly become the only one in the house who ever had any kind of cash on him. He paid for our coffees and pastries and we each gripped our mugs. It felt like we were on the road again, drinking cups of hot coffee together while we journeyed on to our next destination. I think our mom liked those moments, when it was us against the world. We listened to the radio that was being played in the coffee shop. After a few moments of commentary about the recent earthquake, "I Feel the Earth Move" by Carole King came on. We had the *Tapestry* album by Carole King, and we listened to it often. This was the first song on the record, and Sam and I would often kick off some silly dancing moves to it once we put it on—but now, we all looked at each other and just laughed. Our nerves had been so wound up, and for a moment, that song released all the tension from that morning. This big thing happened, and it was over. Now we were all together, and that felt like family again. I wanted that moment to last. I wanted mom to continue to be kind to Paul, to want him there, to need him there.

When the coffee was finished and we had diluted our fears, we parted ways. Paul stayed in Shoreline to work at the kite shop and mom brought us home. Paul was always finding ways to make money. There he would help instruct people on how to set up and fly their newly purchased exotic kites at the park near the village. They sold all kinds of kites: butterflies, dragons, koi fish, you name it. Some kites were several layers deep with many strings that required some serious skills to get them off the ground and to keep them in the air and flying. It was a great job for a kid his age, and he had enough pocket change to buy himself food, cigarettes, and basic necessities—like shoes. But in a pinch, Paul would bring out his quarters, even if Mom didn't make him feel like he was wanted most of the time. At least on that day, he knew that he was.

DOUBLE-JOINTED MUSIC LOVERS

By the time Sam was in fifth grade, she spent most of her free time dancing around the apartment and singing. She was always showing off her ability to do the splits. The best I could do was put one leg behind my head, and only my left one.

Sam and I both had a love for our record player, and we would play it most days in the evening and on the weekend. Two of our favorite albums were "Faith" by George Michael and Michael Jackson's "Bad." We loved singing along to all the songs, but we especially loved "Dirty Diana" by Michael Jackson. We couldn't resist singing and dancing around the house like we were in one of their videos. These were the latest albums in the whole album collection we had; the majority were '70s albums Mom preferred us to listen to, by artists like Kenny Rogers, Dolly Parton, The Mamas & The Papas, and Carly Simon. But we wanted to dance.

Sam was a natural performer—double-jointed and coordinated. She was well proportioned, but smaller and stockier than Paul and me. Sam could pick up on any dance move after the first time she saw them. She also had a voice that could belt out Whitney Houston like nobody's business.

I loved to dance and sing, too, but couldn't perform a coordinated move if my life depended on it, and my voice didn't quite have her range;

she got the voice and I got the height, it seemed. We'd been the same height for going on four years.

When we played dress up, I put two fruits in my shirt to resemble breasts and pranced around like a supermodel. Though Sam would dress up, she would always remark that I had a better body than her. Our mom fanned the flames by agreeing with her. I would have taken her budding breasts over my flat, boy chest anyday. Her nose was a fine one with a regular size and shape, and her chiclet teeth had grown into a wide, perfect smile that shared real estate with her high, rosey cheekbones. Overall, I didn't think I had anything over her, but I'd let her be jealous over something this small, because it was moments like this where I felt beautiful.

When it came to Sam's voice, our mother was nothing but jealous. Mom couldn't sing; in fact, she couldn't even carry a tune or keep time. Regardless, Mom dreamed of being a singer someday—maybe even being in a family band with us girls, with her as the lead singer. She'd fantasize over this idea, and tell us she could be the next Crystal Gayle. She held back her praise of Sam's voice, simply out of spite.

We had a small tape recorder that Mom used to record her thoughts and people, generally without their knowing. We'd find an unused tape or one we felt she wouldn't miss, and record ourselves singing, doing comedy skits, laughing. I would do funny characters of people in our neighborhood, like the pimp or the IV man, and Sam and I would die laughing. Speeding up our voices as we played back the tape made us sound like chipmunks, which was even funnier. We'd laugh and go far away from where we were at that moment—we were talented, we were dreamers, we were comedians, dancers, spokespeople for beauty products, announcers for games. We would always sing together when walking back home from school. We'd sing church songs, mostly, since those were the songs we knew the most. It made things feel a little like home again. Our voices harmonized easily. Though, to really get on each other's nerves, whenever one of us would start singing, the other would start singing, too—but louder. It would always end with one of us yelling at the other to shut up and stop copying them. Sisters being sisters, I suppose.

Sam convinced our mom to enroll her in ballet, jazz, and tap classes through the Parks and Recreation program. The classes were really affordable: only thirty dollars for a ten-week class. The studio was just up the street from where we took the school bus.

She was a natural. The woman who owned the studio was able to provide Sam with a pair of old tap shoes. Luckily, ballet shoes were not too expensive, so Sam was able to get Mom to buy a pair that were just under ten dollars. I was impressed at how Sam was able to not only find the class, but to enroll in it by finding a way for Mom to pay for it—which was no easy job. She was ingenious at finding solutions to problems that required the engineering of a mother saying yes.

Having her hobby was very special to Sam. She could express herself, and she could be pretty. Everything she was taught in dance class, she picked up on immediately. She would tap dance in the house any time she could. I loved the noise, so any time she performed, I was her most admiring audience member.

One Saturday afternoon, she came home from class and announced, "Mom, my teacher wants me to be in the final ballet performance. She's going to give me a part where I get to do a pirouette and leap across the stage!"

This is where I witnessed a very creative sell. If it was going to cost money, you had to already have a plan in mind. If you got our mom to say maybe, you just needed a little more nudging to get to "Yes." Sam's plan was to minimize the cost of the outfit she needed for the reception. The costume included a leotard, a tutu, and white tights. This would cost about forty dollars.

"My teacher says I'm one of her star students. If I'm in this performance, I get to have one of the main parts. It will be the highlight of the show. I can use the tights and the outfit for next season, so it's not like you have to buy them again," she explained, going on and on, dazzling our mom with thoughts of fame and a bargain.

Eventually, Mom broke down and agreed to buy her the outfit. Sam was able to get every piece she needed right in the nick of time.

The day of her performance, we took the 1 Easy city bus to our elementary school. While we were waiting at the bus stop, Mom took a picture of Sam in her outfit, posing in her ballerina stance. We still had a roll of film in our 110 camera. Sam was in a white tutu and pink leotard with sequins, her blond hair combed back and in a bun, shining in the sun. She wore white tights and ballet shoes. She was so beautiful.

When we got to our elementary school auditorium, Mom and I sat in the back and patiently waited to see Sam perform. She came out, did several routines, and—just like a swan crossing a lake—she leaped across the stage, like she said she would. She was in sync with her co-stars and was even lifted from one side of the stage to the other by a boy. She hadn't told us about that part.

As we three looked at the picture of Sam a week later, I went on and on about how beautiful she was. Our mom stayed silent. I'm sure that my compliments meant something to Sam, but she was waiting on a compliment from our mother, who was generally judgmental of others and rarely had more positive things to say than negative ones.

"Don't you think she's beautiful, Mom?" I insisted.

"You seem a little chubby in this picture, Samantha. Isn't dance supposed to make you skinny?" Mom said, as if this was a normal observation that anyone would make.

Either she didn't grasp the magnitude of this comment, or she was being spiteful. Sam looked like Mom did when she was her age, so you would think Mom would relate more to her, but maybe that was the problem. Mom always complimented me on my humor, my looks, and my silly nature, but Mom always hesitated to give Sam a compliment, to be on her side, to fight for her. We knew Mom didn't like Paul—he was a male, and signified all that she hated about men, about our father. But what did Sam signify that Mom seemed to dislike so much?

Was it Sam's intelligence, which was high (according to her grades and ingenuity in fixing anything that was broken)? Was it her incredible voice, gifted in range and timing that could keep rhythm and tone with any song effortlessly? Sam seemed to have gotten all the good stuff that Mom didn't. Maybe if Mom acknowledged that, she'd feel it would somehow mean that her own dreams to be those things would be over. Those dreams seemed to be all she had.

Sam carried herself differently shortly thereafter. After that performance, she stopped going to the dance class. Even her super powers couldn't keep up with this obligation, especially without the power of a parent's approval and praise. She told Mom she didn't want to go anymore because it was too expensive. Our mom seemed neutral on the topic. She didn't agree or disagree; she didn't fight for her to stay or try to offer up other ways the classes could be paid for. This neutrality is what probably hurt the most. Though Sam never told me she was hurt, I knew she was.

Later that year, Mom bought a sewing machine. It was her intention to learn how to sew and make us clothes, so we could have the latest fashions for much less money. She started out strong, going to the fabric store and picking out patterns and fabric. Every pattern she picked were '70s styles—bell bottoms and button down shirts with large collars—which no one wore to school, but I was happy that she was interested in making clothes for us, so I didn't remind her it was the late '80s. I loved watching her while she was learning to sew, and I reveled in the moments she was teaching us. For Sam and me, getting a sewing machine was better than a VCR. At the time, it seemed every house had at least one of those—and if you really had money, you had a Nintendo. Our household prize was a Singer sewing machine.

One of Mom's first projects was making me a costume for Halloween. She found a great clown costume pattern at the fabric store on sale for one dollar. It required two kinds of satin fabric: one pink and one orange. She worked on this project for two weeks, off and on. Even though she didn't have a job, her attention never stayed on any one project for too long. She would waver through really big highs from working on a new project, to big lows for being poor or other thoughts I wasn't privy to. We were still on welfare and she was starting to talk about going to college.

When my costume was ready, I put it on; it was mostly accurate. It fit very well on my left leg, a little long on my right arm, and the body was a little short for my torso, but I was so proud to wear a costume my mom had made me. I planned to wear it to school later that week for costume day. Through her sewing she was paying attention to us, and that was rare and special.

On the weekends, when I knew I could take over the sewing machine, I would find fabric from clothes I didn't wear anymore and make my own clothes. My first project was a bikini. I found some old jeans and tore them up. I made my own pattern, then proceeded to sew. It was harder than I had anticipated, but ultimately it resembled a bikini. The bikini top was shaped like hearts, and the bottom I made out of the pattern from my underwear. When I was finished, I wore my bikini in the house all day long. My sister rolled her eyes at me each time she saw me.

"Are you going to run around in that all day?" she asked.

"Yes, I am!"

I was almost ten years old and still didn't have any boobs—or even the promise of any. I was all knees and elbows, as my mom would say. My sister, however, had inherited the German figure—meaning she actually *had* a figure by the time she was twelve years old. As she developed, I just kept getting taller.

Sam wanted to be tall and slender like me, like a dancer, or like one of those performers at the Circus Circus, so I knew it annoyed her to see me prancing around the apartment. But I didn't care. I flaunted my figure around the house and danced around with very little care. Mom told me how beautiful I was, and how I had the perfect body, and how maybe one day I could be a model. But I knew what I looked like, and I didn't have the heart to tell her she was wrong. Sam didn't have the heart to tell me Mom was wrong, either.

ELEMENTARY
ENTREPRENEUR

My first school crush was on a boy named Cesar. He reminded me of Billy Joel, but had the caramel-colored skin of String Bean from the Bronx. Whenever I could get a moment to stare at him, I would. I would be playing on the rings at recess, and he would be swinging on the monkey bars. Those who played on the monkey bars were the cool kids because it required skills and risk taking. They would lock one leg around the bar and do several spins in quick succession, then jump off and land on their feet.

All the girls I played with at recess had a crush on at least one boy at school. I thought that I could capitalize on those crushes by creating a game. I started to sell "Love Tests." I typed out a test, each with ten questions asking things as basic as, "What boy do you like?" "Which famous WWF wrestler do you like?" and "Do you want to get married and have kids?" I sold each test for ten cents each. I thought I could make an easy profit if I could sell more love tests than what I would draw in a raffle at the end of the week.

So the rules were that for each love test that was bought, you got your name in the drawing. The more Love Tests you bought, the more chances you had to win. Each name drawn would win a pack of Now and Laters, which only cost me ten cents each. I decided I was going to pull ten names that Friday after school. At the minimum, I had to sell ten Love Tests. Everything after that was going to be pure profit. I ran out of twenty love tests the first day and I had already made one dollar in profit. I asked that each person who bought a love test return them to me filled out, then they would get their name in the drawing. This way I also got to see who liked who at school. The next day, I put a twist on the pitch: if you bought more than one love test, you had more chances that the boy you liked would like you back.

Candy was hard currency in school if you could get away with having it and distributing it. Getting caught with it also had big consequences, like going to the principal's office, getting a note home to your parents, and possibly getting expelled. The racket I was creating had to be low-key. How was I going to keep the raffle a secret, though? More and more girls wanted to take the test and be in the raffle. By the end of the week I had sold over fifty tests. The night before the raffle, I read and categorized all the submitted love tests. I read all the secret desires of the girls who had bought a test from me and counted up how many girls liked which boys and all the answers on the tests. I wrote out on small strips of paper each of their names; one strip for each love test they had bought. I had fifty strips in my backpack. I had made four bucks in profit for one week of sales. I knew I was only going to raffle off one dollar of candy, so as my own reward, I bought a bag of bubble gum balls for myself and a few extra packs of Now and Laters and took them to school that morning.

At school that day, my business was catching on. Some boys came up to me asking if I had Now and Laters. Apparently, one of my friends spilled the beans about the raffle and the guys wanted to buy some love tests so they could be part of it. I had a few love tests left, but I couldn't sell them to the boys because some of their names were on them as choices for boys that the girls liked. This was a girls-only love test. From my extra Now and Laters stash, I sold a few packs for a quarter each, at a fifteen cent profit. I made another forty-five cents' profit by lunchtime.

I told all the girls that we would meet after school near my school bus to do the raffle. Only seven girls had bought all the love tests, so there wasn't too big of a crowd. I started drawing single slips of paper out of my bag, and each time the lucky girl would get to choose the Now and Laters flavor she wanted. After I was done with the raffle, I waited at the school bus to get on. Then the principal walked up to me.

"Hi Mary. Have you heard of anyone selling candy at school?"

"No, I haven't," I stared up at him and bold-faced lied.

"Okay, well you know we're having a really hard time with candy at school right now. Many kids have been caught with it in their classrooms this week," he said.

"Yeah, I know." I heard that a kid had been busted with some Now and Laters I'd sold him earlier that day.

"Well if you see anything, let me know, okay?"

"Sure, I'll let you know."

He's onto me.

I got on the bus thinking I was going to get caught. I had sworn to myself that I wasn't going to make or sell any more love tests. Before the bus took off, the principal stepped on to give an announcement.

"Kids, I want you to know that bringing candy to school has big consequences. You can get expelled. We do not allow candy at school. Do you understand?"

"Yeeeessss," said the kids in unison.

I tried to slither down into my seat so he couldn't see my face, but couldn't quite get low enough. My backpack was on the floor and I reached for it slowly, hoping I could bring it close to me—but I accidentally grabbed it from the bottom, and it was still open. All the gumballs started running out along the grooves of the floor toward the front of the bus. Kids started yelling as gumballs rolled past their feet. Kids started picking them up. Shit.

Luckily no one knew where they came from. *At least I didn't have any more evidence*, I thought. The downside was that I'd lost all my candy. Gumballs rolled toward the principal, hitting the tops of his shoes.

"Whomever these belong to, know that candy is not allowed on school grounds. If you are caught with these, you will be expelled," he said sternly.

I had been warned. I decided my candy business needed to close. Part of me enjoyed breaking the school rules, and the other part—the follow-the-rules girl—didn't. But I learned that not toeing the line was fun, especially because I made a little money, I got to sell my crafts, and I was able to spark my imagination.

MUSINGS: FACED WITH REALITY

I held on to this idea that someday I would look normal. I would analyze the faces of the kids around me, then look at mine and see the differences between what was normal and what I looked like. As an adult, I no longer do that. I find the faces that have genuine kindness in them, no matter what they look like. There is a kindness that shines through certain faces. I've analyzed the forehead, the chin, the cheeks, the nose, the lips, every inch of the human face all my life, and nothing conveys kindness like the eyes—especially the corners of the eyes. A face holds so much power, so much pain, so little regard, so little in vain. It does do what you want it to do, and I realized that it can do so much for good. It can have a kind smile, even if the lips are misshapen and scarred. It can have a kind profile, even if the nose is wide and flat. It can speak a kind word, even if teeth are missing. This is what I learned when I faced reality.

CHAOS COMFORT ZONE

The bustling, complex, multicultural world of New York imprinted upon me, and this helped me find a clear path amongst chaos. Any kind of chaos.

Many times, when I was younger, I would spend time nurturing my mom in hopes she would return the favor. I would often be the one encouraging her to move forward with her life, pumping her up when she was down.

"You're not that fat, Mom."

"Things will get better. You're doing the best you can."

"Want me to help you with your spelling?"

Even though I was the one giving this attention, I was getting it back simply because of the interaction. With love, you can make any house a home, and that was one thing that I always wanted: to have a clean house that felt like a home full of love.

My mom had severe ADHD, dyslexia, and paranoid schizophrenia, all of which made her moods generally unsettling, erratic, and unpredictable. She was always in a state of frustration, but she was able to navigate through most situations because she was articulate. She knew what people were saying, and could pull together the right answer when needed. Her reading skills, penmanship, and spelling left much to be desired, but most people never needed that from her. Living in poverty didn't put the expectations any higher.

She generally saved her outbursts for home. Paranoia was part of her late night hours: pacing in the house, lashing out, writing on pads of paper or envelopes or anything else she could find. But normally, it was somewhat hard to spot. Authority figures were generally the focus of her paranoia, which I could see in her suspicious writings.

I was in this town because my father was a gay man, but really because of how my mother felt about how the world and how her family responded to her feelings. I knew from an early age that something was really wrong with my mom, and I couldn't fight my disappointment in her. Mom always seemed to sabotage the peacefulness that my sister and I tried to create within the home. Because her mind was constantly going through what-if scenarios and was generally uneasy, she was like a tornado.

Sam and I would roll our sleeves up to get the house clean and organized, usually after weeks or months of it being filthy. This meant hours and hours of teamwork, because cleaning was not something our mom did. All we ever wanted was a clean home, an engaged mother, and a slice, even a small one, of predictable normalcy. Part of that was coming home from school to a clean house. Sweep, disinfect, scrub, clean, organize paperwork, make beds, wash clothes in the tub or sink and hang them outside to dry, and throw out all the trash. Despite all these efforts, we'd always come home from school to see that Mom had gotten ahold of the house and had made a complete mess of it. She would mess up the papers that we had organized because she thought we had thrown things out. She would make some food and leave it all out on the kitchen counter: the pot she cooked it in, the utensils she used, all of it. She would scatter things on the kitchen table and in the living room, as if seeing the order made her uneasy. By the time we would get home, she would have gotten herself in a bad mood, too. When Sam and I explained our frustration at the state of the house after all our effort, she would do us the courtesy of not apologizing, instead minimizing the situation.

"I needed to find some papers. Besides, the house isn't that dirty."

Could she not hear our frustrations? Did they even matter?

Her state of peacefulness was never the same as ours, clearly. Chaos was her comfort zone. Consistency was thrown out the window—it made her feel uneasy and restricted. Nevertheless, it was quite disheartening to be on the other end of her tornado. We couldn't understand why she had to live in chaos. When we'd come home and see the house trashed after a weekend of cleaning and a day of delightful anticipation at the idea of a clean home waiting for us, we were crushed.

The level of stress and uncertainty around our mother's moods became attitude-shaping for all three of us kids. We had a list of topics that we knew would set her off, and generally avoided them like land mines. But when we were upset or pushed to our limits by what we felt was her cavalier behavior, we'd pull out the big guns and try to hurt her with our words, which was all we had. We knew the cost for those outbursts, however, and in the end we'd pay for them, one way or another. The worst triggers were telling her that we hated her, or that she was a bad mother. Like bullets, she'd take the hits, get stunned, and then fall—on her bed, to sob. She'd be depressed for days and our guilt would be overwhelming.

We were trapped in a life cycle that we did not want, one that we were actively trying to change and that didn't seem to have a way out. I knew there was a life outside of this chaos. I knew there were normal people in the world, and I definitely knew that I would someday be one of them.

DIRTY BOXES AND CLEAN SIDEWALKS

Whenever we traveled from place to place, Mom's boxes and boxes and boxes of papers would follow us. By the time we were living in Long Beach on Henderson, we had a closet filled, three stacks high, with boxes of papers. At least thirty boxes filled the closet. Mom still had papers from her divorce, testimony from my surgeon from when he worked on me as a baby, and his statements regarding my mom's character ("She is a very loving mother and I have never witnessed her acting in any other way"). I'd even found a photocopy of my dad in the paper before he officially came out. He was holding a large poster as he stood in front of a movie theater showing the movie *Cruising*, which was released in 1980 with leading star Al Pacino. It was about a psychopathic killer going after men in the gay community. My dad's sign said, "Give 'Cruising' a Bruising in Nashville, Stay Away, God Says 'Have No Pleasure in Sin' Romans 1:32." The guy standing next to him had a poster that read, "Homosexuality is Sin." It was strange to think that two and half years later, my father had come out of the closet himself, and I was holding a picket sign in front of our church, and one of them called him a faggot.

Sam and I would often go through these papers and try to take out the circulars from months or years before, just to chip away at some of it. If Mom caught wind of us cleaning out the boxes, she would fly off the handle, curse us out, and make sure that we knew we could not mess with her papers. To say that my mom carried around baggage was an understatement.

With a dirty house also came roaches. Even our friends' cleaner houses had them in Long Beach, but not to the level we did. When the light came on in the kitchen, the sea of living brown spots scurried across the floor, escaping the light. The most annoying part of roaches is that they left a sea of poop everywhere. No matter how well you cleaned up, they always left a piece behind for you to remember them by.

We tried using a special chalk that, when traced around your cabinets or other areas, would act like a barrier to roaches. Unfortunately, there wasn't enough chalk in the world to get these roaches out of our apartment.

With the ever-growing mound of dishes and dirt in the house, we got extra guests: mice. The mice came around to check out the mounds of newspapers in our bedroom closet, first. There was plenty for them to bite through, and pee and poop on. Our constant pleas to get rid of the papers to get rid of the mice never worked. Our mom's answer was to buy mouse traps, so we got both the snap and glue types. The most cruel of all is the glue, I soon learned. When you get two together, they'll fight to the bitter end to get out, including eating off their own legs and eating each other alive. Those visuals along with the noises they made to get free, from being chewed away, are still easily recalled in my memory.

Small attempts to wash the dishes were usually met with the lack of dish soap. We would borrow some from the neighbors from time to time, just to get the job done. When the gas went out, the cold water wasn't enough to get the dishes clean, so most of the time, the dishes just sat there, well beyond the mold.

The cleanliness of the Mexican women in our apartment building was very appealing. As we played and mingled with all the kids, we watched their style of cleaning and admired it. There was always dish soap, a small tray filled with soap and water that sat at the edge of the sink. They would have one side of the sink full of hot water, then they would dip their dish in there for a minute, then pull it out, and rub the small pad with dish soap across the dish until it was clean. You would then pile all your soapy dishes into the other side of the sink. When they were all done, you would dip them into the hot water again, one by one. The dishes would get one more round of hot water as they rinsed the soap off, then the dishes would sit in a pile waiting to be hand-dried and put back into the cabinets. Sam and I would watch Reyna, our neighbor, do this after each of her family's meals.

The women would also wash off the sidewalk in front of their apartments, as if to say they had cleaned so much in their houses that the outside could use a little cleaning, too. I found it fascinating. A bucket of hot water with some soap would be thrown over the ground and, using your broom, you would wash away the dirt. The steam would rise and the smell of soap would waft in the air. When I was overwhelmed with the mess inside of the house, I would often start outside, on the porch with my broom. There, I picked up some momentum, a small victory. Then I'd go inside to face the mess, taking my broom and its victory with me.

I loved to sweep. It was my thing. I could sweep from one end of the room to the other, slowly bringing all the pieces of crumbs and dirt to the door or to the kitchen linoleum where I could easily sweep it up and get it out of the house. It was therapeutic. As I would sweep, I always had a sense that I was making a difference. A clean floor always brought a sense of calm to my life. It usually meant everything was finally off the floor, things were in their place, and now you could lie down and relax.

GOODWILL HUNTING

There was a huge Goodwill near our house just off of PCH near the 710 freeway. We would go there once in a while to pick up winter jackets, board games, dishes, blankets, sheets, and towels. Once a month, they had a huge rummage sale. Each bag you filled up was only one dollar. There were dozens of tables set up, all themed with different items. The table full of board games was my favorite. I would go through all the games trying to find one with all the pieces. I would usually settle on a game or two, or even a puzzle. I knew I wouldn't get the satisfaction of a completed puzzle, but a partial one was still interesting to me. If the game rules were missing, or not printed on the game itself, we were usually clever enough to figure out how the game worked—or at least have fun making up the rules. I was learning how to navigate this lawless life of chaos. I was learning how to fill in the gaps and make it work.

COLLEGE BOUND

When my mom decided to go to college, I thought she was making the most rational decision I'd ever seen her make. She was focused and excited to start down an educational path—though this is how she generally got when something was new, but perhaps this would stick and she would follow through?

She applied to Long Beach City College. This community college had two campuses. One was on Pacific Coast Highway, called the Pacific Coast Campus (PCC), and was just one bus ride from our house. The other was further north, off of Carson Street. It was the Liberal Arts Campus (LAC), and took two buses and an hour to get to.

Mom qualified for financial aid, which was how she was able to register for college in the first place. She would have to take a few courses in order to complete her GED, but she was still able to take college courses in many other subjects while she worked on her GED. She took us with her to the PCC so she could start the registration process.

While we waited for her to be seen by the various counselors and clerks, I realized that my mother was going to have a real occupation, even if it was just as a "Student." I felt like things were turning around, and I was feeling proud of her. I'd finally be able to answer the question, "What does your mom do?"

Mom took courses she liked, like criminal law, and electives like charcoal drawing and singing classes. The entrance exam put her in remedial math and English classes. Her semester started right away, and she went from always being around to never being around. She was off in her own world during this time, always going to school, coming back from school, or studying.

By then, our '67 Dodge Dart was no longer a reliable form of travel. The color had faded to green, perhaps from the extra salt in the Long Beach air. It wasn't properly registered, either, and always had a pink registration extension card tapped to the back window. It was a weekly chore for us kids to push the car across the street before the street-sweeping tickets were issued.

Taking the city bus and walking was our main mode of transportation, and because the buses in Long Beach varied in pick-up times, it could take several hours to travel across town.

Often Mom was out of the house before I got up, and wasn't home by the time I went to bed. This meant my sister and I spent most of our weekdays alone and in charge of ourselves. We were responsible for our dinners, snacks, studies, and preparation for the next day. We felt a bigger sense of independence with Mom out of the house.

One morning, I realized I hadn't seen my mom all week. I got worried, but also suspicious. *If she is never home, where is she eating?* I decided I would sleep lightly that night. I would wait for her to get home, then I would wait until she left for school the next day and follow her. I heard her arrive at ten that night. I heard a little noise in the kitchen and the TV turned on. I felt safe with her in the house, but I was paying close attention to whether I heard the sound of fast food bags. I didn't, and fell fast asleep.

By six that morning, I heard her getting ready to leave. I was alert now, and threw on some old clothes after I heard the front door close. I peeped out the window until I saw her leave the apartment building gate. I kept a good distance from her while she walked up the street toward PCH. I figured that if she turned around and saw me, I would simply say that I missed her and was hoping to see her before she left for school. She didn't go to the bus stop, though—she kept walking down the street to a restaurant that we would go to occasionally, called Brite Spot. Here we are starving, barely ever having a decent dinner, and she is having breakfast at a restaurant! I walked up to her booth.

"Mom, what are you doing here?"

She was a little startled. "What are you doing up, Mary?"

"I haven't seen you for almost a week! While you're having breakfast, we're hungry at home."

I started to well up with anger and pain. My cooking acumen and energy were so low that I had resorted to ketchup and mustard sandwiches on moldy food bank bread. I'd even rolled up the end of our toothpaste tube and started eating small pieces of it so I could get a taste of dessert. This quieted most of my stomach pangs just enough so I could fall asleep. I'd stare at bags of pinto beans bought several months prior, knowing the hours they'd need to soak and then cook, so they never seemed like an option. Even if I could have drenched a cooked pot of white rice with soy sauce like Vui, I wouldn't have found what I made appetizing, because while hers was perfect and fluffy, mine always had a porridge-like consistency (I never learned you had to add oil and salt). And here she was, eating bacon and eggs at a restaurant? I felt crossed.

"Come have breakfast with me, Mary. Don't be mad," she said, realizing she had been caught. Of course I was starving and wasn't going to pass up a hot breakfast, so I sat down with her.

"Mom, how are you able to come here for breakfast? We don't have any money."

"I got more money from financial aid than what I needed for my books and tuition. I got a few hundred dollars extra. That's how I've been able to give you and Samantha bus money."

She had been able to give us one dollar here and there to take the 1 Easy to school when we were running late.

"But why are you having breakfast here and not at home? You're never home anymore, and we're really hungry at night," I said, now getting to the heart of it.

"Aren't you eating at school every day? I have food in the house. There's rice and beans," she said.

I looked at her sideways, my arms folded now.

"Mom, we can't just eat beans and rice every day. Bus money and food at school isn't the same as eating at a restaurant or having a hot breakfast at home."

I was so sick of the way she thought. She rarely seemed to see what kind of life we were living. She rarely seemed to feel what we felt.

"Listen, do you want to come to school with me today? Do you and Samantha want to skip school and see what I'm doing?" she asked bluntly. I thought for a moment.

"Well, yeah," I said, not even knowing this was a possibility.

"Okay, let's walk back to the house and get your sister."

Once we arrived at the PCC, Mom took us to the school cafeteria. It sold coffee and bagels, cereals, eggs, bacon, fruit, and more. It was almost like a restaurant. We picked a tray and walked along the line. We were allowed to grab two things and a drink. Sam and I loaded our plates with meatloaf, mashed potatoes, and a hot chocolate.

"First I have a math class, then I have sociology," Mom said as we sat for breakfast. "Then we have a little over an hour to get to the other campus. There, I'll take English, criminal justice, and a music class. I'm getting paid to work part time in the library also, so that will be a few hours in the evening."

"Wait, you're a librarian?" I asked, a little stunned.

"Yes, I suppose so," she said, with no hint of pride. "I'll do that from four to eight. You can read the books in the library while I'm in my other classes; there are record players there, too, so you can listen to music, and places to read newspapers and even listen to recorded classes. As long as you're not behaving badly, no one will bother you."

Since this was our first time with Mom in her world, I knew we would be on our best behavior.

My sister and I sat in the back of Mom's class to make ourselves as invisible as possible. We sat quietly and listened to the lecture. The math class was fairly simple, simple multiplication and division. Sam and I had taught ourselves some pre-algebra that past summer as a way to keep ourselves from being too bored, so none of the examples were new. Our mom wrote notes and raised her hand a lot to have the professor explain the calculations, and then she'd start nodding her head to signify she understood so he could go on.

In her sociology class, we caught a case of the giggles. For some reason, listening to our mom ask questions and acting so differently than how we were used to seeing her gave us a surge of happiness, embarrassment, and uneasiness. We just couldn't contain all these emotions. After the second question she asked the professor, it was nearly impossible to control our laughter.

After a few moments, our mom stopped what she was saying, looked right at us and said, "Girls, you need to leave the classroom, now!"

We got up and marched out. We felt enormous relief being out of her classroom.

We decided to roam the hallways of the campus. I knew then that I wanted to go to college someday. I saw myself walking those halls, being part of that campus, being an adult, going to class, and having grown-up conversations with my fellow classmates. When Mom's class was over, there was no bell that signified its end—students just left their classes. We were sitting in the hallway, trying to look like angels. Our mom came out and looked at us in disappointment, then said, "You can't act like that in the classroom, or I'm just going to take you back home."

"No! We'll be good," we both exclaimed.

She walked us to the bus stop where many students stood waiting in groups. Soon the bus was there, and as we all found seats and were on to our next journey, I realized Mom's life wasn't so bad. After all, I'd already had two breakfasts.

By the time we got to the Liberal Arts Campus, it was around lunchtime, and she brought us to *that* campus cafeteria. It was beyond huge. There was everything there, including a coffee bar and several counters selling hot food. There was a lounge area outside of the cafeteria where you could hang out and look cool with your friends while lying on a couch or in a huge armchair. I liked everything about this place. We all got lunch and sat in the bustling cafeteria.

Our mom was older than most of the people there at thirty-five, and she was not the typical college-brochure type. She was dirty, and her shoes were busted, like ours. She carried her books in a small metal grocery roller cart, the kind old ladies pull behind them. Because she was so heavy, she had developed arthritis in her hip, which meant she wobbled a bit. My mom could hardly notice or care about the snickering around her; she was content to just be in college, taking her classes, and eating lunch. After lunch, we went over to the lounge area. My sister and I watched as students stepped up to get their photo taken for their student ID cards. Out of a bold and rambunctious moment, I asked the girl taking the photos if she would take one of Sam and me.

"Sure, sit right there and look here," the girl said, as she prepared us for our picture.

I quickly went into model mode, pulled my hair up with both hands, and turned my head slightly to the side and smiled. *Poof!* went the camera. Blinded by the light, I remained in my model pose. Once I could see again, I leapt off the stool and was handed a small Polaroid of my picture.

"Wait for a minute and pull this tab," said the girl behind the camera. As I waited, my sister took her model photo, too. We weren't used to having pictures taken of us; we only had a handful of photos. When the picture revealed what I looked like, I was shocked.

"Mom, I'm beautiful!" I told her. I'd never seen myself in such a favorable light before. Maybe it was the red backdrop, or the sweater I was wearing with the lion on it? Maybe it was my sun-kissed tanned skin and blonde hair that shined brighter than usual. My smile showed only my bottom teeth, which I had all of, and I felt so pretty in this picture. Sam was pretty, too. Mom seemed pleased with our momentos of the campus life, and agreed at my exclamation of my beauty.

"You're more beautiful than you know, Mary," she told me. Sam didn't go on about her picture. The flash of light only highlighted her fair complexion and freckles, which she didn't see as flattering. When she got older, she'd use skin bleach to try and lighten them.

We spent the entire day at Mom's college and got home at 10 p.m. that night.

After that first semester, we got used to her schedule. When we complained that we missed her, she would always allow us to take the bus up to one of her campuses and sit in on her classes, as long as we behaved ourselves. She checked in on us more. If she was going to miss dinner, she made sure we had some food to heat up or she gave Sam a few dollars so she could buy ingredients at the liquor store and cook something up. She stopped going to the restaurants and limited her food expenses to mostly campus meals, which were much cheaper than restaurants.

One day after school, Sam and I decided to treat our mom by surprising her with some food Sam had made. Even though we knew her schedule, we were still worried we'd be late because the full trip to the LAC took about one hour, when you factored in the transfer you had to take at the downtown bus station. We were the only ones on the bus when we were about five stops from her campus. We were excited to show Mom how grown up we were, and the bus driver could hear our conversation about wanting to get to the campus on time to make it to mom's music class. I worried the most and every light we caught I'd tell Sam that we were going to be late. All of a sudden, the driver pulled the bus over to the side of the road.

"Why did you stop the bus?" I asked him.

We exchanged worried looks. This wasn't normal bus driver behavior.

He looked back at us and said, "Do you know you girls have been worrying since the moment you got on the bus? We're going to get there; just stop worrying, okay?"

The dramatic gesture shocked us. *Pulling over just to make a point that we were worrying?* It only made us worry even more. *Was this guy a pervert? Was he going to let us off at our bus stop?* Sam and I shot a few glances at each other, silently communicating that if he didn't stop the bus to let us off at her campus, there would be hell to pay. He did, though. And we jumped off as soon as we could, ducking past the college students filing in.

Mom was surprised that we'd brought her food. As we ate, Sam and I spent a good five minutes rambling about the perverted bus driver. Then

Mom said she wanted to show us something. We followed her over to a large wooden announcement board that was protected by glass. It was mainly a bulletin board, but it had pictures of the campus, students at events, and interesting articles. Mom pointed to one of the papers on the board. It was a story Sam had written about the rabbits that roamed around the LAC. Our mom was so proud that Sam had written a story that made it on this very large and public board, that *her* daughter, Samantha Gregory, had done it. She even took several pictures of it on our camera and even got the film developed. Sam was proud, too, and she deserved to have that moment. It was nice to get praise from Mom.

While Mom enjoyed her classes and the independence of the college life, being paranoid meant she was still always suspicious of nice people. A fellow student tried to help her with note taking by typing up the class notes on index cards, but Mom believed the notes were meant to trick her into learning the wrong thing so she would do badly on her exams and her grades would suffer. This was her accusation after getting a "D" on her midterm exam in her sociology class. She reported the student to the dean's office.

She was unable to make friends at school because of these suspicions. It wasn't long before she came home one day with a small metal tool. When I asked her what it was, she said it was a glass cutter. She had a plan to change a poor grade by breaking into the administration office. Her eyes lit up while she told me about her plans and how she would do it. I pleaded with her that, even though it sounded like a lot of fun, if she got caught, she would go to jail for breaking and entering. I had learned that term from a police show my sister and I like called *T.J. Hooker*. I sounded official enough that she listened to me.

BREAKING THE PLATE

One day, my mom was in the kitchen cooking and I had a small blue ball in my hands. I was sitting on the couch and throwing it up high in the air, as if I was making a free throw. I did this mindlessly, over and over as I watched a basketball game on TV. Mom asked me to stop throwing the ball in the house, but I was transfixed on the game. The action of a free throw felt good, and the sound of the ball hitting the ceiling was satisfying to me, *Bah! Bah! Bah!*

After several attempts to get me to stop, my mom came from the kitchen, a plate in her hand, and with all her might, she slammed the plate on my head and told me to shut up. My head broke the plate and immediately split my forehead open. I started bleeding profusely. I wasn't actually in pain; I was more shocked than anything. I turned to her as I grabbed my forehead, stunned at both her action and the blood. I wasn't sure I could stand up, but I tried anyway and quickly got woozy. She stood over me in disbelief—perhaps she didn't realize her strength. She began to panic and grabbed the dishrag, telling me to hold it against my forehead.

"You're going to have to say you fell, Mary," she instructed me. "Say it was the corner of the coffee table. I'm going to go to the neighbors and ask them to take us to the emergency room."

I sat very quietly in the neighbors' car, holding the huge cloth on my head. This was the first time I was physically wounded by her.

When they brought me in to stitch me up, the doctor asked me what happened. I told him that I was running in the house and fell and hit my head on the edge of the coffee table. By this point, my head was throbbing. I remember being very scared, but also kind of relieved that the pain would soon go away. They told my mom that I couldn't go to bed for a few more hours to avoid problems with the concussion I had.

We went to the grocery store and Mom bought some liver. It was sold in a white plastic containers that sat on the butcher counter, not pleasing enough to display like with other meat packaging. I'd never had liver before, but my mom insisted this meal would be good for me, for my concussion. She fried it up, along with some onions and Worcestershire sauce. I'd always loved the smell of frying onions, but the smell of the liver gave it a peculiar, heavy scent, like a musty boy after recess. I was also anemic and our doctor had said I needed more red meat in my diet, so I had been taking little red pills, but she said that this would help me with that.

Mom put the liver on a tostada and handed me a bottle of ketchup. I drenched the liver in ketchup and bit into the soft and tender meat that followed with a crunch from the hard corn shell. I immediately felt energy enter my body. I was so exhausted—emotionally and physically—and I was hungry, too. If this was my mom's apology for hurting me, I accepted it. Us kids were faster than our mom and could outrun and outmaneuver her, which we did on numerous occasions when she looked especially provoked and her facial expression turned into what we knew was attack mode. We'd quickly avoid punches, slaps, or rough grabs on the arms or shoulders as long as we could get to the front door and run out of the apartment. She controlled her physical outbursts and use of objects to inflict pain, at least on me, for many years after that incident. But physical abuse unfortunately became learned behavior for all of us, and it was how we settled arguments when words weren't sharp enough weapons. Though we'd outgrow this method of settling arguments a few years later, there was a period of time where all of us were all out dysfunctional. Luckily, we each tethered to some form of normalcy outside of our home and this helped us to weather most arguments without the use of physical violence.

SISTERHOOD

O ne day at elementary school, a kid commented that my sister was cleaner than me. It stung, but I knew it was true. Sam was always prepared for the next day. She would find what she was going to wear, and if nothing was clean, she would hit the sink or the bathtub and hand wash her clothes, and set them out to dry. I was never that deliberate with the clothes I wore to school. I would be outside playing all night until it was time to eat. I'd come in and watch some TV — maybe some basketball or the Cosbys—and then go to bed. Then I would wake up early in the morning and frantically try to put together my clothing for that day.

After walking about ten blocks from school, we'd be pretty hungry, most days. But we never had the same options most kids had. At least, it was not like what the commercials suggested it should be like: running into the house and grabbing Sunny D from the fridge, maybe grabbing a sandwich from the tray your mother was holding. It was usually pretty damn depressing coming home.

Sam and I would find a way to have some kind of food, though. The fridge was usually barren, with vegetables rotting in the drawer and condiments staring mockingly, daring us to put them on something. Vegetables usually went bad in our fridge because they were bought twice a month with the welfare checks and were rarely cooked quickly enough. It seemed more like Mom's gesture that veggies were important than an intent to actually cook them in time. We also hadn't learned enough about how to cook them either, not that I ever would have because I was more sugar-crazed than anything. Yet somehow, Sam would find a way to whip something up. She'd usually make Spanish rice, which only required some garlic, tomato sauce, rice, and oil. Then she'd start soaking the pinto beans and start on homemade tortillas. She was a pretty good cook by then. She knew how to make a lot of Mexican dishes that she'd learned from our neighbor, Reyna.

Reyna was a first-generation Mexican girl with a traditional family and upbringing. Reyna was not allowed to go anywhere or do anything without her mother's permission. She cooked and cleaned. She went to the laundromat, and when she came back she was in charge of ironing all the sheets. The sheets. She was the Latin Cinderella. Her oldest sister lived down the street with her husband, who was probably around her mom's age. They'd just had a kid, and she was never allowed to leave the house without her husband. Once we visited them, and saw that her sister and the baby had a skin rash, likely due to lack of sun.

We both loved going over to Reyna's, Sam especially. My sister learned how to speak some Spanish, cook Mexican dishes, and make beverages like Horchata, a cinnamon, rice, and milk drink. Reyna's life sat well with Sam; I think it was because it had structure. Sure, she had a lot of demands on her, but she had what she needed. She had a clean home, and there was always food cooking. Reyna couldn't leave the house without an escort though, so she and Sam hung out at Reyna's house most of the time.

Contrary to Reyna, when Mom cooked, it always seemed rushed. Mom didn't have a knack for delicate presentation, or the patience needed to cook anything—even pancakes. The batter went in, she stirred it around until it was clumped like scrambled eggs, then when they were just overdone, she'd scrape the pan for all the mash and burnt pieces and plop it down on the plate. I suppose the butter and syrup made up for it, but I always wondered why she couldn't make a round pancake like at restaurants. Regardless, since Mom was often not home, everything she could have taught Sam how to make, Sam learned instead on her own or from Reyna.

FLYING WRENCHES

When Sam and I argued, we could get pretty violent, especially with our words. On one day in particular, though, our argument was more charged than usual. It was one of those days where we were both unhappy and upset with the filthy state of the house. We only had a few days before we would both be starting middle school. Changes to the school system were taking effect, so now sixth graders were part of the middle school structure. Sam was going into seventh grade and I was going into sixth, so we were starting middle school together. There had been no back-to-school shopping, so we had to make do with the old, dirty clothes we had. We had an epic pile of dirty laundry in the bedroom and nothing to clean it with.

The mess made it nearly impossible to have a space to call your own, let alone fantasize about the possibilities of a new school year. Clothes were thrown everywhere as Sam separated her stuff from mine, then sorted the really dirty from the kinda dirty. She was searching for clothes that I had secretly squirreled away to use the next day for the first day of school, and became more and more inquisitive. Finally, I could no longer hide that I had indeed taken her belongings as my own.

She was so furious. She picked up a long, heavy wrench that was lying on the floor and threw it at my face.

The impact was twofold. The heavy, metal portion of the wrench hit my bottom front tooth and knocked half of it out. At the same time, the handle of the wrench gave me an instant gash above my left eyebrow.

That tooth wouldn't get fixed for another seven years. I still have the scar on my eyebrow and a not-so-obvious fake bottom tooth. I didn't have front teeth up top because of my deformity, and her knocking out my bottom tooth gave me even more of a Jack O' Lantern smile than I had before. Also, where my tooth was knocked in half, a nerve was now exposed. It took until I began high school to have the root canal to remove that nerve. Any kind of contact with it gave me a sharp pain, so I needed to be even more conscious of my mouth and how I ate. Sam apologized the moment she saw what she had done when the blood and pain was everywhere. The whole time we were at the emergency room, she was extra nice to me. Asking if I needed anything and grabbing me little cups of water when I asked.

After we all came back from the emergency room where I got stitches in my eyebrow, Sam took off her shoes. She then stared into one shoe with a perplexed look.

"What is it?" I asked.

"It's your tooth. It's in my shoe," she said as she held it in her hand, looking at it intently. I grabbed it from her and stared at it.

"Was this in your shoe the whole time?" I asked her. Part of me wanted to accuse her of hiding it there. And I thought that maybe if they'd known about it at the hospital, they could have put it back on. But then I realized that Sam would have felt a tooth in her shoe earlier and wouldn't be so perplexed now, so maybe this was one of those unexplainable situations. Nonetheless, I stomped away to the bedroom. I put the broken tooth under my pillow, in case it was still worth something, but it didn't help my mood. Now I really wasn't looking forward to my first day in a new school.

MIDDLE SCHOOL LIFE

The first day of sixth grade actually created a silver lining in my otherwise bleak existence. Sam and I walked up to the front of our Middle School together. I couldn't help but notice the men standing in front of the apartment buildings directly across the street. Some had wife beaters on, they all mostly wore dark pants, and they all had the same black Nikes on, the ones with the white swoosh. My sister told me not to stare and said they were gang members.

Sam walked me to the gym where the new sixth-grade students were, and she and I parted ways as she went to the auditorium with the older kids. I found a spot at the top of the bleachers and watched as more kids filed into the gym. Eventually my name was called and I walked down to the small table they had set up and grabbed my class schedule. I returned to my spot on the bleachers. I now noticed a girl sitting near me who seemed shy. Being that I was new and didn't know anyone, I decided to turn to her and said, "Hi, my name is Mary. What's your name?"

"Imelda," she said quietly.

We started talking about the classes we were in, and it turned out we were in most of them together. She told me where she had gone to elementary school and the neighborhood she lived in, none of which I really knew because she lived in the north side of Long Beach.

She and I began to size up all the kids around us. We even cracked some jokes about them. This almost immediately bit me in the ass. I was making fun of the guy sitting in front of me, who knows why.

He turned around and, without the slightest hesitation, said, "Shut up, you ugly bitch."

I was shocked, but I knew I deserved that.

I knew that I was ugly and I couldn't go around picking on people. I would lose. But I was only just trying to have fun and show Imelda how funny I could be. We made plans to see each other in between classes and after school.

My P.E. class was fifth period, and Mr. Bailey was my teacher. He looked like he came out of a '50s gym teacher catalog: he wore short blue shorts and a white T-shirt, and a black whistle hung around his neck. He was tanned and had nice legs. Boy, did I love those legs.

He lined us all up in six rows, seven people deep. Each of us were directed to sit on a particular number on the ground. That would be our number moving forward. Every time we came to P.E. class, we would have to sit on that number. Once we all got to our spot according to the roll call, he let his humor shine.

"Remember: if you trip and fall on the playground, it's not your fault. Who's fault is it?"

Everyone looked at each other confused.

"It's the ass's fault," he said slowly. We all laughed. "So, if you trip and fall, who's fault is it?"

"It's the ass's fault," the class repeated.

By the end of the day, we found ourselves hanging out on the floor in the hallway, talking about life and the people we had met that day. It was nice to have that kind of connection with someone so quickly, and with someone who didn't make fun of me. She just accepted me. She told me she had a much younger sister who was annoying, and who she had to share a room with. They had different dads, but Imelda had never met her father. Her mom was married to her sister's father and they all lived in a two-bedroom. I'd later learn it was a double-wide in a nice trailer park in North Long Beach. Her mom and stepdad both worked, but she didn't exactly know what her mom did. I thought it was interesting that she didn't know, since I was proud to say my mom was a librarian.

We talked so much that we lost track of time completely. Sam came running up the stairs to find me.

"Do you know what time it is?" she said.

I had no idea, but apparently school had been out for almost two hours. Our mom was worried and sent her to find me. Imelda and I parted ways and I went home, thinking that middle school wouldn't be that bad after all.

I was wrong. With all the new faces I was seeing, those new faces were seeing me, too. There was a new crop of kids, many older than me, who began to insult me on the way I looked and dressed. I kept getting different kids poking me, pulling my hair, or whispering insults in my ear. I tried to ignore them all. *Be still.*

There were many groups at school. The Mexican Cholas all had highly teased bangs molded by hairspray. The higher they could get their pompadour, the better. My sister and I went to Reyna to help us try this look on for size; we each created a small pomp that took so much teasing and Aqua Net hairspray that by the time we were done, our hair was rock hard and our foreheads broke out in small pimples.

Then there were the Black girls. You didn't want to mess with the Black girls—even the Mexican girls knew not to. Black kids were the largest group at school, and with their numbers, they seemed stronger than any of the other groups—except for the Samoans. No one messed with the Samoans. No one.

There were the Asians, who ranged from reserved to slightly popular—though none of them reached true popular status, which usually meant dating, ditching and dressing in the most popular brands. Maybe that was because too few were allowed to dress or act the part, maybe because their culture was more strict, or maybe because this was 1990 and many of our races hadn't melded together yet—most of our parents and grandparents wanted us to keep our cultures separate.

Then there were the white kids. That wasn't really a group at all, because there were only a handful of us. You needed more than a handful to make up a racial group and none of us really hung out with each other.

But it wasn't long before I made more friends at school. My clique quickly became my easy escape from bullies. We were a melting pot, a diverse group of girls from different backgrounds that didn't fit into any one group.

One of my new friends was Sherry. Sherry was a tomboy like me. Her hair was always tied back in a tight ponytail with just small tufts of hair poking out. She wore brandless jeans, T-shirts, and sneakers like me. She was Black, and I was white, though that didn't matter to us. She also had a few more siblings than I did, and her dad still lived at home.

Sherry's spelling was dreadful. She spelled things exactly how you would say them—though she had a slight southern accent, which meant there were a few more Es in everything. I liked that we both had a southern background. No matter how many times I taught her how to spell "beautiful," she would spell it "beuteful."

I only went to Sherry's house once, when she asked if I would come home with her after school so she could show me something. She asked me to stay on the porch while she grabbed what she wanted to show me. As she opened the door, I could see a long hallway full of messy things, just like mine, and that made me like her even more. There was so much clutter packed throughout the hallway you couldn't see into the rest of the house except for a light shining bright like a beacon in their living room. The sense of happiness in her home wafted outside. I could smell frying chicken, cooking greens, and cornbread. I took in huge breaths to soak up the cooking aromas. Soon her older brother opened the door and gave me a large, warm smile. He was my sister's age.

"Is Sherry going to show you the book?" he asked.

"I don't know. She said she wanted to show me something," I told him. He pulled a book from behind his back; it was a children's book his mother had written.

"I drew all of these," he said proudly.

He pointed at each of the pages with his illustrations, then his name, printed at the beginning as "Illustrator." I was impressed. The book later became an internet sensation when someone found it in the public library and was shocked by both the uniqueness of the storytelling and the vast number of spelling and grammatical errors.

Sherry came to the door and saw the book in her brother's hands. She smiled.

"So what do you think?" she asked me.

"It's great! Are you guys going to be rich?" I thought that if anyone had written anything, they were rich.

"I don't know. We'll see," Sherry said plainly.

Another friend was Silvia, who came from a traditional Hispanic family where she had to help her mom clean and cook, just like Reyna. Her parents had her future laid out for her: she would one day be a wife and mother, and that was it. Silvia's father kept a tight leash on her, and she couldn't spend the night at anyone's house. We never hung out after school, either—that was an absolute no-no for her.

Finally there was Kimberly, who was tall like me but fair-skinned and pigeon-footed. She had a full figure; her breasts were large, the kind of large that required her to hold them down with her forearm when she ran. She tried to cover them up with large sweaters and always dressed down, wearing jeans and sneakers, never calling attention to herself with over-the-top makeup or grand gestures. I was rather impressed with her body, because I had always been nothing but a flat board. Kimberly's dad was a skinny Chinese guy, and her mom was a plump white woman. I found the combination interesting.

Though it always seemed a little chaotic at Kimberly's house with her many siblings and pets running around, it was a great place to be. Her mother would always have a hot meal on the stove and made sure I planned to stay and eat. I did a lot of maneuvering with friends in order to eat at their houses, even if it was just a snack after school.

Most days before school, Sherry, Kimberly, and Silvia would meet me on the corner of my block or wait for me in front of my apartment because it was on their way to school. Some days I'd ask them to help me push my mom's Dodge Dart across the street so she wouldn't get a street sweeping ticket. By then it wasn't running. But most days, we'd just walk to school and talk and grab school breakfast together because we all qualified for the school program, and it was an unspoken rule that we wanted to be seen walking together into the cafeteria rather than alone.

SUMMER BREAK

We were one of those families without a home phone. I went through all of elementary and middle school without one. The way I communicated with my friends over summer break was by writing letters. I loved the process, especially when I had matching stationary and envelopes. I loved the act of writing the letter, putting the date in the far right corner, and writing something as simple as, "Dear Sherry, Today I went to the library and started reading Charlie Brown. What are you reading? Sincerely, Mary." They were like little notes in a bottle. Mom always seemed to have stamps, and if I needed a few here or there, she gave them to me without much fuss.

My favorite part of writing was actually getting a letter back. That was where the real joy was. These little twinges of joy kept me going through the summer when bouts of boredom set it. I loved how my friends would tell me about their life, how they were doing and going places that all sounded impossible for me. Silvia went to Mexico to visit family, and Kimberly had gone to Disneyland. I felt included in their adventures in some way, through those letters, but most importantly I felt seen by them, because they took the time to write me back. Their letters were like treasure maps. What they wrote led me to a new world.

BASKETBALL BULLIES

In sixth grade, I wanted to join every sports team. I also planned to take a music class, because the recorder I played in elementary school only whetted my appetite. Unfortunately, you couldn't take music classes or be on a sports team until you were in seventh grade. I was crushed. I figured this was due to the limited number of instruments and the limited athletic proficiencies of eleven- or twelve-year-olds. Whatever the reason, it meant I needed to learn patience.

While I patiently watched my sister learn to play the flute, I took a shop class as my elective with Mr. Beanie. His name was often a source of under-the-breath teasing by the guys, but I found it interesting to be both named after a hat and beans. The first thing I made in shop was a carved wooden plaque that said, "MOM." By the end of the semester, I gave my mom her custom-made gift and it sat in the kitchen on the stove, for years. My brother had made her the same plaque when he took shop class just a few years before, and I remember him giving it to her, but she never put his anywhere in the house so prominently. It stayed in one of her boxes for years.

Every day after school, if I wasn't hanging with Imelda or another friend, I was on the basketball court with the guys. There were four courts outdoors and a huge field where adults in the neighborhood played soccer after school. I wanted to be good enough to make the basketball team next year. I had been playing basketball casually since I was in third grade. By sixth grade, I had already grown to a whopping five feet, eight inches tall, and it added to my skills. Michael Jordan, Scottie Pippen, Larry Bird, John Stockton, The Mailman Malone, and Magic Johnson were all my idols. I was obsessed with basketball.

One day, after playing on the courts for an hour after school, I was walking back home alone. A girl stopped me at the corner. I had my basketball on my hip when she walked toward me. Something about her face—the striking eyebrows, the heavy eyeliner, the tense, negativity-bloated expression—told me I was in trouble.

"What are you doing in my neighborhood?" she asked bluntly, as she stood in my path. She was shorter than me, but bold and scary.

"Nothin'. Just going home from playing basketball."

"I don't like your face. I think you're an ugly bitch and I should just beat you up right now," she said. Her head swung like she was mixing a bowl of cake batter.

"I just want to go home. I live down the street."

"I may be able to let you walk home, but you have to give me your basketball."

"No. This is my basketball, and you don't even look like you play. Why don't you just let me go home?"

"Do you know how ugly you are?"

"Yes, I do."

"What happened to your face?"

"I was born with a cleft lip and palate. I was born this way."

She scrunched up her nose and eyes, trying to figure out if what I said made any sense to her.

"Listen, I'll let you go when you do something for me."

"What do you want?"

"Tell me that I'm better than you. Tell me that I could kick your ass. Tell me that you're ugly and I'll let you go."

I knew this girl was uglier than me, but she wasn't half-baked ugly; she was just ugly.

"Okay, you're better than me. You could kick my ass, and I'm ugly," I told her, still holding my basketball close to my hip.

"No, say that you're *fucking* ugly," she insisted, her head cocked to the side. All her face pimples were more prevalent now.

"I'm fucking ugly," I told her. My face was red, I knew it, and I was about to just start running. It would only be about four blocks to get to the house, and she wasn't athletic by any means.

"Okay bitch, you can go now. Run home, you little punk-ass white bitch," she said, as if she had won something.

Lucky for me, I got out of that without a physical fight—though it felt like one. I knew I had survived a major confrontation, somehow talking my way out of it. A bully of any kind was always an issue. I could take the blunt insults, but this one was a psychological bully—one who needed me to know I was less than her in order for her to let me go. Another hurt soul.

I had grown so accustomed to being bullied that I actually didn't go home and cry that day. I was actually just thankful that I was able to get out of that situation by myself. I didn't need to tell my mom about this one; I just needed to know what to expect the next time I would see her, and create a better plan to avoid her.

Just one week later, my bully appeared in my school. She and I locked eyes, and I knew I'd have to deal with her soon, one way or the other. Her pimples and large breasts made me wonder why she was in sixth grade. *Will she be in one of my classes, God forbid?* I had to see who she hung with in order to see how bad my life was going to be. If she hung with the Chola's, then I'd be okay—they were more obsessed with their looks and clothes to deal with a flea like me.

She caught me in the hallway on her first day.

"Hey Weda," she said as we passed in the hallway.

"Hey," I said, realizing I was over five inches taller than her, and on school grounds. I continued past her. From time to time, we would lock eyes when we saw each other around campus, but she never tried to exert dominance. By the end of the day, I realized she didn't have any alliances either. She must have been a new girl in the neighborhood and wanted to look like a badass that day. Too bad she chose me.

ART THEATER

Riding the city buses around Long Beach meant you could find yourself in parts of town that were actually nice. One such place was the Art Theater. This is where you could see independent films and watch two movies, back to back, for only a dollar fifty. Kids were only seventy-five cents each. Sometimes we'd bring snacks from Denco, the dollar store on Pine.

The theater added charm to the experience. It didn't show movies any of my friends were talking about, but they were still movies. Once inside, they served up some of the best buttered popcorn I've ever had for only a dollar. I was getting a movie experience for a price that was not the norm, for movies that weren't the norm, and I got to see two of them in one night. There was something very special about this cozy little theater.

I never saw other kids there. Perhaps people thought our mother was strange for bringing us to the theater at six p.m. to watch two indie movies in a row, knowing we wouldn't be out until ten or eleven at night, sometimes on a weeknight. I suppose it *was* strange.

One of the first films we saw was *The Accused* with Jodie Foster. This wasn't like any glamorous or sensational Hollywood movie I'd ever seen before. I was riveted by her journey; from being raped to fighting for justice in court. It was graphic and shook me to my core. I realized the vulnerability of being a woman like I never knew I would. I decided to take on those vulnerabilities as part of the armor a woman needed to wear. I also wanted to be an attorney after seeing that movie.

The downside was when we left the theater. The last movies let out late, and we were usually waiting on the last bus. It was usually quite cold at night, especially after getting out of the cozy theater. We clung to our mother, absorbing any heat she had to give us, sorry we had ever agreed to go to the movies. But each time, as if no lesson was learned, we would be at the theater again.

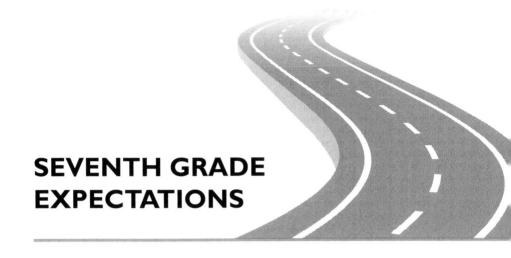

SEVENTH GRADE EXPECTATIONS

When seventh grade started, I knew it was going to be my year. I could sign up for music class and try out for the basketball team—or any team, for that matter. When I walked into the auditorium on the first day of seventh grade, I was told I had to pick a new elective. I stared at my class schedule and wondered what she meant. There wasn't a music class available. I handed the schedule back to her.

"I want to take a music class."

"I'm sorry, Mary. The music program's budget was cut," she said, with a disappointed face, likely mimicking the one I had on mine.

I didn't really have a back-up plan. I had my heart set on music class. I wanted to play an instrument, a piano. I was really looking forward to Mr. Robles's class. I had imagined him showing me how to play an instrument. I had imagined what it would be like to be in his class, what it would be like to perform in a recital, like my sister got to do.

I ended up picking "Office Attendant" as my elective instead. It was an elective that had some practical applications. My role would be to walk the halls and pick up all the tardy slips from all the previous periods. I did this during the last period of school. Once I got back from collecting them, I would organize them alphabetically by last name, have them typed up, and get the list out to all the teachers who had students in their last period who had to stay for detention. Any teacher who had kids in their class on that list, would keep them for twenty minutes after school.

I actually liked this job, because it took me through some interesting parts of the school building, particularly down to the basement where all the English as a Second Language (ESL) kids were. This was like walking into another world. We all called it The Dungeon. Their classrooms were different than ours: they were very large, probably because there were way more kids per classroom. There were only two teachers down there, each teaching about forty-five kids, ranging from eleven to thirteen years old. Whenever I went downstairs to see if they had tardy slips, all the kids looked at me like I was from another planet. I suppose I did look like an alien. I announced myself by peeping into the classroom and asking, "Tardies?" I grabbed the teachers tardy slips, and raced out of the room as fast as I could. I had an irrational fear that I would somehow get stuck down there. I felt the same way with the special ed class. They were all in just one room, away from all the other classes, and somehow this scared me.

I only had thirty-five minutes to walk the entire campus, bring back the tardy slips, organize them by student and last-period teacher, have the secretary type them up, then take the notices back to the teachers who had tardy students in their last period class. One main perk of my job was the power. Because only the teachers who had tardy kids in their classes got the list, they didn't know whether the kid from their earlier period class was going to spend time in detention after school. They just relied on the tardy system to work. If I were to remove, say, my best friend's tardy, well, that could easily get overlooked. And it did.

The next quarter I had to take a different elective, so I chose Spanish. My class was going to be in The Dungeon, and I was definitely not happy about this. The only thing that made this new elective exciting was that my best friend Imelda was going to be in my class—and so was our mutual crush, Giovanni Sanco, but we called him *Gio*.

Gio was not your typical cute guy. He always came to school looking very well-put-together and wasn't a jock of any sort. He would wear black Dickies and a white T-shirt, and slicked his hair back like a greaser. *21 Jump*

Street was on television at the time, and Gio looked like a young Johnny Depp. Maybe that's the look he was going for? If so, he was nailing it.

He was also nice and easy to talk to. He quickly became our secret crush and friend. Imelda and I shared in the pursuit to win him over with our charisma and good looks. Unfortunately, I did not have the looks, and I felt I was the opposite of charming. My tomboyishness, pimply face, and poor-girl clothes made it so that my only bet to get anyone to like me was going to be based on my personality. I was really funny and really good at sports. For some of the guys at school, being good at sports mattered more than what you looked like. What I admired was when someone more attractive and popular than me could have teased me, but didn't. A handful of guys were like this, one of them was Corey. He was always going through the hallways giving people high-fives. Whenever he would see me he'd say, "Gregory!" He was also the first person to give me a compliment on my looks. I dared to wear eyeliner one day, and he stopped me in the hallway and said, "Your eyes are so beautiful and blue, Mary."

My crush on Gio was because of his handsome, sweet, and kind side. He knew the shape I was in. He also knew I was trying to make the best of my situation, and he never teased me or made me feel like I didn't belong. If I was exceptionally hungry, I could tell him and he would slide me a few dollars to buy some fries or an extra lunch from the cafeteria. I would always tell him I would pay him back, and he would always tell me I didn't have to.

My crushes were always with guys out of my league. Really, Gio was out of my league too, but he was a friend and I could talk to him—unlike the other cute guys. While Imelda crushed on Gio too, a deeper crush of hers was on Sebastian Baker, or *Seb*. He and I played basketball together and I was always trying to orchestrate a meeting between the two of them. Imelda was too shy to talk to him directly, so she wrote his name in her textbooks and made him the leading character in all the notes she and I passed around to each other in class.

Seb really seemed like he was in Imelda's league. He was a tall, skinny beanpole, and sometimes I wondered what she saw in him. With looks being the most important thing in middle school social society, they seemed like a match—but he was never brave enough to get to know her. He was shy.

Imelda *would* eventually get the guy though, just not him.

She got Gio.

She eventually dated Gio for a brief moment—though it seemed like an eternity. She got to enjoy the victory of finally getting one of her crushes, and she had a bit of satisfaction seeing Seb's reaction to it, too.

It was a double-edged sword, though. I was happy for her, but when two girls are both crushing on a guy for years and then one gets him, it's only going to *crush* the other. It would take me years until I could say that I got a guy I liked. But in the meantime, I was hurt. I'd pulled away from Imelda and didn't want to hang out with her as much. It wasn't until her and Gio stopped dating that we got close again. I'd felt like there was never going to be a time that a boy that I liked, would like me, for me.

THE NEW NEIGHBOR

Having a new neighbor was always one of the most exciting bits of news, especially if they were around my age…and a boy. When Steven moved in, I got to enjoy the new-kid-on-the-block excitement for a few weeks. He was darker than the other Mexicans in our building, and he was definitely what we called "first generation." He seemed like he'd had a hard life. His father wasn't around; it was just him, his little brother, and his mom. He and his mom would argue all the time, and he was always slamming their front door, hanging over the rails outside his apartment, and crying or sulking. He would sometimes stand there, puffing in and out, looking hard and mean for a good thirty minutes. He was at least fifteen years old. There was always the risk that he would like Reyna first, since she was Mexican and pretty, but she had two things going against her: she never brushed her teeth (her gums were red and puffy and sometimes bled), and she had giant blackheads on her nose. Besides that, she was pretty well put together.

He was too old to play with us girls, though. He always wanted to act tough. He paced around the apartment building, only nodding when others said, "Hi." The only time we got him to play with us was when we had a water balloon fight with the kids in the apartment building next door. The twins with the cleft lips had a cousin who was visiting from Mexico; he was tall and handsome, but didn't speak any English. He didn't have to. He was older, but loved playing with the younger kids, and was happy to be in America, even if it was for a short visit.

When Steven saw us playing with him, he decided to join in on the fun, too. Later that week, the building had a huge party, and in the center of the courtyard all the neighbors shucked oysters and drank beer all night long. Steven and the cousin were able to steal a few Budweisers from the coolers and snuck them over to the alley. I drank a whole beer for the first time in my life with them. It was fun and exhilarating. Sure, I was doing something bad, so there was excitement there—but it was more than that. It was a brief look into what life was like when you got to enjoy yourself and forget about your problems—when you felt like you belonged. The bonus was that the boys were nice to me.

BIG SISTERS HAVE ALL THE FUN

Because my sister was in eighth grade, she could go to Camp Hi Hill, which was Long Beach Unified School District's science center located in the Angeles National Forest. The trip allowed inner-city kids to get out of the city for once—for a whole week. I was really jealous.

Camp came with its own challenges, like getting all the things on the list they gave you. A night gown, travel soap, shampoo and conditioner, boots, flannels, jackets, lantern, bathrobe, towels, sleeping bag, the list went on and on. It looked like the most expensive trip ever. *How is she going to get all this?* We barely had money for the rags we were already wearing, yet alone *new* things.

Somehow, over the course of the three weeks before the trip, Sam was able to beg and borrow her way to camp. The morning she took the giant yellow bus up to Camp Hi Hill, I realized that for one week I was going to be mostly alone, and I started to feel sad. Paul was out of the house most days and nights, and my mom was still in college and rarely around. Luckily, I had enough after-school activities to keep myself busy, but the house got really lonely, really quickly when there was not an adult or sibling around. Most nights, I would whip up some mac n' cheese, throw in some tuna and tomato sauce, and watch a little M*A*S*H until I fell asleep on the couch.

I thought about showing my appreciation for my sister by cleaning the entire house while she was away. That would be no small feat, though. Usually she and I took on that challenge together, and it meant a really long day of endless cleaning. I really wanted her to come home to a clean house. Over the course of the week, I only did what one person could do, but every single accomplishment was met by destruction from our mom. I couldn't keep up with it. Eventually, I resigned. Our mom didn't care that a clean house would have meant the world to Sam, so at that point, neither did I. When she came home that day, she walked in, assuming that I would have kept an unspoken promise to her and cleaned the house. Sadly, it was the same dirty, filthy mess she had come to know and accept. Sheer disappointment hung on her face. It took her almost a week before she really talked to me and shared her camping stories, which she said were filled with fun and adventure and nothing like anything we'd ever seen before.

I had broken our pact, and my resentment turned to guilt. Part of me was still jealous of her latest adventure at camp, but I was mostly ashamed I hadn't found a way to have her walk into the apartment and feel happy. This was a turning point for the both of us. We realized we needed to be there for each other, but couldn't rely on the other to single-handedly deliver on our hopeful expectations.

THE SUBSIDIZED LIFE

Every disappointment helped us get closer to knowing what we didn't want in life, and what we desired in a family. The family we knew wasn't really anything positive; it mostly felt like we were the means for Mom to collect welfare, resources, and discounts to the poor. Food stamps, welfare checks, medical, food banks, all of it—our existence boiled down to the activities around getting this support. I dreamed of how to get out of this life, a way to achieve something that wouldn't constantly disappoint me or be such a struggle. This life seemed like so much work, with such uncertainty.

I began what I know now is called a vision board. I cut out pictures from magazines and glued them on paper—pictures of the kind of house I wanted, the bedroom, the car, the life—and stared at them for hours.

We had moved to a new apartment about seven blocks from our place on Henderson Street. We were now closer to PCH. Unfortunately, this didn't take us far from the ghetto, but it seemed to be a step up from our previous living arrangements. Our mom had finally qualified for HUD, a government program that subsidizes your rent. This was how we were able to "expand" into a different neighborhood and out of a one-bedroom apartment.

Subsidized rent was a real game-changer. Until that point, rent was always one whole government check, so we were left with hard times until the second check came on the fifteenth. Our rent was now going to be forty dollars a month, versus $450 a month.

The new apartment was in a gray twenty-unit building. It was still close to our school so we could walk there. The only difference from our old neighborhood were the skin tones of our neighbors: black, rather than brown. It wasn't much better than where we used to live, as far as amenities. Just different.

We had a Spanish landlord who I was convinced was gay (solely due to his Castilian lisp). A liquor store was through the alley at the back of the apartment building, and a Norms restaurant was just up the street, which made me mildly happy because I enjoyed their food a lot, and it was always a treat to eat there.

A Black family of six lived right upstairs from our apartment. They'd ask us for laundry detergent but called it "clothes soap." They had a slightly southern flare to them, so I was instantly intrigued. They were nice, and since they were a family with the dad still around, I found comfort in them. Their two sons played basketball; one was a few years younger than me, the other a few years older. I spent most of my time playing with the younger one and talking about basketball, because his older brother was never really home.

The neighborhood was fully diverse with its poor people. You had everything from drug addicts, single parents, abusive spouses, drunks, immigrants, and the general down-and-out.

It was the largest apartment we'd ever lived in: it had *three* bedrooms. So far, we'd only had one one-bedroom with bunk beds. The garage had been converted to a bedroom, so it was long and narrow. That was going to be my brother's room. My sister and I would share a room, which seemed like a vacation from our previous sleeping arrangements. Our mom would get her own room. Bushes lined the front of the apartment and covered the window to mine and Sam's room.

Our first night in the apartment, we got our welcoming from the neighborhood. While in the living room unpacking our things, we heard a large crash in our bedroom. Startled, Sam and I ran into our room only to find that our bedroom window had been broken and there was blood all over the shattered glass and newly-cleaned, move-in ready carpet. It was frightening, because we weren't sure what caused this, and by the time we walked out front, there was no one around. The exciting sense of a new beginning faded just as fast as it had begun. Our mom spent that night cleaning up the glass and the blood and finding a way to secure the window until the next day when it could be repaired by our landlord. Sam and I slept in Mom's room.

The extra income from the cheaper rent didn't seem to last long, either. We had an electric stove and heater, the kind of heater that radiated down from the ceiling. By the time the first month's electricity bill came, it was so high it was nearly the same monthly expense as our previous rent. Somehow, getting a leg-up in life always seemed just out of reach.

BASKETBALL DIARIES

B y the time the seventh-grade basketball season approached, I was confident I would make the basketball team. I had practiced nearly every day before school during most of sixth grade, and almost every weekend leading up to seventh grade. I loved playing basketball. I would walk up to my middle school on the weekends and play all day with all the guys on the school courts. I would even get there by eight in the morning and play until three or four on weekends—that's how much I loved basketball.

When I went out for the team, I was confident I would make the team. During the tryouts, I didn't perform like I expected I would. For some reason, playing with girls from the eighth-grade basketball team really showed my weaknesses. Since I had never been on a basketball team before, I wasn't actually familiar with some of the scrimmages or dynamics of the indoor court. When the coaches were looking, I couldn't even make a simple layup, a layup I had practiced for months and that I could do anytime on the courts outside.

The day they were posting who made the girls' basketball team, I was filled with excitement. All day I was confident I had made the team. My thoughts raced all day: *I am the Larry Bird of East Long Beach. There's no way I didn't make the cut.*

After school, I tried to walk into the girls locker room to go look at the list, but the door was locked. The only door unlocked was the one into the gym, so I peered in. Everyone who had made the team was sitting on the bleachers across from the door I had opened. The coach was giving them a talk.

The coach stopped, turned around, and said, "The list is in the locker room, Mary."

All the girls looked at me, and from their faces, I could feel a twinge in my stomach. I walked into the girls' locker room, slowly walked up to the list, read the names. The list went on and on...name by name. I read down the list until I hit the bottom, then I started from the top again. My name was still not on it. My heart swelled with sadness. This was all I had worked for, all I wanted since sixth grade. The disappointment came over me, and I started to cry. I couldn't stop the streams of tears rolling down my face.

Alone in the locker room, I felt embarrassment at the fact that I now had to walk past all the girls who *had* made the team. I looked at other exits, but the cleaning crew had already locked the other doors and put large chains around them with padlocks. After a few more minutes, letting the last of my tears leave my eyes, I started to pull myself together. My pride needed to be restored.

I tied my hair in a new ponytail and patted my face down with a little cold water from the sink. I stared at my face in the mirror. I deliberately put on my *I don't care* face. My plan was to push open the door from the locker room, but it was a double-door so I knew I couldn't open it discreetly. I would open it, turn toward the wall, and walk straight to the door to the exit.

After a few deep breaths, I pushed open the door of the girls' locker room with a shameless force. Everyone was already performing scrimmages and didn't take notice. With this unexpected victory, I saw the girls' coach and decided to walk up to her.

"Why didn't I make the team, Ms. Dardy?"

"I'm sorry, Mary, but you didn't perform well when you tried out."

I held my stoic face, but I was shocked that she had actually called out what I knew had been the case. I knew that my tryout sucked. I looked around at the other girls who were on the team in my grade. None of them practiced like I did. How is it that they made the team and I didn't? I was baffled—then it dawned on me.

Maybe it's because of how I look.

It was somehow easier to believe this than to truly accept my performance as a reason. I didn't want to say this, though, because otherwise I would have started crying, so I said something to Ms. Dardy that even shocked me.

"I would like to still be on the team, if there's a way."

She thought about it for a moment, then said, "You can keep score at the games, if you like."

I immediately agreed to my new role on the team and asked if I could stay while the girls practiced. She agreed I could.

I was at all the practices after school, and at all the games. I was going to make keeping score and supporting my team my top priority. There was a lot of excitement at every game, more than I had anticipated. I was responsible for helping the team and cleaning the floors before and after practice, and I was able to sneak into a practice with the team here and there.

I didn't stop playing basketball—in fact, I was even more committed than before. I leveraged my proximity to the coach and showed her how I perfected my free throw and three-pointer. I still went to the basketball court on the weekends and played with the older guys. I tried to get better. Making the team the following year was my top priority.

I eagerly fulfilled my role as the scorekeeper and pseudo team mate. The basketball season came and went, and by that summer I played so well I was sure I would make the team my eighth-grade year.

My brother was mostly still doing his thing, only home long enough to sleep. He never stayed too long because he didn't fit in in our neighborhood. I didn't fit in either, but I fit better than he did. Paul was into rock 'n' roll and wore Led Zeppelin tie-dyes and ripped jeans and he had long hair like Axl Rose. There weren't very many white boys that lived in our neighborhood—in fact, I can't recall any. He stuck out like a sore thumb.

By eighth grade, I spent more time on my social career at school and how I was going to finally get a guy to notice me, though still committed to my first love, basketball. My mom was still in college and taking courses, mostly in the arts. She hadn't achieved a degree yet, and her interest had started to wane. She still wasn't employable, unless she could find a job as a daydreamer.

It was getting more and more important for me to have some of the things my best friend had, especially sneakers or clean clothes. I could get away with being dirty and tomboyish in sixth and seventh grade, but as an eighth grader it was my duty to be better than all the scrubs.

I managed to put more and more time into myself, from my hair to my clothes. If I had to wash something by hand, I did it. If I had to find a way to get prettier, I would.

I always reminded myself that once I reached fourteen years old, my mom said I was old enough to get my nose fixed. I would dream about it. I would hope and pray that I would be able to go back to Nashville and get the surgery. My mom always said that this was the age Dr. Temple said I would need to be in order for him to do any more surgeries on my nose. This was because, he told her, your nose stops growing by the time you're fourteen.

I didn't have an option for my teeth, except that I was starting to go to the dentist at our local hospital to take out the nerve from the bottom tooth my sister had knocked out. Because he was a specialist who had worked on cleft-lip and palate cases, he suggested we see a panel of specialists at the hospital so they could discuss my case and decide how to best proceed. Based on their recommendations, my surgeries would be covered by their hospital. My first and only visit with the panel was awful. A bunch of doctors sitting around a large conference table reviewed my dental charts and asked me questions.

"Let me ask you, Mary, why do you want to get your teeth fixed?"

Are you serious, I thought to myself. *Don't you have my charts right in front of you? Just take a look at me!*

215

"I want to look normal. I'm made fun of everyday because I'm missing teeth," I told them. I felt they had asked me the most obvious question of the century.

"What do people say about you?" one of the doctors asked. I felt an ocean of emotions crashing on the surface of my face, the tide in my throat.

With my head down I said, "They say I look like a witch. That I'm ugly and a snaggle-tooth." At this point the tears were starting to fall. *Can't you just look at me and fix it and stop asking me these questions?* I thought. But all that came out was, "Can you guys fix what I look like?"

The room was silent for a long while as the doctors looked at each other.

"Mary, we can help you. Perhaps you can help us as well. Could you draw for us the type of nose and lip you would like?" a female doctor asked.

I thought this was silly. I wasn't a doctor—and what if I drew it wrong? I said I could, if it helped. A few questions later, my mom and I left the meeting. I left feeling exposed. I wasn't certain I was going to be able to work with them. They asked really dumb questions, and didn't seem interested in doing the work. I eventually had the nerve in my bottom tooth taken out, and nothing else went anywhere with them and their fancy panel.

Despite my looks, I was doing quite well on the sports front. I made the girls' basketball team in eighth grade and finally felt like I was part of something bigger than myself. I still had pursuits for boys that never had much traction, but at least I could pour myself into basketball and escape life for a while on the court.

I also made the track and field team, and was slated to do the long and high jump for our school's track and field season. A lot of the same girls on the basketball team were on the track and field team. I was really enjoying my time on the teams. I had games almost every week—though unlike the other girls, I never had a family member attend any of my games. My mom was always in school or on the campus, working. My sister was hanging out with her friends after school and starting to date. I didn't know where my brother was most of the time. I didn't bother to invite anyone from the house, either. Part of me was embarrassed with how my mom looked, and I didn't want people to attend and embarrass me.

When we bused in to a school in a nice neighborhood for a basketball game, it was always a strange experience. Most of the neighborhoods were clean, and their gymnasiums were full of family members of the team members, sitting in the bleachers, holding pom-poms and cheering. It was like everyone rallied for those teams. I know I wasn't the only one who felt out of place. Many times we'd step out of the bus and our team would look at each other in amazement. It gave us even more of a reason to win. We were the melting pot of Long Beach—we had Asians, Samoans, Black girls, and white girls on our team. Depending on the school, the other teams were either all white or all Black. There was always a surge of power I felt whenever we would step into a school that I knew had more privilege than ours who I felt we could beat. Our team practiced and worked hard. We were good. We had the desire to win. Many of those victories went deeper than the game.

Throughout the season, we were neck and neck for the championship against Rogers Middle School. These kids lived in the Naples, Belmont Shore, and Belmont Heights areas—the wealthier parts of Long Beach. Though I knew nothing of these neighborhoods until I was a little older, at the time, going through them felt like going through a different world.

The last, deciding game against Rogers was more than a game against another team—it was to show that those rich girls weren't better than us. It was classes: rich versus poor. Our team gathered all our supporters to come to the home game: the boys, the teachers, and family members came. I was inspired by the team and asked my mom to come. I downplayed the importance of the game, partly to not make her feel bad if she couldn't come, partly because I didn't want to feel self-conscious if she could. She didn't end up coming.

This game was neck and neck. By the end of the second quarter, we were down by one. Our coach told us to cool down, because our trash talking was leading to excessive pushing, and she didn't want the game forfeited for bad sportsmanship.

By the end of the third quarter, one of the white girls on our team, Tracey, was ready to have a fight with the other team's point guard. This was broken up, but Tracey had built up a penalty free throw for the other team. The opposing team made one shot and tied the game.

By the fourth quarter, we were up by one. With the last four seconds on the clock, the point guard from the other team stole the ball from Tracey. Tracey scrambled after her, but she was going full steam ahead for her victory layup. Tracey got enough on the ball and on her to foul just as the game the buzzer went off and the call was made by the ref: "Foul, number twenty-two, two shots."

By this time the entire side of the bleachers was roaring and stomping to create as much distraction as possible. I was standing near the basket, watching our opponent take a shot. *Please miss. Please miss.*

"One, tie game."

Damn. What does this mean? Do we get a tiebreaker match?

The point guard bounced the ball and peered up at the hoop like it was hers. She threw the ball in the air.

"Basket, game over. Roger wins," the referee announced loudly.

The gym was loud; the other team screamed with victory. I saw them huddle together, happy, their fans coming off the bleachers. I looked over at our school's side. Our teachers tried to look supportive, but the disappointment was palatable for everyone.

We poured into our locker room, mad and defeated. Tracey began to slam her fists against the locker doors. Our coach rushed in and told us we needed to go back out there and show good sportsmanship by giving high-fives to the other team. No one left the locker room, though. Tracey glared at our coach, her face hot with anger, tears streaming down her face. I sat on the bench, my head hanging low.

It hurt so badly to be so close and not beat those rich girls. I understood that as a team you had to take a loss together, even if it was painful. You fall together, but you always show sportsmanship—so we rallied each other to get up, to wipe off our defeat, and to go out there and show our sportsmanship. This had nothing to do with money. This was about character, and we had character.

INJUSTICE AND RIOTS

I 992 taught me many valuable lessons. There seemed to be a relentless pursuit of justice in my community. Our teachers were picketing outside our school so we could get a traffic light installed to replace the crosswalk that went across four lanes. Just a week before, one of the students was hit by a bus's side mirror while running across the street. It was strange seeing our teachers protesting; it was an activist role I hadn't ever seen before.

The infamous Rodney King beating was all over the news those days while the trial was underway. The cops who had beaten him were accused of excessive force. An impending verdict hung in the air. The trial had been going on for a while, and the community already had their concerns about the jury. Ten white people, one Asian, and one Latino. Not one Black person on the jury. There was no doubt that if these officers were found anything other than guilty, there would be huge outrage. So far, the racial tension I had experienced was due to being a poor white girl, a minority in my neighborhood and school.

It was Wednesday, April 29th, 1992, and news about the verdict was discussed at school—mostly by the teachers. I knew it was that day, but there was no doubt in my mind that the police officers involved in his beating would be convicted. By the end of the day, I had already forgotten about the verdict and was hitting the basketball courts with the guys. Around 5:30 p.m., I decided I should head back home, so I left the courts. I was less than a block from my schoolyard when everything changed.

"Fucking white people!" shouted a forty-something Black lady as she pushed open her apartment gate. I immediately looked over at her as I locked my basketball into my hip. She ran at me quickly. I was just a few steps ahead of her, but within reach for her to deliver a sizable whack on my back. *What the fuck?* I thought, while I kept walking away. I knew I was white, but I was still just thirteen years old, and this was a grown woman! As I looked at the woman to give her my annoyed face, I caught out of the corner of my eye, two Black guys running toward me. I'd been playing ball with them, so I knew I wasn't getting jumped. They ran up to me and guarded both sides as they pulled me away from this situation and toward the light that I had to cross to get back home.

"Yeah, you better walk away, you white bitch," the lady screamed at me.

I turned around to look at her and she stared me down, her eyes furrowed and shaking with rage. By then I wasn't sure what happened, but I knew I needed to get out of there.

I looked at the guy on my left and asked, "What's going on?"

"The verdict was announced, and those officers were found not guilty." He looked down at me, disappointed with both the verdict and this woman's behavior, but he knew I had to keep walking. I felt like he wanted to tell me, *You're fucked, white girl.* A spiral of fear and disbelief ran through me. The only thing on my mind now was getting home, and fast.

My escorts walked me the remaining five blocks to my apartment. We didn't speak, we just walked—fast. We had to ride this only wave to get me home safely. I could feel the climate around me rising. The air was now saturated with distant and frequent yelling, expletives thrown out like exclamation points. Clanking, bottles breaking, fires smoking, this all took over the sounds of birds or cars or whatever the normal sounds were from our neighborhood. We were in a predominantly Black neighborhood and I wasn't sure what this would mean. There was a lot of commotion in my building, but there were no kids playing or screaming or laughing like usual. Once I stepped into the apartment, my mom grabbed me and gave me a huge hug. Gripping me, her face looked terrified.

"Where were you?" she asked frantically.

"I was playing basketball at school. Some Black lady just hit me on my back."

I told her about the two guys from the court who walked me home. Relief finally set in on her face. She was clearly distressed, but still distantly worrying about what this all meant.

"Are you okay? Where's your sister?"

"I don't know. Maybe at her friend Suzette's?" My sister had been secretly dating a guy named Raymond, who was from El Salvador and didn't speak any English. Her best friend Suzette had introduced them. I felt a lot of pride knowing my sister's secret. My mom proceeded to call Suzette's house and spoke with her mother—she was able to confirm that Sam was safe at her house and would stay there until her mom felt it was safe to drive her home.

The news was playing in the background. The beginnings of the Reginald Denny beating were underway. I watched live as Reginald Denny was pulled out of his truck and beaten to a pulp. He was a white man in his early thirties, a construction dump driver who had a delivery that day in Inglewood. He didn't have a radio in his truck, so he had no idea that as he made his way down Florence Avenue, his usual shortcut, he was going to be at the epicenter of an historical riot. His truck was stopped on Normandie, then he was pulled from it and beaten by four men. They threw appliances at him, kicked him, and slammed what looked like a ceramic lamp on his head. Blood poured everywhere and made his hair stick to his face. I'd never seen anyone beaten like this, in so much color. The beating was as real and awful as what those cops had done to Rodney King—their weapons and their power were different but powerful nonetheless.

I watched in horror, in fear, in sympathy, in understanding and hope that he would be rescued and the beating would stop. I was still feeling the sting of my own assault, though seeing this beating on TV distracted me from the bump growing on my back. I had nowhere to go, either. We had no car, and no friends or relatives who lived far away from these riots.

My best friend lived in North Long Beach, about eight miles from where I lived, and when I called her that night, she told me that her neighborhood was just as bad. I had been so used to being profiled as white and poor. Now I was white, poor, and the same as the oppressor by association.

When you're poor, you are discriminated against, but being poor *and* Black is a completely different kind of injustice in America. It was Black against every race now. Women were pulled out of cars and assaulted, old men were stripped naked and spray painted. There was so much deep pain and anger below the surface that it was now bellowing through the fibers of individuals, each on their own journey for justice. It showed itself in fist fights, looting, screaming, fires, surges of adrenaline and comeuppance. Yet, in all this injustice, there was a valuable lesson we were all learning: that there are those who are between the lines of what America represented. We learned what the in-between of social and economic justice meant, that those who were generationally recipients of bad promises and were put down for their reliance on public assistance were given the denial of a conviction—and this made our in-between society grab the line with both hands and pulled it down. They attempted to hang the biggest sign ever hung: "Without Justice, there is no Peace!" They were expressing their hurt in a destructive way, but it was more justified than the verdict. I could now see this injustice clearer than I ever could before. I could now feel the stinging on my back, a physical reminder of this lesson: *Be resilient.*

I couldn't leave my house or walk the streets of my neighborhood. Sirens, smoke, and looting surrounded our apartment. I couldn't walk outside without expecting a beating, so I didn't leave. If I *had* left the apartment, I could have been jumped or stabbed. Everything around us was chaotic. All I could live on was the news and a sliver of hope that this would be over soon.

It was three days before Rodney King went on television to ask for peace. I was really hoping for peace too, but when I looked outside our window and at our neighborhood, it didn't look like peace would happen. Finally, my mom had enough and was getting cabin fever. She was going to brave the outside and walk down a few blocks to the liquor store that the neighbors said was open. Why? Because she wanted some diet soda. I was on pins and needles the entire time she was gone, hoping that nothing would happen to her, thinking of her like I did my brother when he went out for groceries during the winter storm. She returned home safely.

Sam had finally come home, because Suzette's mom was brave enough to drive her to our house early that morning. Sam told me she had been staying with her boyfriend those past few days. When she was at Suzette's, it always meant she was with Raymond, too. They were so in love, from what she had told me. She swooned over him, telling me all about him while we laid in our beds some nights. She told me how cute he was; how he had brown skin and perfect white teeth, light eyes, dark hair, and a perfect body.

After she was home for a few days, Suzette called Sam to tell her that Raymond had been arrested during a nightly sweep of the streets. Suzette's boyfriend has been with him but he was able to get away. While Raymond was detained, the police found out he was here illegally. The protocol during the riots was to ship all illegals back to their own countries if they were arrested. Raymond went back to El Salvador, and Sam was devastated. From that point forward, she made it her mission to be reunited with him again—by any means necessary.

It was another two days until Edward James Olmos was seen on TV, helping to clean up the neighborhoods and signifying that the riots were over. I was so relieved to see him on television. I had seen him in *Stand and Deliver*, the 1988 movie about a relentlessly devoted teacher who believed in the inner city kids he taught more than they believed in themselves. He was the father you wanted, the mentor you needed. When I saw him on television, I knew that every race was watching and was being inspired by his actions and his words of peace. He was able to take the negative energy in the air and peel it away. He exposed all the layers of anger and injustice, he assured the world that they had been expressed, and ensured us that now was the time to heal. He called for no more killing. He was able to deliver this message with a broomstick in his hand. He was in the war zone in L.A., and he was brave enough to start to rebuild and inspire others to help.

Once I knew there were more people who wanted to help than wanted than to hurt, I knew it was almost over. Any more violence was going to be self-inflicted and defeat any efforts to heal the city. He asked us to think about what the violence was doing to our communities and toward other human beings. He pointed out the correlation between this violence and the human rights that were being fought for. By the sixth day, Monday May 4th, I was still not in school. This was now three days of absenteeism. My school decided to call, and it was Ms. Dardy, my basketball coach, who phoned the house. My mom picked up the phone.

"Yes, she is here, and safe," my mom assured her. "We have no means of getting her to school. Are you willing to come pick her up and take her home? Okay, yes, she'll be ready then. Well, she was attacked during the riots, but she is okay. Yes, the riots are the reason she has been absent. Okay, well I'm glad you understand."

When mom was on the phone, I worried that she might figure out my coach was a lesbian. I'd never wanted to mention that to her, for fear that she'd see her as a threat like she did men or that she'd accuse me of being gay like she did my brother, or worse, tell me I couldn't play basketball anymore. I wondered, *how will she react if she meets her?*

It was strange seeing my mom interact with someone from my school, even if it was just a phone call. At that point, she really hadn't been involved with anything. All the packets of papers you get at the beginning of the school year had long been filled out and forged with her signature by me, along with all the field trip authorizations and missed school excuses. She never took the time to be involved in those kinds of things.

This time, she was clearly communicating with the administration office and with my teacher, my coach. I was impressed by her engagement.

"Your coach is going to come pick you up in a few hours, so be ready to go back to school," my mom told me.

Knowing my coach was going to come pick me up from our apartment suddenly made me very nervous. Besides my best friend's mom, who would bring me back home from time to time, I hadn't been in anyone else's car. Being in a car—like, a real car and not the hoopty '67 Dodge Dart that had since been laid to rest in some junkyard—made me feel out of place. I felt there was a class divide that started with whether or not you had a running car, and then how nice that car was.

She's going to see where I live, I thought. *God I hope she doesn't want to come in.* Ms. Dardy showed up right when she said she would. I was waiting for her outside. There was no way I wanted her to see my house, or even my mom. My mom could see the front of the house from the living room window. Ms. Dardy rolled up in her green Honda Civic and rolled down the passenger window.

"Mary, are you okay? Your mom said you were attacked," she asked, the car still running.

"Yeah, I'm fine. It happened the day the riots started, when I was walking home from the basketball courts. The guys I was playing with walked me home," I explained, as I walked up to her car door.

"Okay, well, get in. We need you at school."

Need me at school? I thought. *Why do you* need *me at school?* I turned around to the window and waved at my mom, to let her know I was getting in the right car.

As I walked into the administration office, everyone was asking me how I was doing and telling me they were happy to see me. I was surprised. I had just gone through a pretty traumatic last few days, from seeing and hearing the riot from our apartment to fearing that someone would break in and hurt us. I suppose I was pretty shook up, and probably looked like it, too. I realized that my school cared about me. It was nice to feel that kind of love and attention from the staff and the other school kids. They were all genuinely concerned about how I was doing. They knew where I lived.

I was actually happy to be back on campus. Even though school could really be a battlefield for me, it was my home away from home. I came back different; I had felt the flexed power behind mobs of people and what can happen to communities when injustice and class wars go unchecked. I was in my community, my school, and I felt an acceptance that I'd never felt before.

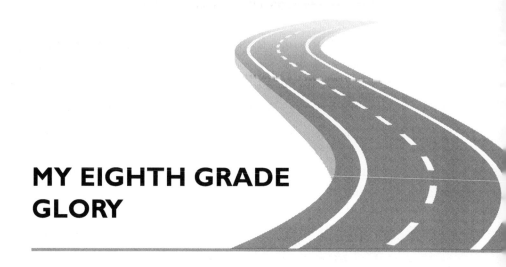

MY EIGHTH GRADE GLORY

I was skinny with long legs and big knees, and I had a cheetah run that made me unstoppable. I'd made great strides with improving my situation at school, as far as popularity was concerned. Wearing a jersey on game day helped a lot, too; it signified I was part of a team and had something going on. I'd even made a few allies with my tardy slip business so far that year. My love life, however, was no more improved than it was the year before.

The crushes I had often fizzled away when they got the girl they wanted. Honestly, I wouldn't know what to do with a guy that I liked if he had actually returned the affection. I was too awkward and insecure to know how to handle a relationship.

Meanwhile, Imelda, while not your typical beauty, was actively exploring her options and batting a thousand. She had already gotten the first kiss out of the way—with Gio. She had given up on her other crush, Seb, for a few months by then, and suddenly she was marketable. It wasn't too long before she had met a new guy and was going to second base, third base, then hitting a home run. This was devastating to me, because it made me feel bad at being a girl, let alone all the other things that made me insecure.

This affected our friendship, because now *anything* made me jealous about her life versus mine. Knowing she had kissed Gio burned me, because he seemed like the guy we both couldn't get. Now she *could* get him, so what did that say about me? The new friends she had made recently who could "relate" to her new adventures all turned out to be temporary friendships, but made me jealous of their kinship in the meantime.

I quickly realized that I now knew someone who had been *there*, who had *done it* and seen it all. Imelda had game, and I could use that to my advantage. I took some tips from her and worked on my flirting. I spent hours trying to get my wink down. I figured out which side of my mouth looked better to smile from and found simple ways to stand so I could show off my rump, which showed some promise.

It all paid off when I finally had a makeout session. Marcus had been playing basketball with me at the YMCA for about a year. He was a tall Black guy, slender, with a cute face and a pretty smile. He had small eyes with long eyelashes, which I found cute. He was pretty shy, so it took more work on my part to let him know I liked him enough to want to kiss him.

Our flirting took place in a racquetball court. We small talked about basketball, the latest game we'd seen, if either of us were seeing anyone, where we lived. We sat with our backs against the wall and stared at the far end of the racquetball court as our conversation softly echoed. The lights were only on for as long as you had turned the knob to keep them on, so suddenly they shut off. I figured this would help, I didn't think he wanted to kiss a girl with a facial deformity and missing teeth. I didn't blame him.

All I wanted was to get to this first milestone while being in middle school. I hadn't kissed anyone since Vegas, which didn't count because it wasn't a french kiss. I had practiced kissing on my hand, on a mirror, in the crease of my elbow, and my pillow several times before, so I felt like I knew what I was doing. I straddled him, sat on his lap, and leaned in for a kiss, not sure where to go because of the total darkness, but following the heat.

Wow, I am actually doing this.

What seemed like an eternity later, we both came up for air. I felt like my grin could be seen through the blackness of the room. I felt like one of the girls now. Monday couldn't come fast enough. I couldn't wait to tell Imelda what happened with Marcus, face-to-face, like she had told me about Gio or the other guy. When I saw her at school, I rushed to give her all the details of my weekend and "the kiss." She asked if she could come to the YMCA with me that next weekend, so she could see the guy in question. Part of me worried that Marcus would see her, and would prefer to give her his kisses. I told her that the weekend coming up wouldn't work out. But she and I did go together a few weeks later and she got to meet him. Luckily, there was another handsome boy there and she put her eyes on him.

DRIVE-BYS

We had been regulars at the art theater for a few years. One night, the movie *Zebrahead* was playing, a movie about an interacial couple and the stigma of it all. As we filed into our seats, I spotted my social studies teacher, Ms. Braxton. She was a slender Black woman who kept her hair short and wore both typical teacher outfits (warm colors and lots of layers) and African dresses with scarves, hair wraps, and beautiful jewelry. She was sitting with a white man who seemed to be her boyfriend, by the way they were talking and smiling at each other. That moment made her seem even more real to me—like a person, not just a teacher. She turned around and saw me looking at her; she seemed puzzled to see me there. It was a school night, and it was already eight o'clock. She was likely wondering why I wasn't at home. She didn't come over to say "hi," just briefly smiled and turned toward her date.

A few months later, I sat down in Ms. Braxton's first-period class. She had been crying and looked very distressed. She was trying to collect her thoughts as the bell rang. She said she wanted to make an announcement when class started. My mind thought about hate crimes and I wondered if something had happened to her or her boyfriend.

"Class, I want to share some bad news with you. It's very difficult to tell you all this, but we were informed this morning that Lance Timmons was shot and killed in a drive-by last night."

I looked around the room and saw all the Chola girls crying. Lance was in my first period class. He was a white boy with blond hair that he slicked back to craft a perfect pompadour. He dressed and acted like a Cholo. He hung out with all the Cholas, and though he only spoke a few words of Spanish, he always spoke English with a Mexican accent. He lived just down the street from me, and I always found it interesting that he was able to be accepted by the Mexican community. I wondered if perhaps one of his parents was Mexican.

I could still feel his presence in the classroom from just the day before. Even though I didn't know him well, I did observe him often. He was kind and never teased me. I thought about what it meant to no longer see him in school; what it meant to be killed. I pondered the pain and the blood and the sorrow of knowing everyone who knew you would be mourning your loss. I had a pit in my stomach. I couldn't cry; I didn't have that inside of me for him, but I was sad for him. I was sad because he was young, just like me, and he was one of the nice guys.

I tried to imagine what could have happened that fateful night. Why would someone have wanted to shoot him? I heard kids at school mutter that he was in a gang, but I never saw him throw up signs like the gangsters outside our school. Maybe he was in a different gang than them. Every class I went to that day, there was at least one girl crying. Every teacher was either sad or crying or had been crying that day. This was before the times when schools recognized that grief counseling was necessary during times of loss or great tragedy. There were no school shootings then, not like in today's time, but kids still died. Usually it was accidents or illness, but this was murder. Everyone had to deal with the loss in their own way, and a few of the Chola girls took a few days off school.

After about a week, it seemed everyone had forgotten about the killing. We got less scared to die, and we got back into our more selfish way of being.

NEW BEGINNINGS

Graduation day from middle school was full of mixed feelings. I had already signed up for the basketball tryouts for Poly High School's freshman team over the summer. I was going to have an orientation in just a few weeks so I could pick out my classes. My interest was in sports; nothing else really mattered to me. It was all a big mystery what I would be doing and who I'd be doing it with in high school. Imelda would be going to a different high school than me, the one right across the street from her house, so I wasn't sure what life would be like without my best friend. I'd have to find a new group of friends and a new dynamic without her at the helm. Though Kimberly and Silvia would be at Poly, it wasn't going to be the same.

Sam gave me reports about the new school. It had more people and more cliques than middle school. She said that races really stuck together. There were rich white girls who only wore shorts and sandals, metal guys who hung out by the trees, hippies who were in band or in art classes, and the Asian girls who wore their hair long and were all very pretty and thin. She said it would make middle school look like a picnic. She also told me that she didn't fit into any of the groups, and hung out by herself near the front gates of the school with all the rest of the outliers. I told her I would find a way to be popular and wouldn't end up sitting with her when I was there. I felt a sense of defiance. My eighth-grade year had been better than any year I had ever experienced. I was on a roll, or so I thought. But she insisted I wouldn't fit in and definitely wouldn't be able to achieve cool status.

That summer, we moved to a place farther east: 16th and Cherry. They were renting a failed commercial condo project to those with HUD. Apparently they couldn't sell the condos because the neighborhood wasn't nice enough for the customers they were looking to sell to. The neighborhood was far from gentrified. The bonus for us was that the apartment was more modern than we had ever seen before, with a large living room, two bedrooms, a nice hallway closet, and a master bedroom with a master bath. There was a balcony that looked out to the alley, and the back of the laundromat that was next door. A fake owl sat on the back of the laundromat's roof. We were closer to the art theater, too—now only twelve blocks away, to be exact. Our neighborhood got a little more diverse, as well. It was now a mix between hispanics, Blacks, Asians, and pacific islanders. Just north of us, about three blocks, was Signal Hill. South, about seventeen blocks, was the beach.

Paul hadn't been around before we moved, so Mom hadn't let him know where we would be moving to. She gave the neighbors upstairs our new address, just in case Paul came around and asked. The new place didn't have a room for him this time, either. With HUD, once you downsize your number of bedrooms, you can't ever qualify for that number of bedrooms again. Even though there were three of us still in the house, Mom decided to only take a two-bedroom apartment, so Sam and I took the master bedroom with the master bathroom.

My brother was already seventeen years old, nearly eighteen, and it was becoming rarer and rarer to see him. There were some talks I'd overheard about him moving in with our Aunt Evelyn in Texas. Those would sometimes be heated fights. Paul had wanted to move out of California and get back to Nashville, back to his dad. Since he didn't have the support from our mom, it seemed like his best chance of getting out of poverty (and off the drugs he was probably on) was to move in with Aunt Evelyn.

Paul's behavior when he was home was very erratic, and Mom thought he was on drugs. He'd come home in the middle of the night and sleep until the middle of the afternoon. He would sleep so deeply he wouldn't get up when he had to pee. That was usually when the fighting between Mom and Paul started. She'd yell at him for peeing on the floor, and he'd scream at her for being a bad mother. He'd usually leave the house while slamming the door and calling our mom a bitch. She'd swing right back and use her same old line and call him a faggot, "just like your father." She'd yell out to the entire apartment building that he was a piss pot, good-for-nothing son-of-a-bitch. I always found that insult amusing because she was de facto calling herself a bitch, but I don't think she got that.

To be fair, Paul wasn't looking good. He was barely topping 135 pounds and he was already six-foot-two.

Mom decided to ask her two sisters for help. Aunt Ruth was the closest to Linda in age, only five years older, and she still lived in her home in Tennessee. From what I knew, Mom hadn't talked to her since we left Tennessee for good, about eight years ago at that time. Aunt Evelyn bought a plane ticket for Paul to get to Texas. All Paul needed to do was get himself to the Los Angeles Airport. Once in Texas, he would live with Aunt Evelyn and she would help Paul get back to school and get his GED. Aunt Evelyn was a lawyer by profession, quite smart and strict, from what Mom told me. Aunt Ruth was a high school math teacher. Between the two of them, they were able to make anything happen, so it seemed. A few weeks after moving into the new apartment on Cherry Avenue, Paul showed up after getting our address from the upstairs neighbors in our old apartment. He was only at the new apartment for a night or two, then got a ride to LAX on the back of his friend's motorcycle, with only a backpack and ragged clothes on his back. Within a few hours he was living with Aunt Evelyn in Texas. *He did it,* I thought. *He got out.*

ONE FLIES OVER THE CUCKOO'S NEST

It wasn't long before our mom felt that she had made a bad decision. She hadn't really kept in contact with her family for the nearly nine years we had been gone, and she never spoke highly of anyone from her family. She still had Sam and I in the house, and with Paul turning eighteen and living somewhere else now, it wasn't going to be too long before she couldn't receive benefits for him. We had finally started receiving food stamps just a year earlier, and they were making a huge difference each month. We weren't having to stand in food bank lines anymore, either.

Every three months we had to send in a form to the Welfare office to let them know of any changes in our household. This meant that the next time Mom submitted her form, Paul's portion of the check and our food stamps would be gone. Paul hadn't really been benefiting from the money for a long while now, though I know he would have preferred his portion of welfare to continue, because he knew how much his resources meant to Sam and me. Our mom would usually hold back giving him even a little cash until it became an all-out fight and he would leave. Now that he would be officially off the government teat, reality was starting to sink in.

Late at night, I was awoken by our mother.

"Mary, get up. Get up, Mary. I need you to call Aunt Ruth and tell her to send Paul home."

"What? I don't know Aunt Ruth's number. I don't want to ask her to do that," I said, confused and tired.

"Get on the fucking phone and call her. She's taken Paul away from me. She's just going to send Paul back to Tennessee to be with his father. He's going to know where we're living. Tell her that I know what she's done."

Her face was dampened with sweat and tears, worry and fears. Clearly, she had been crying for hours while I slept. She would do that often; she would ruminate on one idea for hours or days, scribbling on pieces of paper she found in the house. Usually this was why we couldn't throw any papers away—almost everything that came into the house was used as her stationary. These papers were her records of events, of thoughts, of her streams of consciousness. Here I was, at the barrel end of one of her manic episodes, and the only thing I could do was go along with it. I picked up the phone and dialed Aunt Ruth's number. I was about to get on the phone with someone I hadn't talked to since I was six years old, and who I had stolen quarters from before we headed out on our travels through the unknown.

Ring. Ring.

"Hello, is this Linda?" my Aunt Ruth asked in a soft, southern accent. She sounded surprisingly like my mom.

"No, this is Mary. Mom wanted me to call you. She told me to tell you that she knows what you've done and that she wants you to bring Paul back."

I read the script Mom had scribbled on the back of an envelope.

"Mary, your mom has called the house about ten times tonight. I'm sorry she's having you call me. I told her that Paul wanted to move to Nashville to be with his father. I am helping him get there from Texas, but Paul has earned the money himself by helping Evelyn around the house. Please tell your momma that, Mary."

I let out a big sigh before I turned to Mom to explain what Aunt Ruth had just told me.

"She's fucking lying!" Mom screamed at me.

I knew this was just one of Mom's dark moods, but now I was in the middle of what seemed like a strange dream. I had been in these before; a part of me was always scared of being woken up by the craziness that was my mom's mind. The accusations would fly, the conspiracies she had worked out in her mind—everyone was out to get her, or had bad intentions, and no one could be trusted, especially the nice and friendly ones. My mom snatched the phone from my hand and began crying and screaming at my aunt through the phone. Once it seemed I could get away and back to my room, I did—and locked the door. Sam had been at her friend Suzette's for a sleepover, so I was alone during this episode.

Paul leaving had been a real change in our mom's life. She had spent so many years running from our family, hiding our whereabouts from everyone. When it seemed someone got close, we would run somewhere else. This was one of her own children who was now gone, and she was mourning his loss in her own way. Maybe she reflected on how she treated him? Maybe this was overpowering her, and she had to blame someone? I learned that trying to understand her rationale was futile. I knew why Paul left, and I understood why he wanted to get away from our mentally unstable mother and to be with a parent who wanted him, not just one who used him as a punching bag or a meal ticket.

I locked my door and closed my eyes, and wished for it all to go away. I wished like I did when Mom said the brakes were out in the Dodge. I wished that I could fall asleep and wake up and it would all be over. I could hear the screaming and crying in the living room, but I hoped she would leave me alone for the rest of the night.

I'd heard the voice of a relative, and it was comforting to me. It had been so long since I had imagined it possible to have family outside of the small circle of four that Mom made us believe we had. I closed my eyes and dreamt of what this meant. Paul had flown out of this Cuckoo's nest—and maybe I was next.

SOPHOMORE YEAR

I'd wanted to be part of the cool crowd. I had spied a few of the groups I wanted to hang out with. The grunge kids, who had flannels wrapped around their waists and holes in their jeans, looked like *my* group. I tried to look cool, and would venture near the groups I wanted to hang out with, just far enough so they could see me, but not close enough for us to actually talk. I wasn't getting anywhere with these groups. Even my basketball teammates wouldn't hang out with me outside of practice or games. I was still mostly hanging out on the benches near the front gate, like Sam warned me I would.

One day, I ventured around the campus at lunchtime. I walked to the track and sat on the bleachers. As I was sitting there, I heard one of my old friends shout out, "Mary!"

I turned around. It was my old friends, Silvia and Kimberly from middle school. They had been spending most of their time in high school huddled up in those bleachers everyday during lunch. A lot of our old middle school friends were there too—like Imelda's crush Seb Baker, and the guy Tiffany Taylor liked, Michael Alvarez. I didn't have any classes with them and, being on a campus as big as Poly High, you could almost never see someone you knew if you didn't have a class with them. I'd been so wrapped up with basketball freshman year that the whole year seemed like a small pause between classes and the court.

I was also part of a focused school program called The Beach Academy. My freshman year was the first year the academy started. It was for kids that didn't score high enough for the PACE or CIC programs, the programs for the overachievers, but who scored higher than the average kids in math and science and thus showed promise. They promoted a concentration of these subjects. It was the beginning of STEM. A lot of my classes were not in the same part of the campus as the rest of the kids in my grade, so it wasn't surprising that this was the first time I was seeing my old friends.

Silvia was going to have her quinceañera soon, and she had invited Imelda to be in it. They were going to perform the special dance as part of the celebration of Silvia coming into young adulthood, as a fifteen-year-old—a woman. Silvia hadn't asked Kimberly or me to be in it, but we also weren't Mexican. I was a blonde-haired, blue-eyed, skinny, toothless tomboy, and Kimberly was a half-Chinese, half-white girl with giant boobs and two left feet. We were *not* going to fit in at a Mexican quinceañera as dancers, but we were invited nonetheless, and that's all that mattered to me.

Silvia confided in me that she had a boyfriend and his name was Carlos, but that her parents couldn't know. I knew her dad was really strict, and if he had found out, she wouldn't be able to have her party. Carlos was in the dance as one of the *chambelanes*, the men who dance with the girls, who are *damas*. He acted like he was just a friend of one of the other boys in the dance.

Imelda and Silvia looked so beautiful in their white dresses full of flowers and accents. Imelda never wanted a quinceañera; she was too Americanized. Imelda's mom was at the party too, and came with Imelda's little sister. As the party went on, I got to meet Silvia's boyfriend, Carlos. He was a handsome guy. He was here in the country illegally, but spoke good enough English that I wouldn't have known. Carlos and I hit it off and started sneaking Budweisers from the cooler once the traditional dances were over and the mariachi started. It didn't take much for me to get drunk, and soon I got up and danced. By the end of the night, Carlos and I were walking drunk through the house, knocking things over, and Silvia's mom and dad were not happy. I ended up sitting on the couch and waiting for a ride home from Imelda's mom. When she dropped me off, I was able to walk straight into the apartment and go to my bed before Mom was any wiser.

The next week, I saw Silvia at school and she told me how upset her parents were that I got drunk. They said I was a bad influence on her, and that I wouldn't be able to go back to her house again. She and I laughed, because little did they know *I* was the innocent one. Silvia told me she had been ditching school to stay at Carlos's apartment just down the street. This seemed really grown-up of her, and I was impressed: she really, really was a woman now. She told me she was going to ditch school the next day, and asked if I wanted to join them. I had never ditched school before. I had never really thought about it. My world revolved around playing basketball, looking for ways to eat, dodging insults, and trying to fit in. There wasn't really any time for shenanigans.

The next day, I waited for them outside of her boyfriend's apartment about twenty minutes before school was going to start. Carlos's place was behind a carwash. Just at the time I would have been walking into school, Silvia and Carlos led me into his apartment. It was a small studio apartment, not too big. There were clothes lying on the floor next to a mattress. I could see a pair of Silvia's underwear next to it. He put on the TV and we sat, watching and talking. Silvia seemed a lot different now. She was never the rebellious type, but she had had her dad's thumb on her for a long time now, and it made sense that she was tired of it. I wondered what would happen to her once the school called her house to say she wasn't there. When I asked her about it, she smiled.

"You know my parents think you're a bad influence on me, right?"

"Yeah. Having a few beers and breaking a small figurine makes me bad?"

"You don't know, Mary. You don't understand. My dad will always have a bad opinion of you. If I get in trouble, I'll just say it was you who told me to skip school."

I was just her scapegoat. If and when she got caught for skipping school, she'd say it was because of me.

Carlos ordered pizza, a small prize for my agreement to be the bad one. I left his place and headed back to school, having forged a late note to give to the attendance office.

I wasn't getting anything out of this arrangement. I had missed school and basketball practice, and none of this made sense for me. I felt betrayed by Silvia. But as I walked into school, I felt like I had gotten a little more wise. I had gotten a glimpse of what it was like to get older and what you would do to see your lover, about what it would take to hide a romance from your parents. I had seen that some people can be willing to sacrifice a friendship for love. These dramas seemed more interesting than going to school and following the rules. I could see the allure, but this life of love wasn't for me—at least not yet.

"Chameleon skin is filled with tiny crystals called nanocrystals and when they move their skin by relaxing or tensing up their bodies, the crystals shift and reflect light differently. Shorter wavelengths of light, such as blue, are reflected when skin is relaxed, and the iridophore cells are close to each other."[10]

Part 3

TRAVELS THROUGH BLUE

Paul had moved to Nashville to stay with our father Jack. After not seeing our dad for nearly ten years, Paul now lived with him and his lover Felix. Felix was only five years older than Paul. Dad told Paul that when he sold the house after Mom left Tennessee, that the courts put Mom's share of the profit in an account, and it was managed by a court-appointed trustee. There was almost $15,000 in the account, and Mom only had until the end of the month to claim it before it would go back to the state as part of unclaimed assets. Paul called the house to let Mom know she needed to get to Nashville, and fast. Within a few days, Mom's sister Ruth, graciously purchased Mom a Greyhound bus ticket to Nashville.

Mom said it would be a three-day travel trip, but she would make it in time to claim the money. She left my sister and me at home alone. It was actually the first time we were ever left alone for an extended period of time, and I was looking forward to it. Before she left, we went to the small Mexican market down the street and picked up some quick-and-easy food; a few boxes of mac and cheese and some Mexican-style rings to fry into fritters that we would drench with hot sauce and lime juice. Then we bought some sugar, tortillas, tomato sauce, and rice. We were hoping this would be a week's worth of food. That night, our mom went on her way, taking the city bus to the Greyhound station. Mom called the house on her second day into her travels, complaining about the riff-raff on the bus, but also content that they stopped often enough that she could stretch her legs and pick up snacks from gas stations.

When she arrived in Tennessee, my brother wanted to see her; it had been almost six months by that time, so they met at the courthouse. After she got the money—fifteen individually wrapped stacks of ten hundred-dollar bills—Paul drove her to a car lot, where she bought a blue 1992 Nissan Stanza for $2,500 in cash. After just one day in Nashville, she started on her way home in her new car. Paul had made sure Dad wasn't around when he met up with Mom, and he later told me Mom had only thanked him for driving her around, not for informing her of the cash. She asked him how he was doing and kept the conversation superficial. But Paul knew that telling Mom about the money meant good things could happen for us girls, and he hoped we'd know he was looking out for us.

By the time Mom got to Texas, she took a break and ended up getting a motel room and taking a shower. It had been five days of travel. I was starting to miss her, and it was lonely not having her home. She called us when she was just another twenty-four hours from the apartment. That morning, Sam and I were very excited and had the house completely cleaned, and wanted to show her that we had been responsible while she was gone. We knew that for the first time in six years, we were going to have a running car. It was only seven o'clock in the morning when Mom arrived at the back gate of the apartment complex. We leaped down to the garage to open it for her after she honked a few times. There was a manual switch inside the gate that we could hit, since we didn't have a clicker yet. She drove in with her blue car—a nice compact four-door, and more modern than our old Dart. Sam and I looked at each other in amazement. This was our family car!

The car hadn't been cleaned in all of Mom's traveling, so Sam and I ran upstairs to grab a few trash bags, some dish soap, rags, and a bucket. We eagerly filled two big trash bags full of trash—mostly drive-through takeout containers, gas station snack bags, and beverage cups and bottles—and cleaned the outside of the car. It was the first time that we were able to truly see ourselves as a little more normal; we had a car, by God, and it was newish! It had been a long time since we had been driven to school in a car, besides the handful of times when my mom had the Dodge Dart and we were in elementary school. We were always taking the school buses or city buses. Since Mom got to the house early enough, she could actually take us to school that day. We really wanted nothing more. As we got in the car and Mom started driving, we realized a few things that we had forgotten in the time we had been without a car. The first was that she drove very slow. She also had a very short attention span, so while she was driving, she would stare at things and point or turn her head all the way to the side as we passed them. It could have been shops, people, houses, anything at the side of the road, causing her attention to stray from her driving. Lastly, as she approached a light, even if it was green, she would slow down in anticipation of having to make a decision to go or stop. Getting to school that morning was more frustrating than I had envisioned, and Sam and I spent most of the time asking her to pay attention to the road or speed up to get through the light.

Besides having a car now, Sam and I couldn't believe all the money that was in our mom's purse. She had twelve stacks of $1,000; I counted them. She intended to keep the money in her purse, on her, and nowhere else. It was pretty scary knowing someone could snatch the money from her at any time, but she kept it around her neck and across her body, and held one arm over it tightly. We all had never seen that much cash before. And as she dropped us off at school that morning, she reached into her purse, and gave each of us a twenty-dollar bill. *Wow,* I thought, *I can actually buy snacks at break time and buy soda, or even eat at the burger joint next door after school.* Mom had also told us that after school we could go shopping at Kmart.

I wanted a shopping experience over an after-school hangout, and I wished the day would go by quicker. Finally, Sam and I piled into the car after school, and Mom took us through the Rally's drive-through. We each got burgers and seasoned curly fries, and I got a root beer. We always called these meals menus instead of combos, though I'm not sure why. We then drove up through Signal Hill all the way to North Long Beach to Kmart. We had gone up there quite a few times before to put clothes on layaway during Christmastime—how Christmas gifts happened for poor kids—but once we got there, it looked like a completely different store. Nothing about the store was different, but the feeling that we could actually buy anything, that felt different. Sam and I eagerly grabbed at the cart handle, the vehicle we would drive to experience *real* shopping. It was so exhilarating. Going up and down the aisles, looking at home furnishings, artwork, dishes, towels, bed sheets, pillows; all of these things were on my vision board, the way I had dreamed of decorating my room and our house, and now we could actually buy them. When we saw something we liked, we'd look at our mom and say, "Can we get this?" Her answer was nearly always, "Yes, you can get it." I was hooked. I had never experienced this in my entire life. I did not know what it was like to be able to buy things without worrying about what it would cost, or having to give up what I wanted for something more practical.

We ended up buying two lamps for our side tables in the living room; each had a clear base and were filled with beautiful light brown and beige seashells. Some were long and spiraly, and others were wide and flat, and some were just round. But they were all sizes; from big to teeny tiny. We also bought a big rug for the living room with large brown, burgundy, and beige swirls all over it. It felt modern and homey all at the same time. We bought a set of pots and pans, dish towels, and toiletries. Real towels, not the ones we had been using that had holes and were frayed at the ends, thin from overuse. Sam and I each got a new pair of pants, shirt, shoes, socks, underwear, and bras. This felt amazing. When we got to the register, it became clear our mom didn't think about what it would look like to pay by pulling out a wad of hundred-dollar bills. So she dug into her purse, clutching it tightly while she pulled out one bill at a time. We had spent almost $500. The people behind us were rolling their eyes and sighing. It felt like an eternity before she had finally pulled out the last bill. Finally, we could go home and set everything up. From the moment we pulled into the garage, Sam and I lugged the bags upstairs, walking briskly up to our third-floor apartment several times until all the loot was safely there. Then we went around the house like fairies, setting everything up, making it just so, and then marveling at the sense of normalcy this brought us. The house felt fresh and clean and full of possibilities.

My mom believed that if she deposited the money into a bank account that the bank would report that back to welfare, that we would lose our benefits and they would take all the money. Because she was paranoid about this, what we were able to do with the money was limited. Our mom had never had this amount of money before, and she didn't quite know what to do with it all. Because she couldn't deposit it anywhere, it would have to stay on her person at all times. She practically slept with her purse. Everything was paid in cash, and every time she paid for something, she clutched her purse tightly and dug deep into it to pull out twenty- or hundred-dollar bills, one at a time. But with this much money, we could finally plan a trip back to Tennessee to get my nose fixed.

Paul had actually also given Mom my health insurance card when she was down there, and assured her that it was active. It turns out that my father had been paying for health insurance for us kids the entire time we were gone, just in case we needed it. Of course, I didn't know that until the moment when Mom pulled my card from her purse, like a bill she had dug out, and waved it around like it was the answer to everything. She seemed happy to go back and finally get the surgery we'd talked about for years, to repair my nose. I asked her how Paul was doing, but she only said that he was "okay." She didn't acknowledge his efforts to bring the money to her attention, or how thoughtful it was to bring me my health insurance card, but I was thankful. I was more than elated to go back to Nashville, and I felt that my dad had been answering my prayers. I was finally of the age that I could get the surgery; I had just turned fifteen years old that summer and had worked my first summer job. All those years thinking about finally fixing my nose and my dreams were finally going to come true. It felt like fate.

Mom made a few calls to Tennessee to set up the consultation and surgery date with Dr. Temple. She was able to get it scheduled in just three weeks' time. I was on the junior varsity basketball team at Poly High School, and during the time I would be gone, I was going to miss a lot of practice and the annual retreat to Poly North. This was a camp that all sophomores went to and learned about other cultures and about tolerance. I figured it would be good for my classmates to go because there was a lot to learn in this area for many of them. Even though a part of me was sad I would miss it, there was nothing I would have wanted more than to get my nose surgery. I gave my counselor the dates that I would be gone, and told my coach and teammates. Mom and I made arrangements to make the three-day trip to Nashville by car.

Sam would be alone in the apartment, but she was about to turn seventeen that December and was already pretty independent. Her boyfriend Raymond was still in El Salvador. She had already saved most of her money—a whole thousand dollars—from her summer job to help get him back into the country. She was already almost a fluent spanish speaker by then, too. Sam was taking Spanish in high school, and since she had a big reason to learn to write it and speak it, she immersed herself. She would write Raymond letters and even buy phone cards so she could call him. She had set up her own P.O. Box so that his letters didn't come to the house either. Keeping her boyfriend a secret from our mom was her top priority.

The night that Mom and I set off, we had gotten a late start. Mom had a Thomas Guide that we were going to use to help us get to Nashville. The guide was a printed, spiral-bound atlas that broke down the roads and freeways for the entire country—the analog version of a GPS system. In those days, there were digital devices offered by companies like TomTom and Magellan, but they were very expensive. A Thomas Guide was the more frugal option. From 1915 until 2014, many Americans used these books to navigate roads and plan trips. I had once used my Thomas Guide to get to the Santa Anita race tracks with my friend Richard's father,

George, and Richard's wife, Evangeline; he insisted I reviewed the guide and knew our route before we got on the road. George taught us how to bet on horses that day, too. But I never used it for any other trip in my adult life. Unfortunately, my mom hadn't actually read the guide before we got on the road; she just plopped it on my fifteen-year-old lap. She had just come back from Nashville, so I thought that maybe she knew she just needed to go in the opposite direction. However, she didn't have a good sense of direction, nor did she really know the freeways, so she just left it up to me, like she did with my brother when we left Nashville for good. That's how we ended up in Long Beach in the first place; she just went where it felt right, but she put all the pressure on Paul to help her navigate the roads. So as we got on the freeway, I took a fifty-fifty guess on whether she should go north or south. Then about an hour into the drive, I realized we weren't hitting the 40 East, as the Thomas Guide said. I turned to her and asked her if she knew where she was going.

"Mary, you have the Thomas Guide. You tell me," she said plainly. I paid close attention to the signs and was able to trace where we were. We were going north on the 405, not south. We had to turn around, and had lost two hours. She turned to me, "Mary, it's already late. Maybe we should go back to the house and leave in the morning." Frustrated, I said, "No, I want to keep driving. I want to get to Nashville." I had been waiting too long for this. I was determined to get there.

RONALD MCDONALD HOUSE

This was the first surgery that I was getting done since I was three years old, so I couldn't remember what it was like to have a surgery.

It took us nearly four days of travel to get to Nashville, Tennessee. My mom was afraid to drive over fifty-five miles per hour, so driving through Texas felt like an eternity. Though some would argue there's no fast way through Texas. Mom would only listen to Bonnie Raitt's *Luck of The Draw* album, and we did so many times that her song, "Something to Talk About" felt like people *were* talking. She and I would belt out those songs while driving through the country and I was thoroughly enjoying this road trip. Whenever Mom would get nervous from driving the rough terrain, I'd calm her down with conversation. When we finally reached the city and I saw the Nashville signs, my heart felt like it had come home.

My mom had found a place for us to stay before and after the surgery. It was called the Ronald McDonald House. This was where everyone from out of town who qualified for financial assistance stayed while getting their procedures. It was a community-style facility, where we ate all our meals together and all the living spaces felt like someone's home. There was an outside patio where at least half the people who stayed there went to smoke.

Since we were there about three days before my surgery, I had enough time to go out there and give every adult a hard time about smoking.

The first meeting with Dr. Temple went great. He talked about how he was going to build a bridge for my nose by using cartilage from the back of my ear. He was going to fill out my lip a little by using fat from my belly button, too. That seemed all very interesting to me. All I really wanted was to have the surgery as soon as possible and to start looking normal. My teeth were another issue, and he recommended we visit a local dentist. We did visit one, but the magnitude of work needed to get my teeth fixed, which would also require braces, just wasn't doable on that trip.

I would later spend seven years as an adult getting additional reconstructive surgeries, oral surgeries, dental implants, and braces in order to complete the repair of my cleft lip and palate.

The day of the surgery, I couldn't have been more excited and nervous. We arrived at the hospital at 6 a.m. They hadn't let me drink anything since the night before, so I was beyond parched. I laid there in the bright room, with my mom holding my hand while waiting for the nurse to come in to get me ready for surgery by starting an IV. Mom was nervous that her baby was going to have surgery, but I was thrilled. It was surreal to know that everything I had hoped for, the day I would get the surgery to fix my nose, was finally here. The nurse came in and gave me all the pricks and pep talk I needed. She told me I would start to feel like it was nighttime and that I would fall asleep as soon as I counted down from one hundred. I thought that this seemed strange, that I would just fall asleep like that by simply counting down, like adults said counting sheep worked, because I had tried several times and that mostly didn't work. I looked at my mom and said goodbye as the nurse started to push me out of the room and walked briskly down the hall. As I was pushed into the surgery room, I felt the high from the cocktail they'd given me kick in, the bright light in the room seemed to pull me in closer, and for a quick moment, it felt like I had died.

The next thing I knew I was awake and in a lot of pain. I couldn't remember ever experiencing this amount of pain before. My first instinct was to put my hand on the area that was hurting. As soon as I did, another surge of pain came over me. Someone's hand lifted mine off my face and told me not to touch it. But like a blind man, I tried to slowly feel around my face, slowly caressing my nose, which had a hard metal brace around It. I could feel the prickly mess of the stitches at the base of my nose. I was, in that moment, both in the worst amount of pain I had ever experienced, but also having a moment of exhilaration knowing that there was a new me under all of this.

My brother knew that I was having surgery, and so did my dad, because the surgery was on his insurance and he had received notices of authorization. They had both bravely come to the hospital to see me. I could hear my mom at the door to my room talking to someone.

"Mary is okay. You don't need to come see her," she said to someone outside the door.

"I'd like to see her, to see how she's doing," a soft male voice said, faint though deep.

"No, she's not seeing anyone," my mother told the person and closed the door to my room.

"Who was that?" I asked her.

"That was your brother and father. They wanted to see you," she said.

"I would like to see Paul and Dad. Let them come in the room, Mom," I told her softly.

"No, I don't want your father to see you," she told me, starting to labor her words as she got more anxious and seemed to be preparing to have an argument.

"I haven't seen Paul in over a year, Mom. At least let me see him. We wouldn't be here if it wasn't for him." I started to cry. I was so close to seeing my brother and my father, just a few feet away. I felt like I was floating, my father's hands on my chest and face, about to dip me into the water. My pain somehow disappeared, and all I yearned for was the sight of him. She insisted that she wouldn't budge, and I cried even harder. The swell of sadness and pain felt like I had pushed the stitches out of my face.

This drew a line in the sand between my mom and me. I vowed that I would get out of her control as soon as I could. That I would come see my family as soon as I was able. She was just being mean at this point.

There was no reason why she was keeping me from my brother, from my father; this was all out of spite. I saw that clearly now. She was a spiteful person, and that was why we had been running from everyone my whole life. She knew she had us kids, at least two of us, that she had some control over, and she wasn't about to let it go. It pained me that I had been used like that. I then knew I would never ever respect someone who would use their kids for power plays. It would take me another five years until I would see my dad. Unfortunately by then, my dad had already changed. He was not the guy I would have met that day in the hospital.

MUSINGS: WHAT MY MOM GAVE ME

Years later, I had a thought while driving to work on the 710 freeway. I realized something positive that my mom gave me growing up. Of all the things that she didn't do, she always supported all the wacky and creative ideas I had.

I think she saw me as the same type of creative person she was, but I was smarter than her, and she didn't want to limit my creativity. And I have come to realize that she did support those dreams of mine and always told me that I could do anything. So in that sense, she helped to create my sense of optimism. And I want to thank her for that.

THE PAIN
PERSPECTIVE

After surgery, my nose felt ten times its normal size. It throbbed, and there was a deep pain that traveled through my entire face. Every word I would utter hurt. Eventually, while lying in the hospital bed, I felt an overwhelming feeling of nausea come over me, and asked my mom for something to throw up in. She quickly handed me a plastic bedpan, and I proceeded to throw up all the blood that had dripped down into my stomach during the surgery. I was shocked at what came out. After almost a quart of blood was out of my body, the nausea went away. I swirled a little bit of water around in my mouth, barely able to spit. The drugs they gave me at the hospital worked well enough to keep me from screaming in pain, but I couldn't really fall asleep. Thankfully, the next day we left the hospital and went back to the Ronald McDonald House.

Once we got through the door, I headed straight to our room. The curtains were drawn, and it was dark. I immediately curled into my bed to sleep. The pain started to wane as I drifted off. It felt like moments later that my mom was calling my name, "Mary, Mary, get up. Mary, we have to go eat dinner. Mary, you can't stay in bed. You have to get up."

"Mom, why are you waking me up?" I asked her, confused. This had been the first time I had slept in what had felt like forever. The pain of my surgery was starting to come back.

"Mom, I barely slept. Why are you getting me up?" The tears almost instantly started to well up in my eyes, partly because of my annoyance and partly because of the pain.

"The woman that runs the place said you have to come to every meal here. This isn't a hospital, she told me. You have to go out and eat with everyone," she explained. I was angry that I couldn't just lie there in bed. I asked my mom for a pain pill. I took it with a sip of water and got myself into some clothes. As I walked the long hallway to the large open kitchen, my face was starting to feel like a water balloon. As I got closer to the kitchen, everyone in the room came into focus. All the different people we had gotten to know the first few days there were all sitting at the long table in the kitchen and had already begun to eat.

When I walked in most of them took a moment to look at me. My only way to save myself from this embarrassment was to put my head down and go sit down where my mom told me to. The only thing was that having my head down made my face hurt. The blood and edema was pooling into my nose and made all the insides of my face feel like they were filling up like a bathtub. I had to lift my head. I did so slowly, allowing the blood and all the fluid to settle back into place. My face throbbed. It felt like a snowglobe, with little pricks and pains appearing and disappearing all over my face like little snowflakes, and also like my face was encased in a fluid bowl. I peeked at my plate and acknowledged that I wasn't sure how I was going to eat my food. I could barely swallow water, let alone chew food. "This kind of pain is normal after a maxillofacial reconstructive surgery," I was told. "It's just gonna hurt." I peered down at my green beans and potatoes. Each bite took a bit of artistry, fork on plate, slowly rise to mouth, open mouth a little, put fork in mouth, close mouth slowly, pull out fork, slowly chew, take a sip of water. Phew. Repeat.

My face was pounding, and little drops of edema and blood were flowing out of my nose around the nostrils, which were now almost completely closed up with dried fluid. I had to chew quickly because it was getting harder and harder to breathe. I'd slowly wipe the drops from my nostrils, never really getting it all. The bright lights were making my head pound, so I kept my eyes slightly closed. This was feeling like a living nightmare. I was despising the woman that ran the place. Why couldn't I have had just one night to sleep? But I got through a few bites and asked to go back to the room to sleep. My mom looked over at the women who ran the place, and with her nod, I slowly got up and walked myself back to my room to lie down and wait until my pain medicine kicked in and I could fall asleep.

As I laid in bed, I thought about a couple we had met there. They were having their first child. But there was a problem with their baby; he had a hole in his heart. After my surgery, she went into labor and was at the hospital that night giving birth. I knew that because I overheard other people talking about it at the table while I was trying to eat. I had never heard of anyone ever having a hole in their heart. I thought about myself, how I wasn't perfect, and here I was now having a surgery to fix what was wrong with me. How I was old enough to go through the surgery. Even though I had my first surgery when I was a few months old, it was never a life-or-death situation. I was now worried for them and their soon-to-be newborn baby boy. I wondered how he was going to have an open-heart surgery, being so young. He would be so tiny. I laid there thinking of them, and this helped me fade into sleep.

The next day when I got up for breakfast, I sat there at the table and the woman's husband came in through the back kitchen door, looking very tired, and sat at the table after having grabbed a hot cup of coffee. Everyone wanted to know about his son, and he went on and on about how beautiful his baby boy was. He said he looked totally normal, and it was hard to believe he needed heart surgery. There was a photograph he passed around the table. Everyone agreed that his son was the most beautiful baby they had ever seen. A few days later, they both came home without their baby. The heart surgery had not worked, and their son had died. It was so hard for the house to take. Everyone expressed their love to the couple with hugs and words of condolences. The wife was so sad, still recovering from the birth, likely missing the bundle of joy she had been holding to her body the days before. This put my pain in perspective. In some ways, I felt I had no business giving them condolences. I was just a child. But I hugged the wife and cried into her bosom. I told her how sorry

I was and how handsome I thought her son was, that he would always be known to have been that handsome. She smiled, caressed my hair, and pulled me into her. I felt loved and safe, and I didn't have as much pain anymore. I realized then that being held and having a space in someone else's heart, that helped with pain and dulled it some, even just enough to get you through another day.

One of the men who frequently smoked on the outside patio was going through chemotherapy. He was scheduled to get all his teeth removed that week. He said the extractions were recommended by his doctors to help with the repercussions of chemotherapy. I remember him coming back from surgery and sitting at the dinner table, just like I had after a surgery, full of pain but having to be there. How could he eat anything? All of his teeth had been removed. He sat there, just as I did, and made his best effort to eat something. I believe it was Jell-O.

There was also a woman with ovarian cancer. She was only thirty-three years old and was going to have to have a hysterectomy. I recalled how skinny she was, and I wondered if the smoking had something to do with both of their cancers. These were all learning experiences. We were all going through something quite traumatic, life changing. We were complete strangers going through the same thing together.

UNPACKING

After five days, I was able to get my nose brace off, and I would finally see what my nose looked like. I'd had a lot of swelling and two huge black eyes from all the pressure from the brace and fluid. Before we went to Dr. Temple's for my last appointment, Mom and I had picked up a thank-you card. We handed him the card before he was to remove the brace and dressing. He seemed truly touched as he read it. He said that he had remembered me when I was a baby and had always hoped I was doing okay. He was happy that he could work on me. I told him that I had remembered him, too, and that I had always known his name, that Mom would mention him as the one who worked on me as a baby. I'd learn years later, as I read papers from Mom's boxes before throwing them into the fire, that Mom had asked him to be part of her divorce proceedings as a character witness.

Dr. Temple had me lie down on the table.

"I'm going to take the brace off your nose, Mary, and you might feel really sore all of a sudden. But don't worry about that. That's normal." He pulled off the brace. I immediately felt the cold air in the room envelope my skin. He pinched either side of my nose. I'm not sure why, but it hurt.

"Now, I've got to take the cotton out of your nose. We call it packing, and it's used to help keep the nose in the shape we want after surgery. It may hurt a little, but it will be over soon," he said. And I believed him. He put some tweezers near my face and gently pulled at the cotton. The pull was slight at first, then it turned into a tug, and then it felt like he was ripping out my brains. I gasped in shock and belted out, "Oowe!" Tears streamed down my cheeks because the pain was so sudden and intense.

"It's okay Mary. You're okay." He quickly hovered over with a nasal sucker and pulled out what seemed like more of my insides. I could suddenly breathe through my one nostril. More than I ever had before, and that was scary and progressive.

"Now, Mary, I have to take out the packing from the other nostril. I just want you to relax. I promise I'll be quick." I took in a few deep breaths, and he started to pull out the cotton slowly, like he had on the other nostril. The same sensations came over me, and I again belted out, "Oooowwwwweeee!" He held the packing in front of my face, like you would a child after being born. It was at least eight inches long, and he said, "This was in your nose, Mary." I stared at the bloody cotton, dripping with fluid and redness and goo. He sucked out my other nostril.

"Now sit up, Mary. I want you to look at yourself," Dr. Temple told me.

I pulled myself up and turned myself around to face him. I took a quick glance at my mom, who was smiling. I also recognized faded terror at what had just happened to me, but she was trying to put on a good face. The doctor handed me a small hand mirror. I slowly pulled it up to my face. I started to cry. I hadn't seen myself ever look so normal. I had a bridge; my top lip was fuller and less concave. I turned to the side and saw that my nose was straighter, too.

I still felt like I had been punched in the face as we walked out of the doctor's office, but I was starting to feel that these were new beginnings. It was strange to see myself in the mirror, but each day I was feeling better. I was able to wipe away all the dried edema and blood from around my nose, which still pooled and dried every few hours, but less and less each day. I'd carefully wipe around my lip where I had small stitches from the fat injection. Each day, this new face was more normal to me.

CALIFORNIA FIRES

It was 1994, the Altadena and San Gabriel mountain fires occurred in California. Everyone was watching the fires on the news. It looked like all of California was on fire.

"Isn't that where you two live?" a southern woman asked my mom while she pointed at the TV in the communal living room.

"Yes, we live in Los Angeles, but those fires aren't close to where we live in Long Beach," my mom explained to her.

"Well, all you Californians are too accepting of everybody. At some point, God's going to come down and fix things like this. He's going to burn the whole place down and you'll have to start over. It's full of heathens," the old woman professed as if she was witnessing God's work. We didn't speak much more to her, but I was in shock, appalled even. I didn't know why she thought California was full of heathens. Sure, there were a lot of people of different cultures and we had openly gay communities in Long Beach and San Francisco, but heathens? From the South's perspective, us Californians were just a bunch of lowlifes getting what we deserved. Hellfire and damnation, I suppose. I saw such ignorance and lack of empathy from that woman, and I felt strange looking at my state of California on fire while standing in Tennessee safe and sound. Though Tennessee was my birth state, I realized I was a Californian now.

I was worried about Sam, though. The fires burned for days, and from the way it looked on TV, all of California *was* on fire. But when we called her, she said she was fine and that the fires were nowhere near her. That was reassuring.

ON THE ROAD
AGAIN

Traveling back to Long Beach felt like an eternity. I was no longer in pain, but I was still swollen, and the black eyes I had after surgery had turned into yellow rings. We'd spent over a week in Nashville, and with nearly four days to get there, we had already been gone for almost two weeks. I wanted to get back home and go back to school. I was also excited to see what some of my friends thought of the new me. After the drastic surgery, I almost looked normal. My teeth still needed to be addressed, but if I didn't smile with my mouth open, I didn't look too bad.

Three days into the travel home we were going through Arizona, only half a day away from Long Beach. It was late, and we were hoping to get some food at a diner. My mom took an exit, and before we left the off-ramp, our engine died. We only had enough power to pull into a gas station around the corner. As we pulled in, a man walked outside.

"Ma'am, can I help you with something?" he asked.

"Yes, my car just died coming off the off-ramp. I think I'm going to need a tow," she explained. I looked around, and there were a few other cars that had just experienced the same fate. Their owners looked perplexed at what happened; there was one family of four with two small kids and another car with just a couple. Maybe there was some kind of electromagnetic field set up to trap motorists? It was far-fetched, but looking around at the time, it seemed plausible.

"All right, just go ahead and turn it on." Without thinking, Mom sat back in the car and tried to turn on the car. It wouldn't turn over.

"Haha, I'm just kidding, lady. I know your car won't start," he said while pulling on his suspenders. Oh, man. As we looked around, tow trucks started showing up.

"Well, ma'am, I can call AAA if you want. They can tow you one hundred miles back to California," he explained.

"I don't have AAA," my mom told him.

"Well, I can tow your car to the local car mechanic in the morning. They can fix your car right up. Otherwise, AAA is gonna charge you seventy-five dollars for every ten miles." We didn't really have a choice. However, in hindsight, it would have been cheaper to take the tow back to California. My mom still had about $10,000 in her purse, so she thought about it for a second.

"Okay, you can call us a taxi so we can get to a hotel for the night, and we'll leave the car with you, and I'll call in the morning to see where it is," she told him hesitantly.

We got a hotel room that night at a local Super 8. The next morning, Mom called the gas station where our car had broken down, and he gave her the mechanic's number and address. Later that morning, we took a cab to the mechanic's. When we got there, it felt like a sham. My mom wasn't even the slightest bit knowledgeable of how cars worked, and they could probably recognize a few suckers from a mile away.

"Listen, it looks like your timing belt has broken. We'll need to fix it, but we don't have the parts for your car. It's going to take a day or two to get them," he explained.

"How much will it cost to fix the car?" my mom asked.

"Well, you also need a tune-up and an oil change. It's going to be about $2,000." I was shocked to hear that amount, and to know that we had a few more days in this podunk place. I gave my mom a little nudge. She looked at me while I whispered to her, "That's a lot of money. Are you sure we can't just tow the car back to California?" She paused and thought about it.

"Okay, just order the part," she told the man. We went back to the hotel room, and I just sat around watching TV. All I ate over the next few days was fast food and Sugar Babies from the vending machine down the hall. My stomach started to get really bad cramps. At first I thought it was because of all the candy, but the pain was sharp.

"Mom, I've got to go to the hospital," I told her. It was already getting more and more painful. The cab that picked us up smelled like an ashtray. The smell of the car and my stomach already turning inside out made me feel like I was in a bad dream. The rundown hospital didn't help matters. The lights were dim, and there was hardly anyone there. We stood at the counter and waited for someone to come. I was bent over by that point. We were there a little while before an older woman with brown hair and pale green scrubs walked up and asked, "Do you need some help?" The nurse handed my mom the clipboard of papers and motioned to where we should sit. I sat in a chair next to my mom, hunched over in pain. I'd never experienced a stomach pain like this before, not even when I'd overeaten all my Halloween candy, which I often did. We waited another thirty minutes before I went into the back to see the doctor.

"Okay, put this on," she said as she handed me a gown, so I got undressed, laid on the table, and waited for the doctor. He walked in, greeted us, and got down to business.

"Let's make sure it's not appendicitis," he said as he removed the blanket I had on me and pressed on my stomach.

"Okay, Ms. Bernhardt, has your daughter ever had sex?" I laid there looking at my mom, my eyes wide.

"I haven't," I answered him.

"She hasn't even had her period yet," she told him.

"You are pretty skinny for your age, and you must be a certain weight before you start your period. But you could have cysts in your ovaries. I'll want to examine you," he said.

I looked at my mom, thinking, *What did that mean?* I'd never had a visit to a gynecologist before, and let alone a *man* look at my private parts. But because the pain was so bad, I figured I had nothing to lose. A few minutes later, he came back inside the room with a nurse. My mom stood near the bed, and I put my legs in the stirrups.

"Okay, so I'm going to be gentle, but this could hurt just a bit. I need to put this inside of you so that I can see what's going on inside." As the metal slid inside of me, I could feel a weird pressure.

"Yes, I can see you're still a virgin." The nurse next to him smiled. He slid out the metal piece and placed a finger inside of me, moving it around to see what he could feel. He was holding my stomach down to see if I was feeling pain there. It hurt indeed, and since I'd never had someone put a finger inside of me, I wasn't sure what the sensation was.

"Okay, so she's probably got a few cysts, which is what's causing her this pain. I'm going to give you some pain medicine. Have her take this prescription, and she'll feel better in a few hours. These usually come and go, but once you start your period, you'll probably feel this pain on a monthly basis. Just put some heat on your stomach and take some Tylenol, and you'll feel better," he explained plainly. "Any questions, Mary?" I didn't know what to ask. I just wanted to put my legs down and cover myself up.

"What about the swab you took? When will we get those results back?" my mom asked.

"Tomorrow. I was checking for STDs, but your daughter is clearly a virgin. I'm not sure we need to worry about that," he told her. I felt a little embarrassed that everyone in that room could verify I still hadn't had sex, but I suppose this wasn't the worst revelation my mother could hear.

I began covering myself up while the adults talked a little more. I was actually starting to feel better. Something about the doctor poking and prodding my insides had relieved some kind of pressure.

The next day, we received the call from the mechanic that we could come get the car. After Mom pulled out the last hundred-dollar bill to pay for the $2,100 costs, we walked to the car and loaded it up with our things. We were on the road again, finally.

BACK TO SCHOOL

It was strange walking onto the high school campus knowing that I looked different. I was waiting in anticipation of what others would think of me. My first period was basketball, so I headed to the court early, before anyone else got there. I hadn't played any sports for nearly four weeks, and I needed to get myself in shape. I'd developed my first jelly roll while I was gone. I didn't think I could get fat, but there it was, looking at me. I tossed a few balls, ran a little. I wanted to take it easy at first, to make sure I wouldn't get smacked in the face with a ball. As the girls piled into the gym, the first one to see me was Tiffany. "Mary, you look great!" she exclaimed and went in for a hug. I couldn't help but smile. A compliment from Tiffany really meant something. As the other girls came in, they gave me a few high fives and pats on the back and said they were happy to see me. I asked them about Poly North, and they all said it was amazing and that the exercises they did helped everyone understand each other better. As we were warming up, the coach came up to me and told me that I could sit out if I needed to.

"No, I want to play. It's been too long since I was on the court," I told him.

"Well, if you need to, just let me know," he offered. I assured him I would.

The first warm-up with just a circle of five girls. We had to pass the ball to each other, making the circle bigger and bigger and passing the ball harder and harder. Suddenly, after just a few passes of the ball, Tiffany threw one directly at my face. I tried to catch it, but I only slowed it down a little. The ball smacked me in the face, hitting my nose. It hurt, and the pain made my eyes water and my face flush red. I held my nose and asked if it was bleeding.

"No, it's okay, Mary," one of the girls told me. But I ran out of the gym holding my nose, not sure what the damage was. What had I done? Why did I miss that toss? Why did the basketball have to hit my nose? *All that trouble to get the surgery was for nothing,* I thought. *It's going to look just like it did.* I panicked as I ran to the girl's locker room and stared in the mirror. Nothing had changed about my nose. I was just red from crying. I examined myself from all sides. I was relieved I hadn't broken it or messed it up. I decided then to take the coach's advice and sit out a few practices so I could heal up. That was too close a call for me.

THE NEW ME

I'd been going to school for several months with my new face. I was starting to have the courage to talk to people in groups, the ones I had only looked at from afar. The grunge scene was in full swing at school; all the cool rocker kids wore flannels and listened to Pearl Jam, Stone Temple Pilots, and Nirvana. I wanted to hang out with that crowd, too. A few months before the summer break, I mustered the courage to ask one of them what they were doing over the summer. There was a guy who had been watching me walk home after school for about a year. I would walk just along the fence that led out to 21st Street, next to the football fields. A lot of kids that had cars would leave through the back exit to avoid Pacific Avenue traffic. This guy's friend drove him in his '70s VW Bus, and every time they drove by, he stuck his head out of the window and stared at me, smiling, not saying anything. I thought he was cute. He made me giggle with embarrassment, but I enjoyed those moments immensely. He was more of a hippy than a rocker, but I liked that.

One day, as the bus was driving as fast as I was walking, I asked him what his name was. He said it was Greg, and I told him my name.

"We go to some drum circles downtown. Come check 'em out," he said encouragingly.

"Okay, I will," I said without thinking to ask where exactly these drum circles were held. There was no way my mom would let me out of the house at night anyway, but I wanted to show my enthusiasm nonetheless.

But the summer was coming up, and I was going to get a job through the Summer Youth Employment Training Program (SYETP) again that year. It's a program for low-income families to give their kids the experience of working in different trades, which kept us motivated to stay in school and also allowed us to have a productive summer job that paid. Otherwise, most of us kids wouldn't have an opportunity like this to learn job skills. I was taking full advantage of it and worked at the Belmont Plaza Pool again that year. Sam had worked the previous two summers there, but this year, she was going to work at the police station, so I likely wouldn't see her much that summer.

The kids from the summer program hadn't seen what I looked like now, the *new me*. The year before, a lot of the guys had made fun of my face. One of them even said I looked like a dog. I had mostly ignored them because, overall, most of the kids were nice. I also had the benefit of working with my sister that year, so none of them wanted to get her upset. Now that I had my surgery, I was starting to feel like I wasn't such an eyesore. Before, I had learned how to cover my mouth when I smiled and to tone it down a little so that I wasn't caught with all my snaggle teeth out in pictures. After, I was getting used to people glancing over me without staring and laughing. I was getting comfortable in my own skin, with this new face.

That year, just like the year before, my basketball team had won the championship for our team level. I'd played exceptionally well each year and was looking forward to making the varsity team my junior year. My grades, however, weren't that great, and I was having a hard time keeping a GPA over 2.0. Math was getting harder for me, and so was science. I just didn't have the focus. I was hoping the summer would help me reset and I'd come back stronger the next year.

SETTING MYSELF FREE

That summer, I would be turning sixteen, and I was looking forward to enjoying the fruits of my labor, meaning I could buy clothes and have spending money like my sister did. It was going to mean a lot to me to have money. It would give me options I'd not had since the previous summer. Even though our mother was walking around with over $10K in her purse, we never considered that our money. She held on to it tightly.

I loved my work that summer. I was learning to be a lifeguard and getting certifications. Each day, we began with swimming 500 meters across the large olympic-sized pool. We learned how to rescue people in the water, how to perform CPR, and each day, we were given breakfast and lunch. We had two hours of classroom time each day, then most of it was outside running along the beach, swimming in the ocean, and getting into shape. I ran along the beach in a swimsuit, creating tan lines like you wouldn't believe. By the end of the summer, we would all have our certifications in CPR. I felt proud of the work I did through the program, and how my body was shaping up and forming curves. I was responsible for getting myself to work each morning, each day starting at 7 a.m. I rode the beach cruiser I'd bought with the $100 I found in a liquor store a few years earlier to work each day. I'd ride all the way up Cherry Avenue until I hit Ocean Boulevard. Then I'd head over to Junipero Avenue and take the hill all the way down to the bike path until I got to the Belmont Plaza Pool.

I made $4.25 an hour. My first check that summer had been a whopping $245. It meant a lot to me to hold that check in my hand. I had earned that money. Because we'd never had checking accounts growing up, I was used to cashing a check and holding on to the money. I cashed this check and then took myself straight to the Del Amo Plaza in Compton. My sister told me I could buy really cheap clothes there, and that I'd love the fashions. I hadn't ever been shopping on my own, so I didn't know what to buy or how to shop. I bought a few pairs of pants, tops, and bras. When I got home, I realized that the pants I bought were just a tad too short and the bras were too tight around my ribs. I was already five feet, ten inches tall and had a size nine shoe. I was an A-size cup, but still wider around than the bra I bought. Sam was barely five feet, four inches tall and a B cup, so the fashions she spoke of didn't quite translate to my frame. I was all legs, no curves, and finding pants was harder than I thought it would be.

I waited until the next check to go shopping at the Long Beach Mall downtown on East 5th Street. I knew that mall really well and had grown up walking through its halls and looking at all the clothes and shops and arcades for many years. It was a wonderful place where they used to have runway contests with pretty girls, and give away cars during Christmastime. Sam and I got our ears pierced there when we were in elementary school. There was a huge fountain right outside of the old Bloomingdale's, and I'd sit there and stare at all the sparkly change sitting on the bottom and wonder who got to clean it out and take home the money. But this time was different. I could actually buy things.

I called my best friend Imelda, and Kimberly, and asked them to go to the mall with me. I'd wanted to get a helix piercing, a cartilage piercing located along the upper ear. A lot of kids at school had them, and I wanted to take a step into the direction of *cool*. Imelda had already gotten her helix pierced, and she said it was going to hurt a lot. I braved it and went into one of the cheap jewelry and gun-piercing stores in the mall. I would later learn the art of body piercing and how using a gun is the worst way to get your ears pierced, especially cartilage, but I was young and didn't know any better.

The first shot in my ear was extremely painful. My whole ear heated up with blood and pain. Both of my ears are different; one has a small flap at the top, like someone dogeared a book page. The cartilage on that ear is slightly thicker, too. When it was time for my dogeared ear to get pierced, I hunkered down in anticipation of the pain. My eyes widened as the gun pierced my skin. Within a few moments, it was all over. I was proud of my new piercings.

After that, we shopped around in Mervyn's, a more mainstream store for teenagers and skateboarders. They had clothing like flannels and black T-shirts with skateboard logos on them. Kimberly helped me pick out my first ever flannel. It was blue and black. Next we went to Hot Topic, the kind of store only the coolest metal and alternative people would shop. They sold band T-shirts, piercing jewelry, fishnets, bracelets, chokers, and blared the latest grunge music inside the store. It was cool. It made my stomach get tight when I walked in because of what it meant to shop there. You were shopping on the dark side; even if you weren't cool outside of that store, you felt cool inside of it. I looked around at almost everything. I bought a few small bracelets and a necklace.

When I got home, my ears were burning. I did my best to cover them because now that I was home, I calculated that there could be a chance Mom would overreact to my new piercings. I had come to realize that anything that we showed her that she saw as us growing up or being independent scared her. Sexuality scared her, and she was always overprotective and wanted to keep us from expressing it or being around it. That's the reason why Sam had been hiding her relationship with Raymond for so long and why she had been squirreling away money for close to a year and a half to somehow get him back to the U.S.

Sam had gotten a job earlier that year as a waitress at a restaurant called The Grinder on Broadway and Cedar Avenue near the Long Beach Police Station and Public Library. We used to go there when we were kids after spending the day at the library. We'd get their clam chowder and sprinkle little clam-shaped crackers on top and take big warm bites that would heat us to the core. It seemed almost surreal that she was working there, since this had been a place we ate when we were new to Long Beach. She'd even had a job on the weekends helping a mobile animal vaccine truck. Just like when Paul was her age, she always found a way to work. She went to school, did her homework, and went to bed early. She was living a different life than Mom and me, and she kept her life mostly a secret. She and I did walk to school together some mornings when we didn't have money for bus passes that month—which happened often—or when she didn't have swimming classes that started at 6 a.m. But she was focused on seeing Raymond again, on getting him back, and I believe that's what kept her motivated and working hard.

THE SUMMER OF LOVE

After a few more paychecks, I decided to go see a movie with Kimberly. She had a boyfriend now. He was a handsome, skinny Latino guy with long black hair that he kept tied back in a ponytail. He had a big smile, and he was smart, like her. He was also a little strange, very shy, and they kept their relationship pretty quiet because he was a few years older than her. I had made arrangements that weekend to meet her at the AMC Theater on Pine Street. I wanted to see *The Little Rascals*. I had grown up watching the show and thought it would be fun to actually see the movie and go to the theater with a friend to spend my own money. Little did I know this day would change my life forever.

I had gotten to the movie theater at least an hour before the movie started. I waited at the Johnny Rockets restaurant—a '50s-style diner that served burgers, fries, and shakes while the staff burst out in song every hour or so—near the ticket booth. I was expecting Kimberly to show up any moment, so I got us a seat at the bar. After forty minutes of waiting, and one chocolate shake later, I decided to buy my ticket and go watch the movie. By the time the movie was over, it was already close to 7 p.m. I decided I'd take the bus to go home. I'm not sure why I did it, but instead of going to 1st Street, where all the buses go in Long Beach before heading out to their different routes, I decided I would walk to 4th Street and take the bus that I remembered my mom taking when I was younger. She once got a student loan from the bank on that corner, and I remembered I could take that bus to Cherry Avenue. I walked right out of the theater and headed up 3rd Street until I hit Long Beach Boulevard, then I took a left until I hit 4th Street. I was in the mood to stroll through the neighborhood. I was a little peeved that Kimberly had ditched me that day, so I had a bit of frustration to fuel my curiosity. The streets were dark, and not very many people were walking around. When I reached 4th Street, I took a look up the street, and I could see warm light coming from a building next to the bank's parking lot. I was pulled into the light, and knowing I had a few bucks in my pocket, I wanted to see what it was all about. I walked up to the front door, and a friendly person greeted me. I realized it was Imelda's friend Alex; he was sitting in front of the door with a money box on a small card table, collecting door fees.

"Alex? What are you doing here?" I exclaimed. Surprised to see a familiar face on such a dark street.

"Mary!!" he screamed. "What are you doing here?"

I began to tell him my plans that fell through with Kimberly and that I wasn't sure what I was doing there.

Imelda had gone to Jordan High School with Alex, which was in the north part of Long Beach. Alex had been in ROTC with her, and they had become fast friends. He had been dating a girl from their ROTC classes, but the last party I had gone to at Imelda's house, I had observed him being a real asshole to his girlfriend. "Mary, you have to come in. We're having a drum circle. You're going to love it!" he exclaimed. I had remembered Greg, whom I was intrigued by at school, had told me about drum circles, but I didn't know where to find one. It looked like one was dropped in my lap.

I was drawn in by the soft lights, the smells, all the eclectic artwork, postcards, books. The coffeehouse was called Living Planet and was owned by an early-thirties Black-and-white gay couple. As I stared at all the new sights and soaked in all feelings of a new place, I was overwhelmed by it all. I felt a small pull in my stomach. I knew this was going to change me, and I was looking forward to it. Alex had stepped away from the door by then and waived the two-dollar door fee for me. He wanted to show me what he had been up to since we last saw each other.

"Do you want a cafe latte?" he asked, eager to impress me with his barista skills.

"Sure, I'll take whatever you want to make." I didn't know what I had stumbled into or the names of fancy city coffees. There were tables all around, and the lights were low, just bright enough to see the register and the stage. There were all kinds of hippies sitting around the stage, each holding an instrument. Either a drum, tambourine, or cow bell, you name it. Everyone seemed to be smiling and in a good mood. I hadn't seen this many white people in one place since I had gone to church. I wasn't sure what was happening, but I ran with it. I ordered a cake that had been wrapped in cellophane and sitting near the register. I took my coffee and snack and sat back outside with Alex.

"So how long have you been working here?" I asked him.

"Since the beginning of summer. I met the owners in a club out in L.A. a few months back, and they asked if I wanted to learn how to make coffee and work here. It's all under the table, but it's been a lot of fun," he eagerly explained. I was impressed. Alex was speaking fairly flamboyantly now, more so than I remembered. He opened a pack of Marlboro cigarettes and lit one up. I sat there speechless. I had smoked cigarettes when I was in elementary school with one of the girls Sam and I walked home with after Myesha and Keya had moved. Sam and I would even roll up tea in paper and pretend to smoke cigarettes. But that was experimental. I hadn't thought about that time until right then.

"You want one?" Alex asked me while holding out a cigarette.

"Sure, I'll take one," I told him. Without any hesitation, I grabbed one and lit it up. I was clearly going all out tonight. We sat there and talked and caught up. Before the drum circle started, he told me he had come out of the closet recently. That he had met a couple recently that had given him his first experience. That they were very gentle and liked him a lot and then he started working at the coffeeshop. There was a guy that would come to the drum circles, Scott, who really liked Alex but hadn't come out of the closet yet, and Alex wanted me to meet him. Scott was much older than Alex, by about ten years.

As we sat there and talked, time flew by. Before I knew it, the drum circle had started. I sat around the circle and got lost in the music. I had never seen anything like it. The rhythm of the circle, the beats, the way it made my body want to move. Before I knew it, I was standing up in the circle of women and men who had been brave enough to dance. I'd lost all control over my body; I only wanted to move with the beat. At some point, the beat lessened, and I glanced over at Alex. He was sitting near the entrance, just staring at me. Sweaty and high on the euphoria of dancing, I walked over to him.

"That was so great. I've never danced like that before," I told him while I panted.

"We do this every Friday night. Next week, we'll have a lot more people here. This was just the first week we were kicking it off this summer." Maybe this was the drum circle I had heard about from Greg, and maybe I would see all the cool hippies and grunge guys I had seen at school. Maybe this was it. That thing that propelled me into the cool kid crowd. By the time I got home, it was close to 11 p.m. The TV was on, and my mom was asleep. I slowly creeped in and started to feel nauseous. I ran to the restroom and threw up. The nicotine from all the cigarettes I'd smoked, all the food I had eaten, and all the fancy city coffee was the perfect cocktail, and I felt the effects of these substance overdoses.

The next week, I was there early, almost as soon as I got off work from the pool. Alex and I had made plans to hang out before the circle started at 8 p.m. We mostly hung out at the coffeehouse, and I got to meet all his friends. One of the guys was named Justin. He had long blond hair tied up in a ponytail. He was a college student and had been taking photography classes at Long Beach City College. He was nice, but quiet. I also met the owners of the shop, who were nice and pretty people, Vincent and James. They explained how they got the realistic-sized tree in the middle of their coffeehouse—a local artist had come in and built it. The leaves and the trunk looked so real and gave the "Living" to the coffeehouse's name.

As sure as 8 p.m. came around, so did the cars full of hippies and high school and college kids. As their vans and buses and cars parked in the bank parking lot, the smell of weed wafted in the air. I recognized many of the vehicles as the ones from school. I felt my stomach knot up as a few of the guys got out of their cars and recognized me. This time, they actually came up to me to say "hello," to actually talk, not just a drive-by "hi." I was mostly shy and speechless, but I gave them a "hello" and introduced myself. I had worked on my flirt a little, and gave a few of the guys the eye, a kind of quick wink I'd practiced in the mirror. It was a good substitute for smiling, I thought. I still wasn't brave enough to go over to their cliques and puff on a joint with any of them, but I engaged in conversation when they spoke to me.

I let the night unfold naturally. I met the guy Alex had a crush on. Scott had short blond hair, a raspy voice, and pockmarks on his face and neck from bad teenage acne. He was shy and smoked Marlboro lights. Once the coffeehouse closed, and after I had danced the night away in the drum circle, Scott took us over the Vincent Thomas Bridge to San Pedro to hang out by the seaside cliffs. I'd never done anything like this, spending the night talking, listening to the waves crash against the cliffs. But there was only honesty that flowed from our mouths in the dark moonlit night. Scott told us about how he had felt like he was gay for a long time, that he had just gotten out of a relationship with a woman that he was going to marry. Alex told him that he liked him, and they began to kiss right in front of me. I sat there watching them, thinking about how my own father was gay, and how it must have been liberating to finally be who he wanted to be. Maybe he had had someone like me who he came out to?

We sat there on the cliffs until the sun came up, all huddled together, keeping warm and talking about our insecurities. I thought that I would be in a lot of trouble if I didn't get home soon. So Scott drove me back to Long Beach. After, Scott and Alex were going to go home together, the start of something new. I opened the gate to my apartment building and stood just outside my apartment, staring across at the horizon and noticing the mountains for the first time. Just in front of my gaze was another apartment building, but up beyond that was Signal Hill. I stared at the hill intently, waiting for a moment before turning around and opening the door to the apartment. I was going to walk into either my mother sleeping, or worse, another psychotic episode.

I slowly opened the door to find my mother on the living room couch, awake. "Where the fuck have you been, Mary?!" she exclaimed.

"I was with Alex. We went to San Pedro. I'm sorry I was out late." It all spilled out at once.

"Who is this Alex? I was up worried about you all night. You smell like cigarettes. Have you been smoking?"

"No, I haven't," I lied. I assured her I wouldn't do that again, stay out all night without a phone call. I walked into my bedroom and closed the door. I hoped that she wouldn't press any further. I laid on my bed and thought about the amazing night I'd had. The beautiful and open conversations about real stuff, feelings, deep feelings that I could understand and were changing me. These were real revelations about ourselves, and I was actually witness to the beginning of a gay love affair. My life was starting to become more about how *I* directed it and not how *she* directed it.

Mom had grounded me and said that I couldn't do anything but come home after work and definitely couldn't do anything on the weekends. I'd never actually been grounded before, and the concept seemed funny to me because it meant Mom was somehow being all parenty. Part of me indulged her, as the idea of having a typical disciplinarian mother appealed to me. Though after a few weekends at home, I had to find a way to hang out with my friends.

My friend Kimberly had gone to the *Rocky Horror Picture Show* at the art theater just a few weeks before. She said it was wilder than I would have ever imagined and that I should come with her. She explained that all the virgins, the ones who had never been to the show before, had to let people write the letter "V" on their foreheads and other vulgarities as they stood in line for the show, which didn't start until midnight. That was the rite of passage for anyone seeing the show for the first time. At the end of the show, all the virgins had to go on the stage and show their underwear. One virgin would be picked, and then the cast came out and danced around you all seductive-like. This actually scared me because I wasn't sure if they would actually know I was a virgin.

I called Imelda and told her that I wanted to go and that she should come with me. We planned a sleepover at my apartment for that Saturday night. I thought I would be slick and told Kimberly to call my house to say that Imelda and I needed to meet her up the street to give her back something I'd borrowed from her. Imelda and I simply planned to not come back to the apartment. Instead, we would walk the twelve blocks up to the art theater. I figured it would be worth the punishment to be able to get out and have some fun. But this didn't all go as planned. Kimberly called us from a phone booth just a few blocks up from my house; that part went perfect. Then I hung up the phone and proceeded with the lie. My mom refused to let me leave the house, then she told Imelda that she couldn't leave either. In response, Imelda told my mom that she couldn't keep her at the apartment. She called her own mother and had her speak with my mom. After Mom hung up the phone, she said Imelda could go, but I couldn't.

Admittedly, my mom had never really met any of my friends other than Imelda. Mom wasn't ever really part of my outside activities with friends, and since we didn't have a car for a lot of years and the house was always a wreck, I rarely ever considered my place as a meet-up location with friends. I always had to find my own way to see my friends at their house or in other public places. In fact, I had to remember all my friends' parties, all the social occasions, because my mom was never in charge of our activities or tracked anything like a family calendar. When I was fourteen, I had missed the birthday party Imelda planned in Shoreline Village because I had forgotten all about it. Sherry had come by to tell me that the church had paid for a viewing of the WWF Championship game and was going to play it in their auditorium that afternoon. Since we never paid for cable program specials like that, I was excited and wanted to see the fight, especially since it was going to have a showdown with Hulk Hogan and Andre the Giant. Once the Championship game was in my head, I had forgotten all about my previous obligations. It was only after I had watched the final match that I realized I had forgotten

Imelda's birthday plans. I rushed from the auditorium and ran toward the Long Beach Promenade, where I saw Imelda, Kimberly, Silvia, and a few others from school. Imelda was sad and almost didn't talk to me when I ran up. I apologized for missing her party. I told her that I'd forgotten, which was partially true.

But that night I planned to sneak out to see *Rocky Horror Picture Show*, Mom was against my plans, and it seemed that she was more than aware of what they were. I was miffed as Imelda walked out of the apartment door to go meet Kimberly. I stormed into my room and slammed the door. *Who was this lady stopping me from having fun with my friends, now all of a sudden concerned with my social calendar?* I thought.

MY REFLECTION

A few weeks later, I ventured out to the Living Planet coffee shop again. Things had cooled down at the house, and I was able to go out on the weekends without restriction. While there that afternoon, Justin asked me to be his subject for a class photography project. I wasn't sure why he was asking me, but it seemed as if he saw something in my tall and lanky form. He said he wanted to do the photoshoot the next day at the coffeehouse. I agreed. Immediately after I told Alex, he took me to the mall to buy makeup.

"You have to be pretty, Mary. If you get this foundation, you can cover up those zits on your face." He ended up buying me a liquid cover-up by opening a Bloomingdale's card right on the spot. I stood there while he filled out a credit application where he said that he was twenty years old. They didn't check his credit, or even ask for an ID; they just entered the information into the computer, and bam, he had a $200 credit line. He seemed to know what he was doing. We picked up a few more things, some powder and a few shirts for him, then we were gone, and I was ready to be photographed the next day.

I met Justin that following Saturday afternoon. We went to the basement of the coffeehouse, which was larger than I expected it to be. There were a bunch of old tables and chairs and different kinds of equipment peppering different areas of the floor along with what seemed to be four or five living rooms' worth of furniture. I felt like I was in an underground parking garage but with less lights and a lower ceiling. Being just barely a sixteen-year-old girl and fairly self-conscious, I was excited and honored that he had picked me as his subject, but I was also scared shitless in this basement. He pointed to a '70s couch covered with orange and green floral patterns. There was a small desk lamp sitting on a side table next to it. Justin handed me large headphones that were attached by a long spirally black cord to a Walkman that I placed over my ears. I had on a little brown-and-white sleeveless top that was only long enough to cover just past my ribs. My stomach was exposed. I had on long blue jeans that buttoned just under my navel. I wrapped the spiral cord around my finger, and I marinated there with my head tilted to the side and imagined that I was listening to the most beautiful music. There was no music coming from the Walkman, but I was charmed by having it on my lap and thought about all those years ago living in New York and desperately wanting one for my birthday. Justin took about thirty or forty shots. I was comfortable yet uncomfortable at the same time. I didn't know how to be a model, and I certainly didn't know what I would look like once these pictures were printed. I'd had very few pictures taken of me in my life, and many of the ones I had seen I only moderately liked. It was quite exhilarating to know that someone looked at me as if I was beautiful in some way. They didn't see just a deformity; they saw the entire package. And while I laid there posing, I felt like the total package, too.

A few days later, Justin came back to the coffeehouse to show me the prints from the photo shoot. I was blown away. They were black-and-whites, and I hadn't seen photos of myself in this style before. I didn't realize that my body looked so nice or that the cheap jewelry on my wrist looked so pretty, or that my face had a nice moon shape to it. I looked peaceful while I listened to the nonexistent music on the Walkman. I began feeling an attraction toward Justin the photographer. A few days later, he invited me to go to a show with him in LA, and he invited a few other drum-circle friends from the Living Planet. I felt like I was maturing and that I could hang out with these people outside of the coffeehouse.

As we walked up to the club, I carried myself in a way that said, "I'm old enough. No need to check my ID." The bouncer looked at him, and then at me, then motioned for us to come in. Luckily, I got to experience a time growing up when checking IDs was a lot more relaxed of an activity. As we all walked in, Justin's friends called us over to a large table they were holding for us near the stage. They welcomed us, and we all introduced ourselves. I got a huge rush from this moment because this was the first time I was in a club meeting adults like this. I was dressed pretty cute in my go-to hippie top from the photoshoot and my long beige Calvin Klein corduroy pants I'd gotten at the local thrift store. I noticed Justin's friends look at him, and then at me, then at Justin again, but I wasn't sure what their glances meant. Justin asked me if I wanted to have a beer, and I said yes. He got up to grab beers for us, and I sat with the other hippies and started talking to Justin's friends. I made an effort to pay attention to their conversation and interject interest when it seemed appropriate. They were all at least five to seven years older than me, but I tried not to be too worried about that. We were all here to have a good time and listen to music, and I didn't think they would mind the age difference too much.

Justin was back fairly quickly. He put a cold beer in my hand just as the rock 'n' roll band started to play. The music coursed through my body, and I felt like I was experiencing adulthood through every bang on the cymbal, strum of the guitar, every chorus belted out, sweaty hair tossed back, and beat kicked on the drum.

After the band performed, we all left in different groups. Justin dropped off the other coffeehouse hippie friends at their place and then asked if he needed to take me home. I told him that it would be nice to hang out with him at his place. By this time, I had become a dabbling pot smoker, as all aspiring hippies were; though I never bought it, I hung around those that did. So when we settled into his room, and he asked if I wanted to smoke some weed, I was more than happy to take a few puffs. I began to relax, and I asked him if he would give me a massage. I was being bold, and though he looked happy to do it, he was also a little reluctant. I didn't know what I was doing, but since I was treated like an adult all night, I wanted to act like one now. I insisted that my back was tight and that I needed a massage. I took my top off and my bra, and laid on my stomach, my arms by my sides, waiting for a massage. After a few moments, I felt him reach over to grab his massage oil. I heard the top click open and the sounds of him rubbing oil between his palms. I had never had a massage before, but I knew that asking for one and getting one was very "adult." He started touching my back, and his strong hands on my skin created a heat I hadn't expected. All of a sudden, I was warm and relaxed. The mood was mellow. Bob Marley was playing on his stereo. I took in the smells of the oils, the beats of the music, and the heat of his hands, which were sliding up and down my back like he was pushing and pulling long reams of paper from a mill. As he glided his thumbs further and further to right above my sacrum and then over it, I felt a surge of hormones race through my body. I could not believe how turned on I was getting. I started to moan loudly, rock my hips side to side, and arched my back. As I got louder and louder, he leaned down to my face and asked me to keep it quiet because I was going to wake up his roommates. I didn't want it to stop, but I also wasn't sure where this was going. He didn't either, it seemed, as he slowly stopped rubbing me. Probably to keep me quiet. He laid next to me. I curled onto my side, he wrapped his arm around me, and we fell asleep.

I woke up around 6 a.m. I looked over and saw he was still sleeping, but then I made enough of a rustle that he woke up and swung his arm around me. We began to talk. Though I was only in my underwear, I didn't feel vulnerable. I realized that I wanted to lose my virginity to him. I started caressing his arm and then moved my hand down his stomach. He looked at my face as I was touching him. He asked me if I was a virgin, and I lied and said no. I really didn't want this to stop. I felt comfortable with the idea of losing my virginity to him, though I could see the doubt on his face.

"Are you sure you're not a virgin, Mary?" he asked me again. *Oh man, he used my name.* He seemed to be giving me that last chance to be honest, to tell him the truth.

"No, I'm not," I said sheepishly, hoping he would allow me this bit of dishonesty for this soon-to-be womanly moment I was hoping for. He did. He kissed me slowly, and grabbed for a condom. I hadn't really seen his penis before now, but there it was, all hard and throbbing around while he wrestled a condom on top of it. I wasn't sure what an average one looked like, but I figured he was above average from what I'd seen in pornos. He was tender, just as he was soft-spoken, and that's how he pressed inside of me. I felt a pinch and a sharp pain, and then the anticipation and worry was over; there was no turning back now. A flood of feelings ran through me, and all I wanted to do was feel his kiss and his hips heavy on mine, swaying and rocking. Then I realized I could feel blood down there, a fluid thicker than our lust, that ran down my butt cheek. I didn't care, though; I just wanted him to keep going. We remained intertwined and rocked our bodies together until we couldn't anymore. When we were done, and he pulled away from me, the condom he was wearing was covered in a light pink stain. He looked at me, and then at the condom, and all he said was, "It's okay."

JUNIOR YEAR

I had spent the entire summer becoming a woman. I started smoking cigarettes and pot more regularly. I stayed out late and got home early. I had had sex with a few more guys, older guys. I'd dreadlocked my hair and wore thrift store clothes, bell bottom pants, and a beaded necklace I'd made that summer with a blue eye at the center. It had been a fun and carefree summer.

When junior year started, I wasn't much into basketball anymore. I hadn't even tried out for the varsity team. I became just a regular student. By then, I wasn't just trying to be a hippie and an alternative kid; I was one of them. I'd only been in school for a few weeks before I started ditching classes. I had become friends with some of the kids in PACE, the advanced school program at Poly. One of the girls introduced me to the drug speed.

At lunch, where I'd once hung out with my sister or one of her friends near the school's entrance—the non-cool zone, as I liked to call it—I decided to hang out with the grunge kids. I'd walked over because I had met a few of them that summer. We shared stories from the summer, talked about the pot we smoked and the bands we liked. I was feeling like I was fitting in, finally.

Sam was also doing her own thing. She was a senior now, but spent most of the time at her friend Suzette's place than at the house. We hadn't been on the same schedule for a while, and I spent most nights and weekends at coffeehouses rather than at the house.

I had met Dana at school, and she was a hard-core goth metal chick. She had punky blue hair, wore fishnets and black skirts, and carried around a black spray-painted lunch box for a purse. She liked to go to the Moonbeam coffeehouse where I hung out with friends, just across the street from the art theater. One night, after we had been smoking on the outside patio, she asked me to go inside with her to the restroom. When I did, she pulled out a baggy full of white powder.

"Do you want to do some of this with me, Mary?" she asked plainly.

"What is it? Cocaine?" I asked.

"No, but it's a lot like it. You'll like it," she said. I leaned over the toilet seat to snort a line. Half of it fell out of my nose because of my deviated septum. I snorted it back up, though. A moment later, I lifted my head and could feel a surge of energy fill my body. It felt great, but it also burned my nostrils.

"You like it, huh?" Dana asked me. "Don't worry about the drip; that's going to come in a second when you swallow." I waited for a moment, and then a horrible taste ran down the back of my throat. It was stronger than swallowing Bc headache medicine powder.

"You'll learn to love that burn and the drip, Mary." Dana then leaned over and did a line, too. We headed outside to the two friends that had been sitting with us, Debbie and Leslie. They told us they had been friends since middle school and even went to Wilson High School together. And Debbie lived just down the street. I had never felt so clear-headed. Debbie immediately knew Dana and I had done some speed. She looked at us inquisitively, but knowingly. She told us she had been recovering from slamming speed just that summer, so she didn't want to do any of it, but she knew when someone was on it. This didn't seem to bother her. In fact, it seemed to draw her to us.

"Do you guys want to come back to my place?" Debbie asked after an hour or so of talking. I didn't really know her and Leslie, but they seemed like they were just like me; young and looking for a good time, open to meeting new people, people who were abusing substances to cope with their lives. We all headed to Debbie's house on foot. She lived off of Molino and 4th Street. When we got there, her mom was sitting in the living room with three other people. Her mom was a really slender blonde woman whose boyfriend was tall with brown hair and wore tight jeans and a button-up cowboy shirt. And there was another older couple who her mom introduced as a guitarist and singer that played at their local watering hole. They were all partying in the living room, smoking pot, drinking, who knows what else. They looked at us like we were a bunch of aliens, invading their party time. After Debbie introduced us, she pulled us into her room fairly quickly. We all sat around her room, which was large and full of knick knacks, a big bed, a dresser drawer, purple-colored curtains, and even her own bathroom. Debbie broke the silence and said, "You know, my dad was the first person they ever used the Jaws of Life on." I didn't know what this was, but it sounded serious. I knew about *Jaws*, the movie, but the Jaws of Life? She explained that it was a tool used to cut open car metal after an accident to quickly get a victim out of their car.

"Did he survive?" I asked her.

"No, he didn't. They couldn't get him out in time. He's been dead for almost ten years now. I was just seven when he died," she told us with no sadness, like this was her big reveal to new friends, but she'd gotten over the trauma. The story was rehearsed; she was no longer hurt or shocked by it.

"I'm sorry to hear that about your father," I told her. "I haven't seen my dad since I was six, not since he came out of the closet." I let that settle into the room.

"What? Where were you born?" asked Debbie, shocked by my story. It was easier and easier for me to summarize my life up to that point, too. I dished it out without sadness, but I also was used to people being shocked by it. This was my big reveal.

"My dad's never around. He's this high-powered lawyer, and my mom is this prissy little housewife," Dana shared. "I spend a lot of my time working at the Press Telegram, learning to edit newspaper articles. That's where I got the speed. One of the guys that works there likes me."

We were then in a free-for-all honesty fest, and each of us took our turn to reveal *our* story.

"I don't know my dad well. He's remarried and owns an appliance store down the street. We're not close. I live with my mom and big sister, but I don't see my dad much. But then again, I don't know what we'd talk about if we did see each other," Leslie shared. Leslie had long blonde wavy hair. She was fair-skinned and had a soft, sweet voice. Her clothing style was hip-hop-type baggy pants and a tight halter top. She was tall, too, at least five feet, nine inches, and she had a nice, curvy shape. She was probably the best-looking one of the bunch, but humble and unaware of how to compare herself to the three of us, and that quality made me immediately like her. Dana and I sat there in the circle, waiting for the speed to wear off, then did a little more with Leslie. Debbie refrained; she just watched us snort up the speed and smoked cigarettes with us. We shared a lot about ourselves that night, and I gained a deep, fast, close friendship with them.

The next day, I woke up in Debbie's bedroom. My head was pounding, and my stomach was achey.

"You got the sickness, huh?" Debbie asked.

"What's that?" I asked her.

"It's the hangover from the speed. You're going to feel really bad all day, until you do it again." It was already hot outside, and I still had to get to school. I didn't have my backpack or anything, so getting to school wasn't going to happen. I worried that Debbie's mom would kick me out once Debbie left for school.

"You going to school today?" I asked Debbie.

"I don't know. Let me check on my mom. If she's out cold, I'll ditch."

Dana had left earlier in the morning, so she was likely already in class. The accelerated program she was in had college prep classes that started around 7 a.m. She had told me how many of those classes she was in, and it sounded like she would likely have graduated from college by the time she finished high school.

Debbie walked back into her bedroom after checking on her mom and said, "Looks like we can stay here today."

Leslie was still asleep. She looked like a princess lying there on the floor. I grabbed a Marlboro from the pack on the living room table and sat outside with Debbie to smoke. The front door to her apartment was in the alley on a little street called De Soto. The chances of a cop seeing us and asking us to explain why we weren't in school were small. But you had to be out of sight of them before 10 a.m., or else they'd take you to truancy school, where you had to wait for a parent or guardian to pick you up. That's when you really got busted for ditching.

But the pain was real, the sickness was real, and I started to regret ever having done speed. I felt dirty.

"It's normal how you feel, Mary. It gets worse before it gets better. Around three o'clock you'll start to feel better, trust me," Debbie assured me. I decided that I would try to catch Dana on her way home from school that day, since I knew her route. Around 3:15, I started down toward 7th Street, right past Cherry Avenue. And there she was, punky blue-haired Dana, strutting down the street looking like a badass.

I walked up to her and said, "Hey Dana, I feel awful. How are you doing?"

"Yeah. Me, too. I was sick all morning and almost didn't make it through class. Do you want to do some more?" Dana asked me.

"I do and I don't. If this feeling will go away, then I don't ever want to do it again."

"Well, I have just enough for two. Let's go to Moonbeam. Trust me, this will help, and you'll feel much better. Now you know what the hangover is like." She pointed her head in the direction of the coffeehouse, and I followed. I knew how great I had felt the night before, and I needed a little more of that to get me through the rest of the day so I could get home and rest, a thought that sounded delightful. We did a little more on the top of the toilet, and I started to feel normal again. I decided to go back to "Little Debbie's," what we started calling her because she was so petite and she looked like the girl on the face of their packaging for Nutty Buddy bars, which were my favorite. There she was, sitting on her porch just waiting for someone she knew to stroll by, smoking a Marlboro.

"So you feel better, Mary?" she asked with a knowing look.

"Yeah, I think I'm over the hump. Got a cigarette?" I asked her. We sat on her porch while she described to me her addiction to meth. How she got into slamming it, but started just like me, snorting first, then smoking it, then, bam, a needle up her arm. I never saw myself as someone who would slam anything. I wasn't afraid of needles, but images of cracked-out people from my neighborhood in New York would fill my mind. I didn't want to be like them.

I would continue, however, to do speed for another four months, losing weight on an already slender frame, looking more and more like a speed freak. I decided one day to stop, and the only way I thought I could do it was to only smoke weed. I stopped hanging out with the friends that did speed and started hanging back in my hippie circles. I met a few guys who only ever smoked weed, and I started to slowly get my life back to "normal." But my life would never be normal. I knew that. I still lived in the ghetto, and I wasn't getting out anytime soon if it was up to my mom. My only solution was to keep hanging out outside the ghetto, at the coffeehouses on 4th Street, and meeting new people. I met some really interesting people, those who had all kinds of backgrounds. I even started hanging back with my old group of friends from junior high, like Kimberly and Rose, Kimberly's best friend. In the months I'd been dealing with my speed addiction, I'd also lost contact with a bunch of friends, but I picked up pretty easily where I'd left off. They hung out at the coffeehouses, went to the *Rocky Horror Picture Show* at the Art Theatre, and had friends in common with me. They were my circle.

I was still living at home, and I'd already written off junior year. I didn't have a job, but I also didn't have any opportunities because going back to school was no longer an option and I wasn't planning on working until the summer program started, when I'd go back to the Belmont Plaza Pool to be a junior lifeguard. I somehow checked into the house often enough that my mom didn't think I was a runaway, but I mostly stayed out with friends. The springtime was becoming quite the fertile ground for something new.

PERU

When I was still on speed, hanging out in the living room with other degenerates on an all-nighter at my dealer's house, I pulled out a postcard. I had a few postcards that I had grabbed from Portfolio, my favorite coffeehouse. The postcards featured really great art, unlike the typical postcard that had the city's name and some cheesy backdrop, these had style. They were all free, so I always grabbed a few whenever I was there. I didn't have anyone to write a postcard to, but I still kept them on me for inspiration. But this one night, this all-night binge, I wrote a postcard to my future man. I listed out the qualities that this man would have, and all my thoughts we're concentrated on one manifestation of "the one." The postcard had an out-of-focus red tulip as the cover art, a photo taken by photographer Gabor Ekecs. Here is the simple, yet direct message to my unknown loved one:

"Today is January 24th, 1994. I'm writing on this postcard to hopefully someday give to someone that I love. If someone ever receives this, that means I have finally fallen in love.

"Dear Loved One,

"Once I laid eyes on you, I was in awe. I never thought that I would find someone I'd be in love with and have them in love with me, too.

Love, I thought, was only for other people and not me. I've never been in love until now, until I met you. When we first talked, you moved me not only with your knowledge of life, but also your understanding of lives other than yours. You can relate to just about anything or anybody, and I praise that. The respect you earn from others will never be underestimated. I never received flowers for no reason or compliments from out of the blue. Your aura is of a warming one, like in a comfort zone. You're a crazy, wonderful person. Your style, walk, clothes, and even the way you talk is crazy yet wonderful. You love to explore new things and people. It's easy to see you're in a class by yourself. You're someone people want to talk to and look at. You're an unforgettable human. You make my heart beat fast, and when you're away, I think of you and want to get in your zone, so I, too, can unite in your unique understanding of one's self. Every time our hearts beat the same, I love you more and more. Love, life, the universe, everything is absolutely crazy."

During the El Niño of 1994, it was a deluge in Long Beach. In fact, it was so terrible that the Long Beach sewage system could not handle the amount of rain and flooding; so many cars were lost because streets filled up with water and ruined the engines. Being a pedestrian meant you had a big chance of getting completely soaked as cars drove by. Unless you had to go somewhere, most people were avoiding going outside. If you had a car, it was tolerable, but most folks didn't want to risk getting their engine flooded.

The first time I met "the one," it was in November of 1994. I'd had a fight with my mom and left the apartment. It was pouring rain, and I didn't even have an umbrella, but I was so heated that I just stormed out and started walking south toward Portfolio. As a wet and hopeless sixteen-year-old, I only focused on being away from home, and enjoyed taking refuge in the comfort that Portfolio gave me. So when I got there, I stood outside and took cover under one of the awnings with a hot cup of coffee. I asked a man standing in one of the doorways for a cigarette. He grudgingly dogeared the page of the book that he was reading, stuck it under his armpit, and pulled out a red cigarette roller. He opened up a pack of loose tobacco and sprinkled it across the length of the roller, then pulled out a Zig-Zag paper. I'd only ever seen one person use loose tobacco before, and he was a homeless man in the park in New York that my brother bought cigarettes from. He had rolled a cigarette with his hands. This guy had a special way of rolling the tobacco. He folded the paper into the roller, carefully guiding the paper through and around until one side came out, then he stuck his tongue out and licked the length of the sticky side of the paper and finished with one last spin. He opened the roller, pulled out the finished cigarette, and handed it to me. Just briefly, he cleaned the mouth part of any excess tobacco and began to neatly fold over the paper with his thumb, so my mouth would touch only a well-kept, unfiltered cigarette end.

He gave me the cigarette without even looking at me. I asked for a light, which seemed to be the tip of his annoyance with me; however, he still lit my cigarette. In that moment, I thought he was a pompous jerk. The taste of the cigarette was so strange, though I committed to the experience and inhaled several more times. It tasted of citrus and wet moss, and whatever I thought wet trees in a forest would smell like. With the moisture in the air from the rain and having to smoke outside under the awning, inevitably a drop of rain landed right on my finger directly in the space between where I was holding the cigarette and where I was going to take a drag. Since there was no filter, there was no way to absorb the moisture. At this point, I could no longer take a successful drag, as nothing was coming through. I looked at this sorry excuse for a cigarette and proceeded to put it out in the water-filled ashtray sitting on the table in front of me. This was my first encounter with my future husband. To this day, he does not remember meeting me that night.

I later wrote a poem for our sixth wedding anniversary to signify this first unassuming encounter. It was published in the International Library of Poetry's *The Splendor of Sunrise* in 2001. When they published my little blurb about the poem in the back of the book, in the Poets' Profiles section, they misspelled his name and called him "Pierce." They weren't the only ones who would get his name wrong the first time. The poem was called "Rainy Tuesday."

"Young and scared
Tired and cold
Despite the rain I come to you
'Cigarette please' are my only words
Your disturbed face lifts to say
'Alright then' you begin to roll

A short while later I see again
The one who gives without feeling
I know you, but you've lost touch
I test the grounds and come full force

Who would have known
That tired and cold
Gives new meaning
To love after all"

He had been in Long Beach for just a few weeks when I first met him that rainy night, I later learned, and he was going to go back to his home country of Belgium after that short visit to California. For him, the trip was a way to see his sister and some friends he'd known through the years from various trips to Long Beach. He was also doing some software development work for a small company in Costa Mesa in the hopes of possibly landing a job. He wanted to move from his home town of Liège back to Long Beach, where he felt his life was meant to be.

By the end of February, the work he had done did indeed get him a plane ride back to America, and he would be coming back months later, which is when I would meet him again.

And one day at Portfolio, sometime that April, he showed up with my friend Kimberly. When she walked up with him and a few of my other friends, she introduced him as "Pierre." I introduced myself and then remembered that night in the rain. I asked if he remembered me, and he confessed he did not. I recounted the story with the rolled cigarette and all the details I could remember. I exaggerated as much as I could about how pompous he was. He laughed and apologized for how he acted. He swore that he really didn't remember me and admitted that he can sometimes be annoyed when he's asked to break his concentration from reading. He swore that now that we knew each other, he'd never get annoyed again, and that I could bum a cigarette off him anytime. I believed him.

He was really the most unassuming character. He wore a European black beret hat, backward. It was like a cross between a very typical French beret and a sea captain's hat. He had a little ponytail peeking out that was light brown and wispy. He was short, but probably the typical height of a Belgian, I assumed, five feet, six inches or five feet, seven inches. His shirts were tight and tucked into his pants, which were tighter than what guys normally wore in Long Beach, and he wore a belt. His mannerisms were good, but his broken English and French accent made him seem more reserved and unassuming, and his stutter on top of it all made it hard for me to size him up. Honestly, I thought he was gay. I had already forgotten his name by the next day. Mainly because his strange cigarettes, clothing style, and accent were the most prominent things I could remember about him. All I knew was that his name sounded foreign, and it wasn't one I'd ever heard before. In my mind, it was something like, Pepé Le Pew.

One night, when I arrived at Portfolio, he was there hanging out with one of my other friends, Jane, whom I always described as having three brain cells that were always fighting. Pretty much anyone that knew Jane would always get a chuckle out of that statement because of how true it was. I was a little perplexed as to why he was talking to Jane. She was pretty and curvy, so I figured that might be the reason. I sat down with them and began to draw on one of the big pieces of construction paper laid out on the tables. The coffeehouse put these out on every table; they were held down with coffee cups stuffed with crayons. This was part of the unique charm of the place. It let patrons be creative while they hung out. I loved that. I never really had money to pay for coffee; all my funds were spent on cigarettes. Jane asked if I knew the Belgian man, whom I now remembered as "Peru."

"This is Pierre," she said. *Ah, Pierre!* After we greeted each other, he asked me if I wanted something to drink. I thought that was very nice of him to ask, and indeed I did want something to drink. I wanted a hot chocolate. He ordered Jane and me a drink and came back to the table a few minutes later with both of them in hand. Mine had lots of whipped cream on top and a drizzle of chocolate. My eyes were wide when it arrived in front of me.

We had some light conversation about how he knew Jane, and I gave him a few looks because I wasn't sure he realized what he was getting himself into with her. I asked him how old he was, and he told me he was twenty-seven.

"Oh, that's cool. I'm seeing a guy that's twenty-seven right now, too." He quickly asked me how old I was. I replied that I was sixteen going on seventeen. He later told me that I crushed him the moment I said that I was dating someone who was twenty-seven. He had instantly liked me when I shared my story about meeting him, and then felt like there was no longer a shot with me. Little did he know that *dating* for me was not having a boyfriend; it was just having someone to hook up with from time to time. At that point, I had never had a boyfriend. And quite honestly, I didn't want one. All my friends' relationships had problems. Either they were getting knocked up or just unhappy because the relationship wasn't going well. It wasn't as passionate or as loving as they wanted, or they were pursuing someone that didn't even like them. All this seemed really tiring to me. It was so much easier to have casual relationships, have a good time and leave it at that. You had much cooler conversations and interactions when you weren't desperate to be in a *relationship*.

I'd later learn that in Europe the legal age of consent was a lot younger than eighteen. I had always remembered my mom telling me that my cousin was married at fourteen, and thinking that was so young. But now that I was sixteen, a year older than someone who celebrates their quinceañera and is considered a woman, and two years older than my cousin who got married at fourteen, I was perfectly capable of dating men and controlling what kind of relationship I wanted to have with them.

That night, sitting at the coffeehouse with Jane and the little Belgian named Pierre, I was drawing out an idea of a tattoo I really wanted. It was a fiery sun with long rays that wiggled with sharp pointy ends. There was a crescent moon inside just hugging the right side of the sun with an angel floating next to the moon, suspended and peaceful-looking. I don't know where this idea came from, or why I felt I wanted this tattoo so badly, but I did, and I wanted to follow my intuition. I didn't have any tattoos, so this was going to be a big deal if I got one. I didn't know who would do it, nor did I have the money for it. I just drew it and wished that someday I would find an artist that would plant that beauty right on my young, flat stomach.

Pierre liked the design. We continued talking that entire night. We were so into our conversation that we didn't really notice when Jane left to go hang with some of her other friends. By that time, it was late and I needed to get home, so he offered to drive me back. I insisted that I just needed a dollar to take the bus, that he didn't have to go out of his way. But he insisted, so I figured, why not. Before getting out of his old '74 Beetle, he invited me to have coffee with him the next day. I told him I'd see.

Most evenings, I would end up at Portfolio and see him there after he got back from work. I'd be there with the usual crowd, and I'd talk to him here and there. Since he was new to my group of friends, pretty much any activity we were doing—a party, a stroll around the neighborhood, a joy ride—he wanted to come. I could tell that he was starting to like me. He offered me bus money all the time, he would buy me chips and sodas at the liquor store, and we'd hang out and talk while I waited for the bus most nights. One night, after we'd all come back from a party, I went into my usual routine with him, asking him for a dollar to take the bus back home. He hesitated this time. I teased him and told him I would give him a kiss for a dollar. He immediately perked up and stood next to his car waiting for his kiss. My friends teased me as I leaned into the kiss. "Ohhhh, look at Mary and Pierre," they cackled. I guess I wasn't much of a kisser, though, because within a few seconds he leaned back and told me, "Slow down. It's not a race." I was surprised and a little intrigued by this. When we were finished, he walked me to the bus stop. And just like every night, we hung out and talked while I waited for the bus. We carried on like this for a few more weeks.

In the meantime, I ended up getting that tattoo I'd been drawing right on my stomach. One night at Portfolio, an older biker dude sat next to me. I complimented him on one of his tattoos.

"My old lady did it," he said.

"I like her work. I'm thinking about getting a small tattoo on my stomach," I told him. I described it to him, and he said that it sounded pretty simple.

"My old lady's gonna be here tomorrow. You should come by the coffeehouse and talk to her," he suggested.

I couldn't wait for the next day. Just as he said, she was there, a pretty brunette wearing a sleeveless leather jacket, tight blue jeans, and dark, perfectly dirty black leather boots. We were introduced, and I started describing the tattoo I wanted. She listened carefully and then told me that she could do it if I came by their apartment the next day. She said she liked me and that she would do it for cheap. Just ten dollars.

Their address was just down the street from Portfolio on 4th Street, so I knew I'd get the tattoo and then come straight over to the coffeeshop to show all my friends. The only problem was I didn't have ten dollars. I asked every person I knew that night for money, but none of my friends had any cash they could spare. I thought that maybe I'd be able to convince my mom to give me the money, but I couldn't tell her what it was for. She wasn't in the habit of giving me money, so I knew I could possibly alarm her and set off her mom instincts if I asked and didn't have a really good story. I had nothing. The next morning, I asked if she needed anything at the liquor store, hoping she needed something small and would hand me a twenty-dollar bill so that I could "forget" to put the change back in her purse. "No, I'm fine," she said. *Rats!* I thought.

I collected myself and hoped I would have the courage to tell a white lie to the pretty lady with the brunette hair. While I walked toward their apartment, I gathered a story. I knocked on their door and walked into a small one bedroom apartment with shelves littered with tchotchkes and a big couch that looked like it was from the '70s with thick fabric and brown and orange flowers on it. Their floor had the most typical brown Long Beach apartment carpet, low grade and fuzzy, perfect for hiding cockroaches. I told my white lie when she asked for the ten bucks, "My mom is at work, and I just missed her. When she gets back home tonight, I'll get the ten dollars from her and bring it back to you." She stared at me for a moment, not even fazed.

"All right then. Let's get started." She pulled out a drawing she had made of the tattoo idea I had described to her the night before, but it was different than I had described it in one unique way.

"Instead of the angel, I put the Eye of Horus inside of the sun, next to the moon. Do you know what the Eye of Horus is?" she asked me.

"No," I told her.

"Well, Horus was the Egyptian sun god. When soldiers would go into battle, they would pray to Horus to protect them. See, you have the sun and the moon, so putting the Eye of Horus inside the sun and next to the moon means he'll protect you day and night." I was fascinated by this idea and agreed to her design.

She traced out the tattoo on purple tracing paper. She sprayed my stomach with alcohol and shaved the area where I wanted it placed, just off to the left of my belly button.

"So what does it feel like...to get a tattoo?" I asked her as she positioned the tracing paper on top of my stomach and sprayed alcohol on it.

"You know what it feels like to get scratched?"

"Yeah."

"Well, it's like that for every line I draw," she said plainly. I figured I'd survived plenty of scratches in my day, from girls in schoolyards and my sister, and none of them gave me anything beautiful at the end. I took a deep breath.

"Well, take a look at it. What do you think? Do you want me to change anything? Do you like the placement?" she asked.

I looked down and was amazed as I stared at the purple outline of my future tattoo. She fired up her tattoo gun and a strong buzzing sound filled the room. I was feeling some adrenaline now. She sensed that I needed to be calmed.

"So why don't we do this: I'll do one line, and if it's too painful, I'll stop. Sounds good?"

I nodded. The sensation of the needle did indeed feel like a scratch, but not so painful that I couldn't handle more. She looked at me. "So, how'd it feel?" she asked.

"It felt like a scratch, just like you said."

"Well, you don't wanna go around with one line on your stomach, do you?" She smiled.

Over an hour later, the tattoo was mostly done. She started to shade some of the areas in the wavvy sun rays with three needles instead of one. It felt nice. My stomach was so numb by then, and it had a soft pinkish glow around it with specks of blood rising up through the skin through the different parts of the tattoo. She wiped me off a few times until the blood stopped rising as quickly. She slathered A&D ointment on my stomach, put a paper towel over the tattoo, and wrapped Saran wrap across my stomach to hold the dressing on. I was wearing a halter top that day, so I felt like people would think I had been stabbed. We parted ways, and I assured her I would be back later that night with her ten dollars. I walked over to Portfolio, and upon seeing my friends, I immediately peeled back my dressing to show off my new tattoo. Everyone liked it, so much so that my friend Kimberly pointed her finger right at it so quickly that she found a way to put a tiny scratch in one of my sun rays. My tattoo is still missing ink from that spot.

I covered my tattoo and proudly wore my badge of honor. I was clever enough to conceal it from my family for a few days. I stayed in because I couldn't face going to the coffeeshop without my tattoo artist's ten dollars. I finally had the money a few days later, and started walking toward her house. Halfway there, I ran into a friend who needed to borrow a few bucks. Just until that evening, he said. I gave him five dollars. This seemed like the world to me at the time. The day went on, and by the evening, I had already bought a pack of smokes and an order of french fries from the hamburger shop next door to Portfolio. I figured even saving five dollars to give her was dumb, so I might as well not have any of it. This felt more honest to me. Later that night, a friend of the tattoo artist was sitting at one of the tables and spotted me.

"Hey, Mary! Come over here!" he yelled.

I walked over timidly.

"What the hell, Mary? You still owe my friend ten dollars for your tattoo. You better get the ten dollars tonight."

"Okay, I'll find the money. Give me about fifteen minutes." I looked around the coffeehouse and tried to make eyes with anyone I knew. I spotted Pierre. I walked over to him to make my plea for some cash. He immediately said it was no problem. We walked back to his place, and he grabbed the money. I walked up to Paul, the tattoo artist's friend, and slapped it into his hand. One thing I would never do again was borrow from someone I couldn't pay back.

I finally took Pierre up on his offer to hang out at his place. My friends Travis and Teresa had already hung out there a few times and said it was pretty cool. Pierre had a decent-sized studio apartment furnished with two armchairs, a coffee table, and a large bed tucked into the corner of the living room. He had a large stereo with two detachable speakers sitting on the floor with two large stacks of CDs. He had the Led Zeppelin box set, Nirvana's *Nevermind*, and *Never Mind the Bollocks* by the Sex Pistols, to name a few. His apartment had the typical '40s built-ins, painted over with apartment-colored beige paint ten times before. It even had a Murphy bed built in. He lived right next door to a liquor store, which was just beyond a tall brick wall a few steps from his back door.

He put on an album while my friends and I found spots to sit. Then he came back from the kitchen with glasses of cold Arrowhead water and a large can of Lipton iced tea powder.

"You guys want some iced tea?" he asked in his cute French accent. I'd never had iced tea from a powder before, but I grew up drinking powdered milk, so I was sure it would taste better than that. And it actually was good. I ended up having at least three glasses that evening. He then offered everyone homemade sandwiches. I took him up on that, too. We all spent hours talking about our lives, the music we loved, how our relationships were with our parents, and even why he decided to move to the U.S. from Belgium. As I really got to know him, I found him more interesting than I had previously. I really started liking him, and before I knew it, we were seeing each other a few times a week at Portfolio or at his place with my friends. He'd invite me over to his place nearly every time I saw him, but I never went over unless I was with one of my friends. I knew he liked me, but I wasn't sure I wanted to go all the way. But one day, while I was at my house, I began thinking about him, how nice he was, how he'd given me his work number, so I decided to call him at work. We talked for a few minutes, and I noticed how nice it felt to talk to him. In a way, he was already my boyfriend, but I just didn't know how those things went. He asked if I could meet him at his place after work. I said I would, but that I wanted my friend Teresa to come. As always, he said that was fine. My friend Teresa was my favorite pothead friend, and she liked getting high at Pierre's place with her boyfriend. And the iced tea was nice.

I decided that I would have sex with him that night, so I groomed myself and slathered in Palmer's cocoa butter. When we arrived at his apartment, and while Teresa sat on his couch making out with her boyfriend Travis, I sat on his bed next to him. I leaned over and whispered in his ear, "I've shaved everywhere, and I've got cocoa butter all over my body." He didn't quite know what to say. We kissed for so long that we didn't know when Teresa and Travis left the apartment. I decided that we would go all the way, and we did. He was an unexpectedly good lover. I didn't anticipate how much I would enjoy his tender touch, his soft kisses and lips. *This must be what making love is like,* I thought.

This went on for weeks. I would still go home most nights. But he also didn't mind me coming over to his place during the day while he was at work, I'd been given the key to his apartment and he even showed me the drawer where he kept his cash. He didn't mind if I had friends over to hang out while he wasn't there, either. I could play hostess and treat my friends to homemade sandwiches and Lipton iced tea. It was nice that he trusted me so much. It was also strange having money available to me, going out to restaurants for dinner, brunch on the weekends, and ordering in pizza. I was enjoying my life, and the chains of poverty were slowly loosening. I still didn't fully believe that I had a "boyfriend." I thought that I didn't need one, or maybe what we had was just casual, temporary. It was on my terms, but I liked him more than anyone else I had been seeing.

One night at the bus stop, he asked me a question.

"Would you marry me so I can stay in the country?"

"Yes, I would," I said without any hesitation, surprising even myself.

"Really, you would?" he asked with a perplexed look on his face, likely thinking this would have been a harder sell.

"Yes. It doesn't mean we would stay together forever, but I would just be helping you out and you would be helping me out," I said casually. "I don't know why I'm agreeing, but I think you are a nice person. This would be a good way for me to move out of my mom's place, too."

Many thoughts went through my mind on the bus ride home. What had I committed to? What was I thinking? I'm marrying this guy so he can stay in the country? This was illegal, right? I mean, didn't I want to have some kind of fairy-tale wedding? Isn't that what I'm supposed to want? What would my mom say? Would I be able to pull this off? Am I even convinced that I'm going to do this? He was a nice guy, and I really did like him. The thought of him having to leave the country and not returning for an entire six months, if at all, made my stomach turn. I'd seen movies of girls marrying guys so they could get green cards. Was I one of those women now? Am I even considering it because I love him? I love a man? Does this make me a woman?

I took a few deep breaths and started to visualize what a life with Pierre would be like. I thought about how much he trusted me and took care of me. I liked who I was with him, how I felt when I was with him. I took another deep breath and tried to think about what I could possibly say to my mother that could convince her to let me marry him, which would emancipate me. I knew that my mom was married at seventeen to my dad, who was twenty-seven, too.

My sister had successfully gotten her boyfriend back from El Salvador by this time, and she was living in an apartment with him. My mom was usually alone in the apartment and had begun hanging out with a few people she'd met at the local bars where she would go sing karaoke. One was an older man who had a thing for large women. Mom had brought him over one day because he said he had some clothes he wanted to give me. Everything he had was suited for a church-going girl. That wasn't me. I wore corduroy pants, vibrant polyester tops, off-brand Converse shoes, and was proud of my long blonde dreadlocks by this time. But I humored them and tried on the skirts and blouses he'd brought anyway. They asked me to come into the living room and model the clothes. I told Mom's friend that I'd take them all, with no real intention of ever wearing them. My mom seemed pleased, and so did he. My mom hadn't dated in years, perhaps ten-plus years, from what I knew. And now it seemed she was getting a little lovin' from an old white guy, and this was loosening her up to things.

She had recently discovered my tattoo because the shirt I wore one day was made of thin cotton, and you could see my dark black tattoo just as clear as day through it. But besides her initial shock that her baby got a tattoo, she didn't give me too much grief about it. She just asked me not to get any more, and then complimented me on how pretty it was. I felt that she realized that I must be growing up in other ways, too, and there was nothing she could really do about it. She was doing things I wasn't used to her doing, either, like bringing men to the house and going to karaoke at bars.

Four months before, she had found my diary. I had stuffed it into the couch I had in my room. I had been doing speed, and I was gone a lot back then, and she was rightfully worried and did the kind of search of my room only a worried mother would do. I had also been exhibiting the same kind of patterns my brother exhibited when he was my age, and she wanted to know if I was on drugs. Just like any mother, she always knew when I was up to something. And she found what she needed to find. My diary was also a kind of a "black book." I wrote about having sex with certain guys, and when I did and what it was like, all of it. She had found the number for a male friend of mine named Phil, who I'd written about having casual sex with. He was a hippy steel drum player with a colorful hummingbird tattoo on his right bicep that was mostly covered up by hair. It was nothing serious, but I liked knowing a musician. She called him and outright asked him if we were having sex. He quickly said that he wanted to date me and then asked whether she would give him permission. She surprised him because she told him she didn't have an issue with it. She just wanted to make sure he was aware that I was only sixteen years old. He lied and said he hadn't known my age, then told her that he was twenty-four. He went looking for me that night at my normal hangout spot, and told me that my mom had called him. I was mortified. I knew she would have gotten his number from my black book, which I kept in a bank money bag that required a key to open. My mistake was that I kept the key in the lock. Until that moment, I assumed she didn't even know I had ever kissed anyone before, but now she had proof I was her sex-havin' sixteen-year-old daughter.

But my mom's new life somehow neutralized mine. She was making friends at the karaoke bars. She was meeting gay men and hanging out with them and having a good ole time. All those years of cursing them, trying to shame my brother by saying he was like his father, and now there she was, partying it up and drinking margaritas, laughing, and having a good time with them. I was happy she finally realized that gay men are not all bad, and that it's not a choice. I knew how she had been all those years before, and I was still resentful. But I never hung out with her in those places—I was too young for the bars—so I could only judge what a positive impact this was having on her by seeing that she was happier, dating, and more open to new ideas. So as I rode the bus home, I thought about how I would negotiate this marriage with her. I was about to embark on quite the magic show, but I knew that I had a window of opportunity to actually make this happen.

WE'RE GOIN' TO THE CHAPEL... COURTHOUSE

Between the time Pierre asked me to marry him that night at the bus stop, to the time that he was told he needed to leave the country or find a way to legally remain in America, there was only a three-week window to figure out a solution. Within those three weeks, I would be turning seventeen years old, still too young to get married without parental consent.

Pierre's mom was also visiting Long Beach during some of this window, and so was Pierre's aunt and uncle, Kikki and Mathieu. I'm not sure they knew what to make of me, a six-foot-one hippy girl with dreadlocks, who still had her four front teeth missing and a bottom tooth chipped. I suppose I was quite the sight, but nonetheless, they were all very nice to me. They didn't speak any English either, so who knows what they were saying in French that I didn't understand. I got to meet Pierre's sister Madeleine during this time, too, and she seemed nice as well. We all enjoyed an afternoon in her small front courtyard. I mostly felt comfortable and welcomed. We drank wine and ate really good cheese, and they all laughed and had a good time. The speed at which they spoke French amazed me. But Pierre and Madeleine were happy to translate any conversation they had in French, especially anything that created a huge laugh, so I wouldn't feel left out.

Pierre's aunt and uncle owned a well-established and profitable grocery store in his hometown of Liège, and their tastes were good. Pierre's mom Jeannine felt that Pierre's little studio apartment next to the liquor store would be too much of an embarrassment to show the family, so they never came over to see it. Though during this family visit, his mom decided to spruce up Pierre's apartment and buy blankets she could throw over his olive green armchair and tacky loveseat, an attempt to tie the room together with his simple brown coffee table and typical brown apartment carpet. Pierre had bought all of his furniture from his speedhead neighbor for only ten dollars, which he proudly mentioned from time to time when he spoke about his furnishings. His family was only visiting in town for a week or two, and I only met them a few times while they were here, but it seemed that I passed some kind of test with them, because I didn't hear anything negative about me from Pierre. This was great, but we were slowly running out of time before he would have to leave. I had to figure out a foolproof way to convince my mom to sign off on our marriage.

I spent a few days at home during the week that his family was visiting, and I purposefully mentioned Pierre's name here and there. I told my mom that I was dating a man that was twenty-four, just like Phil. A white lie. The only truth was that I was dating a man named Pierre. Then, one evening, I laid down some of my other truths.

"I've been dating Pierre for a few months, and I love him," I told my mom timidly. This would imply I was sexually active with him.

"Well, it seems like you're growing up, Mary, and you haven't been around much. You do look happier than I've seen you in a while, much better than several months ago," she shared. I didn't have the heart to tell her that I had spiraled into meth use for a few months and she was right to be concerned. That was in the past now.

"He's making good money consulting and has his own place. He's really nice to me and wants to take care of me. I think you would like him if you met him," I suggested confidently. "But he doesn't have a green card and I'm going to have to marry him soon or he's going to have to go back to Belgium. I've already talked to him, and he said he would move in with us to help pay the rent and help out with groceries and other bills. Would you consider letting me marry him so that he could help us out around the house? And if it doesn't work, then I don't need to stay married to him. I can just break it off." I said this so rapidly that I had to take a huge breath when I was done. I sat there, exhaling and waiting for what seemed like the longest pregnant pause possible to end while my mom stared at me, trying to find any cracks in my story.

"Can he move in by next month?" she finally asked matter-of-factly.

"I'm sure he can. I'll ask him and let you know once he's back from work. So you're going to let me marry him?" I asked with part of my heart quivering in anticipation of an explosion of anger or more skepticism about my crazy pitch.

"Okay, I will let you marry him, but only if it's for his green card. And he's going to move in with us to help pay the bills and help out around the house," she told me. My offer for him to move in spoke to her need for financial help, which I knew it would.

The sad part, though, was that I was negotiating for my freedom, and I had no intention of having him move in with my mentally unstable mother and me. No chance in hell! Being manipulative didn't feel good, but Pierre was my way out of it all, and the good part was that I loved him. I had to be smooth and cater to my mom's selfishness and her current financial situation. I was still on the government payroll. I knew I wouldn't have ever spun up an elaborate story and promised all this if Pierre wasn't going to be forced to go back to Belgium. I understood my sister more now than ever. What she was willing to do for the man she loved. I was in the moment of a personal crossroads, and I had chosen a path. I knew it was the best thing for me at the time, despite the lies I would tell. Pierre didn't know I'd promised Mom that he would move in with us.

I had recently turned seventeen, and less than a week later, my mom met Pierre. She had his phone number by then and had called his apartment one morning and asked where we would be that afternoon. He said we would be at the laundromat. It was Sunday. She said she had something to tell us. She drove up to the laundromat in her blue Nissan Stanza. She didn't get out; she just rolled down her window and called to me. I saw her pull in and prepared Pierre to meet my mom.

"She's very large, like I've told you, so don't let that shock you. You have to be really nice to her. If you give her any attitude, she's going to turn on you and there's no going back," I explained to Pierre before we walked outside. By then I actually had given Pierre a pet name. I called him "Booboo." I'd actually played around with a lot of pet names for him—Honey Bear was one, because he had a charming personality like Winnie the Pooh. But I called him Booboo because of a black cat I had named Booboo. When he was a kitten, he had a large, protruding outie belly button, and whenever my mom would put the kitten on its back, she would push the belly button and say, "booboo," and the kitten would wiggle, and she would do it over and over, and he'd continue to wiggle on his back as he enjoyed the attention. He was adorable, and I never forgot how innocent that joy was. I had felt that innocent joy with Pierre, and I wanted to give him a nickname that I felt represented his kindness and sweetness. So I started calling him "Booboo." Not just when it was us, but whenever I referred to him around our friends and then even when I'd call his work and ask for him. It had gotten to the point where most people were calling him Booboo now. I also preferred his nickname to his ical name. The name Pierre seemed a little pompous to me, and I wasn't hung up on his accent or the fact that he spoke French. In fact, what I was more hung up on was that he had a stutter and pronounced things much differently than I did. But I found that cute and for many years never corrected the way he said, "spaghetties" instead of "spaghetti," or "taycos" instead of "tacos." I had an endless amount of patience for these things, and didn't want his name to overshadow the small things that I loved about him.

This was the first time Mom was seeing us together. She stared at him while he extended his hand to shake hers. She didn't extend her hand.

"Hello Linda. It's very nice to meet you. Thank you for allowing Mary and I to get married. I promise you won't regret it," he said sincerely.

She kept staring at him and said, "Well, when do you want to do this?"

He looked at me. I looked back at him. This was the moment of truth. Worry about what she thought of Booboo ran through my mind. She'd never seen me side by side with a man I'd been intimate with before, let alone someone I was going to marry. I wondered what she thought of him and whether he measured up to her standards of who she thought her baby girl would marry. But this was another transformational moment, one that was like jumping on a moving train.

"I would do it today if we could, Linda," Booboo told her. "I can call around, and we can see where we need to go to have the ceremony."

"Give me a call when you know what we need to do," she told him. Then she backed up out of the parking spot and drove away. She never was one to say, "Goodbye," on the phone either. Booboo looked at me with astonishment. This was really going to happen, and we had to act fast. And just like that, it was on.

Because it was the weekend, most official places wouldn't be open. We looked through the yellow pages, called a few hotlines, one of which was for the Norwalk Courthouse. From the recordings, it seemed like we just needed to go there with my mom and sign the paperwork. So I called her and asked her to meet us at Pierre's apartment the next morning. Just like that, at 8 a.m., she was waiting outside. We jumped in her car, and off we went to the Norwalk Courthouse. Things had gone from theory to reality rather quickly. I was nervous to say the least, but it felt like the deed would be done in a few hours and then I could relax.

Once we arrived at the courthouse, we were told that they couldn't marry us that day. You had to make an appointment before just showing up. They asked if we had submitted an application yet. We told them we hadn't.

"Well, you can't get married, then. You have to have an appointment with the courts for the judge to see you. Take these forms and fill them out, and then we can schedule your appointment," the clerk explained as she shoved a stack of papers in my hand.

"How long does getting an appointment take?" I asked her.

"It could be up to a month."

I took the papers and walked away from the clerk's window. I found a place to stand and read what she'd given me. In print at the very top, it read, "Those under eighteen years of age must have a parent or legal guardian accompanying them at time of marriage to legally emancipate the minor." Well, I had that. "There must be a date in court set prior to the request being granted." We only had another four days before Booboo would have to leave the country. *What are we going to do?* I worried. We went back to his apartment to regroup. He'd bought a dozen donuts and made coffee, so we all had something to nervously eat and keep ourselves occupied while we thought of other options.

"What if we called a church and we asked them to marry us?" I proposed.

"Sure, try calling one," my mom returned. I grabbed the phone book and flipped through the white pages quickly. I found a church nearby and called them. I explained to them our situation.

"Well, if you're underage, Mary, the church requires one month of marriage counseling. I can't marry you before I can show you've had counseling first. That's California law," the preacher said plainly. I turned to Booboo and my mom and shook my head, signaling it was a dead end. I thanked the preacher and hung up.

"What about Vegas? People get married there all the time," Booboo suggested. It seemed like a good idea, and I told him to call the Circus Circus. I remembered people walking around the casino in wedding dresses when I was a kid. Booboo called and explained that I was a minor and that my mom would be with us to sign any paperwork. They told him that they could marry us.

"Come on down. Once you get here, we can marry you. You don't need anything but her mom to sign the paperwork," the person on the phone explained. I turned to my mom to confirm she would go to Vegas with us to get married.

"Mary, if this is what we need to do, let's do it," she said. I didn't hesitate or question her decision. I looked at Booboo and said, "Let's go to Vegas!"

It was already two o'clock in the afternoon, and we focused on getting on the road. We needed to keep the momentum going. The headlights on

Booboo's Beetle were shoddy, so we needed to take my mom's car to Vegas. It would be roomy enough for the three of us as well. We headed out on the freeway right after filling up and buying some gas station snacks for the road. I had been eight and a half years old the last time I was in Vegas. A lot had changed since that time.

Pierre had visited Vegas before and had done a trip through the Grand Canyon and to Death Valley with his sister and her husband. He figured we'd be there by 7 p.m., at the latest, and back to Long Beach by midnight. That all sounded good to me as I tried to comprehend the reality that I was getting married and that I wasn't a little girl anymore. I imagined going through some kind of drive-through like in all the movies, then standing in front of a preacher who looked like Elvis to say my vows. It was all a mystery to me as to exactly how it would happen, but many thoughts ran through my mind. My memories of sitting and watching the acrobats practice and perform from the bleachers, dreaming of what it would be like not to be poor, to be pretty, and to be loved. I even went as far back as to remember sitting in the double swing with my sister and listening to her talk about wanting to be married one day with kids. Here I was, the youngest and about to get married.

For hours, we drove, and I created small talk and distractions. Periodically, my mom's car would overheat. Her car was a four-cylinder that hadn't been serviced in a while, and we were loaded: my mother was still over 350 pounds, and her two skinny cohorts still weighed another 250 pounds together. Every two hours, we'd pull over to the nearest gas station, open the hood to let the engine cool, and I'd run into the gas station to grab my mom snacks. Keeping her eating while she was stressed was the best thing we could do. This would ensure she was occupied and cooperative. We did this dance multiple times before we ever saw the glimmer and hope of lights from the distant strip that was Vegas. It took us a whole eleven hours to get there, whereas a normal trip would've only been four to five hours. By the time we arrived, I was exhausted. It was almost three in the morning. We walked into the Circus Circus and went straight to the hospitality desk.

"Hi, we're here to get married. Where do we need to go?" Booboo asked.

"You can't get married here unless you have an appointment. If you want to get married now, you can go over to the drive-through Little Vegas Chapel," the woman explained.

"We called earlier today—I mean, yesterday. We called and were told we could come down and get married, at any time," Booboo explained, exasperated.

"Well, whoever told you that was wrong. You need to make an appointment to get married. We can marry you tomorrow. We have time then," she said.

"Will there be any problem with her being under eighteen? We have her mom here to sign off on it," he told her.

"Oh, you can't get married here if she's under eighteen. You can't even get married at the drive-through if she's under eighteen. You have to go to the courthouse first before you can have a ceremony. You need to pick up a license first. That's going to cost you $380," she explained.

"But no one told us that when we called."

"I'm sorry, sir, but you have to go to the courthouse first."

"What time does the courthouse open?" Booboo asked.

"Eight a.m.," she said. My heart sank. This journey would be a full twenty-four hours before we had the hope of marriage, let alone sleep. What were we going to do for a full five hours before the courthouse opened? That was an eternity. A day filled with disappointment and delays and getting so close to the finish line I could taste it, and we were turned away.

We looked at each other and didn't quite know what to say. We were in Vegas. There was no doubt about that; slot machines were jingling all around us. I turned to Booboo and my mom and suggested we walk the strip. As we walked, I had an overwhelming feeling that I was lost. I had come all this way to make a huge change to my life, and now it wasn't happening. I wondered why. Was this a sign? Was I making the right decision?

We were standing in front of Treasure Island—fake bombs and pirates were swinging across the ship, and heat was coming from the attraction—when I started to cry. The weight of the decision I was making was overwhelming.

"Mary, don't cry. Please don't cry. This will be okay," Booboo assured me.

"I don't know. Maybe I'm not doing the right thing. We keep getting turned away everywhere we go, and now this." My emotions were bubbling up. I could feel the tears ready to come down my face like a hot spring. I started to take a few deep breaths.

"Mary, don't do this. This is going to be okay. We can get through this," Pierre assured me again. My mom was now staring at me and looking for a definitive sign to call it all off. I didn't know what I needed to do. So I took a few more breaths, a few sniffs, and pulled myself together. I needed to pull it together fast. I had to be strong. Booboo was right.

"So what should we do until the courthouse opens?" I asked them both while I wiped my eyes.

"I think we should go gamble," Pierre suggested. I thought about it for a second and decided that made sense. If we could keep my mom gambling for the next four-ish hours, we would be at the courthouse at 8 a.m. sharp and be married by 9 a.m. We could do this.

Mom sat down at a penny slot machine back at the Circus Circus casino, and Booboo handed her a twenty-dollar bill. She grabbed the money, excited to start on her gambling journey. I had only remembered her playing once when I was younger, so it was a bit thrilling to see her that happy again.

"Need anything to eat?" I asked her.

"Yeah, grab me some McDonald's. I'll take a cheeseburger and some fries," she requested. Booboo and I went to search for the food and to have our first moments alone since we started the journey from Long Beach eighteen hours ago.

"Do you think we can keep her occupied until 8 a.m.?" I asked him.

"I think we can. We just can't run out of money before the morning. I don't have enough for the license fee. Your mom has eaten most of our budget. I have to call my sister in the morning and have her send me the cash I need." He sounded a little more worried because he would have to try to wake his sister up by 7 a.m. and tell her that we were in Vegas and going to get married, and then have her wire us at least $400 before 8 a.m.

I thought about the task at hand, and I had confidence that since we'd gotten this far, we would see it through. We roamed through the sea of slot machines and card tables. Booboo played a few rounds of his favorite slot machine, Triple Cherry. He was actually lucky, winning twenty dollars here, forty dollars there. As the coins made their loud bang as they hit the tray, I'd grab a few and sat at the next slot machine. Once I ran out of coins, I'd grab some more from his tray.

"You know, this is going to be our life. I make the money, and you take it," he said jokingly.

"I can live with that," I said and laughed.

It neared 6 a.m., and my mom had gambled forty dollars away and had eaten several cheeseburgers. She had moved to the nickel slots and seemed to be doing quite well. We had an hour to kill before Booboo had to call his sister. It felt like the longest hour yet. To kill some more time, we walked around to the shops selling souvenirs. One of them was selling jewelry.

"We're getting married today, and we need two rings. We would prefer silver," Pierre told the lady at the counter.

"We have these here. They're not expensive. Men's rings are twelve dollars, and women's rings are ten dollars," she said. We took out the rings and tried a few on our fingers. I looked inside mine and noticed the engraving said, "Made in Mexico."

"Hey, so mine is already engraved. How sweet is that?" I told him jokingly.

"Wow, we're fancy! Mine's engraved with that, too." He laughed. We felt good about our twenty-two-dollar purchase, and he put the rings in his pocket. The pressure of waiting for 7 a.m. was beginning to be too much, so Booboo found the desk that had the yellow Western Union sign above it and asked to use their phone. He dialed his sister's number and stared at me while he called. When she picked up, he explained why we were in Vegas and asked her to wire the money quickly. She agreed. Booboo paced and smoked his rolled Drum cigarettes while we waited for the man behind the counter to tell him the money had arrived. My mom didn't know I smoked, so I didn't try to partake. While we waited, my mom and I played the slot machine, taking turns pulling the lever. It kept us both focused on something else. Then it was 7:45 a.m., and Booboo was called to the Western Union table.

"Are you Pierre?" the big burly man behind the counter asked him. "Yes."

"Let me see some ID." Booboo pulled out his oversized wallet that was made to carry large Belgian francs, which seemed almost twice the size of American bills. He laid his ID on the table for the man to inspect.

"Okay, you have a wire from Madeleine. It's $450. Please sign here." She'd sent him a little more than what we needed, just in case. After Booboo signed for the money and stuffed it into his wallet, he asked the man where the Clark County Courthouse was. It was luckily right down the street, only a few blocks away, and would be open any minute.

"Let's go, Mom. We can be the first ones in the courthouse," I told her like it would be something fun we could do. "We can grab some breakfast afterward."

We got in her car and drove the mile and a half to the courthouse. Just as we walked up at 8 a.m., the doors opened. *We are finally here and this is happening,* I thought.

"Where's the county clerk's office?" I asked the man who had just opened the door. "We need a marriage license."

"It's down the hall there, to your right," he said as he pointed one finger toward the end of the hall. I walked with as brisk of a pace as I could muster, knowing that I had to walk slower than my heart wanted to keep pace with my mom and her bad hip. She waddled at a slow pace. When we finally got to the counter, we were the first in line. In fact, there was no one standing behind us either.

"We need a marriage certificate. I'm under eighteen, so my mom is here to sign the form as well," I told the clerk.

"Okay then. Everyone, take out your IDs. Mother, I'll need you to testify that you are allowing your daughter to marry. Do you give consent?" she asked my mother, staring right at her with an impatient expression.

"Yes, I do give consent," Mom said in a soft tone. It sounded almost like she was following orders, but not exactly sure why.

"Well, okay then. Mom gives consent. You two need to fill out the top portion, name and address, birthdays and social security numbers." She took all of our IDs and left to make copies. Then she came back to read the application. "Okay, Pierre, age twenty-seven, born in Liège, Belgium. Mary, age seventeen, born in Nashville, Tennessee. Mother, Linda Bernhardt, we won't say your age. Please sign here, Linda." I stepped aside as the form was pushed to my mother to sign. She looked at me, "Age twenty-seven?" she asked.

"I know, I didn't want to tell you. I just didn't want you to get mad. Please sign, Mom. I want to be done and back home," I said with a bit of impatience. She signed the paper, and the clerk asked Booboo for the application fee.

"That will be $380," she said. Booboo pulled out the money from his oversized wallet. The clerk counted it and started stamping the forms for the license application.

"Okay, now you have to go to the office around the corner. This is where they're going to read you your vows and sign your marriage license. This will make it legally binding. Don't worry, it's no additional charge."

We walked around the corner, Mom still trailing a good few steps behind, and I opened a door that led to a small office. It had a small desk with two chairs in front of it and one off to the side, and a large cash register sat on top of it, the kind you'd find in an old grocery store. There was a beer-bellied man in a light-blue polyester suit sitting behind the desk.

"Well, hello there. You two here to get married?" he asked in a very flamboyant country voice while he aimed a wide smile in our direction and placed his hands on his hips and leaned his body back like he was about to say, *Guuurrrl*. His demeanor was way too happy for that early in the morning. I wanted to imagine he was gay. As he stood up, he revealed a large brass belt buckle that said, "Vegas," on it. I thought that this experience couldn't get any stranger, that I was living through an out-of-body experience.

"Okay, let's start the vows," he said as he slapped his hands together like he was making a deal. My feet were beginning to get a little wobbly. My stomach was feeling hollow. I didn't dare look at my mom; this was already uncomfortable. It was like I could feel my mom watching me become a woman. I stood there in my dark outfit: black velvet bell bottoms, a black halter top with silver print that said, "Rock Star," and some beat-up black Converse. That wasn't at all what I expected being married would look like, but there we were. The man read my vows, saying, "Will you this, and will you that," and at the end of it, I said, "I do." I knew that when you got married, you said, "I do," not "I will." I could hear my mother let out a small cry. She was having an emotional experience, too, and I was starting to feel it, to understand it. The man then asked Pierre, "Will you this, will you that?" and he said, "I will." *Damn it,* I thought. Of course, I went with the traditional response and Booboo went with the grammatically correct one. Then my mom's cries became stronger and louder.

Booboo and I kissed quickly and bent over to sign the certificate application. The man in the light blue polyester suit signed our forms and stamped them a few times.

"Okay, kids, you're married! I wish you both a wonderful life," he said, shooting us that happy and excited smile of his. I smiled, too, and stared at Booboo. I felt a brief feeling of relief. Here we were, married. We had done it. I turned to my mother, who now seemed to realize what had just happened. I leaned down to give her a hug. Her cheeks were wet from crying, and she looked at me. "My baby, you're married. I don't want this anymore. I want to undo what we just did. You're too young to be married," she said in a voice filled with regret.

"No, Mom. It's done. We can't undo it," I told her calmly. She stood up, and we all walked out of the office, resigned to it all. The awkwardness filled the long hallway as we exited the courthouse. All the emotions from the past twenty-four hours flooded over me. But I had to keep it together.

My mom stopped just outside the courthouse doors. "We have to go back in there. I'm going to undo this. You lied to me. You said he was twenty-four. You lied, Mary," she told me. I kept walking down the street, toward the car, farther and farther from the courthouse doors. She followed me.

"Mom, I'm sorry I lied about his age, but everything else is true. I love him, and we're married now. You can't undo this." I wasn't actually sure if there were any "take backs" in the legal system, but I banked on the fact that there weren't. The realization was hitting her like a ton of bricks. She, too, had married at age seventeen, and my father was twenty-seven. This was jarring her to the core. *Just keep walking toward the car,* I told myself. I could hear her crying behind me.

My confidence, if only temporarily, helped to lead her to the car, and I even convinced her to get on the road to go back home. If the next eleven hours on the road were going to start, I wanted them to start ASAP. This time, Booboo insisted on driving a few legs of the trip to help my mom get some sleep on the way home—and likely get us there before we all fainted from exhaustion. It had been a long, long twenty-four hours. Before leaving the city limits, I was already fast asleep, and so was my mom.

I woke up three hours later to hear Mom and Booboo speaking gently to each other, so as to not wake me. He was talking about his family in Belgium, how he had gotten to America, about his sister and how she came to the U.S. as an au pair for a French-speaking lawyer's family. She seemed to be enjoying the conversation and resigning herself to getting to know him. I stirred a little and asked how close we were to Long Beach.

"Just another hour," Booboo said from the driver's seat. We were almost back home, and now I was feeling like the change was real. I was scared of how my mother would react when I would tell her that I wasn't going to go back to the house with her, that I was going to get dropped off at Booboo's. When we pulled up to the liquor store parking lot and parked, Booboo pulled out his wallet and handed my mom forty dollars.

"Here's some money to fill your tank back up and some money for food. Will this be enough?" he asked her. My mom took the money and thanked him.

"Do you want to come get some food with me, Mary?" my mom asked.

"I'm going to stay at Pierre's place today. We're going to get some sleep. We can call you when we wake up, and we can all go get dinner," I said boldly and held my breath.

"No, you should come home with me, Mary," she said like a mother does with her child.

"I'm going to stay with Pierre, Mom. I'll call you when we get up." I started to get out of the car. Booboo did the same, and my mom pulled herself out of the passenger seat and waddled her way to the driver's side. She winced as she fell into her seat. Her hips were probably sore from our travels. As she sat down and got herself situated, she rolled down her window and looked at me.

"Mary, I don't think you've done a good thing. He's too old for you. I think you should call this off, right now." Her tone was beginning to get stronger, as if she was trying to reestablish control over me.

"No, Mom. I'm not going to undo this. I'm going to be with Pierre," I told her.

"You're making a big mistake, Mary. Don't call me later. I don't want to hear from you. You lied to me," she said angrily. I stood there looking at her with no intention to call her back. She backed out of the parking lot, and I watched her drive away. I felt very alone in that moment, realizing that I was now making a choice to leave home for good. And she was right. I had lied.

"Let's go home, Mary," Booboo said to me. I followed him back to *our* apartment with my head hung low. Once we got to the door, he looked at me with a grin and said, "I should pick you up and walk you through the door."

"Yes. Yes, you should." I stood there smiling and wondering how someone his height was going to lift someone my height up and through the door. I did a small hop into his arms, and he grabbed me. Then he walked three steps inside and immediately let my legs down.

"Well, we did it. We're married!" he said as he smiled at me. I liked that at least the gesture of carrying me over the threshold had been traditional.

"We did do it," I told him. I smiled, but then immediately felt my energy depleted. I walked over to our mattress on the floor, crawled into the bed, and without any more words, laid my head down and quickly passed out.

I woke up to the sound of Booboo's house phone ringing. He had answered it and was softly speaking to someone on the other line. I could barely hear what he was saying. He hung up the phone and came over to the bed.

"It's your mom. She's been calling. She says she wants you to come home." I stared at him and rubbed my eyes. It was already 9 p.m., and I'd slept for a good six hours. I wasn't ready to talk to her, but I told him that the next time she called, I would pick up the phone. We ordered Pizza Hut and got our favorite, the Supreme. We hugged each other while we waited for it to arrive. We then poured ourselves water and stirred in some Lipton iced tea powder. When the pizza arrived, it tasted better than ever. The crust was greasy from being a deep dish and the tangy tomato sauce, bell peppers, sausage, and pepperoni were all that we needed to feel at home. I was happy. I wasn't feeling nervous or insecure anymore. I was feeling that sense of home I'd always wanted to feel. My new home. We finished the whole pizza and decided to walk over to Portfolio to share the good news with everyone. I was sure that they would all be shocked, but we didn't care. I figured if anyone got too judgemental, I'd play it off like we were just married for convenience and that we'd call it off in two years when he got his green card. I was still too insecure to accept this new life, or marriage, and what other people thought about this crazy union.

As we arrived at Portfolio, Booboo's co-worker Leo was sitting there having a cup of coffee out on the patio. Booboo had called him during one of our rest stops on our way to Vegas.

"Well you old dog, you, Pierre. Look at you two. You two are married, huh?" he said while he laughed and smiled. Leo had known me for a good year by then; he was a regular like me. Then a few other friends of mine came over to our table. They were all around my age, and hearing the news shocked them, as I expected. But I downplayed the massiveness of my decision and said that it was no big deal, that we'd invite them all to the divorce party in a few years. This seemed to make everything a lot more lighthearted and I didn't have to explain to them how much I deeply loved Booboo, and that for some crazy reason I thought this marriage would work out. I didn't know what a marriage was supposed to be, but I knew what a divorce was, so I stuck to my lighthearted banter as we shared the news.

Over the next forty-eight hours, all our friends were in disbelief as we shared our story. They couldn't believe that we had accomplished what we set out to do and all the twists and turns we had to go through. It seemed the most surprising part for everyone was that it took us eleven long hours to get to Vegas. They hoped it was all worth it. It was. We were going to be in this together, and even though we didn't know what "this" was, we knew that if we could go through what we just went through to get married, we could do anything.

A NEW LIFE

It was easy living this new life. I had made the transition to living at Booboo's apartment and out of my mom's place. His employer, knowing he had gotten married, gave him a full-time position and raised his wages another $12,000 a year. We got a new apartment just around the corner from our favorite coffeehouse almost immediately. But I wasn't completely living this new life. My mother would call the house several times a day and leave angry messages or scream at me for leaving her whenever I picked up the phone. She'd threaten to call the immigration office on Booboo. I was scared, but I also had many years of experience dealing with my mother. I knew a lot of what she said were empty threats, that she was upset at being lied to, and felt excluded. And, she wasn't wrong. I had manipulated her in order to get a new life. I felt I had no other choice, and even though it wasn't right, I also wasn't the only one who had left my mother. My brother was in Tennessee living his life, and my sister was living with her boyfriend. So I told myself not to fear my mother anymore. She had the keys to my childhood, and that story had already been written. She had projected her fears and insecurities onto me for far too many years, and I was now free. Yes, I had gotten freedom from lying to her, but the truth was I loved my husband.

I would still have to work through years of dealing with my mother's paranoia and keep pushing her out of my life. I still had all my own fears. I had just walked up to the diving platform, looked into this new life, and jumped right in. My life had been turning around gradually. But for my mom, it had happened overnight. All of a sudden, I was a woman and had left home. Sure, I was still just a seventeen-year-old, and yes, that was a crazy decision. The odds that it would work out were slim to none. No doubt about it. But I had been observing people and their choices my entire life. I was a chameleon. I knew a good thing when I saw it, because I'd had a whole life of seeing the wrong thing: people doing the wrong thing, and the wrong thing happening to me. I felt no threat here with him. I could be who I was, fully. I could look how I looked, fully. There was no threat here.

This would be the beginning of my life out of the immediate sphere of my mentally unstable mother. I no longer had to wake up to a house full of papers, dirty dishes, the smell of piss, a fridge with no food, and rotten bags of veggies. When you don't have to worry about someone waking you up in the middle of the night telling you how everyone is out to get her, your brain changes. When you don't have to come home to find your mom crying in her bed, convinced she is worthless, and then have to convince her she's not, you start to focus on yourself. But I did want to look back. I agonized any time she called, and each time she did, I would pick up and wait for the moment when it got crazy or mean.

If she needed rent, I'd ask Booboo for money, then drive it over to her apartment. She'd plead for me to come back home, then I'd have to leave feeling torn. One night, I went over there to pay her rent shortly after we moved into our new apartment. I was to pay the forty dollars that was her HUD-assisted rent. The money order cost fifty cents. So I showed up with a money order for $39.50. When I handed it to her, she took one look at it and started yelling at me. "I can't use this for my rent, Mary! I can't give this to them for the rent. It has to be exactly forty dollars."

"I didn't have anything more than forty dollars. The money order was fifty cents. Can't you give them another fifty cents?" I asked.

"No, I can't give them fifty cents. First off, I don't have fifty cents, and it has to be exactly forty dollars or they won't accept it. I asked you for a forty-dollar money order. Why can't you do anything right?" She was now crying.

"Listen, I'll go downstairs, and Booboo and I will get another money order for fifty cents," I told her reassuringly.

"If you don't, you'll be the reason why I lose my HUD benefits. This is on you, Mary."

I got into Booboo's car and closed the door slowly. I asked him to take me to the store to get another money order for fifty cents. And he did. When I knocked back on the door to give her the fifty-cent money order, she opened it, grabbed the money order from my hand, threw a handful of pictures at me, and slammed the door quickly.

I picked them up, and my heart began to sink. She had cut out my face from the very few pictures we had as kids growing up. It was like from a movie when someone cut their old boyfriend out of their pictures. Some of the pictures were only cut and not completely lost. This was one of the biggest insults she'd ever given me. I felt like I was only good for money at this point. I was no longer the child she knew; that's what she meant to say. And she was right. This reality stung. I went back to Booboo's car and started to cry as soon as I closed the door. I could barely contain the tears as I tried to explain to him how mean she had been. These were also my sister's memories. So few and rare were these pictures that a part of me was relieved they were actually now in my possession. Booboo grabbed them and told me, "Don't worry, Mary. I'll tape them back together when we get back to the house." And he did just that, pulling out the tape and carefully putting back together what he could. He would ask me about each picture. I'd give him the backstory of how old I was and where we lived at the time. It was therapeutic. Even though the physical memory was damaged, I realized that the memory didn't have to be. I started to feel like those were the old days. It *was* the past and now my life would change and new memories would be made.

I carried myself differently after that night, and I didn't take as many of her phone calls anymore. I had to disconnect from her, from her grip, and be the person I was destined to be. This didn't stop her from reaching out, but soon my sister and her boyfriend moved back in with her, and they helped pay her rent. My mom would sometimes show up at the coffeehouse and stay for a few hours, waiting for me to show up, then leave. A few of the regulars would often tell me I had just missed her.

I was working a service job at Baskin-Robbins while taking classes to get my GED at Long Beach City College, the same school I had been to many times before while my mom attended it. I was driving an old Beamer that one of Booboo's colleagues had loaned us since he knew we were young and needed the help. I didn't have a license or insurance, but I quickly took care of that and signed up for driving school. Both of our cars didn't have insurance, but the class instructor promised I would have an insured car the day I took the test. It was worth it, and after four weekends of official practice, I took my test and passed.

I had figured out how to get my birth certificate by ordering it from the local library, since my mother refused to give it to me. I had been able to hold on to my tattered social security card from when we filled out the marriage license in Vegas. This had proved to be more important than the birth certificate, because with it you can get your state ID, get a job, and enroll in school. It was strange, but I had started the process to become a bona fide adult, and it felt liberating. I had no problem with the process of getting my official papers and my ID at the DMV. I'd spent plenty of time at these places as a child, and I knew how to navigate them. I knew how to do these things; how to fill out paperwork, find resources, apply for jobs. I'd not only watched my mom do these things, but I had helped her along the way, too.

Booboo got his driver's license and a social security card shortly after we were married. His social security card had, "Not Valid for Employment," across the top, just under his name. We quickly started the immigration process, got a secured credit card from Bank of America, opened a joint banking account, started building our credit and our case to prove to the INS we actually married for love. We worked really well together. We were both determined to make it and fully invested in our relationship and our life. Many challenges arose, yet none were as challenging as the life I had lived with my mother in poverty.

It was just a year later in 1996 that we connected our home computer to the internet using a 56K modem. This opened up many possibilities, but one I hadn't expected. One night after work, we were sitting in the living room and the idea to find my father came up. Booboo said that he could go online and search for my dad, that he was sure he could easily find him. Booboo found three men named Jack D. Gregory in Nashville's online white pages. We decided on a game plan. Booboo would call the first number, and I'd call the other two. I was afraid to actually call. Somehow, I had the feeling like I was doing something wrong, that my mother would disapprove and be mad at me. I had to think rationally, though. I was an adult now, and nothing was stopping me. Not even her.

He dialed the first number. I nervously rolled a cigarette, which I'd now embraced as my primary way to smoke, and waited for the other person to come on the line. It turned out it wasn't my father. So I called the second number. I knew this would be the *real* Jack Gregory; that's how these things worked. It rang five times before someone answered.

"Hello," said a man with a thick southern accent.

"Hello, my name is Mary Gregory. Is this Jack Gregory?"

"No, Jack isn't home right now. Can I take a message?"

"I wanted to know if this is the Jack Gregory who has three children: Paul, Samantha, and Mary."

"Yes, that's brother Jack. He's at church right now, but I will tell him you called."

I couldn't believe it. I had called the home of my actual father. A piece of me felt excited and the other scared. He was real, and I was actually going to talk to him soon.

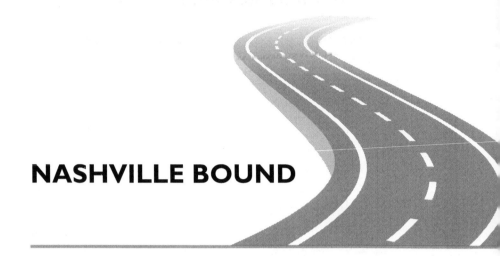

NASHVILLE BOUND

My father did call me back just a few hours later. Despite my nervousness, he seemed relaxed and happy to hear from me. I couldn't remember exactly what we spoke about; there was too much swirling through my mind. He seemed old and somewhat timid. He had a soft southern voice that easily started and finished a thought, and then that would be it; he'd wait for you to speak. He wasn't overly enthusiastic. He didn't push or prod me for information. He just let me know the facts. My brother still lived in Nashville, and my father gave me his number. I immediately called Paul and shared with him all that had happened since he had tried to see me after my surgery when I was fourteen. He encouraged me to come back to Nashville, to see him and Dad. He told me that Dad had been through a lot in the past few years and wasn't the same. He'd had several shock therapy treatments and was on medication for his depression. He said that his ex-lover had really done a number on him, taken a lot of his money, and given him hepatitis C.

Paul was working the night shift at a printing company and would need a few days' notice to change his schedule around before I decided to go visit. When I hung up, I knew that I would be planning a trip to Nashville soon. Booboo was encouraging and wanted me to take the trip.

I was feeling more grown up than ever now, and this new chapter of my new life was just beginning.

I had been on a plane for the first time just a few months before. Booboo's company needed him to attend a meeting in San Francisco, and he asked them if I could join him. They said yes. We had a nice room in a fancy hotel, and while he was in meetings all day, I walked around and perused record stores to find a few CDs Booboo had told me he wanted. But this time, I would be traveling alone and staying with my dad. The same dad that I hadn't seen in thirteen years. I was scared to go, but I was also excited. I would see my brother, too, who I didn't really know well either. It had meant a lot to me that he came to the hospital with Dad to see me after my surgery. I thought that I should at least do my best to visit now that I had the full power to see anyone I pleased.

I coordinated the visit with my dad, keeping the trip to only three days, including air travel. This was my way to keep myself safe, just in case it didn't turn out to be what I hoped it would be.

I made small talk with the few people sitting next to me. I was new to the small talk people expected of you when you sit in such close quarters on a plane. The woman I had sat next to asked me a simple question about where I was going and why, and from there, she wanted to know as much as she could about my story. We talked nearly the full four-hour flight.

As the plane landed, I pulled in all my courage. I hoped that my dad would recognize me and I would recognize him. I'd only seen the picture my mom had of him from when he came out of the closet. I hoped he would be happy to see me and tell me how much he missed me. I prepared myself for that initial awkwardness I knew would be there once we saw each other.

I walked out of the plane and read the signs to the baggage claim. The woman from the plane tapped me on the shoulder and wished me luck before she walked off with her bag. I focused back on the bags turning around, spotted mine, and grabbed it. Then I turned around to search across the airport. Looking high and low, I wasn't quite sure what I was looking for. But then suddenly, there stood my father. I leaped into his arms and hugged him for a little while. I wanted to feel close to him in the hopes of getting some kind of understanding of him. My nerves went away as he pulled back, looked at me, and smiled.

He wasn't emotional, at least not outwardly. I proceeded to follow him to his car. There was some small talk, with me remarking how much of his face I remembered. How our eyes were almost exactly the same, blue and cat-like. I didn't mind any of the simple talk or the not-knowing-what-to-say silence while we drove to his house. I was just fine staring at him. I was with my father! What a journey it had been. We rode in his old black Lincoln, which made me remember playing in the broken-down Lincoln he'd had in the driveway all those years ago, the one I'd explored before we left Tennessee. He was different than I remembered. He was older now, of course, but he was still my dad, and enough of his memory filled in the gaps.

He called Paul, and we made arrangements to hang out that night and the next day. Paul came by around 8 p.m. and said we could spend a few hours before he had to go to work. I recognized Paul's profile as soon as he pulled into Dad's driveway. His hair was long and in a ponytail, and he had put on some weight since the last time I saw him. He looked healthier, older and taller, and free like me.

"There's my little sis. It's so good to see you, Mary!" Paul said with his deep, scruffy voice while he gave me a big hug, lifted me off the ground, and twirled me around a few times. It was a surprising side to see of my brother. He seemed happy, which was wonderful and reassuring.

I spent those few hours catching Paul and Dad up on my life. Paul couldn't believe how I pulled off getting married and got out of the house. He shared what it was like living with our Aunt Evelyn, our mom's eldest sister who lived in Texas, where Paul went first before moving in with Aunt Ruth. He shared how Evelyn and her husband supported him while he got his GED and helped him with transportation to and from school, how they fed him and encouraged him. It was the first time in a long time that he had felt taken care of and wanted.

"Mary, I was really fucked up before I left Long Beach. I was on drugs and desperately needed a way out of the ghetto. Everything changed in Long Beach after the L.A. Riots. Our aunts really saved me. Then I moved in with Dad and his boyfriend," Paul told me.

Dad's boyfriend Felix was awful, from what Paul said. They had gotten in a fight one night because Paul was tired of the way he was treating Dad. But Dad wouldn't leave him, so Paul moved out and got his own place. He told me that Felix was the one who green-lit Dad's shock treatment. After several rounds of that, he said Dad hadn't been the same since. Had I just met Dad two years earlier, I'd be meeting a different person than I was now. He would've been more full of life.

"If I ever see that asshole again, I'm going to kill him," Paul told me. Luckily Dad and Felix had broken up and he was no longer in the picture.

Dad said he used to have a lot of cats. Just a year before, he had ten, but there was only one now. His neighbor poisoned all of them. I asked him why his neighbor would do that, and he said plainly, "He doesn't like gays. He's thrown nails and tacks on my driveway, too. That popped a few of my tires."

It felt strange to be talking to my father and brother, adult to adult. I felt a new relationship with each of them building with every moment. I shared with them that Mom had spent the last $1,200 from the house proceeds on Herbalife. That besides the car she'd bought, the home furnishings from Kmart, and the trip to Nashville for my nose surgery five years before, there wasn't much left of it. Paul and Dad shared how upset they were knowing I was just behind a door and Mom wouldn't let them see me.

The next day, we all drove together to a restaurant not far from the flea market Dad wanted to take us to. We talked during breakfast, and though Paul was pretty tired after having been at work all night, he showed no signs that he didn't want to hang out as much as he could.

During our trip to the flea market, my dad asked me bluntly, "Are you a lesbian, Mary?" I didn't quite know what to say, but I told him flat out, "Well, I am bisexual. I do like girls, but I would rather be married to a man."

It was awkward to say this to my father. My brother sat in the back seat silently. Dad drove near Centennial Park, and as we passed a man running along the road with no shirt on and small shorts, Dad honked and yelled out my open passenger window, "Owwww!" The man looked toward us, and my dad just smiled and kept driving. I looked back at my brother, eyes wide and smiling, too. He smiled back at me and shook his head. Was this what it was like to have an out-of-body experience? Just twenty-four hours after reuniting with my dad, he was asking if I was a lesbian and catcalling men running down the road.

The trip to the flea market was more subdued. I found a bracelet that had been soldered together with seven pennies, three of which had the birth years of my brother, sister, and me; 1974, 1976, and 1978. I had to have it, and my father paid for it immediately. My brother found a cufflink that had the Queen of Sheba on it. He would later get a tattoo of it on his left calf, marking the importance of this day. I asked an old man to take our picture as we stood near someone who had just sold our dad an antique end table. The three of us stood there in the sun, smiling. Looking at it now, we looked like three peas in a pod. The wrinkle in between our brows, our wide smiles, high cheekbones, and our similar heights, there couldn't have been a more obvious familial relationship. I kept that picture in my wallet for nearly fifteen years.

I perused pictures in boxes in my father's basement. I stared at baby pictures of Paul, Sam, and me, family photos of my aunt Carolina, my grandpa Jack, even of my parents sitting together when they were young, smiling even. There were pictures I had never seen before in bountiful quantities, a sign that our parents were once young and happy and wanted to document it. I was connecting to that period of my life when I was just a small child, living in Nashville, when things were more normal than they would ever be again. You never know when normal will go away or when it will return, but looking into the past like I was, through these pictures, I could see the more normal times of my early youth. I was fascinated with this box of memories. It was the largest set of pictures of my life that I had ever seen.

Dad interrupted my journey through the past and suggested we go to the gay church where he ministered every Wednesday night. It would be mostly empty, and he could show me around. We walked into the church and Dad walked right up to the organ, sat down, and asked that I find a seat wherever I wanted. I looked around and saw a few random people sitting by themselves. Some looked sad; some looked hopeful. I found a seat at the front of the church and sat there looking up at the large and powerful pipes. I stared at them and waited for something to happen. I hadn't been in a church for years, let alone one that had a pipe organ. I faintly remember my father playing the organ at our old church.

All of a sudden, the sound hit me. My heart sank under the burden of memories and danced in joy at the same time. The church filled with the sound of the organ; the deep, dramatic, and melodic sounds vibrated my whole body. Magic was happening right then and there, and I began to see the other colors of my prism, the ones that made the full picture of me, through my father playing the organ. I was part sound. I looked around to somehow get a confirmation that this was happening, that I was now all my colors, yet no one looked my way. They each looked forward, toward the pipes, immersed in the sound. I succumbed to the music. I imagined the notes as words from my father and that I was somehow experiencing what it was like to have a dad. This was his way of showing me he loved me. I started to cry. There was no control over it either; it just poured out of me. Several years of pain was allowed to release. These emotions couldn't be held inside anymore, and as the beautiful music went on and on, I cried harder and harder until I had nothing more to let out.

The music stopped, and I felt a deep, calm aura circling slowly around me, and then it went up and out of the room and left me lighter. I knew that my father wouldn't be able to speak to me like he just had with his music, yet I heard all I needed to hear. He loved me. I knew that now.

SISTER'S CITY

I decided when I got back to Long Beach, that I would go to Sam's work and drop off the pictures I had of her as a child that Dad had given me. He'd given me a lot of pictures. She and I hadn't been in touch for over a year. I wanted to give her the same kind of feeling I'd felt when I'd seen the pictures for the first time, and maybe she'd want to see our father again. I wrote her a little note, telling her that I had seen Dad and spent time with Paul. I gave her my number and handed the envelope to one of her colleagues. Just two days later, I got a call from Sam. She had been very moved by receiving the pictures and told me she ended up crying in a bathroom stall at work after seeing them. She was determined to see Dad soon and ended up booking a Greyhound bus with plans to leave just a week later. The Greyhound would take three days to get to Nashville, but she didn't care. She was going to see Dad and Paul. She told me she had moved out of our mom's place and was living in an apartment with her boyfriend Raymond. Not surprisingly, Mom had been too hard to live with, and the moment they had enough money, they moved out.

Sam ended up spending a full week in Nashville. Our aunt Ruth heard from Paul that Sam was in town and wanted to see her, too, so she bought her a plane ride back home, and this allowed Ruth to see Sam while she was in Tennessee. When Sam got back, she shared the same opinion I had about our father, that he was a nice older man but didn't talk much. She ended up going out with Paul and his girlfriend Ima to a few dance clubs. Ima spoke Spanish and loved to salsa dance like Sam, so they instantly bonded and enjoyed the nightlife out on the town. Sam took tons of pictures, and it was nice to see Nashville from her perspective. She had spent more time with Paul than I had. They had even gone to the zoo. Sam felt she'd reconnected with Paul, and this made me feel like we were becoming more like the siblings we were meant to be. This was a new start. And now that we were all adults, no longer living at home, it was our choice now how we would treat each other.

Sam and I started to spend more time together, and we began to get closer. She and her boyfriend Raymond, though, were going through a hard time, and it would just be a few months later that they would break up. I had spent enough time with her in the past few months to know that she was downright miserable. I helped her move out of their apartment one day while Raymond was at work. But Sam found her passion and love of dancing and singing again and wasn't going to let go of it. The confirmation that you are more than just one person in your family, more than their fears and shortcomings, has a magical way to open up your horizons. I had opened mine by getting married, and it seemed Sam had opened hers by leaving Raymond.

RECONSTRUCTING MY LIFE

I had laid down several seeds over the last few years. The journey to repair my cleft lip and palate, along with my desire to go to college, required me to keep my focus. I had obtained my GED certificate, which arrived at our apartment a few months after I had taken it. The date was August 18th, 1997; our two-year wedding anniversary.

When my husband got his next raise, he came home and immediately told me that I could stop working as a cashier at the local drug store, Savon's, and start planning for college. I also yearned to finally get the reconstructive surgeries I needed to fully repair my cleft lip and palate. I wanted to get my "two front teeth" as Santa Claus had always promised me as well as finally fix my lip and nose. This dream was quickly becoming a reality.

After I quit my job, I met with a counselor at Long Beach City College and started mapping out my college career. I would focus on computer skills and the liberal arts. I took the entrance exam in order to gauge my reading, writing, and math levels, and I was quickly put into the lowest math class they offered. I didn't test very well, but my writing and reading results were above average. I began my college career in the fall of 1997. That semester, I received all A's and one C. The C was in a class I took that was to help new college students prepare for college life; somehow I missed an assignment. But I still ended my first semester with a 3.8 GPA.

During my first semester, I also focused on my surgeries. I met with several specialists until I felt I'd found the right team of doctors who would work on my case. I wasn't sure how I felt about being a "case" after all the years we were on welfare and were referred to as a "case." But I had a burning desire to no longer look like a person with a cleft lip and palate. I knew my deformity would never be fully repairable. Someone like me will always have a wide and misshapen nose that's somewhat bulbous at the tip. I'll always have visible scars that run from my nose to my lip. I'll have a Cupid's bow that's crooked, and unless I get dental implants or dentures, my teeth will always be a bit misshapen or missing.

My husband always marveled at my confidence. Someone who looked like me wasn't supposed to act like me, he would tell me. It's that quality that drew him to me in the first place. But my confidence had been built slowly and unknowingly. Maybe it was from spending many of my years having to endure teasing and bullying and hardship that I'd developed a kind but confident "fuck it" attitude. *What do I have to lose?* I would think to myself when times were hard. No matter what I had done in life, no matter how nice of a person I was, I could be stared at or made fun of at any time and by anyone, young or old, so why would I care what someone said to me in passing anymore? Slowly, I realized that caring about others, knowing that some had it worse than me—yes, my life wasn't the worst thing that had ever happened in this world—took the sting out of my hardships and, over time, slowly made me more confident. I'd adapted like the chameleon. I was aware of myself and accepted what I needed to do to survive: be resilient.

How would I look and feel once my surgeries repaired my deformity? What would looking "normal" feel like? I could go anywhere and people wouldn't stare at me. How would having front teeth make me look? I could smile without covering my mouth. I was still going to have to go through the surgeries, but the hope alone was enough to make me ready for the challenge. I had a purpose to work toward. A dream.

My team of doctors—an orthodontist, prosthodontist, and maxillofacial and reconstructive surgeons—all worked together to plan out my surgeries.

We wove surgeries and healing time around my college classes and my life for five years. In this time, I had over seven surgeries, two of which were to build the bone I would need to implant front teeth. I would need several teeth extractions and to wear braces for three years.

The first of the four major surgeries was to take bone marrow from my hip and put it in the gum tissue where my front teeth would be one day. The two holes inside of my lip that I used to do my "milk through the nose" parlor trick to get snacks in elementary school were going to get closed up, and so would the small hole in the roof of my mouth. The little tiny shark tooth that poked out of my top gum as a cruel reminder that I didn't have normal front teeth would get yanked while I was out as well.

I was somewhat prepared for this first surgery, given what I had endured for my nose surgery when I was fourteen. Yet waking up in the post-op room after my bone graft and oral fissure closures, I was in a world of hurt that I wasn't prepared for. The sheer pounding sensation I felt in my mouth, which never stopped, leveled me. Everything felt bumpy and prickly from the stitches, and some parts were slimy as I ran my tongue around my mouth to feel what had happened. My hip ached from where they'd taken out my bone marrow. They'd given me morphine for the pain, and as they took me back to my room, unpleasant side effects set in. I felt hot, then cold, and this all made me feel like I was having a panic attack. I barely made it to a bedpan when the blood that had pooled in my stomach from the surgery came shooting out of my mouth. Luckily, the doctor was able to counter the effects of the morphine quite quickly, and soon, the episode was over. I lay in the bed wondering what it would feel like when the pain meds wore off.

The car ride home the next day was a queasy one, with every bump feeling like a little knife jab to my brain. I tried to turn my face toward the sun so that I could feel the deep, soothing warmth. Once we got into the apartment, I felt just tired enough to lie down and attempt sleep. Booboo ran out quickly to get my pain medicine, antibiotics, and a few other recommended liquids for when I woke up. I drifted to sleep. What seemed like a few moments later, I woke up in a tremendous amount of pain. My face and mouth throbbed, and saliva and blood had dried around the corners of my mouth. I called out to Booboo through the blood-soaked bandages that packed the inside of my mouth. I didn't hear anything. I called for him again with the little energy I had, but still no answer. I would be alone with my pain until Booboo returned home. The pain was building up so strong that I couldn't control my emotions. All I could do was sob loudly and rock myself in an attempt to soothe the pain.

Booboo eventually walked into the apartment, heard me crying, and rushed to my side.

"It hurts. It hurts so bad!" I told him, looking for some kind of relief in his eyes. He handed me a Vicodin pill while he ran to the kitchen to open up some apple juice he'd just bought. I swallowed the pill with care, as each swallow made my tongue put pressure on my many surgery sites. Each swallow carried with it little traces of iron from my blood. My mouth felt like a big open wound.

It took nearly three days before the pain was at a reasonable level. I could make it manageable by sitting under hot showers, which I'd end up doing in the middle of the night when I couldn't sleep. Doing warm rinses with salt water helped, too. I had to be delicate because all the goo and blood had a purpose. It would all help to ensure my surgery sites healed properly.

My face was swollen and puffed up like I was a chipmunk for almost a week, which then luckily resolved the following week. After three weeks, I was feeling better, but definitely still in recovery. It was nearly eight weeks until I was finally healed on the outside. It would be another four months before I would be considered "ready" for another surgery. It would be three years and several surgeries later, before my top gums were able to get dental implants.

NEW KIDS ON THE BLOCK

A few weeks before I was twenty-one, in the Summer of 1999, my husband and I bought our first home. Booboo had just started the second year of his tenure at a high-flying web development company in Santa Monica, and this being the height of the dot com boom, they gave him a pretty unbelievable raise. The pay was more than he'd ever made before.

Our apartment manager sent us a notice that the rents were going up, again. It hadn't even been six months since the last rent raise. Booboo had grown up in a house, and living in an apartment wasn't all that appealing anymore. There'd also been some break-ins recently, so when we got the rent raise notice, we were both open to a new idea. The idea that we could own a home floated into our consciousness. The fact that Booboo was told that his raise put him in a new tax bracket, and if he wanted to keep some of his money, he'd need to find some write-offs, also contributed to this new consciousness.

The MLS system had recently gone online to the public. It's what real estate agents use to list properties for sale. He started browsing for homes, and so did I. The idea that *I* could be a homeowner was exhilarating. We'd often spent entire weekend afternoons perusing the website and getting all giddy when we found something that we liked. A friend of ours had recently gotten his real estate license, so we decided to be his first clients.

We walked into the Century 21 office and filled out the application. We were approved for a home that would cost $250,000. Booboo and I were flattered by this number, but it seemed too high for us and would have put half his monthly salary towards the mortgage payment. Instead, we asked him to look for homes that were $180,000 or less.

We found the house we wanted on our first day of looking with our agent. Though as we drove closer north to view the house, I was reminded about my trek to KMart on Cherry Ave when I was a kid and the neighborhood was too industrial for my liking. Our agent said the house was just another ten blocks away. He took us down a more siloed industrial street and I was not feeling too hot about the location, and I was just about to say I didn't like the neighborhood when he made a right turn into the street. It felt like the ending of *Who Framed Roger Rabbit* when the brick wall comes down and the sunny and happy town of Toon Town emerges and all the cartoons begin to sing. I couldn't believe how pretty the street was. It was stunning. Trees lined the entire block of twenty homes or so, and it felt calm. He pulled in front of the house, which had a long, wide driveway that seemed like it could fit at least five cars. There was the tallest palm tree I had ever seen on the patch of grass near the garage. I knew this was the one.

We walked through the home and though some rooms were small, especially the kitchen, we loved the mid-century architecture and the flow felt like our style. The kicker for me, though, was the outside. They had a built-in grill and corner prep area where I imagined many large gatherings, a large swimming pool that I immediately saw myself diving into, and likely on many summer nights skinny dipping with friends. This was it and we told our agent to call and make an offer that day. Hours later our agent called and said that we wouldn't get the house, because it turned out the seller's agent was now the buyer's agent and her client had seen the house earlier that day, and now they wanted the house as well. We were crushed.

We kept looking for a few more months, but nothing compared to the house we saw the first day. We decided to canvas neighborhoods without our agent, to help speed up the house-hunting process. One weekend Booboo said we should go back to that neighborhood we liked and see if any houses were for sale, and maybe the one we wanted to buy would be back on the market. We knocked on a few doors that had for sale signs out front, but nothing sparked our interest. We went down the Toon Town street. A red "Sold" sticker was stuck to the for sale sign for the house we wanted.

There was a muted green-colored house with an old chain link fence that was for sale just a few doors down. My husband pulled the car in front of it and I pleaded with him not to stop. It looked awful from the outside, and a bit creepy and nothing like the house I wanted.

"Come on, Mary. Let's at least check it out. We have nothing to lose." That was all he had to say to me because he was right. I grudgingly opened their fence to enter their walkway. Booboo knocked. The family was home and we asked if we could look at the house. Once we walked into the hallway, I saw how pleased Booboo looked. He'd been looking for a hallway like this. We both looked at each other and realized *this* was the one. It didn't have a pool, but it had a large backyard with a lot of potential. The kitchen and dining room were twice as big as the other house, and instead of four small bedrooms, there were three, and they were each fairly decent-sized.

The homeowners told us that the house had been on the market for months and they wanted to sell it quickly since they needed to find a home in a better neighborhood where they could send their son to kindergarten in the Fall. The house was $5,000 less than our target budget, too. We told the homeowners we were going to buy their house and that they'd hear from our agent that day. Coincidentally, they were planning to have the house painted in a few days. Since we were going to be the new homeowners, they asked us what color we wanted to paint it. We said a nice yellow but not too yellow. We stopped by the house a couple of weeks later, and I was amazed. I could finally see the beauty on the outside and I was thrilled to call this my home.

I had felt grown-up when I married Booboo, having tied the knot much earlier than anyone I knew and certainly many people didn't think we would work out. The odds were not in our favor. But here we were, four years later, buying a home. No one we knew that was in our age ranges owned a home. Anyone my age would have looked at you crazy if you ever expected them to own a home or be thinking of buying a home before they were even of the legal drinking age. But I didn't do things like most people. And I knew that Booboo and I could handle it. And even if there were unknowns, we could band together and get through anything.

When picking up our keys to the house, just forty-five days after meeting the owners and proclaiming our intent to buy, the handing of those keys felt like a true milestone for adulthood, and made me proud. I'd always wanted to have a house. I remembered ours in Nashville, and I knew in my heart that in all the years that I'd grown up in poverty, that that life wasn't supposed to be my life. That one day I would get back onto the path I was meant to be on. Not because I was owed anything, but because I knew I had been taken away from a trajectory that I had felt had already been written and now I was back to the page at which I was meant to be on.

Our first night in the house we didn't have any of our appliances yet, so everything we had from our apartment that was refrigerated, likely wouldn't last until the end of the next day, so we only cared about having a fresh cup of coffee with creamer in the morning. We sat in our living room, in front of the fireplace, eating our favorite deep dish pizza from Pizza Hut, and marveled at how far we had come, and against so many odds. We still had a long road ahead of us, with the immigration process and my reconstructive surgeries, but we were on the right path, the right page if you will.

CHRISTMAS SURPRISE

I was twenty-two years old when I'd made an appointment with my prosthodontist to review the molds he'd taken of my mouth and to get a regular teeth cleaning. I sat in the chair for a long time, especially for a teeth cleaning. He told me he had something he needed to work on and that he wouldn't be very long. I sat there and waited. Periodically, he would come into the room and shove various instruments in my mouth, then leave again. But this time, he put something different in my mouth and then tightened it. I could feel my metal implants in my gums tighten.

"Take a look in the mirror, Mary," Dr. Obo said to me as he handed me a small mirror and sat my chair up. As I pulled the mirror toward my face, I felt my top lip resting on something hard. I stared at myself in the mirror. I had front teeth. Smiling, I looked up at Dr. Obo. I felt like one of those monkeys who'd learned to communicate and would smile widely at themselves in a mirror. It looked different when my top lip was able to rest on teeth; my lip was more full now. It was pleasing to see.

Dr. Obo looked at me and said, "I thought this would be a nice Christmas present for you." I didn't even know what to say. My permanent bridge was not due to be installed for another six months, but the molds he had taken from my mouth looked good, so he had decided to order a temporary one based on them, without telling me.

"Enjoy them, and smile in your holiday pictures," he told me. *I can smile in pictures,* I thought. After a long pause I asked, "How much do I owe you for these?" I figured they were expensive, and we hadn't talked about costs yet.

"No charge, Mary. I just wanted to give you a present for the holidays."

I left his office dumbstruck by his generosity. I felt like a new person, and all the surgeries finally felt worth it. I couldn't contain my excitement, and I immediately called Booboo to tell him about the gift I had just received. He couldn't wait for me to get home to see what I looked like. I kept looking at myself in the rearview mirror and smiling, trying on this new smile for size. I loved everything about my new teeth and my new face. This must be what being normal felt like. It's no big deal; it just is. I practiced speaking in the car, saying my name and any other sentence I could come up with to learn to use my new teeth.

"Tada!" I said as I walked into the house, feeling utterly exhilarated and my new teeth fully exposed.

"Mary, you look so great! I can't believe it! And no charge? Like nothing?" he asked me.

"No charge. It was his Christmas present to me."

Booboo was used to me having to ask our doctors for discounts for my surgeries. I'd ask every time, and they'd usually knock off about thirty percent. At the time, with how much work I was getting done, these added up to thousands of dollars.

Our friends were shocked and pleased with how I looked. Booboo was beaming with pride. By then, I had a college certificate and would be graduating with an associate's degree in information systems that spring. We had both been busy and focused on bettering our lives, and I was achieving my goals. I remembered singing, "All I want for Christmas is my two front teeth," with my mom and hoping that one day I would get them. This Christmas, I did.

It's very easy to get used to looking "normal." In fact, the moment that I had my dental implants put in, I never looked back at the old me or identified with how I looked before. It was like I had been given permission to be myself. I no longer had that chain around my ankle, the one that said I didn't look normal, the one preventing me from flying. I was free. My new look also changed how I related to other people. I had spent most of my life not feeling normal or at least not the equivalent of others, either in appearance or by means. I had spent so many years berating myself for not meeting this invisible standard, and having the dental implants actually leveled the playing field for me. I was never going to look back.

Being the chameleon—observing, listening, adapting—actually made me quite the well-rounded person. I had overdeveloped my ability to listen to others and to empathize while observing the actions of those with more choices than me. I still had issues with my confidence, this feeling that I'm some sort of an imposter, but it didn't usually last long because I knew that I had something special, and even if others couldn't see it, I knew it was there.

LAND FOR THE LONESOME

Several months later, my mom moved to a trailer in Lancaster, California, on a piece of land she bought from a tax lien sale for $500. Her sister Ruth had lent her the money so she could try her luck at buying a piece of property that she could live on, something away from the city. There were tax lien sales every quarter in Pasadena, California, and Mom had used her resourceful ways to find out how she could be a part of it. She'd asked me if I could help her get to the auction so she could put a bid on a property. I figured it was an easy job and that I could help. I picked her up from her new apartment in a senior living building that was near St. Mary's hospital. When she sold Herbalife, one of the guys from the church who also sold Herbalife lived there, and we visited him and his wife from time to time. Now Mom lived there in a one-bedroom apartment with her cat Booboo, the one I had named my husband after because they were both so cute.

I drove her to Pasadena in the '77 Buick LeSabre that Booboo and I owned. It was a golden brown four-door sedan and had large seats that could fit at least six people total. It was one of the most comfortable rides I'd ever experienced; thirty-five miles per hour felt like seventy because it glided so smoothly on the road you felt like you were on a monorail. It made the trek with my mom that morning more comfortable. Anxiety ran through my body every time I was in a car with my mom, a trigger from our travels through the States. Mom's lingering smell of urine usually sent my stomach into a state. But also because I hadn't really spent much more than a few hours at a time with her since I had gotten married. I'd usually see her at my sister's apartment when she popped over there.

Mom had waited long enough at the auction that all the property they hadn't sold earlier that day was starting to sell at great prices, so she purchased her property for only $500. The land she bought that day was far enough from civilization that I knew she would be happily escaping society, yet she hadn't seen the land before placing her bid. In fact, most people at that auction hadn't either. No one had ways to quickly look up views of the property locations because Wi-Fi and smartphones and Google Maps weren't available at the time. But most people walked out satisfied, having acquired property for rock-bottom prices.

When my mom moved to the land, the local church donated her a pop-up trailer and a working car, which was modest in appearance but running well enough for her to get around town. The blue Nissan Stanza was dead. This allowed her to survive the climate there, which was hot and dry. It was a small town compared to Long Beach. But she still had an apartment in Long Beach as well after buying her property. She was still eligible for subsidized rental expenses through the U.S. Department of Housing and Urban Development program (HUD). Rent was subsidized so much so that she now only paid a mere twenty-five dollars per month to maintain a one-bedroom apartment. When Mom did come into town, she would only stay long enough until she could gather enough money for gas to drive back up to Lancaster, where she would stay for weeks at a time on her one acre of land that was far from most people. My sister had one small child by this time and was in nursing school. I was in my last semester of community college before transferring to Cal State Long Beach.

Sam only saw Mom occasionally, when she decided to come into town and check her P.O. Box for mail. Then one day, Sam received a call from our mom's apartment manager, as she was listed as a contact. Sam explained to me that the landlord said our mother would be evicted if she didn't clean her place up. The cockroaches and mold were affecting the other tenants. The landlord also said that our mother was disgusting, and that she had until the end of the week to clean the apartment.

If you ever lapsed with HUD, or got evicted from your place, you would never qualify for it again. It was one of the most important benefits to maintain, besides social security and Medi-Cal. I had mostly avoided my mother for years, ducking and diving whenever she would pop up around town. If she ever called, I cringed as I saw her number on the caller ID. It would usually go one of three ways. She would ask for money, she would ask to see me, or I would be told that I was part of a conspiracy to ruin her life. I never called my mother because I never knew which Linda I would get. The sweet mother who missed her daughter or the mean one who wanted to blame me for all her problems. It was a gamble I never wanted to take.

Because Mom was obese, finding clothing that fit and that didn't strap her in like armor was nearly impossible, at least with the limited means she had. She wore the same clothes for days at a time. She carried with her a stench of urine which, as an adult, made me nauseous. When I knew I had to forge ahead and interact with my mother, I had to muster as much resistance to bodily odors as I could. There was a part of me that wished she was no longer around. It's a horrible thought, but I thought that if I never had to deal with calls or unpleasant interactions with her again, my life would be better.

We were asked to meet the landlord at the apartment later that day. So my sister and I drove over to the address we were given. We'd never been there before, but it turned out it was next to the liquor store where I'd bought Now and Later candy to sell as prize winnings for the love tests I sold in elementary school. It was also where I'd bought twenty-five-cent off-brand cream sodas and where Sam and I would have to duck and dive from the bullies who wanted to kick our asses because I looked deformed.

We walked up to the apartment door number the landlord had given us. It was on the ground floor of a two-story apartment building where each door faced the street. Mom's apartment was closest to the alley right next to the liquor store. Figures. I knew her living situation would somehow be the essence of poverty. Her door had a black security gate that Sam and I banged on in an attempt to wake our mother up. There was no answer. After a moment, a man came up to us. He asked if we knew the woman that lived there. We told him we were her daughters and asked if he had seen her lately. He told us he hadn't seen her for a while.

I pulled the antennae to my cell phone out—it was 2002, just about seven years after cell phones were available for most people, and my phone looked like a candy bar and required you to use the antenna to get reception. I began to call the apartment manager's number to see if she could let us in. Sam was crouching low and peering into the crack of the blinds Mom had in her apartment. There was just a slight opening in one of them, enough to see into the living room. There was a faint outline of a lump in the living room. We both saw it and then began to bang on the door even harder, but there was no movement.

"There's no way that's Mom," I said as I scanned for any sign of life. The phone kept ringing and I ended up getting the apartment manager's voicemail. We then called Mom's number. The phone rang, and with each ring, I felt sick to my stomach. Once her voicemail kicked on, I hung up. I dialed a few more times, keeping my ear to the window to see if I could hear a phone ringing inside her apartment. After the third time, I gave up and left a voicemail.

"Mom, we're trying to reach you. We're at your apartment. You need to call me back," I said.

Reluctantly, my sister and I left the apartment after deciding we would come back when the manager called and could let us in.

The next day, after not receiving any calls from Mom or the apartment manager, I went up to my business law professor after class to ask for advice.

"Would I have enough cause to break into my mom's apartment if I felt she were in danger?" I asked her in my most lawyer-like business speak.

"Mary, if you think your mom is in danger, you have every right to open the door however you see fit." She looked at me as if I was crazy for not having tried that the day before. I had noticed that the metal gate had some give around the lock. I immediately called Sam and told her I was going to go back over to Mom's apartment to open the black metal gate with a flat-head screwdriver. I had seen someone do that in a TV show before, probably *MacGyver*.

By the time I pulled up, Sam had stepped out of her car and was waiting for me at the bottom of the steps. I wedged the flat-head into the small opening between the lock and the doorjamb. I hit the back of the screwdriver hard with the fleshy part of my palm. It popped the gate open. Then I turned the wooden doorknob slowly, hoping it was unlocked. It was. I opened the front door gently, not knowing what I would find. A strong stench of mold and decaying bodily fluids assaulted my senses. I hesitated and looked at my sister before we walked in, scared to discover what the lump in the middle of the living room was. But we walked in and got closer to it. I pushed it with my foot. We each breathed a huge sigh of relief as we discovered it was just a pile of clothes and blankets.

As we walked through the apartment, the adrenaline was pumping through my body and making my stomach sour and my neck tighten. This was the type of filth we were raised in, dirty clothes on the floor, every surface piled with empty containers and plates; the smell of mildew and urine permeated the apartment, and there was no homey feeling whatsoever. I walked toward the bathroom. The toilet was clogged with unflushed bowel movements and toilet paper. The bathtub and sink were full of dirt and grime, too.

Her bedroom was full of dirty, wet, and moldy clothes. When I opened her closet, it had the same set of boxes of papers I had grown up with. They were stacked up five high, each in its own level of decomposition and leaning awkwardly in various directions. They were full of holes from the years of mice running through them and chewing on their edges. The papers had stains and frayed ends. A waft of the mice pee scent hit me, and I was right back to being ten years old living on Henderson Avenue. Those boxes had been towed around my whole life, as a memory of our life in Nashville and proof of our mom's hoarding. As I stared at them, I felt a surge of unidentifiable sorrow rush over me. How many times had I lugged those boxes around? How many times had I seen mice scurrying through them as they lined the floor of our entire closet? Now, they sat there, misshapen and unattended. I grabbed the top box, but hesitated for a moment because all I wanted to do was toss it into the dumpster and finally rid myself of those memories, yet I pulled it onto the floor and started to sift through the papers, traveling through the past. I found her old divorce papers, old ads from the local grocery stores, receipts for food, old college paperwork, a wrapper from a piece of candy. I found the wooden stick I'd brought back from Camp High Hill. I'd sanded it down and had everyone sign it; from counselors to bunk mates. I sat there looking at the only living catalog of my previous life with Mom. Those boxes were like an unorganized library. I let out a sigh, put the stick in my purse, then grabbed another box, and threw it to the floor to look through it. There didn't seem to be anything else that I hadn't seen before.

I walked out of the bedroom and back through the living room and then into the kitchen. I flipped on the light and watched as roaches scurried everywhere. Some were even crawling up the walls. Their droppings littered the counters and floor and gave the kitchen a cold, grimy feeling. When I opened the fridge, a cliché soured pint of milk rested on the top shelf. In the fridge drawers, decaying vegetables laid in bags of gooey brown liquid. She had a small bottle of ketchup and mustard in the door, and suddenly I remember my youth.

An urge to vomit rushed over me. I ran outside and leaned over the alley wall, trying to catch my breath. After dry heaving three or four times, I took a deep breath and stood up. I placed my hands on my hips and walked along the alley, staring at the ground, just as if I'd finished running a mile and was trying to catch my breath. My eyes were red and watery from bending over. It would take a lot out of me to do what I knew we had to do. We had to clean this apartment, or my mom would lose it. This would mean throwing out the soiled bedding in the living room, washing and salvaging any clothes she had, cleaning the bathroom and kitchen, and making it livable. The manager arrived a few minutes after Sam and I had figured out our game plan. She gave us a key to the apartment.

"If you can clean your mom's apartment this week, I'll reconsider throwing her out," she said with a no-chance-in-hell look on her face. She didn't know us.

When I got home that day, I reached out to my friend Lolli to share what was in front of us. She had gone to computer school with my husband in Belgium and had visited California a few years earlier. She always wanted to move to California, and specifically to Long Beach—she had fallen in love with the town and the city, just like my husband had. And she was someone who worked hard for what she wanted, so she eventually achieved her goal of moving to Long Beach. Lolli was also fiercely loyal to her friends. I told her about cleaning up my mom's apartment, and she immediately offered to help. I explained to her that it was a real mess. Like a filthy kind of mess.

"I'll come by tomorrow, and we'll each take a room. I'll take the bathroom," she offered. I panicked because, though I knew we needed the help, the bathroom was the filthiest room of them all. But there was no talking her out of it. I accepted her help and then set off to buy all the supplies we needed for the next day.

When we all arrived at the apartment the next morning, we had our war faces on. There would be no crying, no breakdowns; we were there to get the job done. Disinfectant was thrown everywhere, bags of trash and furniture hauled to the alley. As layers and layers of clothes were lifted up and thrown into large black bags, strong smells of mold lingered like spider webs. It would get so pungent I had to turn my head away or even stop what I was doing to get fresh air. Sam and I decided we would buy Mom new bedding and hauled her mattress to the alley. We also needed to buy her bed sheets, towels, a shower curtain, and even some food, if she were actually going to stay there. So Sam and I split up the costs and bought her what she needed to live in her apartment and get back to the city. We worried about her living in some distant plot of land that was off the grid.

After three days of cleaning, scrubbing, and disinfecting, we were done. The three of us sat on the stairs while we waited for the manager to arrive and do her walk-through. My muscles were still tense while I rested, still working even while I sat there, twitching and pulsating. I had a general buzz all over my body, like an electric shock was just wearing off. We were all exhausted, mentally and physically. We had done all this work with the assumption that we would find out where our mom was and have her come back, at least long enough to keep her apartment. When the manager finally arrived, we took her through all the rooms. When we walked outside, I asked her, "Can she stay?"

"Yeah, it looks good enough to me," the manager replied.

The only leads we'd found in Mom's boxes were the location of Mom's property and her P.O. Box address in Lancaster. Based on those two locations, we figured we had a good chance of finding her. I prepared myself for another exhausting mission.

Sam had visited Mom once before in Lancaster and knew roughly how to find the property, which was difficult unless you paid close attention to where you had to pull off the road to find the path that went half a mile down a dirt road. This ultimately led to a barren plot of land with a water tank and a trailer against the backdrop of a large rock formation in the distance. When Sam visited Mom, there was nothing to do there, so they ended up going into town to eat.

Sam had a memory like an elephant and never used any kind of GPS. She knew every place Mom might be. The gas station, the post office, and the Chinese buffet restaurant would all be locations we would look first before looking for her on her plot of land.

It took us two hours to travel to Lancaster from Long Beach. We scoped out each known location where we thought she could be, even checking the movie theater parking lot for her car. Our last stop was the post office. As we pulled into the parking lot, we saw her car. As we walked up to it, we could see she was asleep in the reclined driver's seat. I knocked on the window with my knuckle.

"Mom!" we both said as we leaned in close to her window. She woke up out of her slumber with a confused look. Then she wiped her eyes and sat herself up enough to roll down the window.

"What are you girls doing here?" she asked. It was strange to see her like this, asleep in her car in a busy parking lot during the day. We explained to her that we'd cleaned up her place and that her manager threatened to evict her if we hadn't.

"What? Those people are crazy," our mom said. "I've had mold in the apartment for months, and they ain't done nothing about it. I can't live in that apartment. I want to live out here on my land."

"Mom, if you get evicted, you'll lose your HUD benefits, and you'll never get them back," I told her.

"Fuck those bastards. I don't want to go back," she exclaimed. "Why would I come back? I've got a water tank put in on my land, and I have what I need. The man at the church helped me put it in."

We had put ourselves, and my friend, through an emotional hurricane over the past few days. Feeling drained and exhausted, a simple 'Thank you' would have made things okay. But our mom rarely thanked us. Seeing Mom living in her car like that brought me back to us kids traveling across the country when we'd left Nashville. I saw that this is the life she went right back to, where she could run away from her responsibilities, leaving other people to pick up the pieces. I wondered why the hell I was trying to bring her back. Why was I so concerned about her losing her housing benefits when she didn't even seem to care? Why did I put myself through all that? Why was I even here, staring into a car already filled with trash, and the stench of urine. She was comfortable with running away from life, and I never would be. All I wanted to do was run away from her.

"Can one of you girls run into the post office and grab my mail?" Her question pulled me from my travel through time. I grabbed her keys and headed inside.

We decided to all go to the Chinese buffet to grab some food before heading back to Long Beach. When we got to the restaurant, our mom struggled to lift herself out of her car. Though she was heavy, she used to be able to walk; though she waddled, she never needed a cane. But this time, she could barely walk straight, and we had to hold each arm to guide her. She'd always had bad hips, and as she shifted her weight to her right hip, she would have a tinge of pain and breath in between her teeth with a "sssccccehhhee" sound, and then she'd fall into her other hip, and the process would continue until she would sit down. But this time, she winced as her weight shifted to her right hip. "Ooooh," she said. I was brought right back to when I was a child walking downtown Long Beach on Pine Avenue and hopping around to avoid stepping on the cracks, or I'd break my mother's back. To the times we walked the streets of our neighborhood and people would say she was the zero and 1 was the one; we made a ten. I needed to get out of there, to run away from her, but I sat down and ordered food. We awkwardly conversed through Mom's two rounds of plates I fetched for her at the buffet table. It was decided that she would come back to Long Beach to square up the apartment, and maybe even live there for a while so she could get her manager to fix the mold problem. We seemed to convince her that it was better than living in her car, and it would give her some time to get her life sorted out on her land. We gave her money for gas. She did come back, but only for a few days and then she headed back up to Lancaster, to be on her land. She lost the apartment and her HUD benefits the next month because she failed to pay her rent.

RECLUSE AND NEAR DEATH

In the summer of 2005, I got a call from a social worker at the Antelope Valley Hospital in Lancaster. I was told that my mother had been found on the ground at her land by the pizza boy. She'd had days of heat exposure and was now recovering, but I was told that she almost died. I called my sister immediately and we decided to go straightaway to visit her.

By this time, Sam had a four-year-old and a two-and-a-half-year-old. We took Sam's minivan and strapped both girls in the back seat, and with a DVD playing in the center console to keep them occupied, we hit the road. The drive was a very long two hours, and Sam and I began to talk about our lives. I shared the anxiety I was feeling about never knowing when Mom would call or if she would threaten to call Immigration Services on my husband. We'd been married ten years by this time, yet she would still call the house and leave messages angrily recounting how I'd duped her in order to marry Pierre. She never let go of anything; she hoarded memories as well as papers.

When we finally arrived at the hospital, we decided I would go to Mom's room first so that Sam could manage the girls. The Antelope Valley Hospital was just like any other major hospital I had ever been to. Because it was nighttime, the lights were dimmed, and I felt like I had to whisper and tiptoe through the halls. After finding my mom's room, I slowly walked in. She was lying on the bed nearest the window. The curtains were drawn open so the big dark sky was visible and had the effect of making my mother appear as a small blip on the planet. She looked frail and, somehow, both clean and dirty at the same time. There were fresh blankets on her bed, but her leathered forearms were dirty, and the skin slightly drooped off her arms, likely due to severe dehydration. I'd never seen my mother in this state before, so helpless physically. I'd always known her to have physical challenges, but none of them ever actually stopped her from doing what she wanted.

In this hospital bed, she seemed powerless. I wondered how much strength I'd acquired over the years from following my mom's example; I felt weak at the knees, seeing her like this. Her eyes were closed, and her body and face were turned toward me. This kind of weakness made me feel sorry for her. The great sense of compassion I felt slowly started erasing past grievances I'd had with her. I suddenly felt a huge sense of guilt for having avoided speaking with her over the past several years. But I tried to forgive myself because here I was by her bedside, committing to doing anything to help her. I could see her vulnerabilities, her humanity, and her sickness all at the same time. *Could she remain in this life a little longer?* I thought.

"Mom, it's me, Mary," I whispered gently toward her face as I leaned in closer to rub her arm. Her skin was no longer the chubby, pale white skin I'd always known, and I mourned for that loss now. She opened her eyes slightly, and without hesitation, she began to cry as soon as she recognized my face. As soon as she caught her breath, she said, "Mary, I almost died!" She was crying in a way I had never seen her cry before. Her voice was light yet raspy, likely from being parched.

"It's okay, Mom. You're going to be okay," I told her. I kept gently rubbing her hand and forearm, wanting to feel a connection, but also because this was so surreal that I had to keep touching her to ground myself in reality. Mom was a recluse, and this way of life seemed to have caught up with her. Her frailty was everywhere I looked as I scanned her body. She seemed smaller now. It was possible she'd lost up to a hundred pounds since the last time I'd seen her almost four years ago.

"What happened to you, Mom?" I finally asked her. She tried to gather her breath while tears streamed from her eyes. She slowly exhaled and told her story.

"I was stepping out of the new trailer I got from this preacher a month or so ago. My hip went out, and I misstepped and fell onto the ground, so hard I couldn't get myself back up on my feet. My hip was hurting so bad that I thought I had broken it. The guys who live down the way from my land would pass me each day, and I would scream to them to help me, but they just looked at me and laughed and kept driving." My heart went out to her. She always carried around an emotional cocktail of suspicion and anger, but never one of disappointment.

"My dog Poopy was with me the whole time," she said.

"You have a dog?" I asked. I never knew her to really care for dogs. I'd thought of Sugar Foot, the small white dog we'd found as children that disappeared a few days after we had it.

"Yes, I've had him for about nine months now, and he's very sweet."

"So how long did you stay there on the ground?"

"I was there at least three days, Mary. I thought I was going to die. The boy that delivers me pizza just showed up yesterday and rescued me," she said as she belted out more tears as she remembered this near-death experience. "I usually buy pizza from him every few days, and I hadn't called him, so he got worried about me. He knows I can't walk very well, so he usually drives up and delivers the pizza straight to my trailer. I don't have to get out or anything."

As she talked about this simple routine of ordering pizza, I just stared at her and felt an enormous distance between who she was and who I was. But I also felt that I understood her life. I could see that the pizzas, this delivery boy, her dog Poopy, and her trailer were all part of her life, and she'd found normalcy in it. I wanted her to be safe, though, and if she had neighbors who drove by her day after day and laughed at her while she sat there baking in the heat, then she needed to rethink living out in the middle of nowhere.

The social worker who had called me walked into the room and wanted to speak outside. I listened intently as she explained to me all the realities of Mom's present condition. "Besides severe dehydration, we also did an x ray, and she's got a large tumor in one of her ovaries. It's the size of a grapefruit." I'd known about this tumor since around the time I'd gotten married, but I also didn't know whether Mom had gone through with the procedure. *Who doesn't want to get a grapefruit-sized tumor out of their body?* I'd thought at the time. But we weren't talking about just anyone. I couldn't recall a time growing up that my mom had been to the doctor, except when she went to the emergency room on Mother's Day when I was eleven because she broke her foot after tripping on some blankets we'd left on the floor. She never saw the doctor, even if she had the flu; she'd just stay at home and tough it out. But if us kids were sick, she'd have us at the doctor's office or emergency room before you could say, "Ah-choo!"

"Obviously, she's got a bad hip, and the hospital's recommending she see a specialist. She's likely got hip dysplasia." The social worker went on and on with the list of issues Mom had and what she thought could be done about them. "Your mom's first problem is her living conditions. She's told us that she relies on support from people around town to get by, and when they don't come through, she can sometimes go without food or water for days. Your mom also shared with us that she's been diagnosed with paranoid schizophrenia and that she hasn't been taking her medication."

The words, "I knew it," wanted to jump out of my mouth so I could breathe again. Yet, the lump in my throat prevented me from speaking. I had only ever known my mom to deny she had any mental health issues. Knowing that she had actually been diagnosed, and had been given medication, brought the trauma I'd experienced as a child, young adult, and even now as an adult standing in front of a social worker after my mom nearly died, to the surface like a radiator emitting heat. The words she said after that became a bit of a blur as I stood there gobsmacked.

For years, I knew my mom was paranoid and even labeled her as such when we'd go at it. It was always met with something like, "I'm not paranoid. People are actually trying to destroy me." I could never have imagined her seeking treatment willingly, and with this new information, I was suddenly mad at her for not having done it earlier. Mad at her for never being the mother I needed. Mad at her for not telling me that she had been diagnosed and was getting treated. Mad at myself because maybe one of her phone calls I avoided was actually a call when she would have told me this. I'd already written her off by this time and never wanted to speak to her again. I'd always known that Mom's mental illness would be the death of her, but I never considered that Mom's mental illness made it nearly impossible for her to get treatment.

I suddenly realized what an enormous feat that would have been for her to get help. I tried to imagine the steps she took to get treatment; calling and seeing a doctor, them giving her the diagnosis, her taking that prescription to a pharmacy, and then picking up medication that she would likely then take with a swig of a two-liter bottle of diet Coke, as she always liked to drink her soda. I felt a deep sense of both hope and sadness. This stirred deep in my chest and all I wanted to do was to go back into the room and hug my mom. This new reality of her mental illness being labeled and spoken, had me reeling. But this social worker had no understanding of how much pain and loss were part of those two words, "paranoid schizophrenic." How devastating they had been to our lives. As she continued to speak, her words were like little S.O.S. messages washing up on the shore. I was eagerly bending over and picking them up. Eager to read what was inside, yet frightened at what the messages contained.

"I think your mom needs to be in an assisted living home. She could get the medication she needs, possibly even her hip and tumor surgery. She's going to need physical therapy to fully recover from this event. Her way of living is unhealthy," she said as if this wasn't painfully obvious. All of what this woman was saying to me made sense, but I zeroed in on the fact that Mom hadn't been taking her medication.

How was I going to convince our mother to move into an assisted living home? It seemed like the last thing Mom would do, even if she had almost died on her property. I mean, that was her little island away from society where she could be with her thoughts, off the grid.

"I would love nothing more than to know she's getting help," I told the social worker, hoping she could see I also needed real and effective suggestions.

"If you give me the word, and you can convince your mother, I can arrange to have a bed for her by tomorrow afternoon at a facility not far from here," the social worker told me.

I'd always known of my mom's fear of being "put away." For as long as I could remember, I knew she was unstable. That something was off. And there I was, in my late twenties, being given the chance to make a decision on what bed my mom would be in the next day. It was a surreal moment, and I didn't feel like growing up in that way. Not knowing if I was being a cold-hearted person for being receptive to what I was hearing or whether I was actually going to help her weighed on my mind.

I told the social worker I had to discuss this with my sister. Then I went downstairs and prepared Sam for Mom's situation. I watched my nieces while she went to Mom's room. A potentially traumatizing event could be unfolding in my sister's near future, yet she had to see Mom to make the decision we had to make. I chased my nieces down the halls of the hospital, entertaining them as well as myself.

When Sam came downstairs, she looked a little older to me.

"So, did you talk to the social worker?" I asked her.

"Yes. I think we have no choice but to get her into that nursing home while she recovers," she said. Sam was always good at making hard decisions. She had a sageness about her. You knew that if she made a decision, that she was making it because it was the practical thing to do. I agreed with her, and we gave the social worker the green light. I went back up to the room and was able to convince my mom to go with the plan and that it was for the best. However, she needed reassurances that when she was better, she could go back to her trailer on her property and continue to live as a recluse. I assured her that all of this was temporary and that once she had regained her health, that she would be able to go back to her property. I focused on the positive outcome that could come from this, and the idea of having a healthy mother was alluring. I thought that the biggest hurdle for her mental health was her acknowledging she was mentally ill, which had already happened, and that meant that she could get better. I was hopeful I would meet my real mom, without all the paranoia.

The night of the transfer, I got a call from the nursing home.

"Is this Mary Gregory? The daughter of Linda Bernhardt?" the admittance nursed asked. I confirmed it was me.

"Your mother is screaming that she wants to leave the nursing home. She says that we can't keep her here. She thinks we're going to steal her social security checks." I rolled my eyes as I let out a huge sigh.

"We only temporarily ask for social security checks to be endorsed to us while the patients are here. That helps to cover the costs, but she doesn't believe us. If she won't sign the form to grant us her checks, she has to leave tonight. Does your mom have some place to go?" I told her that she didn't. I put the phone to my chest, hoping for some kind of strength to do what I had to do next.

"Can you put her on the phone? I'll see if I can talk her into signing the form," I told the nurse. While I waited, I searched the house for the hidden pack of smokes I had around in case of emergencies. I lit one up; the flick from the lighter was loud enough for my husband to come into the kitchen and give me the *you're smoking again?* look. I gave him the *I know, but I've got to deal with my mom* look right back.

"Mary, get me the fuck out of here!" she proclaimed. "Everyone is crazy here. They want to take my money. They want my social security checks. I want out of here, Mary," As she spoke, her voice went from crying to screaming to pleading.

"Mom, listen to me. They aren't trying to take your money. They need to be paid for your stay, and your social security is enough to cover it." In my most lawyer-sounding voice I tell her, "Write on the form that you are not allowing them to receive payments past the day of your stay and that doing so would be an act of fraud. Ask them for a copy of the form." I was hoping that my semester in business law was allowing me to fake it enough for her to believe me. She did. She signed her papers, but by the time I got off the phone, I had smoked three cigarettes.

Mom had been there a few days when I decided to go visit her. I wanted to pick her up some things she needed, like clean socks and underwear, clothes, towels, and toiletries. This seemed to be a good time for her to continue to remain clean, and I wanted to support her as much as possible.

When I came to visit, I could see that the hospice facility was full of interesting characters. I was half expecting a bunch of old people sitting around in wheelchairs with blankets on their laps, maybe in a small common area with a TV playing a soap opera where everyone gathered around to watch in silence. But it was different than that. Young and old people roamed about a vast and well-lit facility. It was clean and had wide hallways with rails on the sides, and it was bustling with different people with disabilities in all shapes and sizes. The staff greeted me with smiles when I checked in at the front desk. When I told them I was Linda Bernhardt's daughter, one small Filipino woman looked over at me and said, "Oh, you're the girl we talked to the other night. Your mom is much better now. We gave her something for her anxiety. You know, she cried that whole first night. It was really sad. But she's better now." I'd been holding my breath the whole time she was speaking, prepared to hear the worst. I was relieved that things were better now. She walked fast, and I followed her while smiling at all the different people who walked past me.

My mom's room had the lights down, and as we walked in the room, the little Filipino nurse spoke loudly, "Linda. Your daughter's here. Linda, wake up." Seeing how frail she was in the hospital made me afraid to see her frailty once again.

"Mom, I'm here," I said reassuringly as I walked slowly toward her bed. She opened her eyes slowly as she adjusted to looking at someone.

"I need you to get me some things, Mary. Write them down. Here's a pen and use the back of that envelope over there." Her voice was scratchy and hoarse. "Oh, and I need you to call this doctor. I need to see if I can schedule a hip surgery," she said while handing me a business card she had no doubt gotten from the hospital. "That's why I fell in the first place. I'm sure I have hip dysplasia."

I started executing my mom's orders. I called the doctor and set up an appointment for her. Then I went out to buy her the things from her list. It took a few hours to gather it all, and by the time I returned to the nursing home, I was ready to begin the journey home.

"When are you coming back, Mary?" my mom asked me with an almost childish look on her face.

"I'll be back in a few days, and I'll bring Sam," I told her reassuringly. Before I walked away, I gave her a hug and then kissed her on the forehead. She turned her head away from me and drifted off to sleep. I felt reassured leaving the facility, as if my mom was going to be okay.

A few days later, my sister, her two daughters, and I were on our way up to Antelope Valley to visit Mom. Sam really wanted them to see Mom, and she thought her girls could help cheer her up. When we arrived, Mom was sitting outside on the porch in a wheelchair with a blanket across her lap waiting for us.

"Mom, Sam and the girls are here," I said with a hopeful smile. Our mom sat there looking somewhat spaced out, not reacting much at all. I leaned down lower to get eye level with her, so she could see it was me.

"Hey, Mom, look, it's Sam and the girls," I said as I waved my hands like a traffic cop toward the girls, who were standing next to my sister. Each girl stood quietly while holding one of Sam's hands, waiting for Mom to acknowledge them, not close enough yet to hug her.

"Mom, can't you say hi? Don't you want to see the girls?" Sam asked as she stared at Mom in amazement. Our mom continued to ignore her and the girls' presence. My nieces began tapping on Sam's thighs to get her attention.

"Sam is here with the girls. You should say hi. The girls are beautiful. Just look at them. Your grandchildren are right here," I told Mom. I was starting to feel nauseous. This was feeling like a *Twilight Zone* episode. I stared right into my mom's face, waiting for something to come back. *Why is she doing this?* I thought. *Is she on medication?* My sister stared at our mom and said, "We're going. We drove two hours to see you and you can't even acknowledge me and your grandchildren?"

My sister was a nurse by this time, and my mom had told me on my last visit that she thought Sam was the reason she was in the nursing home. I tried to explain to her that it was both Sam and me that had agreed to put her there while she recovered, but she clearly didn't believe me. When I got in the car, my sister was tense with anger. We had only driven a block before she pulled to the side of the road and began to cry.

"Why does she fucking hate me? Did you see that? She didn't even acknowledge me or the girls. She's never loved me." Her hurt was coming through with such a force I could only cry with her.

"I know, Sam. You don't deserve this. She loves you, but she's sick."

"No, Mary, she only loves you. She's only ever loved you," she said in her deepest and saddest tear-filled voice. Our mom had always seemed to have more concern over my life than she ever did of my sister's and brother's. She had moments with Sam, but it was true; I was more important to Mom. I got the sympathy and the benefit of the doubt more than Paul and Sam. I felt guilty for this, yet I couldn't change our mom's feelings or actions. Our mom was no PTA mother by any stretch, but of what she concerned herself about with us kids, I was higher on her priority list. This was certainly not something I bragged about. I mean, we're talking about only having it good compared to my siblings, not actually having it *good*.

The girls sat in the back quietly, waiting for their mom to stop talking. Her youngest, knowing that her mom was in pain, said, "We love you, Mommy." The words consoled Sam enough for her to stop crying and start the car back up. We drove off and headed on the two-hour trip back to Long Beach. I could see and feel that a change had happened that day for my sister. She didn't want to talk anymore about the significance of the disrespect our mother just exhibited to her and the girls. It was heartbreaking, and their relationship would never be the same again.

THE THANKSGIVING PHONE INCIDENT

By November 2006, my brother planned to come to Long Beach and bring his girlfriend Nicole and our father to visit so that the family could celebrate our first Thanksgiving together—something us kids hadn't done since before leaving Nashville over twenty years ago. Sam had broken up with her children's father by then and had a new life and apartment. She had offered to host our father, while I offered to host Paul and Nicole. With Dad being at Sam's, he could spend more time with her and the girls.

Both Nicole and Samantha were great cooks, some of the best I'd ever known. A few visits to Nashville had proven to Sam that Nicole could cook, but Sam was no doubt the west-coast champion when it came down to home-cooked Mexican dishes. She used all the authentic ingredients at her disposal and seemed to know how to cook anything.

Thanksgiving always felt more like a mad list of to-do's and stressful shopping than the wonderful bliss it seemed to be for cooks and for my husband, who had a real fondness for the holiday. We started with the planning of the Thanksgiving dinner at my house. Sam, Nicole, and Booboo were chiming in. I only wanted to speak when a decision around the menu came up.

Booboo and I had spent our first few Thanksgivings together at our friend Emily's parents' house, but since we bought our house, we'd been hosting dinner there for our friends, with one of them usually offering to cook the feast. But my husband was developing more of an interest in cooking. We always expected a stream of friends to come over throughout the day. Our friends were our family, too, and we were happy to host more than just family.

During the planning of the dinner, wine was being consumed, and plenty of it.

Sam mostly sat quietly, not chiming into the discussion much. She was not okay. Nicole kept building upon her plans as dishes were described and approved by Booboo and me. My father sat quietly, too, which I was accustomed to at this point. I knew he only ever spoke when there was a need to do so. Dishes upon dishes were discussed until we had a final plan.

The next day, Nicole and I went forward with the dinner plans and went shopping for all the Thanksgiving ingredients.

Thanksgiving morning started at 5:30 a.m. with Nicole getting up to start getting the bird ready for the oven. I had woken up around 7 a.m. to see and smell the house slowly brewing with a Thanksgiving smell. A smile crossed my face, and I was looking forward to the day's festivities. I called my sister's place around 9 a.m. My dad answered. He said that it would be best for me to come by and get him early rather than waiting for Samantha to be ready with the girls. I drove down and picked him up without going inside; he was standing on the sidewalk waiting for me.

During my normal rounds of morning calls to get an idea of who was coming, I called my sister again to get an ETA. I left a voicemail just in case she was too busy or was out shopping for something to bring to the dinner.

I also called our friend Sandra, who would be celebrating with us since her family was in Michigan, but I got her voicemail, too. Eventually, my phone rang around 11 a.m. with a call from an unknown number. This was strange since it was Thanksgiving and I knew everyone who was going to call me. It turned out to be a friend of Sandra's. She told me that Sandra was experiencing extremely painful period cramps and couldn't walk. She was going to pick her up from her apartment and take her to the hospital. Within thirty minutes, I was called back and told which hospital Sandra was at, and so I turned to my family and let them know I would be back soon, but that I had to help out our friend. My dad was gracious and told me that I was doing the right thing. Nicole was cooking and drinking and being merry and wished me the best. When I arrived at the hospital, I could see the immense amount of pain Sandra was in. She was curled up like a snail, holding her stomach so tight and breathing like she was in labor. After an hour and a half, she had received a pain shot, which started to take effect after about fifteen minutes. Once it was certain she could go home, her friend and I agreed I would be responsible for her, and I insisted she come straight to my house so she didn't have to be alone on Thanksgiving.

When we arrived at my house, I immediately went through my closet and found a shimmery brown dress she could wear. With her thin figure and caramel-colored skin, I knew she'd look like a classic beauty in this dress. I wanted there to be no trace of hospital on her at all. As soon as I could find a beer and grab a smoke, the phone rang. From the caller ID, I knew it was my sister.

"Hey, Sam. Where are you?" I asked plainly.

"I know what Paul said about me," she said.

"What do you mean?" I was puzzled.

"I heard Paul on my answering machine."

"I just got back from the hospital, Sam, so I don't know what you mean. So what time are you coming over?" I asked her again.

"I'm not coming over. I heard what Paul said about me. He said I'm just like Mom."

"What?" I turned to my brother, who was sitting at the kitchen table, so I signaled to him that something was wrong by giving him my puzzled face and pointing to the phone and mouthing, "She's pissed."

"And don't act like you weren't there. I could hear you laughing in the background."

"I wasn't here. I just got back to the house. I was at the hospital with Sandra."

"You're lying, Mary. I know you were there, and I know you were laughing at me." I looked at Paul and asked, "Paul, did you say that Sam was just like Mom? She says she's not coming over."

"Let me talk to her," he said while grabbing the phone from me. He went outside and I could see him pacing along the patio. They seemed to be arguing. I looked at my father, Nicole, and my husband to try and get clarity from their faces. Nicole offered up what could have happened.

"I think Paul forgot to hang up the phone the last time he called Sam. Paul was so frustrated with not getting ahold of her. He called and called at least three or four times since you've been gone, and she wouldn't answer the phone. He finally got upset and thought he had hung up the phone, but he said that she was acting just like your mom."

This was not good. This was one of the biggest insults we could say to one another. We all knew how crazy Mom was, and there was a special and unspoken rule that none of us were like her. My friend Sandra stood there in the pretty brown dress I lent her and slowly found a seat to sit at quietly while this was all unfolding. Our father had been sitting there at the kitchen table, quiet, and I felt he might have an answer.

"Dad," I asked slowly. "Do you know why Sam hasn't answered her phone all day?"

"Sam and the girls went shopping early this morning. She wanted to have her own Thanksgiving dinner. She's not coming today," he said in a soft southern drawl. I stood there while the blood rushed out of my face and turned my head to the backyard to see my brother still pacing and talking to our sister. This was news to us all. Paul then came back into the kitchen. Before Paul spoke, I blurted out, "Dad just told me that Sam never planned on coming. She went shopping this morning with the girls," I told Paul quickly, so he knew that some of his frustrations weren't completely unjustified.

"What?" he yelled out, enormously puffed up from the frustration and argument he and Sam had just had. He had shared with Sam that he had been frustrated that she wasn't picking up, and that he'd spent so much time trying to organize this dinner, flying out from Nashville with Dad, and felt disrespected because she wasn't there with the girls.

"Dad, I don't understand. Why didn't you tell us that Sam wasn't coming? This was supposed to be a family Thanksgiving. That's why we're all here," Paul said in exasperation.

"Well," he said, like he usually started off his sentences, "Sam said you guys didn't ask her to make dishes the other night, so she figured she wasn't welcome." This didn't make much sense, but the other night was coming back to me, slowly. The fawning my husband did over Nicole and her cooking, the days before when we rolled our eyes at Sam's kids running around wild in restaurants. Paul and I weren't parents, so we didn't have much patience for misbehaving children. Sam had just barely broken up with her ex and was still sorting out her life. There was a huge difference between our lives and hers. She'd been more financially insecure than Paul and me, and though that didn't change how we felt about her, it did change how she felt about us. She was also a mother, which changes priorities. And though we judged her for how her children behaved, she also equally judged us on our excesses and immaturity, especially our smoking and drinking.

Although the intention was there for a family Thanksgiving, perhaps all of this judgment would never have allowed for a "normal" family dinner. It was too late to say anything to change the day, as it had already been written a few days before. After all, was this what all the other families did? Fight with each other and accuse each other of being the worst or not good enough? If so, then I suppose we finally had our first and last family Thanksgiving. We were normal after all.

"Chameleons pretend to be dead when in danger. They wear a blank stare and simply fall to the ground when they are attacked by enemies. They only move again when they feel safe."[11]

THE CALL

It was late summer 2007 and I was studying for my real estate exam, the one I had failed just four months before.

I was in the middle of my own chaos running a loan origination business during a financial and real estate meltdown; I was quite literally in a vortex. The stress of work, the constant despair and struggles all around me—homeowners losing their homes, retirements, and dignity—weighed on me. My own foundation was starting to crumble. My mood was getting dark, and I couldn't see a glimmer of hope ahead of me, no way out of the financial burden of running my own business. It had become clear that I was not any good at managing my relationship with Sam either. We were heading into a whole year of not talking.

My business was struggling. I tried to remember why I had opened it in the first place, why I had chosen the risk at all. All I could think of was how I could have worked somewhere else. I could have been safe in some large company, wearing just one hat, and judging people who got adjustable-rate mortgages.

But of course, like most entrepreneurial twenty-seven-year-olds, I was confident that I could handle running a business. What could be so difficult? A year later, I was drowning in debt. It was starting to feel like another test of survival. I was in a space where duality was becoming normal. I was hiding my financial despair from my spouse, family, and close friends. I was working almost sixty hours a week to bring in the income that would only feed the debt dragon and keep the doors open long enough to work another day. I didn't want to be at the helm of the business anymore. It was scary to be in that position with the economy crumbling all around me.

And then the phone rang in early September, and it would change the course of my life. It had been several months since my mom had phoned me. Another Mother's Day had gone by where I didn't call her or even return her messages. Some had even been sweet messages, with no trace of negativity or anger, but I didn't have the courage to call her back. The last call I'd had with her left me feeling helpless. She told me she was leaving the convalescent home to stay with a guy she had met who was there recovering from a drug addiction. She walked right out of that place with him and into a car that she'd bought for $500 from another patient there. She told me she wasn't going to go back to her property alone, so she needed this guy to protect her.

"Yes. Yes, Mary Gregory is her daughter," Booboo said to the person on the other line. I looked up at him once he said my name. His expression changed as he looked at me. I knew this concerned my mother.

"Mary, you need to take this call. It's about your mom," he said as he handed me the phone. "It's the coroner's office."

There was a tingling in my neck as my muscles stiffened. I prepared myself for the call I never wanted to have. I closed my eyes as I took the phone. I could suddenly see white sheets flapping in the wind like laundry drying in the sun on a clothesline. As a child, I'd run through these as my mother hung them up. I suddenly remembered this good time as a man with a deep voice started to speak slowly and calmly.

"Hi Mary. This is Jim Tucker from the Antelope Valley Coroner's Office. I'm sorry to tell you this, but your mom was found dead in her car two days ago. Looks like she had been living in her car. She died from heat exposure from the recent heat wave." I rested my head on the countertop. The man on the other line stayed silent, as if he knew what was coming next. Like a newborn just delivered, I was waiting for the cry to come out, but it began so far deep within me, that I was certain *this* was what it was like to take my first breath.

I realized this call was inevitable, maybe even an unavoidable experience with how Mom lived. I felt Booboo's hand on my back, tapping it, helping the breath come out, gently saying, "Let it out, Mary." And when the breath finally came, I felt a calm cover over me for a moment.

"This is really hard to hear. I wish this hadn't happened to her," I told the man. He apologized for having to give me the bad news. He assured me that she had died quickly, most likely she was asleep in her car when she had the heatstroke. This gave me some comfort.

"You will need to identify her body, so I suggest you find a mortician close to you who can pick her up and bring her to you. Once you can identify her, we can finalize her death certificate." These details were overwhelming, so I gave the phone back to my husband, who took down all the information I needed. I sat down on the closest chair and covered my face and cried. Cried like when I was a child and felt helpless, like when we lived in Vegas and I wanted to see my mom but had to wait all night before she got off work and came home. This was a new loneliness, one I had never felt before because now she was never coming home. I had to mourn the loss of her now, and admit to myself that I'd left her long ago. I felt an enormous sense of guilt for that. I lifted my head once my husband was off the phone, my face red and dewey from my tears. Booboo leaned in to give me a hug, but somehow I didn't want a hug because I'd have to lift my head and body and I didn't have that in me. I watched the tears hit my pants. I stared at them for a little while as if they were the only things that existed. I felt Booboo's reassuringly warm hands on my shoulders, not rushing me to do anything.

I lifted my face, then I turned to look at him and said, "I have to call Sam." When the answering machine came on, I left her a message asking her to call me back. I then called my brother. He answered right away, "Hey, Sis, what's up?" It's always how he answered the phone when I called. I asked him if he could sit down.

I told him that Mom had died. He immediately roared out a loud "Nooo!" Then he started crying, and I would interject here and there saying, "I know." After a few moments, he took a few deep breaths and asked me what happened. I explained all that the coroner had told me. He told me he would take the rest of the day off and call our aunt Ruth so she could let the rest of Mom's family know.

I'd seen the news about the heat wave, but I didn't take it seriously, nor did I think my own mother would be one of the first people claimed by it.

I tried calling Sam's house again. She picked up just as I was leaving a message that I was going to come to her house to speak with her. It seemed she was still screening her calls.

"Yes, Mary. I got your calls. You don't need to come to the house," she said soberly.

"Sam, it's about Mom. She's died."

"She's been dead to me for years, Mary. I told the girls she was dead a long time ago." I was speechless. Her words felt like a sudden shallow wound, not hurting at first but deep enough to know it's going to take a long time to heal.

Through the years, I saw the layers of disappointment add onto her like paint over beautiful wood, and the only people who had never let her down were her children. And like with any relationship, there's not just one incident that ends it, but years of them. And at some point, one draws a line and decides they're done.

I've always known siblings to judge each other, either silently or vocally. But I never thought it actually changed how they loved each other. My sister wasn't perfect, nor was my brother, and neither was I. We all made our own relationship and reproductive choices, and at that time, they were all very different from each other, with my lifestyle and choices more aligned with my brother's. But the scale that I believed we used to weigh love for each other and our nieces, that scale would never change for me, though it seemed to be different now, at least for Sam.

I knew what we had learned from our mother growing up, and that we were all capable of writing off family. That we could justify ending relationships with our family members. That we could rationalize why they weren't worth our time because of their lifestyles, or because we felt judged by them and not supported, or because they made us feel left out. This was in our DNA. I had heard this reasoning from my mother my whole life, this very rationalization as to why we weren't in contact with our family. Both of our parents were the black sheeps of their families. To think this didn't have an impact on how we would grow up and live our adult lives would have been shortsighted. Did Mom die in my sister's mind the day we left the nursing home after my mother had rejected her and the girls? Had that been the final straw?

My friend Lauren arrived at the house and started cooking for me, insisting I needed to eat. She opened her purse and handed me her cigarette pack. I took one out and took a long, hard drag. My husband watched me and then started to lecture me about smoking, but Lauren turned to him and said, "Let Mary smoke. She needs it right now." She was acting like a protective big sister. She fried up eggs and spam, and I watched her cook comfortingly. I despaired in brief moments of pain, laughed when she tried to cheer me up, and then disappeared back down into sadness again. I sat there eating her cooking, and I was brought back to Vui, and Reyna, and all the smells of other homes I could remember, of fragrant ingredients that wafted in the air and stuck to the furniture and made you feel comforted. Food was a color in the prism of my childhood.

Many of my friends came over, dropping by one by one, to give their condolences. I wanted to be alone, but I needed this show of love.

The next day, I planned out how I would get to the tow yard to collect my mom's things from the car she had died in. My business partner offered to drive me there. Within the first fifteen minutes of getting on the freeway, we were sideswiped by a semi that was changing lanes. He apparently hadn't seen my little black Altima in his right-side mirror. There was little damage to my car, but I was unnerved by it, having barely mustered the strength to trek there in the first place.

We got to the tow yard, pulling into the dirt parking lot on an oppressively hot day. I went inside to discuss the situation with the woman at the front desk. She told me that they normally charge $240 for a tow, but they would waive the fee for me.

"Here are the keys to your mom's car. It's the blue Toyota Camry out back. You won't be able to miss it." She handed me a wad of keys. Dangling from it was Mom's key charm that said, "Spoiled." Reality hit me hard then. *These are definitely her keys,* I thought.

We walked outside and past the main gate that had been left wide open for cars to be towed in and out of the outside garage. Orange caution tape marked an X across the car's back window. It read, "Caution, Biohazard." I knew this was the one. As I approached, I noticed the driver's door had been removed. I thought about my friend Debbie, whose father was the first person they used the Jaws of Life on. He hadn't survived either. My mom was still over 300 pounds, which probably didn't make the body very maneuverable. "Caution, Human Body Found" was written on the back driver's side window in white marker, like the kind you see for car prices on small car lots. I felt like a cruel joke was being played on me. This advertisement of my mother's death was so public and obnoxious.

I peered inside her car. I saw a small red cooler on the passenger seat with the lid flipped up. Inside were small squeezable mayonnaise and relish containers, and a few bottles of water stacked on their sides. Her purse was on the driver's seat. It sat there wide open and stuffed with papers, grimy from dirt. This was a familiar sight growing up. When I popped open the trunk, I could see she was down to just three boxes of papers. I thought about how far she had come to reducing the baggage she obviously still carried around. I dug into the three mismatched boxes, desperate to piece together what was still left of who she was. One box still contained her divorce papers, and between the papers, there was a *Moral Majority 1983 Clean Up America Poll* Dad never mailed in; he was out by then. The few divorce papers that were left, only four or five of them, told of my mom's recount of my father coming out to her. How she knew who the person was that he was likely having an affair with because of how he talked about the man while they were making love. How she had just bought the man's wife a baby shower gift because she was expecting. How my dad didn't want her to keep the house, and asked her to move out. He said he would be too jealous to see her living in the house with another man and that he loved his home too much for us to stay there, so he wanted us to leave. How she pleaded with him to think of the children and how we would be affected with the divorce and having to move.

These were conversations and details I had not known before, and to see them in print in an official transcript, all tattered and old, I wondered if we left Nashville that day because our mom was afraid of our father. I'd seen them argue before when I was little, and it was coming back to me now how violent Dad could be, how loud he would get when they yelled at each other. It was scary. And for a mother with small children, it seemed she did the best she could given the circumstances. I grabbed her things and came home.

There it was, the front page of the *Los Angeles Times* article dated Wednesday, September 5th, 2007, titled, "Heat blamed in the deaths of at least 16." In plain print, "In Lancaster, the body of Linda Bernhardt, 53, was found in her car by a passerby about 12:45 p.m. Sunday in the 700 block of West Avenue I, said the sheriff. Bernhardt appeared to be living out of the vehicle. Her body was sitting in a reclined position, as if she died while sleeping."

I had found a morgue in Long Beach to go pick up my mother a few days after the coroner had called me, which was three days since her passing. I'd never used a morgue before, so the choice was completely random. They were near my house and had "Sons" at the end of their name, so I thought of *Six Feet Under*'s Fisher & Sons and decided to use them. Unfortunately, it would take them five days to actually pick my mother up to bring her back to Long Beach for cremation, and by then, eight days had passed. Before cremation, the coroner instructed me that I had to identify her body or they couldn't issue a death certificate. Not ever having to identify a body before, I did not know what eight days looked like for the dead. Eight days for the dead is awful.

I had called my sister to let her know I would be at the funeral home and that if she wanted to come by to see Mom, she could. She offered to help with the costs to cremate the body. After the cremation, I would have the ashes sent to my aunt Ruth in Tennessee so Mom could be buried next to her father in the family plot. Mom had been a daddy's girl, from what she told me, so it seemed like it would please her that she could lay to rest next to the only person she never had a bad thing to say about.

Sam was at the funeral home before Booboo and I arrived. She was sitting on one of the chairs in the lobby. The funeral home was small and nothing special, and the sitting area probably only held five people comfortably. She handed me a check for $300.

"This is what I owe for Mom's cremation, right?" she asked me.

"Yeah, that's it," I told her. I studied her, hopeful for a conversation, but she wasn't up for small talk.

A young man came from the back and addressed all of us.

"Are you here to see Linda?" We confirmed. "I'll bring the body into the main room for identification."

We sat there for a few minutes in uncomfortable silence. Then a man came around the corner pushing a body in a black body bag through the hallway that led to their main room. It started to hit me again, the feeling of true loss. My mother's body had just passed by me on a gurney in a body bag. And I knew it was her.

The young man came into the lobby and told us that we could come view the body. I looked at my husband and started to walk unsteadily toward the small room. It had five rows of pews on two sides, probably able to sit fifty people comfortably. My mother's body was at the front of the room. Her upper body was uncovered, and her arms were resting on her belly. I recognized her profile the moment I walked in. There was no music, no flowers; this was a quiet and raw experience, meant for identification and a small goodbye. As I got closer, I could see that her face and neck were clearly black from decay. I hadn't expected that. I thought being frozen preserved the body, but I was gravely mistaken. The body still decomposes. She looked as though she'd be in a fiery car crash, blacked from the intense heat and smoke. It was my mother. There was no doubt. But her slightly sunken face and withered nose drew me in for an intense examination as I tried to reconcile this face with the one I had known all my life. Her arms and hands were even smaller than when I'd seen her at the hospital a few years before. They were not the pudgy hands with grease spots that I remembered.

My sister stood across from me, staring at Mom, too. We both cried and said our own goodbyes. My husband sat in the front row farthest from the body. He didn't want to interfere with our experiences, but I could see from his face that he knew this was shocking for us.

"Mom, I want you to know that I forgive you for everything. This isn't the way I wanted you to go," I told her. I grabbed her hand, feeling the stiff coldness. I called my brother and put him on speakerphone. He said his peace to her as well, that he wished that they'd had a better relationship, and that he loved her.

We left the room and waited silently in the lobby for the young man to come to the front desk. He apologized for our mother's condition and said that they were sorry they hadn't picked her up sooner. Seeing my mother in that condition was now something we would have to live with forever. I confirmed it was my mother, signed the document to authorize her cremation, paid for the services, and walked out to the front.

I sat next to my sister on a bench, and we both stared at the street for a moment as cars passed by.

"If I die, don't ever let my daughters see me like that, Mary. No matter what, I don't want my daughters to ever see me in that condition," she said plainly.

"That was a surprise to me, too. I've been working with them for over a week. This was supposed to be an identification of Mom's body, not a viewing, but had I known it would be that bad, I would have asked them to make her look better."

When I got home, I plunged into my drawing book and started to doodle. I let myself go and wrote down all my words and feelings with manic impatience. I had been put through the wringer. Heart and soul.

My husband and I arranged for a visit to Tennessee to bury my mother that December. It would be cold and strange and tough, but it had the potential to revitalize the connection I'd lost to my Tennessee family. At least I hoped it would. I thought about what it would be like to go back to my aunt Ruth's house, the house with bacon grease by the stove where I stole quarters from her big five-gallon water bottle that sat in the kitchen corner. My aunt Jean, whom I never remembered meeting, was coming in from Atlanta, Georgia.

The first night we arrived, my brother and his wife drove us to our aunt Ruth's. As we pulled into her long and steep driveway, I remembered that as a child it felt like it was hundreds of feet down a hill. It was just as cold that night as the night we left Tennessee when we were children. We walked toward the back door that led right into Aunt Ruth's dining room and kitchen. My aunts were illuminated by the soft glow of the kitchen light, and vertical blinds were pulled back so we could see her and Aunt Jean sitting there talking at her messy table with their hands wrapped around a cup of coffee. As we got closer to the door, I saw my mother's resemblance in both of these women. My stomach started to tighten as we all started to pile into the house.

"Mary and Paul, look at you!" my aunt Ruth said loudly as we walked through her back door. We gave her and our aunt Jean a big, warm hug, like you do with older and rounder relatives, that good kind of squeeze. Our aunts seemed so short compared to Paul and me, who are both over six feet tall. Aunt Jean seemed to have the shyness of my mom's personality, while my aunt Ruth had a teacher's straightforwardness. I introduced my husband to everyone, who all thought that "Pierre" was such an exotic name. I said hello to Uncle Henry, my aunt Ruth's husband, who almost immediately started to help us settle into the house, assigning beds and rooms to everyone. He set me up in my cousin Chloe's room, the one with all the horse posters. It was strange to be there over twenty years later sleeping in the same room I had the night we'd left on our travels through Tennessee.

My husband and I slept in separate beds, so he got my cousin John's room. He and I decided to sleep in different beds shortly after we got married, when we realized we had incompatible sleep habits. I flailed my arms and legs when I slept, and he was an angel. We'd heard on *John and Ken's* KFI AM 640 radio program one morning that 50 percent of all divorces stemmed from incompatible sleep habits. We decided then that we would sleep in separate beds to give our marriage the best shot we could. We made it fun and said that we slept like Ricky and Lucy, from the *I Love Lucy* show, which seemed to help people understand that a young couple could be happily married and still sleep in separate beds.

I was struck by the resemblance to my mother in my two aunts. Even their hands were the same as hers. My aunt Jean had a playful and immature demeanor just like my mother, and my aunt Ruth had a forwardness like Mom, blurting out direct questions and opinions, laughing and smiling, which set off another round of laughing when she'd realized she'd amused herself. We talked the whole night about the positive things our aunts remembered about our mom. They even revealed some of the not-so-pleasant memories of how they treated my mother when she was younger, leaving her out of things and never wanting to play with her because they were much older than her. My mother had always felt left out, an insecurity obvious in so many decisions she made.

They revealed to me that my mother was thought to be mentally handicapped and placed in classes for the mentally and physically disabled until she was out of elementary school. This was done to her because it wasn't well understood how to integrate kids with dyslexia and other learning disabilities into regular classes, so this was how it was addressed. I'd already made up my own theories about my mom's disabilities, but she never said she thought she had dyslexia. I did know how hard it was for her during college, especially for her to spell. It was sad to say that even by the time she was in college, she'd not been formally tested for learning disabilities. She eventually dropped out because she couldn't keep up her grades and no longer qualified for financial aid, though she tried. As we all talked, I realized the depths of my mother's inadequacies and felt I understood her better. She had gone through all those years of being misunderstood, and then having older and *smarter* sisters on top of it. No wonder she felt like she never measured up. Maybe Sam's intelligence reminded her of her sisters? I appreciated how open my aunts were to share their regrets. They needed to mourn their baby sister's death, too, and part of that was fessing up to their own mistakes. It was humbling to see their genuine openness. They were the familial anchor we needed.

The next day, we made plans to see my grandma Edith. I'd mentioned to Aunt Ruth that I also wanted to see Aunt Sophie, since I'd not seen her since Paul broke his arm climbing her tree. Aunt Ruth told me that I could see them both the next day, but I'd have to convince Edith to see Aunt Sophie because the drive would be very long to get there from her nursing home. Aunt Sophie was my grandma's second to youngest sister. It had been over fifteen years since they'd seen each other. I had my work cut out for me, but I didn't have anything to lose and insisted we visit Aunt Sophie. My husband had heard my stories several times before and wanted to meet them both.

My grandmother was now in a nursing home, nearly in her nineties, and it had been just a year or so since she recovered from ovarian cancer surgery. My aunt Sophie was still on her farm and as fit as a fiddle, from what I heard. I knew I could make this reunion between these two sisters happen.

Grandma was happy to see me, at least as much as she could muster past her grumpy and salty disposition. She was smaller than I had remembered but still had her white hair and strong personality, and her face still looked like she'd sucked on a lemon. She was a little skeptical of my husband, giving him that untrustworthy stare once I said his name was "Pierre" and that he was from Belgium.

"Where's that?" she asked.

"In Europe," he quickly replied.

"Do you speak Belgian?"

"No, I speak French."

"Oh."

"I call him Booboo, though," I quickly chimed in.

"What kind of name is that?"

"It's a pet name I have for him. Pierre seems like a harder name for people to remember, and I think it's cute." Her expression didn't change.

I had a flashback of my mother when I told her about Pierre all those years ago. Maybe a certain kind of paranoia existed in the south and my mom couldn't help her instincts not to trust a man named "Pierre" from Belgium. Was this just too foreign and made him sound suspicious? He also had an accent that lended him to enunciating the wrong vowel sound in common words, which I found cute, but proved English was his second language.

Grandma Edith took a moment at some point to really look at me. I stared in her eyes, not saying a word, and she stared back. She was a bold old woman, not afraid of anything, but I saw her soften as she looked at me, and I thought that maybe she saw her daughter in me.

"I'm sorry about Linda. It's so sad how she died. You kids must be heartbroken." She began to cry softly. We all got quiet and watched this tender moment. I hugged her, and after a few moments, I assured her that Mom was in a better place. I asked Grandma Edith to come with us when we visited Aunt Sophie, and she agreed.

We decided we'd visit her the next day, and Aunt Ruth drove us to Aunt Sophie's house. It was about eighty-five miles away from Aunt Ruth's home, which was half-way between Nashville and Knoxville. As we pulled in front of the house and the noise from the gravel stopped, a small old woman with her white hair pulled into a high bun came out, smiling and waving her hands. I recognized her face, and I couldn't stop smiling. I hopped out of the car and waved back at her. I opened the passenger door to let Grandma Edith out. Her face was resting in a sour position, and she didn't make any moves to get out. As Aunt Sophie walked toward the car, she noticed that her older sister was in the front seat. She started smiling even wider.

"Is that you, Edith? Oh my, it's so good to see you!" Grandma Edith barely said anything to her sister, just looked ahead and sat stubbornly in her seat. But Aunt Sophie didn't seem to care. She kept talking to her and asking her how she was. Aunt Sophie and I put our arms out to help Grandma Edith get out of the car, but she swatted at our hands. While we moved out of her way, I leaned down to give Aunt Sophie a hug and asked her if she remembered me.

"Oh yeah, I do. I remember when you alls was here with your momma before you left town. Your brother broke his arm after I told him to stop playing in the tree."

Eventually, we all went inside as she reminisced about her family and her farm. I asked her if I could go see the house that had burned down, the one I remembered so vividly when I was a child. She took me to it, and there it was, just as charred and untouched as over twenty years before. A burned stove and living room furniture, the random pieces of their belongings displayed like pieces of art in a museum. Then a small donkey walked up to me and nibbled at my hand, startling me.

"Oh, that's Rastus. He's a nice boy," Aunt Sophie told me. I petted him and then walked over to the alpacas she had in a large fenced area. I'd never seen an alpaca in person before, and she had about six of them in all kinds of colors. As I stared at them in amazement, one of them spit on me.

"You can't look an alpaca in the eye like that, Mary. They'll get defensive," Aunt Sophie warned. Then she led me to another part of the farm where two white horses strolled right up to us and let me touch them. They were impressive. But after they greeted us, they continued on their walk. After that, we walked to the tree where Paul had broken his arm. It was as big and majestic-looking as I had remembered it, with long branches whipping in the air, showing off their leaves. My memories of her and the farm had now come full circle. By the time we walked back to her house, my grandmother was ready to go. But Aunt Sophie offered everyone a cup of coffee, which Booboo and I immediately accepted. My husband leaned into me and whispered that he thought Aunt Sophie was the sweetest little old lady he had ever met. Later that night, he told me he felt that Grandma Edith wasn't kind enough to her sister. He wondered how such a sweet old lady like Aunt Sophie could have a sister as sour as Edith. But I later learned why.

My grandmother's life was never easy. She was born in 1918, the oldest and big sister of her five younger siblings. She grew up on a family farm in the hardship of the 1930s Great Depression, had a mother who was ill much of the time, so she did most of the housework and childcare and helped her dad on the farm. Once the family moved to Loudon County (relocated by the government who took generations of family land now under Norris Dam), Grandma Edith worked and at age sixteen started working at a clothing mill in Loudon until she managed to save enough to pay her way through beauty school and open a beauty shop.

Her formal education ended about the 5th grade, which seemed about right by the handwriting I'd seen in letters or postcards that found their way to us from time to time, but she was a smart and hard-working woman who never quit. She married my grandfather in 1943, had her first son, Hank in 1944, Aunt Evelyn in 1945, Aunt Jean in 1947 (Grandpa Walter was in the United States Army Corps of Engineers rebuilding Japan after the atomic bombs for a short while), then Aunt Ruth in 1948, (then a miscarriage), and then my mom Linda in 1953.

Being the mother of five close-together kids would have been enough for most women, but she also worked full time in her beauty shop. Grandma Edith did a couple of loads of clothes in a wringer washer and hung them outside in freezing weather before going to the beauty shop with Aunt Evelyn babysitting the little sisters. Grandma Edith loved her children, made sure they were clean, fed, and had clothes to wear, but with that many children and a job, she never had the time to be the "good parent." That was Grandpa Walter's job. He was the kind of daddy that hugged his children and played with them when he was home, but with that size family, he took every construction job he could get, traveling as far as New York to make enough to feed, clothe, and house his family.

After all their children were out of the house and started families of their own, Grandma Edith still worried and worked to make sure her children and grandkids were taken care of. When Grandpa Walter developed Parkinson's in the mid-'60s after he was injured in a construction accident, she devoted her life to taking good care of him throughout his illness until he died thirty years later. She loved her family and was proud of all her children and grandchildren – but she was just about always a tired woman. Aunt Sophia was the middle daughter, fourth in the line of all six children and some might say the prettiest. She went from being a farmer's daughter to a farmer's wife.

That night, after visiting with Aunt Sophie, I wrote a poem for my mom, one that I intended on putting in the ashes box Aunt Ruth had out on the kitchen table to use at Mom's burial ceremony the next day. I never did, though. I kept the poem, too shy to slip it in there before we headed off to the gravesite. At the time, I was not confident in my own writing and poetry, and felt the poem was a silly gesture. I didn't want my mother to have some poem she may not have liked with her for all of eternity. It was called, "Your Hands." I wrote about what an eerie yet comforting feeling it was to see how much Aunt Ruth's hands looked like my mom's. I wanted her to know that with her gone, there was a lot I had found comforting in those hands. Seeing them again, on her sister, made me realize both the strength and vulnerabilities she had being our mother. Those hands had held us, fed us, cleaned up after us, written volumes on many pieces of paper, cooked and eaten food, slapped us, grabbed us, and even held the wheel as she drove through parts of America. Now these hands were no longer blackened from decay; they lived on through her sister.

The next day, we went directly to the cemetery for the funeral ceremony. There were several family members there that I'd not seen in over twenty years. Some I didn't remember much, but they all remembered me. My grandmother, too old and frail to walk up to the area—or too stubborn—stayed in the car but could still see all of us. There we were, only about ten of us, all together standing in a large circle. Each person spoke a little something about Linda. My brother and I were standing close together, and when it came to him, he shook his head and looked at me to say something.

It was a family tradition for us growing up never to have any close family around. We didn't grow up with our cousins, aunts, uncles, grandmothers, or grandfathers around. It felt like we had been broken off from the family quilt, but now, through this loss, it felt like we were being sewn right back in. Even though we have not grown up together, we were still family. In loss, we had come together, and in love, we could start to grow a stronger bond. I was letting go of all my mother's guilt and reasons for being estranged, and there I was, standing with my brother and reunited with my family. I knew that any life I wanted to have with my family moving forward was my own decision and not our mother's. It was liberating.

We made arrangements to see my uncle Hank, and his wife Gladys the next day.

As we pulled up, Aunt Jean pointed to Uncle Hank's blue double-wide trailer. When I walked in, some of his home was what I could remember, like the big living room and wood paneling. Where most religious people would have a painting of *The Last Supper*, they had a picture of Elvis looking over the dining room table. My cousin Natalie came out, hugged me hard, and immediately wanted to show me her tattoos. One was Dale Earnhardt's name and his racecar number, which was placed right above her butt. Dale Earnhardt had already died by this point, but she said she was proud to have his name and race car number on her back. Uncle Hank had gotten old, but he still wore blue jeans and a white T-shirt with a pack of smokes rolled up in the sleeve. We reminisced about the wooden boxes he made for my mom and Paul before we left Tennessee. I told him how treasured they were by all of us. I'd stared at the beautiful rose he'd carved into Mom's box and the triumphant eagle he'd carved into Paul's and would peruse them for little hidden treasures and mementos that they each kept in them. His wife Gladys was still lovely, kind, soft spoken, and a little nervous. She was an attentive hostess and brought out a few photo albums. We all sat around and looked through them while she explained who was who and what was what. Before we left, Natalie insisted I look in her room. She had a large confederate flag hanging on the wall, and she said, "I bet you don't see those very often in California, huh?" I assured her I didn't. After leaving their home, Aunt Jean wanted to know what I thought about seeing everyone. I told her that if I had been alone, I might have felt nervous. I turned to my husband to see what he thought of the visit. He looked at me and said, "It's like I just spent an evening on the set of *My Name is Earl*. It was fantastic."

THE SECOND CALL

I had finally gotten through the loss of my mother. Well, you never get through that, but I was certainly feeling less dreadful than I had for several months. It was the holiday season of 2008, and that Thanksgiving was my husband's turn to cook up the best turkey he could and to have friends and family over to taste his creations. We were the place everyone ended up at after spending a day with their family and the shenanigans that usually came with that. So we went into the season of invitations, cooking plans, and cooking assignments with glee. I believed that Thanksgiving was going to be special.

The day of, I was bustling around the house, preparing for guests to start trickling in. Then I received a call from a man who said he was the preacher from my father's church.

"Your father, Reverend Jack, he's had an episode. He's been taken to the hospital. He's claiming he can't see. The hospital says they don't know why he can't see, but they're going to monitor him today." I called my brother, and he rushed over to the hospital. After his visit, he called me to tell me that Dad had a stroke.

"I think after the holiday, we can get him in to see some specialists, but this ain't looking good, Mary. He's definitely missing his eyesight,"

Paul told me. I called our father to check in on him. He sounded weary, which troubled me.

"Mary, I don't know what's going on. I don't know if I'm going to be okay. Did you know that my old lover Felix has HIV now?" he asked me plainly.

"No, I didn't know," I told him.

"Well, he does. Isn't that just awful?"

"Yeah, it is awful, Dad."

Just a few years before, our dad let Felix back into his life, and within months, he had convinced Dad to sell his house. He moved into one of those huge senior living towers where the rent includes all your meals served in a huge cafeteria where all the other residents meet up and mingle around mealtime. I'd had a salad there with him one night. It was awful. Our dad was barely sixty years old at the time, and it seemed premature to put him in a place like that. My sister and I made an emergency visit to Nashville to try and stop Felix from prepping the house to be sold, which he was doing by selling off Dad's antique furniture. The house was so packed with antique furniture it was hard to move around. We tried to talk some sense into him, but Felix was a con artist, and he had our father's ear and heart. We were powerless against him. I wasn't raised around my father during the time that he and Felix were a couple, but I knew of the cheating—which led to him giving our dad hepatitis C—the stealing, and the manipulative behavior. He was the one who, fifteen years prior, signed off on our father getting multiple shock treatments for severe depression, which ultimately caused irreparable changes to Dad's energy levels and memory. He went from having a vibrant personality to a very subdued one, from what Paul told me. He spoke slowly and thought long before speaking, which was how I knew him. When Paul was living with them, Dad and Felix got into an argument, and Paul stepped in. He got into a fist fight with Felix and helped Dad kick him out of the house. Paul thought he was gone for good, since it had been over ten years since Dad had seen him. But Felix popped into town again and worked his magic on Dad.

"Do you think you caught it from him?" I asked Dad. Part of me was thinking his recent illness could have stemmed from a compromised immune system.

"Oh no, Mary. He didn't want to have sex with me when he came back into town."

I've always heard that your other senses are amplified when you lose your eyesight. I wondered if his memory was heightened now. I closed my eyes while my father talked to me, and I hoped I could get a better understanding of what he might be feeling. It would seem that if you lost your eyesight as an adult, you'd panic and feel alone, but he was calm, even chatty.

He was sent home after a few days and told he could recover there, but that his eyesight may not return for a while. At that time, the senior living center was just what he needed; they provided the extra help to get him to and from doctor's appointments and made sure he took his meds and ate his meals on time.

But in just two weeks, I was called by his preacher again. He told me that my father was back in the hospital. He said that I needed to come soon and that it didn't look good.

Christmas was nearing, and the prices for flights were through the roof. I called nearly every airline and requested bereavement prices, but the best prices offered was $800 each way. We decided that it was best that I go, so I booked the trip and was there two days later. I called my sister and left messages to let her know all the details of where our father was and his condition.

I arrived in the evening on December 20th and planned to stay until the 22nd. I spent several days by my father's side in the hospice care facility he had been moved to. I didn't know then that it was a sign that someone wasn't going to recover, so they're kept comfortable and out of the larger hospitals. It was personal, quaint, and the staff was compassionate.

Dad's preacher was there every day that I was. Friends streamed in and out of Dad's room. Many came and told lighthearted stories about our father Jack, and he'd smile and laugh, while keeping his eyes closed, barely muttering a word here and there. Sometimes he'd put a full sentence or two together, but he had to labor to get the words out. He'd squint when he heard a new voice, probably hoping he could see something, but then he'd give up and close his eyes again. I was slightly jealous of how other people interacted with my father and how he would respond. It was easy to see that they all had a day-to-day relationship with him, and all I'd ever had was a few days here and there over the past ten years. I realized I didn't know how to talk to him to make him laugh. I didn't have any funny memories either. It all made me feel uncomfortable because I just didn't know what to say to him, and there we were, near his final days. I accepted that I'd just be by his side as long as I could and soak it all in.

I had called my sister the last night I was there to see if she wanted to speak to him. It was the end of the day and just a few hours before I would take a red-eye flight back to L.A. I'd gotten her on the line and asked if she wanted me to hold the phone up to Dad's ear so she and the girls could speak to him. She spoke for a few moments, and Dad made small grunting sounds here and there, and finally he said, "I love you, too."

As the final hour before I left approached, my heart was heavy. I leaned in and whispered in his ear, "I'm sorry I have to leave you like this. I know this is the last time I'll see you. I want you to know that I forgive you for everything and that I love you." He moaned a labored moan, almost like it was painful. Then he said, "I love you, too, Mary." Then a contented look settled on his face. I grabbed my things and walked toward the door to leave. My brother and his girlfriend Nicole joined me. Just as we were all near the door, Dad started to speak. We all turned back toward him.

"I want you all to know this. That life is what you make of it. You only have your integrity, so make the most of it. Please be true to yourself and be kind to others, please promise me that." We stood there, astonished. He'd barely said a complete sentence to me in two days, and then such a profound message came out just as we were about to leave. It felt as if he'd saved up all his strength to deliver it.

"I promise," I told him.

We all walked to my brother's car and went to the airport in near silence. I wrote down what Dad said so I wouldn't forget. We had just heard our father's last words, and it felt as if they became greater than him. I flew back feeling like I'd gotten something special from my dad.

We celebrated Christmas every December 24th. It was when Belgians celebrated it. And that Christmas, my mother-in-law was in town, so we prepared a family dinner with some close friends. I was moving around the house, lighting candles and putting the final touches on the house before guests arrived. Our phone rang, and when I picked it up, Paul told me Dad had passed away a few minutes ago and that he was holding his hand when Dad died. That he didn't think he'd ever be the same again. I asked him if there were other people there, too, and he said that a stream of family members and other friends had come by that day to see Dad, including our aunt Carolina, his older sister. It seemed only right for him to die on Christmas. Just as I had felt more like I became a grown woman when our mother passed, my brother said he now felt like he needed to become a better man. That he had a bigger purpose and responsibility than himself, one to our family. It seemed that now my brother was now officially grown up.

My husband printed a picture of my father, and we put it in a frame and set a candle in front of it. As our friends and family arrived, everyone gave me their condolences.

THE FUNERAL

By January 5th, Booboo and I were in Nashville, standing in front of a small white church and being greeted by some of our father's friends and family. It was a modest church and only had enough seats for about sixty people. I could see that everyone was either gay or lesbian, and this gave me great comfort. Sam still wasn't taking my calls, but I left messages and texts to let her know the funeral details. We were hopeful that during this tragic event, we'd be able to connect as siblings and come together. Though with each death, it seemed Sam was becoming more and more estranged.

Once you walked into the church, I could see my father's body in his open casket, his full head of grayish-white hair poking out. As I walked toward him, I started to cry. My brother had asked that his beard be cut, to give him a nice, clean look. I'd not seen my father without a beard for several years, so it was a bit shocking. I was surprised at how good he looked, so peaceful and distinguished. I leaned in and gave him a kiss on his forehead. It was ice cold and dewey. He was dead. I moved toward my seat next to my aunt Carolina. She leaned into me and whispered with a soft, southern accent, "Oh Mary, this just breaks my heart. Jackie was such a sweet man." As we pulled away from each other, we realized we were both wearing the exact same long black coat. From the furry trim to the materials, except mine was large and hers was small. She had large, red, beehived hair, and her coverup was just a shade darker than it should have been. Her eyes were sparkly blue, just like mine and Dad's. She had large and rosey cheekbones and a wide, white smile with a small gap between her two front teeth. She looked like a southern belle. Her husband sat next to her, as did mine next to me. My brother was in the row in front of me with his girlfriend Nicole. I'd never been at a southern funeral in a little white church, but I was ready for whatever came next.

A large Black man sat at the front of the church and settled into the piano bench. I didn't know what was about to happen to me, how every cell would vibrate with beauty as his voice sang out like an angel, effortlessly carrying a song of love and healing that hit every part of my heart. I cleansed myself with his music; his words and melody shook the shelves of my heart and let everything fall to the ground. I had never heard a man sing like that before. His voice echoed around the room with bass and boom that vibrated through me. I wasn't sure I could stop crying, that it would ever end as long as this man sang. Another woman came up and sang hymns, though I didn't know any of them. I'd stopped singing church songs when I was a child and only knew a few Bible school songs that I'd sing with my sister when we walked home from school. The preacher stood up and talked about my father's contributions to the church; volunteering for food drives, playing the piano in community senior centers, and always being available to counsel someone who was struggling with how to come out to their friends and family. The ceremony was short and sweet, as my father would have liked. I knew he would be genuinely missed by the congregation.

My brother and I stood outside the church, and as people slowly walked out, they each gave their condolences. Some even shared fond memories. One man told me that my father had been the only preacher who would officiate same-sex marriages anywhere in the south and that he would drive to nearby states in order to hold those ceremonies. He once married a gay couple in Kansas City, and they held the ceremony in an old underground bank vault. He'd never told me any of this before.

We all slowly left the church and drove toward the cemetery. As we drove behind the hearse, I noticed people politely pulling over to the side of the road and turning on their lights. I learned that this was a show of respect for the dead. I was deeply touched by this. I looked up into the sky and noticed the clouds looked like a long procession of horses galloping in the same direction we were going. It was so remarkable that I took a picture of it. As we arrived at the cemetery and walked toward the canopy that had been set up with chairs for close family and friends, I locked eyes with my cousins, Amy and Al, and their mom Janice. I knew by their faces and eyes that we were related; I just didn't know how. Amy looked just like my sister. They immediately told me who they were, and I was stunned. They were my father's little brother, Al's, children. I hadn't seen my cousins since I was a kid, and I didn't even remember them. They said my uncle Al wasn't able to attend the funeral, but they wanted to be there. His wife Jan said Al was suffering from the first signs of dementia, and this would have been too hard of an event for him. I honestly couldn't even remember my uncle Al. I later learned that he was a musician, guitar player, and actor.

The preacher had arranged for a Military Funeral Honors ceremony. The honor guard detail was beautiful, and ended with my brother receiving the American flag folded perfectly and respectfully. Paul had cried during the funeral, but at the burial ceremony, as the guard handed Paul the flag, he stopped crying and looked proud. I saw him change before my eyes.

Our cousins waited for us to walk back to our car, and they asked us if we wanted to have lunch with the whole family the next day at Buca di Beppo. We all agreed, and it became a family reunion. Our cousins brought their spouses and kids, and even more cousins and their spouses came. There were fifteen of us at a long table, talking to each other like we'd known each other our whole lives. I felt close to them immediately. It seemed our personalities were similar. We were bold talkers and loud laughers. All of the women even made more plans to go shopping the next day, which allowed me to see the playful and carefree side of my family.

I was attracted to my spouse in part because of the family he brought with him. He had a particular kind of comfort and contentment while existing around his family. He knew his place in the family tree, and he was loved. Every family member had a funny story to tell about him when he was a child. They could easily poke fun at him, and he would play along. He could joke with his sister or his mother, his aunts or cousins, and everyone had a good time. There was no animosity or resentment, and I was drawn to that over the years. As I was getting to know my whole family tree now, Booboo supported me and helped make the integration easier. While I was making new family connections, the connection with my sister was even more strained.

Sadly, within the next two years, two more family members would pass. First, our uncle Al, my father's youngest brother, who I'd only got to meet twice. The first time was in 2009 after his brain surgery to remove the tumor they believed was causing his dementia. They found a spot on his lungs and, soon thereafter, diagnosed him with lung cancer that had spread to his brain. He was the spitting image of my father. The second time was in early 2010 when he was lying on a gurney in his living room, with hospice care and a drip of morphine going into his veins. By February, he was gone. Before he left this world, he shared with me that he always knew that he was his father's favorite. That Jack Sr. always felt that my dad was too soft, so he preferred his youngest son. I learned Al had been in the movie, *Hey Vern, It's My Family Album*, in 1983 with the legendary Jim Varney. He had a short role playing, *Mistake Worrell*.[12] I remembered the funny character Jim played named Ernest P. Worrell, who had the catchphrase, "KnoWhutImean, Vern?" He was such a hick. I used to love watching this series on television, and we even watched a few episodes from the show when I was in elementary school during rainy days. I especially remembered the dairy farm commercials that used to come on during cartoon breaks. I was surprised that my uncle knew him and had been part of a production with him.

When Dad came out of the closet, some of his family rejected him. I could imagine how my dad became the black sheep by leaving his family for a man. The world was not ready for an out-and-proud gay divorcee with three small children. But Dad's boyfriend Felix didn't help either. Many felt he was too flamboyant and that he put it in everyone's face. Felix would often dress scantily and overtly show affection, which compounded everyone's unease. When my grandfather passed a few years after my parents divorced, Dad and Felix showed up to his funeral. They were quickly asked to leave, and his brother Al ended up escorting them out. Felix apparently showed up in black short shorts and a cut-off T-shirt. He was also kissing my father, appalling those who attended.

My grandmother Edith would die in August of 2009 at the age of ninety-one. I flew down to Tennessee to go to her funeral. Paul was one of the pallbearers. As he helped carry Edith's casket to her gravesite, I was emotional, as I stood in the same circle I had less than two years before. She was laid to rest next to her husband Walter and her youngest daughter Linda.

We soon learned that after our mother died, Grandma Edith had put Linda's portion of her inheritance into her kids' names. It wasn't a lot but it was definitely enough to be able to make some financial choices. There was never a thought in my mind that we came from a family where there was an actual inheritance to be had. We were the children of black sheep, so this kind of thing did not happen to us. But thinking about my grandma and how sour she seemed, how my mother never felt that she loved her, knowing that Grandma Edith was still going to give our mother an inheritance, made me see the soft and tender side of my grandma. Had my mother been alive, this would have allowed her to have a better life than she'd ever had, and maybe she would have forgiven her mother for her past mistakes, and realized that she'd never stopped loving her. I reached out to my sister, leaving a message once again on her home answering machine, giving her the numbers and information she needed to claim her inheritance. Being that the economy was in a recession and I was burned out, I'd felt like Granda Edith gave me a one-way ticket out of hell. I was eternally grateful.

SISTERS

I'm sure that there have been many books written by many authors on the subject of siblings, but there must be a special category for sisters. At the time of writing this chapter, my sister and I had not spoken in over ten years. I had not seen my sister since September 2007, since the day we had to identify our mother's body.

It felt as though the one who birthed us also took away any chances we had of sisterhood. We each went through difficult stages of self-doubt and insecurity as children, and Sam and I rarely had our emotions validated. Those scars from Mom's extreme paranoia, our poverty, lack of security, and little emotional intelligence displayed in our home, drastically reduced our ability to communicate our feelings and, in some ways, created an animosity between Sam and me that never went away.

Although having such difficulties growing up could have made our relationship stronger. It did, for a while. When I helped Sam leave her first boyfriend Raymond after I returned from visiting Dad the first time, we got so close. We shopped at thrift stores together, swap meets, went on the same diets, and even worked out at the same gym. But we made different choices. She wanted to be a mother, and she never quite found suitors who were kind, supportive, loving, and fun, like she was. I always wanted to be in control of my reproductive choices. I'd seen so many friends and people growing up who were trapped in bad economic situations and relationships because they got pregnant, and I never wanted to put myself in that situation. But I recalled the time when Sam and I were kids, swinging on the double swing and her telling me that she wanted to be a mom one day. I didn't have the urge to reproduce like she did. Within four years of meeting her last suitor, she had two beautiful girls. She had to work so much harder than I did to get through college, to be able to support herself, and ultimately to be able to leave the father.

Her choices put strains on our relationship, but so did mine. My husband was too different and eccentric for her. She found him controlling and too worried about my well-being. From Sam's perspective, Booboo checking in on me if he hadn't heard from me in hours, his annoyance whenever the phone rang and broke his concentration, along with his curt and nonexistent phone etiquette, looked controlling and was quite annoying to her. Sam thought I was too codependent. Perhaps I was. It would appear that with the childhood I had, I would be susceptible to that. Though if true, it made my sister despise him even more. The two people we chose to be with couldn't have been any more different. Her children's father controlled the money in their household. We'd go to lunch twice a week while we were in community college together, and sometimes I'd have to pay. Though I never cared, this was embarrassing for her, and likely very painful. My husband's career was skyrocketing at the time, but he was working all the time too. We were doing well financially, and I was quick to offer help whenever it seemed to be needed, but once accepted, this only furthered the grudge Sam had with my husband. We talked endlessly about how her partner and his family treated her and I'd share my exasperations with balancing my surgeries, school, and my workaholic husband.

For her daughter's first birthday, I was at the park with her from 9 a.m. until dark waiting for the father's family to show up. They did, but only moments before we decided it was late and needed to pack up. They even considered her ambitiousness as a negative thing, though it was a quality I admired in her. I was proud to say my sister was a nurse, and I understood how deeply her achievement meant to her and what it said about her abilities and her future.

My experiences with my husband's family couldn't have been any more different. Both sides of his family welcomed me my first time to Belgium by having a party in the middle of the Brussels airport, with champagne and a sign that read, "Bienvenue, Mary!" Years later my father-in-law, André, took my husband and me on a trip around Paris, stopping at every location in the movie *Amélie*. He had planned it out for months. It's where I had Camembert cheese for the first time; I took my first bite as we passed Notre Dame in a covered Bateau Mouche in the rain.

When our mom and dad died, there really didn't seem to be a reason for her to be my sibling anymore, to have to "deal" with me, my husband, or my friends. There was no living connection through our parents. In a way, their death detached us from an invisible umbilical cord that connected us as sisters. Her strongest and most important connection was now with her children.

"A chameleon will grow throughout its entire life, shedding its skin when necessary. This symbolizes change, maturity, and renewal."[13]

NEW SKIN

The previous four years had taken their toll, and all I wanted to do was shed my skin and show my real colors. I'd been in that skin for too long. I took an inventory of my life that fall and realized I needed to make major changes. I decided to walk away from my start-up and take a sabbatical. Thanks to Grandma Edith, I didn't have to be afraid of that bee sting. I took steps to remove myself from the company and to come clean with my husband about the debt it had accrued and to make giant leaps toward repaying it.

I started a co-ed softball team just a few months later. It was partly because of the advice I'd received from the psychologist I saw briefly after my mother died. She reminded me that I had been consumed with work and had lost the friendships in my life that made me happy. I had lost the ability to express what was keeping me from feeling joy, and I worked on getting my voice back. Pulling away from my company was hard, but it was a distance I so desperately needed. I was going to reassess my life and my skills, but in the meantime, I was going to go back to what I knew gave me joy, and that was playing sports.

I'd never played softball in my life, but the idea of putting together a team, practicing, and building new relationships was an unknown I eagerly walked into. I put together a ragtag group of friends, and we all learned how to play softball together. We only won one game our first season, though the victory felt like a scene from the movie *The Bad News Bears*, and we celebrated like we were kids. The team has been going strong for nearly ten years at the time this book was written and had several championships under its belt.

I joined a prominent entertainment company in the second year of my sabbatical. It turns out, the skills I learned being an entrepreneur during the Great Recession and the grit I developed from the life I had as a child prepared me for the world I thrive in and the problems I can solve at work. Who knew?

My last therapist helped me to understand and process the angst I had toward my parents, my sister, and even my spouse, who at times put me second to his work.

It turned out that never being a mother wasn't what was missing in my life. What I wanted most was for my husband to relieve me from the responsibility of abstaining from reproducing. This was discussed at length during our 20th anniversary stay at our favorite winery, Ponte, in Temecula. If he didn't want children, that was fine, but I now needed that burden to finally become his, I felt it had been mine for long enough. I had by that time, become much more aware of the biological and physiological effects birth control chemicals were having on me, and I wanted out from under them. So we again discussed the obvious solution, a vasectomy. The irreversible nature of the procedure had always been an obstacle for him. The possibility of it changing what sex felt like, forever, was too great a risk. But what was said that night convinced him that it was the right thing to do, and the first phone call he placed when we got back home from that weekend was to get the process started.

Soon after his procedure, we started to fold into each other and work on our marriage, to remember who we were, but also to acknowledge who we had become. We realized that we had changed so much over the years, and that we had put other people and our careers ahead of our marriage, and that it was time to acknowledge that and find our new truth.

I recently read that being in a marriage is like being married to a different person every few years. Because we change so much through the years, it's almost impossible to be the same person our spouses married, though we cling to who they were when we fell in love with them. We resent our partners for changing and even mourn that change. When I began writing this book, I was mourning those changes in him and in me.

Writing this book has helped me understand my parents, my siblings, and myself much more than I ever had before. I spent so many years as a young person never really being able to solve my mother's problems. No matter what advice I'd give, I was powerless over her mental illness. I couldn't stop an episode of rage she was having if she thought she was deceived by someone in one of her college classes or from her past. This would usually spawn from a comment someone had made to her a few days before that she'd spun into a full-fledged conspiracy theory. But I would still try to talk her down from the ledge. This was an experience I could later use to talk down escalating situations. "Normal people's problems" seemed like child's play compared to hers. This was why it was hard for me later in life to spend time around people with severe mental illnesses. I was not confident I could help them, nor did I have it in me to try.

I do acknowledge that during my time as a youth, mental illness was frowned upon and that my mother had very good reason to be afraid that if she had gotten mental health services, that she could have been deemed an unfit parent. I'll give her that. However, not obtaining those services until much later in her life had tragic consequences on herself and us kids. Schizophrenia is a deep struggle I've seen up close and personal, and I wouldn't want anyone to go through that struggle alone, especially untreated. It seemed that her illness wounded her, the kind that left scars that you couldn't see. Her heart was so thoroughly hurt that the only way to escape was for her to cry for hours and then fall asleep, or to pace around the house and murmur under her breath because her thoughts were racing through her head. Years of untreated schizophrenia seemed like the aftermath of a car accident; parts of her body always seemed broken and never really healed from past trauma. She always seemed to be unconsciously protecting herself from past injuries in her heart and mind.

I had injuries in my heart, too. I decided to open up my wounds and let others touch them, to learn about my life growing up. I wouldn't offer information about my past, but if someone asked me questions about my life, I'd pleasantly go as far down the information rabbit hole as they wanted. I was embarrassed about some parts of my life, but telling my story allowed me to make it hurt less. It was also in the forgiving of others and admitting my own weaknesses and faults that I was willing to move forward in my life, without giving my mistakes or the people who had hurt me power over the good and wonderful parts of myself.

I hadn't checked in on myself in a long time—to see who I had become and what I wanted the rest of my life to be—until I embarked on this journey. When I finally took a step back, I realized that the part of me that hadn't expressed itself because of my fears of not being worthy enough was the *writer* in me and that I had to write this book in order to become who I was meant to be.

I traveled through my past, through all the colors I could see, and I relived all that I could remember. I sat with my child self, and I put the truth, the unfiltered light, through the prism of my childhood, and I finally saw all the beautiful colors within.

POST SCRIPTUM: MENTAL ILLNESS AND HELP

Throughout my life, I've experienced both sympathy and intolerance for mental illness. I was ignorant to the benefits of mental health, and I didn't seek out therapy until I was in my late twenties. My first experience wasn't that great, but I'm glad I kept an open mind to it. My second experience was transformational. It took a lot out of me, and it left me sad, confused, and even hurt at times, yet I kept going back to work on myself and my marriage. I kept going so I could continue to peel away the layers I'd added on through the years and to ultimately find myself.

If you are suffering from a mental illness and have thought about seeking support or treatment but don't know the various mental health services available to you, then please visit the National Alliance on Mental Illness website to find support services near you. Please continue to seek help until you find the right healthcare professional for you. Even when you feel better, if you can afford to do so, please continue to feed your soul with all the good stuff that therapy has to offer.

Through writing this book, I discovered that I needed to share my EMDR session with my readers. I had to open up about myself and what it really took to get through the dark times and to address my trauma. I had to let myself know that sharing my childhood PTSD story was not a weakness, but an expression of strength that could possibly inspire someone else to seek help for their trauma. It wasn't until years later that I realized exactly how this EMDR method and therapy helped me, I had developed a better way to express my feelings, and I was clearer on what I wanted in life. My professional life skyrocketed, and I no longer felt like the insecure girl who kept dropping her lunch tray.

I'm now part of my company's leadership team, and this success is directly related to what my therapist helped me overcome. I will admit, there were some days after therapy sessions that I wondered why I was going to them. Sometimes I didn't even know what to say and felt almost like a fraud. But deep inside, I knew I needed to keep going and to work out my issues.

There shouldn't be any stigma for having a mental illness or PTSD. The most important thing you can do for yourself and those you love is to seek treatment and to keep trying until you find the help you need. It can be a long road, but it's worth traveling.

ACKNOWLEDGEMENTS

Thank you to my continuous cheerleaders, friends, and family who supported me. A special thank you to my aunts (Ruth, Evelyn, and Jean), Amy Gregory, Jeannine Mockel, and the late André Adriaans. To my brother, Paul, thank you for helping me fact-check events, names, locations, and always being just a phone call away. I appreciated that immensely.

To Pascale Cleyman, Lauren Kim-Jablon, Richard Novac, Amanda Novac, Chelsea Meissner, and Imelda Nunziato, thanks for always being my advocate. To David Nadal, who gave me the appreciation and admiration for good storytellers, and who let me enjoy many nights while he played guitar for his daughter until she fell asleep. To Courtney Roberts, my accountability partner, thanks for inspiring me to keep getting to the finish line. To Michael Roberts, thank you so much for your amazing cover artwork. Thank you to Lisa Biagiotti, my fellow writer in arms.

Thank you to my powerhouse of female mentors and friends; Paula Laus, Marjorie Gilberg, Lydia Colaresi, and Laura Sperrazza-Novak. Also, special thanks to the early believers and readers of my first few drafts, Michael Gioan, Mike Weber and Jacob Noor, my first editor. To Jim Moore, who encouraged me to read the book, *The Glass Castle*, after hearing a few tidbits about my childhood. I was left inspired by Walls's honesty and drew strength from her journey.

And lastly, to my husband, Booboo, who always encouraged me to take the time I needed to finish my book, "You don't rush art," or "It will be done when it's done," were always welcomed encouragements and delivered just when I needed to hear them the most.

ENDNOTES

Introduction

1 **"Experts suggest that parents discuss with their children ways to handle negative social situations related to their cleft lip or cleft palate.":** Leonard BJ, Brust JD, Abrahams G, Sielaff B (October 1991). "Self-concept of children and adolescents with cleft lip and/or palate". *The Cleft Palate-Craniofacial Journal.* **28** (4): 347–53, wikipedia.org/wiki/Cleft_lip_and_cleft_palate#Psychosocial_issues.

2 **"A congenital cleft or fissure in the midline of the upper lip, resembling the cleft upper lip of a hare, often occurring with a cleft palate.":** dictionary.com/browse/cleft-lip?s=t.

3 **"Research has shown that during the early preschool years (ages three to five), children with cleft lip and cleft palate tend to have a self-concept that is similar to their peers without a cleft.":** Tobiasen JM (July 1984). "Psychosocial correlates of congenital facial clefts: a conceptualization and model". Cleft Palate J. 21 (3): 131–9. PMID 6592056, wikipedia.org/wiki/Cleft_lip_and_cleft_palate#

4 **"Self-concept may be adversely affected by the presence of a cleft lip or cleft palate, particularly among girls.":** Leonard BJ, Brust JD (1991). "Self-concept of children and adolescents with cleft lip and/or palate". Cleft Palate Craniofac. J. 28 (4): 347–353. doi:10.1597/1545-1569(1991)028<0347:SCOCAA>2.3.CO;2. PMID 1742302, wikipedia.org/wiki/Cleft_lip_and_cleft_palate#

5 "Changing skin color is an important part of communication among chameleons. A chameleon's skin changes colors in response to its emotions, such as anger or fear, changes in light, temperature, or humidity.": Alina Bradford (2015). Live Science, livescience.com/51061-chameleon.html#skin_of_many_colors

The Beginning

6 "Jack Sr., a locally famous musician who played the clarinet, saxophone, and was the band leader for the Nashville WSM radio show, "Waking Crew," which he had led since before World War II. He also played each weekday on WSM TV's "Noon" show. Roger Bissell. *Jack Gregory— Unforgettable*, rogerbissell.com/id22n.html

P.S. 17

7 "Children who are judged as attractive tend to be perceived as more intelligent, exhibit more positive social behaviors, and are treated more positively than children with cleft lip or cleft palate.": Tobiasen JM (July 1984). "Psychosocial correlates of congenital facial clefts: a conceptualization and model". Cleft Palate J. 21 (3): 131–9. PMID 6592056, wikipedia.org/wiki/Cleft_lip_and_cleft_palate#Psychosocial_issues

8 "Children with clefts tend to report feelings of anger, sadness, fear, and alienation from their peers, but these children were similar to their peers in regard to 'how well they liked themselves.'": wikipedia.org/wiki/Cleft_lip_and_cleft_palate#Psychosocial_issues

Sellin' Snakes

9 "Unlike other animals, chameleons continue to grow throughout their lives. As their old skin gets too small, they will shed it in bits and pieces, dissimilar to snakes that shed their skin all at once.": Alina Bradford (2015). Live Science, livescience.com/51061-chameleon.html

Opening quote to *Part 3 – Travels Through Blue*

10　"Chameleon skin is filled with tiny crystals called nanocrystals and when they move their skin by relaxing or tensing up their bodies, the crystals shift and reflect light differently. Shorter wavelengths of light, such as blue, are reflected when skin is relaxed, and the iridophore cells are close to each other.": Adrienne Kruzer (2019). The Spruce Pets, thesprucepets. com/chameleon-color-changes-1238534

Opening quote to *The Call*

11　"Chameleons pretend to be dead when in danger. They wear a blank stare and simply fall to the ground when they are attacked by enemies. They only move again when they feel safe.": Suvigya (2018). Savage Facts, savagefacts.com/18-colorful-facts-about-chameleons/

The Funeral

12　"He had a short role playing, *Mistake Worrell*.": rexnjenine (2008) youtu.be/BlX_GFS5Uvk

Opening quote to *New Skin*

13　"A chameleon will grow throughout its entire life, shedding its skin when necessary. This symbolizes change, maturity, and renewal.": What is My Spirit Animal, whatismyspiritanimal.com/spirit-totem-power-animal-meanings/amphibians-reptiles/chameleon-symbolism-meaning/.

ABOUT THE AUTHOR

Mary E. Gregory writes essays, poetry, and screenplays. You can find her poetry on UrbanHonesty.com. Born in Nashville, Tennessee, she now lives in sunny Long Beach, California. She is happily married to her culinary-inclined Belgian husband of twenty-five years, Pierre. You can connect with her on maryegregory.com, by email at info@maryegregory.com, on Facebook: @UrbanHonesty, or on Twitter: @msmaryegregory.

Made in the USA
Columbia, SC
29 August 2020